Introduction to American Education

Planning for Competence

Introduction to American Education

Joseph F. Callahan

Leonard H. Clark

Jersey City State College

Macmillan Publishing Co., Inc.
New York

Collier Macmillan Publishers
London

Macmillan Publishing Co., Inc.
866 Third Avenue, New York, New York 10022

Collier Macmillan Canada, Ltd.

ISBN 0–02–318230–X

Printing: 1 2 3 4 5 6 7 8   Year: 7 8 9 0 1 2 3

To Jane E. Callahan *and* Maria A. Clark

Preface

The ambitious goal of this volume is to supply you with a multitude of general concepts about American education. It is expected that as you continue your professional studies you will eventually have a broad base from which to operate. You will be able to place in the proper context the new and specific ideas you are confronted with, and you will evolve a skeleton framework for organizing the corpus of knowledge about education that you will acquire through your experiences.

Modules 1, 11, and 12 establish the boundaries of this panoramic orientation. They set forth the functions of the school and hence the need for teachers. They also describe some of the qualities and strengths that effective American teachers apparently possess, and they offer helpful information to be used when those just beginning to teach are faced with career decisions.

Modules 2, 4, 9, and 10 dwell upon the aims of education and the existence of the school as an institution in the community. The role of the citizen in the local school districts is explored, and the impact of the controversies caused by the divergence of the opinions of citizen critics is examined.

Modules 7 and 8 examine the curriculum in the elementary school and in the secondary school.

The remaining modules focus upon functional operations in general. Module 3 describes how the schools are organized to operate, Module 5 establishes the legal justification for this operation, and Module 6 describes how this operation is financed.

J. F. C.
L. H. C.

Contents

Introduction to
American Education

To the Student

Welcome to an adventure in learning.

Now that you have begun to think seriously about a career in teaching, it is our guess that you will find adventures of this sort very helpful in planning to meet the challenges that await you in the classroom. It seems safe to predict that not only will you increase your background in educational theory and methodology as you work your way through these modules, but also you will improve your chances of becoming an effective teacher when the time arrives to put theory learned into practice.

Probably you have not encountered many books organized as this one, calling for such active participation on your part. From this point forward, you are expected to become a sensitive, self-motivated learner engaged in making frequent and sound judgments about your learning. You will be the one to control the rate of progress through the various modules and you will decide when you have mastered the knowledge presented in each. We have tried to help by (1) listing the objectives of each module, (2) providing a comprehensive set of questions to test your mastery at the end of each module, and (3) providing an answer key for your use in evaluating progress. Those with little time to spend on study can move through the various modules and finish quickly so long as they study attentively and demonstrate the mastery called for on each test. Slower-paced individuals, who wish to ponder and probe various areas and who decide to read extensively from the selected readings listed in each module, can establish a pace that suits their purposes.

It is not intended that any student will be able to prepare himself for a teaching career solely by completion of this kind of study program. Teaching is a human activity. It deals with people, with children, parents, and fellow professionals. It involves various kinds of knowledge, judgments, and decision making; it requires communications skills, human relations techniques, and a host of other attributes for the cultivation of which human interaction and professional expertise are necessary. But faithful and zealous use of this learning tool will add depth and meaning to your classroom sessions in education courses. Mastery of these modules will carry you beyond the initial steps of preparation so that you may place into context more of the campus lectures about education which you hear, and ask questions about schools and students that go beyond the layman's level of significance.

The sections of the book are called modules, for essentially they are self-contained units that have cognitive values by themselves. Each module contains a rationale, a list of objectives, a post test, an answer key, and a list of selected readings. The rationale attempts to establish the purpose of each module and, in some cases, the link with other aspects of pedagogical knowledge. The objectives inform you very specifically what you should know and be able to do as a consequence of your study of the module. The test and the key inform you of your progress toward module mastery. The general study plan recommended is as follows:

1. Read the rationale to acquaint yourself with the task you are addressing and, if possible, with how this module fits among the others that you will study.
2. Examine carefully the module objectives. Find out what will be expected of you upon completion of your study.
3. Read through the module, checking back from time to time to see how well you are mastering the objectives. Review what you do not understand.
4. Take the Post Test. Evaluate your success by using the answer key. Where your answer differs from that of the author, search out the sentence or paragraph in the text that confirms your answer or his.
5. If you score less than 85 per cent on any test, reread and retake the test until your mastery improves.
6. Try out your knowledge by exposing yourself to some of the suggested reading. Your progress should accelerate as you bring more and more knowledge to each book that you read.
7. Engage in interaction with fellow students, professors, and members of your family on the topics studied, whenever possible.
8. Enjoy the experience. The profession needs zealous seekers of knowledge who enjoy learning and who, in the process, develop a capacity for infecting other people with the same "felicitous virus."

What Teaching Is

Harry L. Brown

Jersey City State College

module 1

What Is Education? / Work of the Teacher / The Professional Teacher

RATIONALE

"Education." "Teaching." Two words you probably have used most of your life. But have you ever attempted to construct a definition of one or both of these terms? If so, in all likelihood you have found your goal very elusive indeed. As with so many of our most fundamental concepts (justice, beauty, equality, truth, community), *education* and *teaching,* too, are defined differently by different individuals. Usually the differences have been most aptly articulated by those who have given the most attention to education and teaching. Philosophers, educators, and some of our most informed citizens have been intrigued by the problem of defining the meaning of these terms. As a result, they have presented us with dramatically different answers to such questions as What is education? What is the function of education in the American culture? What is the argument pro and con formal education or schooling? What educative functions should we expect the schools to fulfill in our society? What does "to teach" mean? What is the proper role of the teacher within the American culture?

Why is it that people answer these questions so differently? And if they do, what difference does it make? When the answers of those who have conscientiously considered these questions differ greatly, you might even ask why it is important for prospective teachers to pay attention to the questions, or to the answers. How important is it for teachers to work at developing answers to the questions for themselves? And, do one's answers to these questions and their corollaries have much effect on one's functioning as a teacher?

These are fair questions. It would be extremely difficult to catalogue all the factors that generate the various notions about education and teaching. However, consider the following statements:

1. Education implies teaching. Teaching implies knowledge. Knowledge is truth. The truth is everywhere the same. Hence, education should be everywhere the same.[1]
2. It is the function of the school to place in the possession of the succeeding generation the "common core of ideas, meanings, understandings, and ideals representing the most precious elements validated by study of the human heritage."[2]
3. The school should be viewed as "a form of community in which a concentrated effort should be made in developing habits of critical inquiry in the solution of personal and social problems." Education is "a process of living and not a preparation for future living."[3]
4. It is the function of the school consciously to influence the attitudes of students to be prepared to participate in the construction of a new society, the outlines of which may be seen only dimly by farseeing prophets.

Do you agree that these four statements posit considerably different conceptualizations of the functions of education and schools in the American culture? Of

---

[1] Robert M. Hutchins, *The Higher Learning in America* (New Haven, Conn.: Yale University Press, 1936), p. 66.

[2] Charles A. Tesconi, Jr., *Schooling in America: A Social Philosophical Perspective* (Boston: Houghton Mifflin Company, 1975), pp. 69–70.

[3] Ibid, p. 81.

course, you would want to know a great deal more about these four positions, but do you now have a preference for one position over the others? If you do, how do you think you might behave differently as a teacher, in comparison with a friend who subscribes tentatively to one of the other three positions? Do you think the position you feel most comfortable with would affect your choice of subject matter or the methods of instruction you might employ? Would it affect the way you might view your students or organize your class? Try to infer from these statements what you think proponents of each position might say about the nature of human beings and about the process by which human learning takes place.

It is unlikely that you will encounter anyone who subscribes without qualification to any one of the four statements we have presented. However, almost certainly you will be able to recognize those associates who (1) place greater emphasis and value upon the importance of the universals of education (Perennialists); (2) stress the disciplines, traditional values, and logical methods (Essentialists); (3) think that the schools should pay attention to the present concerns and interests of students and employ problem-solving approaches in instruction (Experimentalists); (4) sincerely believe that the schools must become more active participants in the processes by which society "recreates" the culture (Reconstructionists).[4]

Does one have to subscribe to a particular school of thought in order to become an effective teacher? Apparently not. Most of us probably have had "successful" learning experiences mediated by teachers whose views on education and what it is important to teach varied widely. Can it be that one does not need a philosophy of education in order to be an effective and inspiring teacher? There are individuals who seem to be "born" teachers. They have, seemingly, acquired the art of teaching by instinct and intuition. Such individuals are extremely rare. For most of us, our quest for the status of "professional-teacher," and, possibly, "artist-teacher" (as opposed to "lesson-hearer" or simply "scholar") includes a continuing effort to invest such terms as *education, teaching,* and *human learning* with greater meaning for ourselves. In this quest, attention to the thoughtful formulations of ideas about education, and the functions of educational institutions in these formulations, as well as attention to what others have said about teaching and learning, can be helpful. It is also essential that, in our efforts to define the foregoing terms we examine our experiences as teachers, observing carefully how our behavior and techniques affect students and their learning. By subjecting our own experiences to close, critical scrutiny, we can test the formulations others have presented, and we can further the process of perfecting the definitions that will serve in the future as guides in our practice of teaching.

The foregoing discussion suggests that professional teachers will find that their definitions of education and teaching will continue to evolve, taking on deeper meanings throughout their careers. We consider it very likely that when we attempt to distinguish professional and artist teachers from pedestrian performers, we will find that teachers in the former category have an abiding interest in the art of teaching and the scientific foundations of that art; they take pride in perfecting their art; they can explain why they find that their work provides them with rich opportunities for creative expression and personal satisfactions. Recall your own

---

[4] The terms *perennialism, essentialism, experimentalism,* and *reconstructionism* are frequently used to identify major streams of current educational thought or philosophy. Authorities differ in the classifications they employ. For useful, brief discussions, see Tesconi's, *Schooling in America,* op. cit.

teachers: have you ever had an exceptionally fine teacher who did not enjoy teaching and who did not appear to be thoroughly caught up in his or her work?

Subjects such as these will comprise the subject matter of the learning modules in this volume. This module will concern itself with (1) what education is, and (2) what teaching is. It is hoped that it will provide you with a background that will help you understand the teaching profession and make your study of succeeding modules easier and more rewarding.

Objectives

This module is an introduction to teaching and the teaching profession. Upon completing your study of this module, you should be able to

1. Explain the difference between education and schooling.
2. Define education in its broad sense and in its narrow sense.
3. Explain why educationists believe that education should be lifelong, and not limited to the classroom.
4. Tell why societies provide schools for their youth.
5. Explain the principle of education for complete living.
6. Describe the major thrust of, and the implications for education of the Seven Cardinal Principles, the 1938 Educational Policies Commission Report, and *Education for All American Youth.*
7. Explain why many experts consider teaching to be an art—not a science or a performance.
8. Explain strategy, tactics, and operation, and give examples of each.
9. Describe the general pattern of good teaching, sometimes called the *teaching-learning cycle.*
10. Describe the teacher's role in each of the following: mentor and guide; policy maker; bureaucrat; mediator of the cultures; liaison with the community.
11. Describe the professional teacher functioning in his roles as learner, thinker, planner, doer, evaluator, team member, and member of professional organizations.

MODULE TEXT

As we pointed out in the Rationale, *education, schooling, instruction,* and *teaching* are so much a part of our vocabularies that at first glance it seems unnecessary to examine their meanings. But before we go any further in this series of modules, we ought to define them, in order to avoid misunderstanding.

What Is Education?

The unabridged edition of the *Random House Dictionary of the English Language* defines education as "the art or process of imparting or acquiring powers of reasoning and judgment and generally of preparing oneself or others intellectually for mature life."

In Carter Good's *Dictionary of Education,* education is defined quite differently: "the aggregate of all the processes by means of which a person develops abilities, attitudes, and other forms of behavior of positive value in the society in which he lives."

As you can see, these definitions make several quite different assumptions about education. The *Random House Dictionary* definition limits education to the intellectual development of the learner. By implication, this insistence that education is preparation for mature life seems to confine education to childhood and youth. Good's definition is much broader. It does not limit education merely to the intellectual, or to preparation for mature life. Rather, it assumes that education includes everything of value that a person might learn—intellectual, psychomotor, social, emotional, and so on. The differences in these definitions illustrate the many and various conceptions of the meaning of education current in our society. These different conceptions stem both from the looseness of common usage and from differences in philosophy.

In general, however, the terms *education* and *teaching* may be viewed in two ways. The Random House definition illustrates the narrow view, whereas the Good definition is an example of the broader view. Let us first turn to the examination of education in the broader sense. To most educationists, this is the real meaning of education.

Although many people thoughtlessly equate *education* with *schooling,* a few minutes' reflection should show the narrowness of this view. Schooling is what takes place in school. In its broad sense, education is much more than that. It includes all the learning experiences that shape us into persons. Even if we differentiate between learning and education, education is and should be lifelong. It takes place in school and out, at work and at play, from the cradle to the grave. Education may be the result of instruction by teachers, or self-instruction, or even learning from the situations we get into. Probably most education consists of learning experiences that occur outside of school, through other agencies. One may learn much from men's and women's clubs, the theater, the mass media, working with civic groups, and the church. The world of work is also educative, so much so that we have created the phrase, *on-the-job training.* Furthermore, social, emotional, and vocational learning are fully as much a part of education as intellectual learning. The social or emotional or vocational ignoramus is just as much an educational failure as is the intellectual ignoramus.

This broad-scale view of education has many implications. Because schooling is not the whole of education, other agencies have educational roles and responsibilities. If education occurs from cradle to grave, people need opportunities for planned educational experiences after they have completed their formal schooling. If education is to be a continuing process, schooling should not be merely a preparation for adult life or vocation, but rather one step in a lifelong process. If education concerns emotional, social, and vocational aspects of life, then the range of its planned learning activities must be expanded both in school and out.

The impact of this broad view of education can be seen in the world-wide movement for lifelong education, which is continuously gathering strength. The reason for this movement's growth seems to be an increasing realization that, in this rapidly changing world, the formal education one acquires during childhood and youth will leave one obsolescent during later life unless one's education is renewed and revamped during adulthood.[5] Accordingly, it is felt that adequate opportunity for both formal and nonformal learning in professional as well as general sectors is essential. Dave continues,

> For many kinds of learning a rich educative environment in the home, community and educational institutions is necessary. Here learning must be as natural and effortless as possible. Apart from incidental learning, a variety of provisions in the form of paid study leave, inservice programmes, on-the-job training, etc., will be necessary to create ample opportunities for learning at any time in life.[6]

Efforts should be made to see to it that people are motivated to take advantage of these opportunities and that their experiences result in a high degree of educability. As defined by Dave,

> Educability is the readiness to profit from learning opportunities. It includes skill in the techniques of learning, ability to plan and implement one's own programme of learning, ability to utilise effectively different tools and media of learning, ability to carry out independent learning with self-reliance and confidence, ability to profit from inter-learning in a group or inducted learning of a formal system, ability to select from and take advantage of a variety of learning strategies and situations, ability for self-evaluation of progress, and so forth. Education, in one sense, becomes a process for the enhancement of educability, and in the other, utilises educability for producing recurrent learning at different stages of life and in diverse areas of growth.[7]

These concepts of lifelong education and educability represent a considerable shift in emphasis and orientation from the more narrow view of education as schooling.

Activity

Turn back to the four positions described in the Rationale of this module, and the questions and discussions which follow them. What implications do these have for your own thinking of what education and teaching are?

Schooling. Up to this point, your attention has been directed primarily toward the larger, philosophically oriented context within which we use the word *education*. As the Rationale for this module suggests, the perfecting of definitions for the words *education* and *teaching* in the broad arena probably will be career-long or even lifelong pursuits of the professional or artist teacher.

Nevertheless, though we invite you to enter upon the long-term inquiry into the meanings of education and teaching within the broad human context, you, as a beginner preparing for a career in teaching, will probably find it most helpful to consider the terms *education* and *teaching* within a narrower framework. Within these more restricted boundaries, education may be viewed as something that takes place in a formal setting (school), under the direction of a person who serves as

---

[5] R. H. Dave, *Lifelong Education and the School Curriculum,* VIE Monographs 1 (Hamburg: UNESCO Institute for Education, 1973), p. 14.

[6] Ibid, p. 23.

[7] Ibid, p. 23.

teacher. Education in this sense is something identified as "formal education" or "schooling," to distinguish it from "education" employed in the broader sense.

In this module we are using the word *schooling* for the formal portion of education. Ordinarily, *schooling* is a word not much used in pedagogical circles. We use the term in this module to emphasize that school learning is not all of education, but only that part of education received in schools. As a rule, schooling is construed to be formal, disciplined, and somewhat arbitrary; therefore, when one uses the term *schooling* metaphorically, as in the phrase "one schools himself," the word connotes formality and discipline.

Why Schools? All civilized societies, and a good number of primitive societies, have maintained schools. The first schools probably were not very formal, but they were schools. In the earliest times, evidently, cave-men artists used to sit young people down and teach them to draw. In aboriginal tribes today, men teach groups of boys the skills they will need as hunters and providers. Interestingly enough, sometimes they use quite sophisticated teaching methods—games and simulation.

Ancient peoples invented schools for the same reasons that modern peoples maintain them: to serve as the formal institution for introducing the young into the organized life of the society. Principally, they wanted an institution that would

1. Teach children customs, mores, and traditions in order to preserve the culture of the society and to promulgate the ideals of the society.
2. Give young people the skills and knowledge necessary for making a living as adults.

Most people still want that sort of institution. The educational processes employed in the schools and the goals to be attained by the schools are an outgrowth of the society, and reflect its core values and traditions. The balance that is struck varies among societies between the objective of preserving and advancing the central interests of the society on the one hand, and the needs and interests of individual members of the society on the other. The differences stem largely from the nature of the core values—those things that the culture holds most dear. Thus, for instance, Kaiser Wilhelm is purported to have instructed his Minister of Education to give him "loyal, God-fearing, servants of Imperial Germany."

Of course, when society changed, the schools changed. What was once a small informal group of children often became a large, formal, sophisticated, bureaucratized institution, extending from early childhood well into the third decade of life. As the nature of society and schools changed, the purposes of schooling changed with it.

Schooling in the United States. In the early days of the United States, the schools were places where it was hoped children would learn moral values and to read, write, and figure. Secondary education was selective in character and classical-academic in orientation. The European roots were unmistakable. Secondary school was not for all youths. It was primarily conceived as preparation for college and entry into a limited number of professions: the ministry, medicine, and law, primarily. Emphasis was placed upon classical-liberal studies, and the calls of Herbert

Spencer, Benjamin Franklin, and others, for more practical studies, for example, the sciences, made only small inroads into this tradition. In addition, some vocational schools and courses were made available for young men who wished to become businessmen, and whose parents could afford to pay the fees. And this is pretty much the way things remained until almost the beginning of the present century.

However, the increasing pace of industrialization eventually began to exert its influence on the social fabric of the nation. One result was an increasing awareness that a public school system encompassing six to eight years of study was insufficient to meet the needs of the American society of the late nineteenth century. The celebrated Kalamazoo Decision served as the cornerstone for the construction of a system of universal, free, public secondary education throughout the United States. With the authorization to collect taxes to support secondary education, the transition of an institution (originally designed to serve a select minority of the population, identified largely by birth and means, and providing a classically oriented college preparatory curriculum) gradually began to take place. The transition is not yet complete; furthermore, in the minds of some critics, errors have marred the shift. Still, the American secondary school of today can be characterized as free and open to all; offering a variety of programs designed to serve youths of diverse social, racial, and ethnic backgrounds who have various interests and capabilities, and who are at various stages of accomplishment. The most frequently stated objective of American secondary education is that it serves equally well all American youths. In short, by the mid-twentieth century, Americans had become imbued with the notion that all of the children of all of the people were entitled to at least a secondary-school education.

Unfortunately, when we Americans decided to educate all of the people, we never really decided what we were going to educate them for, or how we were going to do it. To this day we have not faced up to the enormity of the task and the problems it brings with it. That we have not done so is not really surprising. It is not a simple task to decide what should make up the curriculum of the school, or how instruction should proceed. What are the core values of the American culture? What are the understandings, sensibilities, and skills new citizens need in order to participate as full members in this society? What conception of man and of institutions, and of the relationships among them, does this society choose to present to the new partners in America? These are not easy questions with which to come to grips. In all likelihood, the implicit, if not explicit, judgments of individuals on these issues are more diverse today than they have ever been. That this is so may help to explain why the schools frequently appear to be centers of conflict and confrontation.

Stated Goals of American Education. Professional educators and government officials have formed numerous task forces, study groups, committees, and commissions to determine what the goals of American education should be, and to so describe the needs of American children and youth that the statements of goals and needs can be employed in constructing appropriate school experiences and programs. Perhaps the most influential of these groups was the Commission for the Reorganization of Secondary Education. Near the end of World War I this commission, influenced by Herbert Spencer's insistence upon the need for a practical education designed to prepare young people for the future, developed a statement describing seven broad life-oriented areas of educational objectives. Although formulated by a commission on secondary education, these objectives apply to all education.

These objectives became known as the "Seven Cardinal Principles." They provided an impetus to the transition of the secondary schools and are a useful guide to professionals and citizens planning new roles for education. The objectives enunciated were (1) Health, (2) Command of the Fundamental Processes, (3) Worthy Home Membership, (4) Vocation, (5) Citizenship, (6) Worthy Use of Leisure Time, and (7) Ethical Character. A cursory examination of the written statement of goals or objectives for secondary education for almost all secondary schools indicates that the Seven Cardinal Principles are still alive and influential in American education.

Another major effort to formulate goals for American education was undertaken by the Educational Policies Commission of the National Education Association in the late 1930s. In this 1938 report, *The Purposes of Education in American Democracy,* the Commission set forth forty-two specific objectives for American education. These objectives fall under four broad areas:

Objective of self-realization.
Objective of human relationships.
Objectives of economic efficiency.
Objectives of civic responsibility.

These areas go far beyond the practice in early eighteenth and nineteenth century schools. They touch on all areas of human life and living. Not one area is omitted from the list. They represent a theory common among modern educators and accepted by many but not all laymen: to wit, education should prepare pupils for complete living. According to this theory, schools should not only carry out the goals of preserving the society's culture and promulgating its ideals, but should also provide all the skills, knowledge, and emotional capabilities one needs in order to live the good life. The same orientation and preparation for living, can be identified in the 1944 statement of the Commission, which identifies ten goals for secondary education in terms of needs of youth. These are

1. Vocational skills and other attributes necessary for success in the world of work.
2. Physical fitness.
3. Good citizenship.
4. Successful family living.
5. Consumer skills and attitudes.
6. Understanding of science methods and scientific facts.
7. Appreciation of beauty in art, music, literature, and nature.
8. Ability and inclination to use leisure time well.
9. Respect for others.
10. Skill in thinking, expressing, reading, and listening.[8]

---

[8] Educational Policies Commission, *Education for All American Youth* (Washington, D.C.: National Education Association, 1944), pp. 225–226.

As one might expect, these guidelines for American education have not been without their critics. On the one hand, some critics have argued that preparation for living as represented in these two formulations constitutes too broad an assignment for any institution. They argue that the results are that the institution loses focus or purpose because it has no basis for establishing priorities among competing objectives. As a response to that general line of criticism (which became particularly strong during the late fifties and early sixties), the Educational Policies Commission issued, in 1961, a statement entitled *The Central Purpose of American Education*. In that statement, the central purpose of education is identified as the "development of the rational processes." "These processes involve the processes of recalling and imagining, classifying and generalizing, comparing and evaluating, analyzing and synthesizing and deducting and inferring." The Commission attempted to draw two connections between these rational processes and the 1918 and 1938 statements of goals. On the one hand, the materials to be employed in expanding the students' capacity to employ rational processes could be drawn largely from the life-need areas identified in the earlier statements. On the other hand, as the student developed his command of rational processes, he would augment his power to "apply logic and the available evidence to his ideas, attitudes, and actions, and to pursue better whatever goals he may have."[9]

Criticisms of American education from another direction have grown in the late 1960s and early 1970s. The central theme of the criticism appears to be that there is something drastically wrong with American society, and that the schools, quite apart from doing anything constructive to change conditions, have been co-opted by the State and may even actively participate in the perpetuation of the existing unsatisfactory conditions. By and large the critics do not speak with one voice; their analyses of the ills of society and of the extent of the complicity of the schools differ. In general, when remedies are proposed, they are apt to be short on specificity. Many have either abandoned the thought that the public schools can play any significant part in righting the ills of America, or they see them as having a capacity to do so only if the concept of schooling in America is radically transformed. Some sense of the diversity of the criticism may be obtained by a study of the writings of George Dennison, John Holt, Charles Silberman, Christopher Jencks, Paul Goodman, Ivan Illich, Jonathan Kozol, and Herbert Kohl.[10] Less apocalyptic writers and critics have placed great emphasis on the importance of the affective, social, and vocational aspect of education. In theory, our schools are still committed to the doctrine of education for complete living.

John Goodlad's remarks to a Convention of the Association for Supervision and Curriculum Development indicate that perhaps American schooling is ready for a change. ". . . it is exceedingly doubtful that schools, as now generally conceived and conducted can make much difference. The changes called for are profound. . . . We must think of schooling as a concept embracing the fostering of knowledge, wisdom, and a host of qualities of mind and character—in effect a society's way of educating, if it is to make a significant difference."[11]

---

[9] Educational Policies Commission of the National Educational Association, *The Central Purpose of American Education* (Washington, D.C.: National Education Association, 1961).

[10] Some of these criticisms will be considered in later modules.

[11] John I. Goodlad, Main Address at 1975 ASCD Annual Conference (ASCD *News Exchange,* **1:**17 (May 1975), p. 1.

Activity

Now review the description of the Seven Cardinal Principles, the 1938 report of the Educational Policies Commission, *Education for All American Youth* and the *Central Purpose of American Education.* Do you believe that proposing such broad scope for American education is realistic? Do you think that it would be better to limit schooling to the intellectual pursuits? How broad should school education be, in your opinion? Do you think schools should take an active role in repairing the ills of American society?

The School Curriculum. Very seldom does the curriculum keep up with the theory of education and the goals to which the profession gives lip service. The purported goals of our schools are "education for complete living," but the curriculum is more likely to support intellectual academic education. If the schools have failed in recent times it is probably because the curriculum has not kept up with its mission. The curriculums in many of today's schools are carry-overs from old curriculums constructed to meet the needs of their clientele before the schools took on the task of educating all the children of all the people. In spite of recent reforms and innovations, few curriculums have been brought in line with the educational objectives or the clientele of the time.

Teaching in the Schools. We stated earlier that formal education is the major vehicle employed by advanced societies to induct the young into the life of the society, to acquaint them with the society's ideals and goals for men as individuals and citizens, and to equip them with the knowledge, skills, and attitudes requisite for functioning as good citizens. The process by which this formal effort at acculturation takes place within schools is called teaching.

As with the word *education, teaching* has broad and narrow definitions. The broad definition states that teaching is what a teacher does as part of his job. Let us consider this definition later. For now, let us turn to the narrower definition which is the heart of the larger definition. According to this definition, teaching is helping someone learn, that is, helping someone acquire (or change), some skill, attitude, knowledge, ideal, or appreciation.[12] In the school situation, teaching is one component of an interactive process, and student learning is the other. In evaluating the effectiveness of teaching, ultimately the essential questions are "Did the students learn?" "What did the students learn?" "How do we know?"

As you read this statement, you will immediately realize that this definition is a simplification of an extremely complicated process. In the 1974 Presidential Address to the Philosophy of Education Society, Kingsley Price emphasized the complexity of teaching.

"Teaching cannot be described, correctly, as the performance of a thing like the performance of a pharmaceutical tablet; and if it were, that description could have no point. It cannot be described, correctly, as a mechanical performance like the performance of the drill; and if it were, it would carry with it the false point of causing

---

[12] Leonard H. Clark and Irving S. Starr, *Secondary School Teaching Methods,* 2nd Ed. (New York: Macmillan Publishing Co., Inc., 1967), p. 4.

the expectation that everyone who has been taught a subject will certainly be able to use his mastery of it in the realization of any human purpose to which that mastery is appropriate. It cannot be described, correctly, as an artistic performance like the performance of the sonata; and if it were, the description could accomplish nothing other than itself in ordinary circumstances. It cannot be described, correctly, as a moral performance like that of Jones' writing letters to his parents; and again, if it were, the description could accomplish nothing other than itself . . . Teaching is a great many different actions engaged in with the intention of bringing about mastery of the subject taught."[13]

In short, teaching is not a performance, or a skill, or even a science, but an art. In the estimate of Travers and Dillon, it is one of the "great performing arts."[14]

To help pupils learn, the teacher must assume a number of roles and functions. Among the roles he must assume are planner, policy maker, guide and mentor, curriculum builder, doer, evaluator, team member, bureaucrat, and professional. These and other roles will be discussed in greater details later in this module and in Module 12.

Teachers use many sorts of operations or tactics to carry out their teaching functions. Usually the teacher organizes these operations into strategies by which he hopes to help pupils learn. By *strategies* we mean a general approach or plan to a relatively large goal. A strategy, then, includes the selection of suitable subject matter, the general organization of the subject matter for instruction, and the modes of instruction. Teachers construct strategies to carry out a variety of purposes:

1. To make pupils' ideas clear.
2. To present new or different materials.
3. To show pupils how to do things.
4. To affect or change attitudes, ideals, opportunities.
5. To give security.
6. To motivate.
7. To evaluate, or to measure.
8. To guide or direct pupils' work.
9. To arouse, to direct, or assuage emotions.

The operations mentioned earlier may be thought of as the tactics by which we carry out the strategies we are attempting to follow. Many tactics can be used to carry out each strategy. For instance, some tactics one can use to make pupils' ideas clear include

1. Asking pupils to forecast the implications of a statement or idea.
2. Asking a pupil to define what he means, in his own words.
3. Asking a pupil to illustrate what he means.
4. Asking a pupil to justify or cite the authority for a statement he has made.

---

[13] Kingsley Price, "The Sense of 'Performance' and Its Point," 1974 Presidential Address of the Philosophy of Education Society, published in *Educational Theory*, **24**:313 (1974); reprinted in part as "Is Teaching a Performance?" *Educational Researcher*, **4**:7 (March 1975).
[14] Robert M. W. Travers and Jacqueline Dillon, *The Making of a Teacher* (New York: Macmillan Publishing Co., Inc., 1975), p. 7.

5. Asking pupils to summarize.
6. Asking pupils to outline.

Similarly, examples of tactics by which one might show pupils how to do things include

1. Demonstrating.
2. Showing better methods.
3. Correcting faults.
4. Using films or videotape.

Examples of tactics a teacher uses to control pupils include

1. Tells pupils what to do.
2. Sets goals.
3. Reprimands.
4. Accuses.
5. Supports.
6. Encourages.
7. Grants or denies permission.

Other operations may be used to clarify, to give security, to unify the group, to diagnose learning problems, and so on.

Alert teachers also find that they must use different strategies to teach facts, concepts, skills, and attitudes. The strategy that works well for teaching facts may prove useless for teaching attitudes or concepts. For instance, oftentimes facts can be taught by purely expository strategies, but to teach deep understanding, that is, to teach concepts, one must provide the pupil with opportunities to examine the concept from several angles, and to turn it over and over in his mind. Rather than by exposition, attitudes are more successfully taught by strategies that (1) provide the pupils with models, (2) appeal to the emotion, or (3) apply group pressures on them. Skills can best be taught by demonstration and practice strategies.

In recent years, the notion has gained increased prominence in education that the teacher does not have to be the direct agent of all the formal educational experiences made available to students. The long-term implications of this point of view cannot be the subject of examination in this module. However, it should be noted that a number of new resources have become available, and deserve the attention and careful evaluation of the professional teacher. These include learning modules or packets devised within the individualized instruction-programmed instruction format, instruction by TV, and computer-assisted instruction. Moreover, efforts to diversify staffing and instructional assignments, in order to make the school schedule and calendar more flexible, have been the subject of discussions and experimentation. Professional teachers have a responsibility to participate in experimentation aimed at determining the utility of these processes in the educational effort. As the worth of new procedures and resources is proved, teachers have a responsibility to students and to their profession to integrate them into their teaching procedures.

A General Pattern for Teaching. Although there are many different teaching strategies, and although different objectives require different teaching strategies, most good teaching follows one general teaching pattern, no matter which strategy is used. This teaching pattern is sometimes called the *teaching-learning cycle,* or the *teaching cycle.* It has been described variously by different authors, but in spite of superficial differences, the authorities are all in basic agreement. According to the model we shall follow, the pattern consists of five basic steps:

1. Diagnosis.
2. Preparation.
3. Guiding learning.
4. Evaluating the results of learning.
5. Follow-up or follow-through.[15]

These will be discussed in Module 13.

Work of the Teacher

The larger definition of teaching is, in effect: Teaching is what a teacher does as part of the job. What then does the teacher's job encompass?

Guide and Mentor. First and foremost is his role as guide and mentor. (This is the role we have been speaking of as the "narrow" definition of teaching.) This role includes instruction and guiding learning in both curricular and extracurricular subject matter. The role also includes a guidance function. In a sense all teachers must be guidance counselors. That is, they must help pupils understand themselves —their strengths, weaknesses, and problems, and must help them to make the choices (decisions) that will make their lives more successful and complete. In this role, guidance is quite informal, and consists largely of helping pupils find information, making suggestions, referring pupils to agencies that can help them, and in general sharing with them the results of their larger experience and information. Much of this guiding is done in impromptu conversations—snatches of talk before and after school, between classes, during breaks, and at other odd moments. Even so, the teacher's guidance may be more influential than that of any other adult.

Mediator of the Culture. In his role as guide and mentor the teacher also acts as a mediator of the culture. A society provides schools so that the children will grow up to be good members of the group. It is therefore expected that teachers will induct pupils into the ways of the society. Through teaching young people the beliefs, values, and traditions, as well as the social and intellectual skills that the society prizes, the teacher fulfills this role. He is also charged by the community with the responsibility for interpreting the culture to the pupils so that it will be meaningful to them, thus enabling them to fulfill their societal roles. He executes this mission in his formal teaching, but he may be even more influential in his informal contacts with pupils. It is this sort of learning that is more likely to be communicated by what the teacher does, and is, than by what he says.

Policy Maker. The teacher is also a policy maker. He sets the tone and the philosophical direction of the education in his classes. But on the larger scene he has a considerable role in establishing system and school educational policies. Although the responsibility for determining educational policies rests with the boards of education and the state government, few school boards or legislatures would dare to enforce an educational policy that was anathema to the teacher.

[15] Leonard H. Clark, *Strategies and Tactics in Secondary School Teaching* (New York: Macmillan Publishing Co., Inc., 1968), pp. 2–3.

In this connection we should note that curriculum building is primarily done by teachers. Even in school systems in which the curriculum is laid out and mandated by local or higher authorities, the teacher determines what is actually taught, for once the door is closed on his classroom, the teacher is king or queen. In many systems, school policy and the curriculum are largely set by teacher committees and study groups.

Bureaucrat. The teacher is also something of a bureaucrat. As a bureaucrat he not only has a hand in shaping policy, he must also carry out the policy. Some of these bureaucratic duties are quite mundane: keeping records, filling out requisition slips, taking attendance, issuing supplies, supervising corridors, and a score of other trivial, seemingly menial, tasks. But this is also the fate of all lawyers, doctors, professors, and other professionals, particularly when they work in a bureaucracy. Both the large and small tasks are essential to make the bureaucracy work. Without the working routines of bureaucracy, hospitals, court systems, and schools would be chaotic.

Liaison with the Community. By the very nature of their work, teachers represent the schools to the community. They interpret school policy and practices on formal occasions such as parent conferences and parent-teacher's meetings. They also interpret school policy and practices in their dealings with pupils in school and out, and in informal, social intercourse with adults in the normal business of community living. This role of liaison officer is extremely important; community members are more likely to derive their ideas about their schools from what teachers and pupils say and do than from board of education public relations programs. Good liaison with the community usually results in sympathy and support, but lack of liaison results in dissatisfaction, unrest, and lack of support.

The Professional Teacher

The essence of teaching is that it involves intellect and activity. A teacher is a learner, a thinker, a planner, a doer, and an evaluator. The professional teacher is one who perfects his art in all these activities through thoughtful reflection on his teaching role and by continued study in order to fill in gaps in his knowledge.

Professional Teacher: Learner. What should a teacher learn in order to be able to exercise the greatest wisdom in the selection of the subject matter content and the methods of instruction, and in order to bring the greatest skill to the teaching act? The answer to this question goes a long way toward defining the subject matter deserving the continued attention of the professional teacher. And this obviously encompasses a much larger area than that which only constitutes the disciplines or fields of study he identifies as his teaching specialty.

In the broadest sense, subject matter appropriate for the teacher includes all things that help him arrive at increasingly better answers to the questions posed earlier: What is worth knowing? What conditions do we need to establish in order for students to learn it well? In answering these questions, what factors do we take into account when selecting content for teaching? What do we take into account when selecting the strategies and tactics we shall employ in the instructional process? There is probably no complete answer, but there appears to be conclusive evidence that the following subject matters deserve the attention of teachers throughout their careers: (1) the substance and structure of the individual's teaching specialty or specialties (for example, mathematics for the mathematics teacher); (2) the psychology of children and youth; (3) human learning; (4) society and culture, with particular emphasis upon how they impinge upon children and youths; (5) techniques of teaching, organization for instruction, and the improvement of instruction; and (6) techniques of evaluation and the improvement of evaluation.

These subject-matter areas will be elaborated upon in other modules, and we hope the prospective teacher will understand why they are considered to be essential for the professional teacher.

It is not our intention to overwhelm the prospective teacher with this recitation. But it is very much our intention to establish that teaching is a demanding activity. What one needs to know is extensive, and this is one reason why we have emphasized the term *professional teacher*. We have also emphasized that the task of becoming a professional teacher requires a long-term, even career-long commitment. The acquisition of the knowledge and experience base required for professional-level teaching takes time and perseverance, but there can be great personal rewards and satisfactions for the person who enjoys learning and helping others to learn.

There seems to be a tacit assumption that the only appropriate way to acquire knowledge is one involving formal classroom settings. Teachers certainly are encouraged to continue formal study in the areas suggested here. However, the teacher's avenues for broadening his knowledge, understanding, and skills are extensive. He can learn much by perfecting his skills of observation and using them as he goes about the day-to-day business of living. A rich dialogue within a professionally oriented faculty group is an excellent source of intellectual stimulation. Workshops, institutes, conferences, and conventions also provide opportunities for communication and stimulation. Individual inquiry into intriguing questions often can be one of the most personally rewarding activities; research often produces meanings for teaching that go well beyond the topic chosen for direct attention.

The Professional Teacher: Thinker. The work of the teacher is professional in yet another sense. Teaching is not a matter of mechanically filling out prescriptions or following cookbook-type recipes. If it were, teachers' work would still be important, but it would be technical rather than professional. Teaching is a much more highly intellectual task. It requires teachers to be diagnosticians, prescribers, and implementers. To perform these roles, teachers must apply theories, concepts, and broad principles from many fields of knowledge to specific pedagogical situations. The activities involved in this process—conceptualizing the problem, bringing to bear relevant information, making value judgments, planning the responses, and carrying them out—are all intellectual acts. It is not likely that the professional teacher need ever suffer from a lack of intellectual stimulation.

The Professional Teacher: Planner. By planning we mean a systematic approach to determine: (1) What do I want the students to learn? (2) By what means can they best be helped to achieve the learning goals? (3) What materials, equipment, facilities, and conditions are required to facilitate the accomplishment of the learning goals? The teacher usually has much latitude in developing his own approach to planning. The important thing is for planning to take place, not that a specific approach be employed. To some degree the nature of the fields of study (social studies, mathematics, and so on) may contribute to variations of the process. Some teachers attempt to involve their students in the planning process. (This approach has a twofold instructional value: (1) it demonstrates the value of planning as a life activity, and provides experience, with guidance, in the development of skill in that activity; and (2) it is likely to stimulate a higher degree of involvement in the subsequent learning activity, because students tend to have a psychological "stake" as a result of participating in the planning process.)

The Professional Teacher: Doer. The "doing" aspect of the work of the professional teacher is the visible part of the iceberg. It is here that everything comes together to contribute to student learning. All that has been done before is prologue and all that follows is epilogue. When it is done with care, directed by informed intelligence, and warmed by serious concern for young people, the results may be art.

Two observations are germane about the "doing" phase of the work of the professional teacher: When selecting teaching strategies and tactics, it is possible and legitimate to select those that are compatible with one's own personality. Since there is an almost infinite variety of methods and tactics that can be employed effectively by a skillful teacher, fitting the strategy to the teacher and the class becomes an important judgment act.

The second observation is that it probably is necessary for the professional teacher to have achieved a mastery over a variety of teaching methods and tactics. When students discuss teachers whom they do not rank very highly, a frequent complaint is that they are bored with classroom routine. The professional teacher must have command of a sufficient variety of methodologies and tactics so that he can work with students with a variety of characteristics, without sacrificing educationally desirable outcomes.

These points will be developed in later modules.

The Professional Teacher: Evaluator. All of us have known, since we were very small children, that teachers are evaluators (givers of grades). When we played school, didn't most of us want to be the teacher—the person who used the red pencil and distributed the 0's and *F*'s with such delight? Shevikov and Redl rightly ask, "What do you want to be anyway, an educator, or an angel with a flaming sword?"[16]

Evaluation is an important subprocess in the over-all instructional process. It represents another dimension of the work of the professional teacher, one requiring thoughtful and skillful application. For the professional teacher, evaluation is not the simple matter of recording symbols on report cards. He sees evaluation as a process that begins with goal-setting and has as its functions the providing of continuous and valid information which can be used in assessing the progress that is being made toward achievement of the goals of instruction. The professional teacher is interested in knowing whether the results he anticipated are being

---

[16] George V. Shevikov and Fritz Redl, *Discipline for Today's Children and Youth* (Washington, D.C.: Association for Supervision and Curriculum Development, 1964).

realized. If they are not, he wants to initiate new activities or procedures. He wants his students to have valid information about their performances. They need that information as they plan for the future and set goals for themselves. The professional teacher accepts responsibility for reporting accurately to parents the achievements and problems of their children.

The objective of the evaluative process is to make it possible for the persons who are involved in an enterprise to know if, and to what extent, the goals of the enterprise are being achieved. In evaluation relating to instruction, the process involves three separate operations, each requiring different skills of the teacher for their execution: (1) the collection of data in relation to the goals of the learning experience; (2) the assignment of values to the data (determining their meaning); and (3) reporting the assessments.

In the first operation, the teacher looks to his goals and decides what information is needed in order to determine whether or not progress is being made in the achievement of goals. He determines how the data will be collected, and sets in motion the procedures that will yield the data. In this procedure he uses measurement instruments and data-gathering devices and techniques such as tests, written work, observation of pupil performance, and so on. Paper and pencil tests and examinations tend to carry an excessive load in the evaluative process in many class situations. The professional teacher uses these devices when they are appropriate, but he knows that there are many other evaluative techniques, and he has them in his repertoire.

The second procedure involves the teacher in assigning meaning or significance to the data collected in the first phase of the evaluative process. Here the teacher relates the data of the first phase to some external criterion and makes a judgment concerning its significance. To illustrate this procedure: suppose that in measuring a board, we find that it is two feet, six inches long. That fact alone gives us little basis for assigning value to the board. When we add that the objective we are attempting to achieve is to replace a shelf that is two feet, nine inches in length, we can then judge that the board we have measured will not serve our purpose. The external criterion is not met. In the instructional setting, what does a raw score of 40 mean? If a student succeeded in completing 10 of 12 items in a work sample, how shall we evaluate that accomplishment? We cannot say, until we relate these scores to external criteria. In general, those criteria will be related to our instructional goals. These two procedures are the same as those in the evaluation phase of the general pattern of good teaching.

The third procedure in the evaluation process involves the teacher's recording, very clearly, the judgments arrived at as a result of second-phase activities. The key word here is *communication*. Very frequently, report cards and other devices employed by teachers and schools do not meet the communication test, and the result is that those who need or deserve accurate information simply do not receive it.[17]

The Professional Teacher: Team Member. Under ideal conditions, all the individuals who come together to make up the school consider themselves members of the community that is the school. In such a setting, the outsider quickly senses

---

[17] The treatment of the evaluation process in this section has been derived from a formulation found in Harold Hand's book, *Principles of Public Secondary Education* (New York: Harcourt, Brace, Jovanovich, Inc., 1958.)

that students, teachers, aides, cafeteria workers, secretaries, administrators, and custodians find the school a good place to be. They take pride in their school. Each person in the school makes his contribution to establish and maintain this closeness of community. Teachers, because they work so closely with students, and because they are in more permanent positions in the school community than students, who come and go, are in a unique position to assist in maintaining the tradition of the school community. Their sensitive treatment of students under stress can do much to create the climate of mutual respect and concern so necessary for the generation of a sense of community within a school.

We like to think that the professional staff of the school constitutes a team. A team in the sense that individuals and groups (administrators, guidance counselors, supervisors, department chairpersons, teachers, and instructional aides) work together to achieve commonly accepted objectives. Each person and each group makes unique contributions to the whole. All are aware of the importance of the contributions of the parts of the organization, but are equally imbued with the notion that the whole is greater than the sum of the parts.

Wherever the concept of a school professional team is a functioning reality, professional teachers have had a most significant role to play. By their actions teachers demonstrate that they genuinely enjoy working with their colleagues, and they recognize that the most pressing tasks a school staff must confront (instructional tasks and problems) cannot be dealt with except in a spirit of mutual cooperation.

The Professional Teacher and Educational Organizations. The professional world of the teacher extends beyond the walls of the classroom and the school. As a professional person, he has many opportunities to join and participate in the work of organizations that have as their purposes the advancement of education and the promotion of professional growth and careers of their members. The values of affiliating with other teachers to pursue common goals and to secure a voice on the educational issues that concern the society are sufficient for us to recommend such affiliations to all teachers. We make no recommendations as to particular organizations. The choice has to be a very individual one. We do advise that you learn as much as you can about the organizations that interest you, their goals and programs, before you make a decision to join.

The Professional Teacher and Educational Issues. *"Accountability." "Technology in Education." "Compulsory Education?" "Career Education." "Student Rights."* Are you acquainted with these terms? Do you know the issues associated with them? These represent but a few of the current issues in the field of education, some of which are the subjects of subsequent modules. How they are eventually resolved could dramatically affect education in the future, altering our conceptions of teaching and the roles of teachers.

Controversy is no stranger to the field of education; issues are always abundant. In another aspect of his life as a professional, the teacher is expected not only to keep abreast of the issues, but to be well informed about them; and to make critical assessments of the alternatives presented by them for education, the practice of teaching, and student learning. One reason for affiliating with professional organizations in education is that most of them do exceptionally fine work in highlighting issues in education, and in relating their meanings to their members.

A Final Comment

If we have convinced you that education is serious business, and that teaching of a quality deserving the adjective "professional" is a demanding activity, we have accomplished some of the objectives we had for this module. We hope, too, that we have established a background and set a tone for your involvement in the modules that follow. It may be that in our zeal we have erred in the direction of dwelling too exclusively upon the awesome responsibilities associated with teaching. Much is expected of the teacher, and the financial rewards are not always commensurate with the responsibilities. But the personal satisfaction is enormous. When you know you have done something well, and all of a sudden the mind's lights shine in the eyes of your students, you know that it is all worth it. Teaching "is a profession to be proud of, and the professional teacher glories in being able to say, 'I am a teacher!' "[18]

SUGGESTED READING

Bagley, William C. *Craftsmanship in Teaching.* New York: Macmillan Publishing Co., Inc., 1912.

Barzun, Jacques. *Teacher in America.* New York: Doubleday Anchor Books, Doubleday & Company, Inc., 1954.

Highet, Gilbert. *The Art of Teaching.* New York: Vintage Books, 1955.

Kelly, Earl C. *In Defense of Youth.* Englewood Cliffs, N.J.: Prentice-Hall, Inc., 1962.

Schlosser, Courtney D. *The Person in Education: A Humanistic Approach.* New York: Macmillan Publishing Co., Inc., 1976.

Silberman, Charles E. *Crisis in the Classroom.* New York: Random House, Inc., 1970.

Stuart, Jesse. *To Teach, To Love.* New York: Penguin Books, Inc., 1973.

Tesconi, Charles A. *Schooling in America: A Social Philosophical Perspective.* Boston: Houghton Mifflin Company, 1975.

Travers, Robert M. W. and Jacqueline Dillon. *The Making of a Teacher.* New York: Macmillan Publishing Co., Inc., 1975.

Van Til, William. *The Making of a Modern Educator.* Indianapolis: The Bobbs-Merrill Co., Inc., 1961.

Wilson, Charles H. *A Teacher Is a Person.* New York: Holt, Rinehart & Winston, Inc., 1956.

POST TEST

1. Explain the difference between education and schooling.

_____

_____

[18] Clark and Starr, op. cit., p. 461.

2. What difference is there between formal education and schooling?

_____

_____

3. Name at least three institutions or agencies other than schools that contribute to one's broad education.

_____

_____

4. From the viewpoint of this module, should schooling be entirely intellectual?

_____

_____

5. Do most educationists consider the meaning of education to be broad or narrow?

_____

_____

6. Name the principal reason why educationists recommend planned lifelong education.

_____

7. In the modern world, educationists claim that a principal educational objective should be educability. What is educability?

_____

_____

8. What was the principal reason for establishing schools in the first place?

_____

_____

9. George Counts, other critics of education, and modern activists have held that the schools should become the instruments for building a new social order and to cure the ills of modern society. Is this thinking compatible with the principal reasons for maintaining schools?

_____

_____

_____

10. How long has universal public education through the secondary school been an American ideal?

_____

_____

11. What are the major areas of educational objectives, referred to as the Seven Cardinal Principles?

12. In what major ways do the goals of the 1938 NEA statement and the 1944 statement, *Education for All American Youth,* differ from the Seven Cardinal Principles insofar as major areas of educational objectives are concerned?

13. According to the Educational Policies Commission's 1961 statement, what should be the central purpose of American education?

14. Define teaching in its broadest sense.

15. Define teaching in its best narrow sense.

16. Kingsley Price, Travers and Dillon, Gilbert Highet, and others, state that teaching is not a performance or a science, but an art. Why do they say this?

17. What is the difference between a strategy and a tactic?

18. What are the five steps in the teaching-learning cycle or pattern?

19. Who determines what is actually taught in the classroom?

20. In his role as mentor and guide—besides actually instructing and guiding people in both curricular and extracurricular subject matter—what does the teacher do?

21. Why must the teacher be something of a bureaucrat?

_____

_____

22. From whom do the parents and other citizens derive most of their ideas about the programs, worth, and effectiveness of their local schools?

_____

23. A professional teacher must learn his business. To do so he must become knowledgeable in six general areas, according to this module. What are the six areas?

_____

_____

_____

24. According to the module, what is the basic difference between a technician and a professional?

_____

_____

25. If you were asked what the one best way to teach is, what would be the only correct reply?

_____

_____

_____

26. Why does the author of this module believe that to be a truly successful teacher one must act as a member of a team?

_____

_____

_____

27. What stand should a teacher take on the question of equal rights?

_____

_____

Current Status of Schools and Education

John C. Forbeck

Shaker Heights, Ohio

module 2

Criticism / Function and Purpose of Schools / Adequacy of Curriculum Offerings / Competency of the Teaching Staff / Some Problems of the Present Decade / Alternatives for Consideration

RATIONALE

Pressure to succeed in school, increasing world over, encourages behavior that is antithetical to goals of rational self-transcendence. Children steal answer booklets, copy each other's work, falsify records, in order to appear to have obtained minimum standards set by the system. Education, the individual, and mankind are corrupted. Little wonder, then, that we have much-schooled men devoid of self-understanding and good will toward humanity.[1]

Can this be a description of the schools we know, by a prominent American educator who has had an opportunity to observe a multitude of schools? If so, what a shocking commentary on the American school system, the American people, and the accomplishments, to date, of the great American experiment in universal education!

Can it be possible that the many noble minds that have contributed to the growth of our national school systems in the past two hundred years knowingly fostered the system's development toward this end? Is it possible that these consequences have resulted by unconscious drift?

If the deplorable state of schools that Goodlad describes has resulted from failure to recognize and implement worthy and lofty goals, when did the decline begin? How did it become so well-established that a sweeping condemnation such as Goodlad's can be tolerated as having any resemblance to fact?

These questions, and similar ones that may be provoked by this module, all teachers should be able to answer. If the quoted condemnation does not represent the convictions of most knowledgeable educators, it does reflect the persuasion of some individuals or some groups of citizens. It is very possible that it describes accurately the mind-set of some parents whose children will be in your first classroom.

On the premise that if you are ignorant of history you may be doomed to repeat it, we shall examine in this module some of the criticism that has been leveled at the schools and education. Our major thrust will be that there are things that need to be changed in education, but that, because it is impossible to please all observers and critics, the changing of education will be no simple chore. A move to the left will offend those who demand a move to the right. Actions responding to clamors for more tradition will alienate those who shout for more innovation. The position of the author of this module is that teachers must be constantly aware of what is being said about their programs. Unless a teacher succumbs to hypersensitivity about criticism, knowing what the critics of our programs are saying or writing about them should serve to strengthen defensible programs and help to eliminate unsound programs.

For as long as they have existed, schools have had their critics. In each era vocal individuals, groups, and agencies have taken positions of opposition to what has been proposed or effectuated. Most recently, in addition to local citizens' groups and Parent Teachers Associations which have boycotted individual schools

[1] John I. Goodlad, *School Curriculum and the Individual* (Waltham, Mass.: Ginn/Blaisdell, 1956), p. 259.

and picketed the offices of the superintendents of schools, other groups such as The Citizens League, The Committee for Economic Development, The Council for Basic Education, The National Association for the Advancement of Colored People, and so on, have raised their collective voices for one reason or another. Those opposing rising school costs have demanded Spartan quality-control measures to bring about promised economies. Those more concerned with the alleged decline in excellence of student achievement have focused their attacks on such problems as faulty curriculums, inferior methodology, inadequately prepared teachers, or ineffective administrators.

Criticism of the schools will never cease, nor should it. Effective utilization of criticism, however, can render it a benefit instead of a drawback.

Objectives

In this module you will read about the positions taken by critics of education over the decades. You will note that in each area commented upon the demands have been incompatible—for more and for less, for increase and decrease, for higher and lower, all at the same time.

The goal of the module is to provoke you to think about the various positions that have been taken. You should be aware, as you begin your career, that battles have been waged over these topics in the past. You should also be aware that at some time in your career you will be forced to declare yourself "for" or "against" proposals that will be similar to, and even identical with, some of those presented here. By becoming familiar with the causes of some of the past criticism and controversies, you should be helped to formulate some guidelines upon which to base your decisions in the future.

Upon completing your study of this module, you should be able to

1. Cite a minimum of four areas that have been singled out for criticism.
2. List the steps in sound program development taken by school districts that have been successful in modifying the curriculum.
3. Designate the types of individuals who should be involved in the development and implementation of a goals- and objective-setting process.
4. Identify the five general types of critics of the school.
5. Identify the characteristics critics have attacked as "traditional" or "progressive" education.
6. Give four criticisms directed against the competency of the teaching staff.
7. Cite three disadvantages of a small high school.
8. Cite three disadvantages of a large high school.
9. Cite three causes for the increase in teacher power.
10. Show knowledge about the American Federation of Teachers and the National Education Association by labeling statements about their tenets as true or false.
11. Cite at least three valid changes that should be made in teacher education programs.
12. Describe the changes in the role of accreditation agencies in today's schools.
13. State the changes from *traditional* to *reformed,* as described by Fantini.

14. State the optimum enrollment for a high school, as recognized by the National Association of Secondary Schools Principals study.
15. List three ways that schoolmen in past eras have responded to attacks of radical critics calling for abolition of obsolete institutions.
16. Cite three facets of philosophy on which all of the current alternative schools are based.

MODULE TEXT

Criticism

In keeping with the precedent established early in our history, schools across the country today are the recipients of frequent criticism. Today, the biggest difference between this and previous eras might well be either the wholesale participation of ever increasing segments of the population in the criticism or the widespread discussion and circulation of opinions about the various items causing discontent.

The integrity of most critics of the schools cannot be doubted. Their credentials frequently are impeccable; their motives are sincere. Of course, vested interests and ulterior motives may constitute the prod to action for some complainers, but more often the prod is really a long-suppressed and vague feeling of dissatisfaction with what is being taught and how it is being taught.

Schools in America are in a unique position. They belong to the people. Although administrative efficiency may demand delegation of powers to professionals for day-to-day operations, control of the schools resides in the hands of citizens. In those cases where civilian boards of education are elected, this power is demonstrated every time a school board election is held. Where there are appointive boards, neighborhood citizen groups, ad hoc committees, and demonstrating action-factions serve to communicate the message.

Educators who make the error of forgetting that the people are the source of power for the schools are usually the ones most seriously hurt by criticism. When educators neglect to keep their patrons informed about new developments and experimental programs in education, or when they introduce actions before the community understands enough about the new goals and objectives, the patrons then probably get that "vague feeling of dissatisfaction" referred to earlier.

Categories of Critics. Critics of the school appear to fall into one or more of five categories:

THE SINCERELY INTERESTED. People sincerely interested in education but who are impatient with the rate of progress being made in solving the persistent problems facing the schools usually complain thus: Some problems should have been resolved years ago. The research, the expertise, and financial resources have been available but they have not been utilized vigorously enough to set things straight.

In this category are those equally sincere people at the other end of the change continuum, who find changes being foisted upon them too rapidly. These critics see little necessity for new teaching methods, new textbooks, new promotion practices, new courses, or new report cards. They want the schools to be more like what they remember them to have been years ago.

THE POLITICALLY ORIENTED. People in this group generally give little thought or attention to the problems addressed by the schools or the methodology practiced therein. They become concerned, vocal, and active only when their suspicions have been aroused by intemperate public utterances about the motives of those directing education. Innuendo and/or accusations about the political base or ideology of the power structure involved with the schools galvanizes them into action.

THE DISAFFECTED. People in this category are, predominantly, those adults whose experience, while students in school, was not positive and reinforcing. Some of these people have emerged into adulthood with deep-seated resentments and antipathies toward education. On one occasion or another they or their children have found themselves out of adjustment with the curriculum, the discipline, or the personnel in the school. Their theme usually is that the "shabby" or "devious" or "fraudulent" treatment accorded them is "typical of school people." For anyone, except the privileged few, to expect different kind of treatment is, in their view, an error.

The disaffected readily believe negative gossip, and they are inclined to ignore positive reports about accomplishments.

THE ELITISTS. Category four includes those people who are not in sympathy with the American ideal of equality of opportunity for all American youth. They resent the efforts of the school to adjust to the many levels of intellectual ability exhibited by children, and to its efforts to respond to the many psychological and sociological needs of the children. Fundamentally, people in this category tend toward the elitist fringe in society, usually because they possess (or think they possess) some or many of the characteristics they believe qualifies them for preferred treatment—according to their own theory of education.

THE SELF-SERVERS. The last group is made up of those self-serving individuals who criticize because they stand to gain financially or personally by change. Some seek tax reduction and hence oppose all changes in the schools that might necessitate additional funds. Others seek political advancement and prestige. By exploiting people's feelings of dissatisfaction, they collect the support they need to obtain nomination for public office. Then by promising to bring about changes that will remove these dissatisfactions, they get themselves elected.[2]

In all probability, the largest number of critics fall into categories one and two.

Types of Criticism. In many cases, constructive criticism of the schools has been positively influential. Often it has brought citizens together to support increased taxation, to endorse new building construction, or to effect other measures designed to solve local problems. The destructive criticism, on the other hand, has divided communities, precipitated emotional confrontations, and resulted in damaging consequences to staff members, students, and citizens.

Successful district staffs and boards of education attribute much of their progress to the fact that they cultivate constructive criticism. Districts have been able to grow, to change, and to innovate because they have been willing to recog-

---

[2] Based on Nolan C. Kearney, *A Teacher's Professional Guide* (Englewood Cliffs, N.J.: Prentice-Hall, Inc., 1956), p. 268.

nize the presence of problems and to solicit help in their solutions. After all, problems do not go away merely because they are ignored!

Districts of this kind organize themselves to recognize criticism at its inception, to prevent its becoming a sensitive issue. They provide for good human and public relations, good interaction among citizens and staff, and a steady flow of communications throughout the year. When a misunderstanding occurs, or when suspicions are voiced that all may not be well with a particular program, inquiries are launched to collect data. At this point there needs to be no denial or defense; there is merely an acknowledgement of the criticism and the inauguration of the plan of inquiry.

Successful districts often begin their inquiry by inviting key critics to visit the school to observe the program in operation. Meetings are set up for public discussion of the areas under examination. The school personnel who are involved in implementing the program to be discussed are, of course, present at the meeting. In many cases, the most vocal critics are appointed to citizens' committees or advisory councils, which continue to work in concert with the school staff to make sure that sensitive concepts or areas of concern are respected. The major advantage of these procedures is that they ensure that the criticism will have a genuine basis in fact, and that the misleading and mischief-causing kind of criticism—which derives from hunch or gossip and which cannot be combatted successfully because its point of origin cannot be found—will be eliminated.

Many schools achieve their goals by skillful treatment of community opinion-makers. Every community has its share of people who occupy positions of power or social prominence who are not reluctant to speak out on any topic. Often such people influence the thinking of other people in their social circle far beyond the point merited by the cogency of their arguments. Citizens of this kind do not like to be ignored. Involving them in committees and councils reassures them that their ideas, wrong or right, are at least being listened to and weighed. It provides an avenue of release for their frustrations, and contributes greatly toward the diminution of that "vague feeling of dissatisfaction" with the schools which flourishes where the professionals alone are in charge. When opinion-makers serve on committees and councils, they often become substantial agents of support for the school programs. When investigation reveals the need for changes, they can make valuable contributions as committee leaders working toward rectifying the situation.

Where doubt and dissension prevail, faculty morale problems generally follow. Successful school systems concentrate upon cultivating school staffs that are united in the desire to provide the best possible instructional program for the children of their community. They attempt to retain the dynamic members, to eliminate the foot-draggers, and to achieve a stability of membership which results from a conviction of the worthiness of a system. Each staff member is well-informed and is expected to reflect to the parents with whom he comes in contact a genuine concern for the students and the school. Each is expected to feel at ease with the district's goals, policies, and program plans. Each staff member can then be expected to accept the criticism leveled at anyone or any program without taking offense, and then move toward the resolution of doubt through the inquiry process.

Negative criticism often stems from inadequate knowledge about existing conditions. It has sometimes been the result of agitation by special pressure groups with definite goals which are in conflict with the established objectives of the school district. Often, negative criticism has resulted in arousing community malcontents looking for a cause to rally around, and has attracted those citizens who were generally ill-informed about their schools.

Controversial Issues. Nearly all the issues over which serious debate can be conducted have been in existence for a long time. Some assume more crucial importance than others at times because of the economic or social climate enveloping the country or the school district. During the eighteenth and nineteenth centuries, for example, "when the American people were rejecting aristocracy in favor of an emerging democracy," the curriculum of the schools, supported by vocal action of the critics, moved from elitist programs toward universal public education. In the late nineteenth and early twentieth centuries, as social problems again changed, the traditional curriculum was challenged by the progressive critics "who favored the education of the whole child."[3] In more recent decades, in a reaction against progressivism, right-wing critics attacked the curriculum because they suspected it of being socialistic, communistic, atheistic, and unpatriotic. Since then there has been a succession of waves of critical attacks, most notably attacks favoring

1. Academic education as opposed to progressive education.
2. Rigorous, disciplined learning as opposed to the alleged mediocrity inherent in progressive curriculums and teaching methods.
3. The study of mathematics and science as opposed to the study of the humanities.
4. Programs for the education of disadvantaged and alienated children.
5. Relevant curriculums as opposed to the subject matter usually offered.

In general, though, the issues that cause controversy are always with us. People always have strong beliefs on such matters as

1. Progressive versus traditional schooling.
2. State versus federal financing.
3. Method versus content.
4. Spending versus austerity.

Usually, however, the adherents and opponents of the various positions are willing to go along—without excessive protest—with the middle position (a compromise between the extremes) that the schools usually seek to follow. And so, despite cyclical periods of intense concern, the factions live side by side and do not become embroiled in conflict unless a cause célèbre arises.

Areas of Criticism. When the "celebrated causes" set the factions working against each other, the following areas, among many others, often elicit the most heated debate, or result in the most dramatic consequences.

---

[3] William Van Til, *Curriculum: Quest for Relevance* (Boston: Houghton Mifflin Company, 1974), p. 2.

1. The function and purpose of the schools.
2. The adequacy of curriculum offerings.
3. The competency of the teaching staff.
4. Urban education and the present decade.
5. Alternatives for consideration.

Not all of the various attacks upon the schools are referred to in the paragraphs that follow, nor are the many complicated facets of the major battles that were waged. Exhaustive studies of both can be found elsewhere.

It will suffice for this module if you, the reader, are alerted to the fact that public opinion does differ and does change, and you are thus enabled to put into perspective whatever future opposition you may encounter in your professional career, or in the endeavors of the school in which you will serve. Now let us look at a few of the debates.

Function and Purpose of Schools

Public education has been extended to include activities affecting many aspects of the child's life not formerly considered the province of the school. Critics claim that the extension has occurred without full public cognition and/or approval. At the instigation of professional educators, they contend, schools have engaged in social work, in psychological testing and counseling, in cooperative work-study programs, in home arts programs, and other nonacademic functions. These services, they protest, should be performed by other agencies. Therefore, responsibility for them should not be assumed by the school, nor should attending to them be permitted to distract the school from its fundamental tasks.

The schools' critics who hold the opposite view lament that the schools have been turned into hothouses nurturing conservatism and the status quo. In their view, only the privileged of the upper classes can make use of the education that is presently offered. This education, they say, is based on verbal proficiency, is highly textbook-oriented, and favors mainly those students from privileged environments who have retentive memories.

Schools have tried to resolve antithetical demands and expectations of this sort in various ways. One of the most successful has been the use of citizens committees. By being very careful about selecting a representative cross section of the community for committee membership, and by making good use of professional staff members, communities have been able to use the committee process to define the functions and purposes of their schools and to compile district policies for the guidance of school personnel. Committee chairpersons have publicized the meetings, invited contributions of ideas from all in attendance, and have discussed conclusions at length with district boards of education, in open sessions to which the public have been invited. By thus controlling conditions for research, discussion, and the circulation of conclusions, these districts have been able to eliminate attacks of the most destructive kind. Committees can examine complaints in the light of district policy and then either accept or reject them, and, if it seems desirable, initiate a reexamination of the policy.

A written philosophy of education for the school system specifying the school's general objectives and goals is helpful for these committees. So is a written description of the ongoing program of evaluation and review of the school curriculum. Generally these documents establish the guidelines, within which operating committees must function when recommending changes affecting instruction. To establish the bases for decision making, these documents generally:

1. Describe the kinds of data used in establishing the current levels of achievement and specify by test name, by grade, and by month of the year when each evaluation should be administered.
2. Indicate how data gathered in previous years can be used to compare progress of students recently tested.
3. Name the districts that are similar in socioeconomic backgrounds and academic aspirations which can be used as comparison groups.
4. Specify the action which should be taken to meet the needs of students who have failed to achieve and the provisions which should be implemented for students enrolled in experimental programs that are declared defective.

In each case, steering committees comprised of teachers, administrators, board of education members, community citizens—especially members of forceful minority groups evidencing interest in particular aspects of school life—have been called upon to do the work. Where laymen and educators work cooperatively on program improvement, it has been found that resentment and dissatisfaction with school efforts have been held at a minimum.

Adequacy of Curriculum Offerings

The Traditional Position. If the various curriculums offered in contemporary schools were to be placed on a continuum, traditional education would be placed at one extreme and progessive education at the other. Traditional education is subject-centered. It emphasizes the basic skills and, frequently, a great deal of memorization. The most conservative of traditional curriculums are dominated by basic subjects such as history, geography, and arithmetic, which are taught to all children at the same grade level, and in the same way. If a child does not master the material, he is forced to repeat the grade until he does. Critics of the traditional approach claim that the curriculum is narrow, limited, and irrelevant to the needs of both the pupils and contemporary society. They also believe that the lock-step teaching procedures (which ignore individual differences) and the demand for mastery are downright harmful.

Supporters of traditional education believe that schools should concern themselves only with the intellectual development of the pupils. They believe that the social, emotional, physical, and moral development should be the responsibility of the home, the church, and other agencies—not the school. If these institutions do not provide for children properly, then, the traditionalists say, it is up to the community to provide other means. The school should not do so, because assuming the responsibility for other than the pupils' intellectual development tends to defeat its intellectual mission. Provision for special services such as psychological consultations and medical and dental examinations, and the teaching of such courses as Art Appreciation are not, they maintain, the proper business of the school.

Educational Traditionalists find much of contemporary education anti-intellectual. They shudder at the introduction of what they consider to be watered-down courses (for example, courses in home and family living, and consumer mathematics) particularly when these courses are given the same curricular weight as such traditional courses as French, algebra, or U.S. history. The claim is that students of superior ability are not challenged because they are permitted to elect courses lacking in intellectual rigor; that students who are not able to master the curriculum are pushed through to graduation by social promotion and credit for "no-content" courses such as driver education.

The Progressive Position. Progressive education, at the other end of the continuum, is child-centered. Here the focus of classes is on the child's own personal adjustment problems—intellectual and emotional—rather than on organized knowledge. Subject matter is not important for its own sake, but only as it happens to apply to whatever problem is being studied. It is not so much that knowledge is downgraded, but that it is perceived as a tool with which to solve problems. Thus, a particular bit of subject matter is of great importance when it is needed, but is not of much importance when it is not needed. In such a context, the subject matter to be included in the curriculum consists only of the subject matter needed to help solve problems. The logical placement and development of subject matter according to the disciplines does not apply.

Progressivists believe that the school's responsibility is to develop the whole child—not only the intellect. In fact, they believe that intellectual development is so intimately interwoven with the other facets of human development that it cannot be isolated from them and treated separately. As they see it, the school program must treat the whole child, or it is a failure. Furthermore, they believe that unless the school assumes the responsibility for the social, moral, emotional, and physical development of children, no one will, because in modern society the church, home, and community have proved themselves to be inadequate for this task.

Progressivists are upset by the almost exclusively academic tone of contemporary school curriculums. It is their position that such curriculums are obsolete relics of past centuries, when education was a prerogative of the socially elite. In their view, now that the country has moved away from an agrarian economy and has begun to confront the complex problems of an urban era, the genteel aims of the Renaissance are no longer satisfactory. Upwardly mobile members of the laboring classes expect the schools to provide for their needs and the needs of their children, just as in the past they provided for the children of the elite. When the attempts to teach all the children of all the people resulted in large numbers of drop outs and academic failures, the people became disenchanted with elitist academic education. What traditional education labeled as pupil failure caused by disinterest or disinclination to perform, Progressivists viewed as the failure of an out of date curriculum and the memorization of textbooks.

Many students, parents, and other laymen join the Progressivists in their attack on what appears to be an overemphasis on the academic. There is little in the curriculum, they say, for those who are not book-oriented or college-bound. In secondary schools particularly, students and parents alike have resented the second-class treatment of all who do not plan to go to college. Sympathy and support for the feelings of frustration caused by the continuing stress on academic subjects in the curriculum have come from alumni who have found that the school has given them little that they can use in the practical workaday world. Many of these alumni, feeling victimized by the school and its curriculum, have voiced great dissatisfaction, and have demanded a change. These parents, students, alumni, and laymen demand that secondary schools of today must not be specialized vocational schools for students aiming at the learned professions. They demand a school that meets all the needs of all the students—a position anathema to the Traditionalists, who see this as heralding the end of intellectual education.

School Size and the Curriculum. School programs, as we have seen, may be criticized because they are too traditional or too progressive. They may also be criticized for many other things. One of these is the richness or poverty of the programs offered; another is the size of the school. Small high schools have been criticized because they are not able to provide a rich enough intellectual diet. Small size has some advantages of course. Where there are only a few students, it is easier to learn to know the students and their needs, but it then becomes economically unfeasible to offer the many courses and various sequences required for a comprehensive program. Consequently, students compelled to attend a small school may be at a disadvantage because of the location of their parents' homes; they are in a position inferior to that of students from larger districts with their more numerous resources and richer offerings. On the other hand, large schools have been accused of neglecting the cultivation of some of the personal and social qualities needed for success in society. Their sheer size has tended to make them impersonal. The opportunity for students to slip into anonymity has been tremendous. Furthermore, it has been charged that large schools have offered too many frill courses, too many impractical subjects, too few how-to-study courses, and that too little emphasis has been placed upon critical thinking, creative expression, and development of leadership abilities.

The National Association of Secondary School Principals has conducted studies which reveal that the most functional high school should have approximately one thousand students in a four-year program. Because of the facilities available and the populations available, this ideal is impossible to attain in many areas. Schools within the inner cities are known to house nearly four thousand students, whereas in small suburban areas and farming districts there are high schools with only two hundred pupils. Both extremes create problems that are difficult to resolve. The small high school today is pressed with a financial burden if it attempts to offer all the courses and activities which are considered by laymen to be both prestigious and necessary. Furthermore, classes in small schools are so reduced in size that teacher-pupil ratios are expensive to maintain. At the other extreme, where three to four thousand students are housed in one building, a variety of course offerings can be made available, with teacher-student ratios somewhat higher and therefore more financially realistic. However, so large a mass of students in one building often creates difficulty in control and organization. In addition, the disabling malaise of bigness and anonymity often sets in, and is counterproductive.

A Middle Ground. Just as school administrators have tried in their schools to combine the best features of large and small schools, educators in general have tried to combine the best features of traditional and progressive education. As we have said, concern about the adequacy of the curriculum and the merits of traditionalism and progressivism has been the source of much of the controversy in our schools. But because each theory has its shortcomings and its attractive features, probably the only reasonable solution to the choice of curriculum in any school district is a compromise position—a middle ground that is neither one nor another, but a combination of the best elements of each. However, no position can be made to suit all the people all the time, therefore school personnel must learn what the predilections of their community are and take these into account before moving toward or away from a particular position. The schools that have been most successful in introducing modern programs, and which have experienced the fewest tragedies regarding these programs, are those that have done the best job of interpreting to their constituents the what, how, and why of the program. Their "middle ground" has been broad enough to accommodate convictions across a broad spectrum. Voters who lean toward traditionalism have not needed to revolt when minicourses or time-modules were introduced, because these innovations did not necessarily destroy the quality of study previously established as the standard. Supporters of the Progressivist stripe have not needed to resist the implementation of structured programs and sequences because developmental needs and student-centered problems could be accommodated within the context of the resulting curriculum schedule.

Kinds of Scheduling. Scheduling is another area about which a wide range of comment has sprung up. In recent years, in order to make their programs more flexible, some forward-looking secondary schools have "retooled" in order to convert to modular scheduling of their total program. In flexible scheduling, the school day is divided into short modules, that is periods of 10 or 15 minutes, instead of the usual 45- or 50-minute length. Pupil activities and classes are scheduled to be one, two, three, or more modules long. Thus, in a school using 15-minute modules, one activity might be scheduled for 15 minutes and another might be scheduled for two hours. In some schools the students move continuously about the building. Theoretically at least, this varying of the meeting time of activities or classes makes it possible to match the length of time scheduled with the nature of the activity or class. In another scheduling variation, some newer school programs have literally hundreds of various minicourses built on four- six-, or nine-week plans so that students can change courses at regular short-term intervals. At least one secondary school has so individualized its curriculum that each student in the school has a "personalized" schedule that is different from that of every other student.

The contrasting extreme has been the traditional six- or seven-period day used in other schools, where every student moves through the building on a regular time schedule, period by period. In these programs, every class and every part of the curriculum has a uniform time-slot designated for instruction. In the traditional scheduling approach, too, the curriculum itself has many traditional patterns, such as English I, II, and III, or Math I, II, or III.

The variety of scheduling techniques and of curricula used by different districts, and the mobility of many families throughout the United States (resulting in the exposure of students to the varieties), have caused much criticism by laymen. In some affluent districts, administrators have been able to "sell" highly innovative programs to their communities. Other districts have convinced their voters of the desirability of a traditional approach. In a nation so mobile and communicative as ours, such differences in policy are bound to lead to clashes of opinion, particularly as families moving from district to district find themselves confronted by new, seemingly incompatible, school programs.

New Curriculum Problems. Relatively new problems currently facing the schools have created a slightly different base for critical comment and reaction. Schools still struggle to achieve the aim of secondary education proposed in 1961 by the Educational Policies Commission—the development of the ability to think. They endeavor to encourage the transfer of learning from one context to the other in order to secure the optimum development of every student's rational powers. But the rapid social, economic, and technological changes that are taking place are creating new reasons for students to challenge educational practices. As they and the adults in many communities demand evidence of quality in education, increased pressure is on schools and teachers to deal more adequately with disadvantaged groups, with problems dealing with race, with sex, and with the relevancy of accumulated knowledge to the tasks at hand.

SEX EDUCATION. Two significant areas that have received intense scrutiny and that have caused considerable debate are sex education and drug education. The increased number of early marriages, of early divorce, of premarital pregnancies, and known cases of venereal disease have led to a demand for more sex education in the schools. Consequently, family-life programs have been proposed in great number, in an attempt to meet the apparent need.

The introduction of instruction in sex education has caused conflicts in many school districts; many parents and other concerned citizens are convinced that sex education has no place in our schools. In some cases these opponents are right-wing conservative; some are parents who find sex education objectionable on moral or religious grounds. In other cases, the opponents simply object to the teachers appointed to the sex-education classes, and/or to the method and materials being used in the courses. Others consider the schools to be improperly prepared for this role. It is their contention that such a psychologically important subject as sex education should not be taught by teachers who may have few qualifications for the job, or who may themselves suffer from sexual disabilities. When one adds to this criticism concerns about what the course content should be, whether or not the class should be coeducational or sex-segregated, and the philosophical and moral positions expressed in the texts and other instructional material, the reasons why conflicts over sex education have continued so long become strikingly apparent.

DRUG EDUCATION. In the late sixties and early seventies, many programs in drug education grew out of the fear that in some parts of the country addiction was reaching epidemic proportions. Ignorance on the part of young people, curiosity, peer pressure, or the desire to rebel, it appeared, had begun to influence children to turn to drugs, even in the early grades of elementary school. And so courses of study were developed and units concerning drugs were incorporated into teacher preparation programs in order to equip future teachers to address the problem. Experienced teachers were requested, or required, to attend workshops and in-service programs to prepare for the emergency.

In many communities major conflicts concerning the drug problem resulted from disagreement about the treatment of drug offenders. Hard-liners took the position that offenders should be punished with jail terms or fines, and soft-liners favored using educational and therapeutic measures, reserving the full penalties of the law only for major offenders. Some critics were also concerned that introduction of "drug education" would intensify rather than help the problem. They were afraid that the attention given by the school to drugs and the drug problem would serve to create interest and experimenting with drugs among pupils who would have remained untouched if drug education courses had not been introduced. The problem of drugs and drug education still continues unsolved.

Competency of the Teaching Staff

A considerable share of the criticism of the educational enterprise has been directed at teachers—both as a group and as individuals. Their training, the quality of their dedication, their native ability in contrast to representatives of other professions, their subjectivity or objectivity in dealing with students, and especially their requests for increases in salary have been the subject at one time or another of attack by different people and groups. In the main, the critics have generally contended that

Too many poorly trained and incompetent teachers are permitted to retain their positions. The methods they use are antiquated, they remain in one system too long, and they fall too easily into a rut of routine performance.

Teachers place too much emphasis upon grades. There is a lack of uniformity in standards set by different teachers so that students experience difficulty in adjusting to the varying demands upon them. In some cases, the thirst for knowledge on the part of students is destroyed, only to be replaced by an obsessive pursuit of higher marks.

Teachers are inclined to be too mobile, hopping from school to school as advantages are to be obtained. They reveal little serious interest in and dedication to the community they serve; display little professional zeal for the improvement of education but much active interest in higher salaries. They are often unsympathetic to extracurricular activities.

Frequently in their dealings with students, teachers are rigid and authoritarian. They appear not to understand the pupils whom they teach. They play favorites, often antagonize marginal students, and alienate those in need of disciplinary action. Some are vindictive and make use of sarcasm and ridicule to preserve unfairly their superiority over students, a superiority that they seem to need.

The Change of Teachers' Status. Historically, teachers have relied heavily upon the benevolence of lay boards for their protection and well-being. Having selected teaching as a career not because it would lead to wealth, but because of an interest in working with children and a desire to help young people, teachers assessed their own worth on the basis of service to society. They did not quarrel much with the financial compensation for their efforts established by officials outside of their profession.

In the past half-century, however, the situation has radically changed. Of late, there has been a significant rise in the number of teachers actively involved in various types of teacher activity, including membership and participation in teachers' organizations. Educators, like other groups affected by the changing social and economic conditions, have felt the need to organize in order to improve their status position, to satisfy their need to belong, and to improve their economic standing.

With few exceptions, educators' early efforts at organization followed the structural pattern that had already become standard in the schools. Organizational policies naturally were dominated by administrators. Only gradually did teachers develop a spirit of responsibility for the growth of the profession, and gain a role as participants in policy making.

TEACHER MILITANCY. By the 1960s, teacher militancy had become a force to be reckoned with. According to the Bureau of Labor statistics, although there had been 91 strikes by teachers between 1940 and 1962, between 1965 and 1969 there were 296. The number of full-time executive secretaries of local teachers' associations grew in that decade from 25 to 150.

The treatment of teachers in the mass media has changed radically during this period, also. The image of the unselfish, dedicated schoolmarm has been modified to that of the hard-nosed negotiator or strike-leader. The fact that neither image is, or has been, completely accurate may help to account for that "vague feeling of dissatisfaction" on the part of those citizens responsible for the criticism of teachers.

For their part, teachers and their organizations discount the militancy attributed to them. They view their efforts as modest attempts to change their longstanding organizational weakness, and to upgrade their position as a profession. Their big push, which has constituted the major change, has been for input at the local level. Prior to the 1960s, most of the organizational efforts and resources were devoted to and channeled through state associations. If they wanted their salaries improved, teachers attempted to move the legislature to effect a raise in the state minimum salary. For protection against unwarranted dismissal, they worked for a state tenure law.

When teachers began pouring their organizational efforts into the local organization instead of into the state association, boards of education and district administrators naturally tended to overreact. Their hasty condemnations of the newly visible teacher militancy reflected their shock at the radical change in a previously impotent organization. Militancy was widely condemned as unprofessional and completely inappropriate for public employees by both school administration and lay officials.

EVOLUTIONARY CHANGES OF ATTITUDE. Gradually the attitude of most citizens has changed in the direction of tolerance or acceptance of increased teacher militancy. As other groups of public employees exerted their collective power to gain some of the advantages they demanded, the resentment of the teachers' position subsided into one of toleration for employment disputes. Teacher strikes, once shocking, began to seem less catastrophic, and less likely to lead to the dissolution of the nation. In consequence, the series of strikes in 1967–68 by the United Federation of Teachers in New York City, which closed schools for fifteen days in 1967 and fifty days in 1968, culminated in victory for the teachers, a rallying of public opinion for their position, and an increase in prestige for the union, in the view of at least one author.[4]

---

[4] Myron Lieberman, "Teacher Militancy," in Dwight Allen and Eli Seifman, Eds., *The Teacher's Handbook* (Glenview, Ill.: Scott, Foresman and Company, 1971), p. 721.

The Membership Dilemma. The rise of teacher militancy poses a dilemma concerning the role that should be played by professional staff members. Is it legitimate for teachers to exert pressure to achieve their goals in the same fashion as other groups, or are they obligated to avoid militant tactics? "Rightly or wrongly, most white-collar and professional groups tend to regard militant tactics as 'unprofessional'; hence to be avoided."[5]

For many teachers, the dilemma is extended to affect their decision about membership in The National Education Association (NEA) or the American Federation of Teachers (AFT).

The NEA, the largest of all professional educators' organizations, represents more than seven thousand local associations. Its purpose is to promote the welfare of teachers. In this connection, its research division "has made more significant educational studies on a national level than any other single agency in America."[6] Recently it has been very aggressive in its attempts to better the economic and professional status of its members.

The largest national teacher union is the American Federation of Teachers (AFT), which is affiliated with the AFL-CIO. Its goal is to provide a high-level, nonindependent organization for teachers who are convinced that without a *united* effort teachers will be unable to compete with other organizations in our society.[7] Economic determinism and collective bargaining are basic tenets of the AFT.

The goals of both these organizations are similar, but "the professed method of attaining these goals are considerably different. Many teachers have been very wary of the labor movement in education, and are concerned with its effect on the professional status of the teacher. However, there is little evidence that teachers belonging to either the AFT or a local union organization have lost status within their communities."[8]

COLLECTIVE BARGAINING. With the advent of collective bargaining between teachers' organizations and boards of education, every teacher may have more incentive to become a supporting member of a teachers' organization. The changes which aggressive organization have brought about have resulted in improved economic welfare for teachers at present. These changes are also beginning to produce counter demands by citizens: they want accountability. Some teachers also feel that the short-range gains have been achieved at the expense of community understanding and sympathy for school problems. They feel that these processes have set up an adversary relationship between teachers and administrators at a time when unity and cooperation are important. They are also concerned about the need to find a way in which teachers will be able to guarantee to an investigating public the quality education the public is demanding. How can teachers resolve the multitudinous problems surrounding the concept of accountability without "self-governance," for example? Under existing conditions, teachers have either too little control or no control over the factors that might render accountability feasible or fair.

[5] Ibid.
[6] Edward W. Smith, Stanley W. Krouse, Jr., and Mark M. Atkinson, *The Educator's Encyclopedia* (Englewood Cliffs, N.J.: Prentice-Hall, Inc., 1961), p. 235.
[7] Ibid., p. 243.
[8] Ibid., p. 244.

TEACHERS' ORGANIZATIONS. Teachers' associations and unions, have usually been stronger, and have played a more dominant role, in the secondary school than in the elementary school. The age, education, and experience of teachers at this level, as well as the predominance of males and breadwinners on the high school staff help to account in part for this development. Of late, however, because teacher organizations have experienced considerable change, these precedents may no longer prevail.

Today, teachers' organizations are more powerful than ever before. Concern about the apparent growing surplus of teachers in many subject fields, about the survival strength of current tenure laws, the future availability of jobs, and the declining pupil population, among other things, has moved them toward increased demonstrations of viability. Today, there is more pressure from the associations than ever for a role in decision making at various levels and for more input and control over the professional destinies of their members.

Such participation in decision making is not entirely new. A variety of participation plans, which include consultation with teachers of stature on matters pertaining to school personnel, have been extant for some time in secondary schools. On some staffs, the design of the plan has helped to elicit and utilize the opinions of the entire staff in matters relating to program objectives and curriculum. In cases where teachers have worked with strong administrative leadership, staff contributions have aided curriculum improvement and have resulted in educational programs of merit. In some other cases, though, where concessions to staff were made begrudgingly, or where teacher clamor for involvement in school policy making has been especially vehement, curriculum action has been even more impervious to change.

Some Problems of the Present Decade

The increase of the school population after World World II, along with the social and economic adjustments of a very mobile society, created difficult problems for almost every educational district. Criticism intensified in the postwar era because of the lack of ability of some districts to respond quickly enough to the continuing changes in the schools. School district administrators and teachers faced not only an enormous housing problem and a teacher-shortage problem, but also the problem of meeting the needs of the new groups of students who did not plan to attend college. Now, although the over-all student population has begun to show signs of modest decrease, the plight of the noncollege-bound segment of students still appears to be the critical area of focus in the eyes of the public.

How to make education for a career truly viable is somewhat problematic under present conditions. Employment patterns reveal dramatic decreases in the number of blue-collar jobs available, and predictions are that the average wage earners of tomorrow will change occupations at least three times in a working career. Government sources have attempted to address the problem of the noncollege student by funding and by offering manpower training programs for specific groups whose problems are sizeable and serious. Industry has begun to offer short-term training programs for the hard-core unemployed to help them retool for new jobs. The U.S. Department of Health, Education, and Welfare, with the blessing of the President of the United States, has poured millions into the encouragement of interest in experimentation with and staffing of new programs dealing with career education in the schools.

Educators who have been involved with this movement feel that the career-education models that are beginning to emerge (that is, the cooperative programs in the distributive and industrial trades, and especially the regionalization of vocational schools along county-district lines) should be made high-priority items in schools throughout the country. The fact that students can retain their academic standing and remain in their program in their district high school while, on a part-time basis, engaging in technological education at the county school, should do much to remove the stigma that has traditionally been attached to vocational education. In the future, no student should have to graduate from high school still lacking in saleable skills.

Accreditation Process. With the changing role of secondary schools, and the availability of space for many more pupils in the higher-education area, the accreditation of schools is viewed with less trepidation today than it was in the fifties. At that time, parents interested in quality education would have been reluctant to send their sons or daughters to schools that were not accredited by national agencies of good repute. Today, many alternative schools, both private and public, are totally lacking in accreditation. In many cases, students graduating from nonaccredited schools are now invited to enroll in and complete higher-education programs. The most universally accepted accrediting agency—The Commission on Secondary Schools—maintains six regional associations: The New England Association, The Middle States Association, for the Eastern United States; The Southern Association, for the Southern United States; The North-Central Association, for the near Midwest; The Northwest Association, and The Western Association. Some or all of these groups have begun developing programs for accreditation of elementary, middle, and junior high schools, as well as of high schools and institutions of higher education.

Originally, these accreditation systems and programs were established to standardize the quality of instruction in the various secondary schools that had come into existence. Until that time, well-intentioned schools had no measuring rod against which to evaluate their efforts. Universities too were lacking in facilities and machinery for judging the readiness of applicants for college-level work. So different were the products of the many and various schools who requested admission, and so different had been the preparation of these students by the schools from which they graduated, that the universities welcomed the coming of the accrediting agencies. Until recently, many colleges, especially the prestigious universities, would not even consider the acceptance of a student who graduated from a secondary school that lacked accreditation. Today, the pressure for accreditation and the prestige resulting from accreditation have diminished considerably. Of late, the agencies themselves have reduced their efforts toward standardization, and have begun to place greater emphasis on the quality of programs, and on the extent and purpose of innovative secondary school programs.

School Staff. The secondary school today is staffed by individuals of many levels of education. The typical secondary teacher holds a Bachelor's Degree and often a Master's Degree. Many prestigious high schools have teachers who hold the doctorate (they are financially reimbursed for this advanced training).

It is not uncommon among schools at the secondary level for 50 per cent or more of the total staff to hold the Master's degree. School systems offer various inducements to encourage teachers to continue their education as they become more experienced. They also offer other inducements, such as sabbatical-leave opportunities, and so forth, which seemingly create a holding power. The resulting tendency toward reduced annual turnover appears to foster a stability that facilitates school organization.

Teacher Education. Criticism has been leveled at colleges where for years programs in teacher education have been traditionally offered. Some institutions who train teachers tend to produce teachers who are inadequately prepared to meet the needs of today's society, it has been said. Other criticism includes the following: The needs of society have been altered vastly in recent years, and teacher education has not kept pace; programs designed for teachers in training have not been able to keep abreast of the "knowledge explosion." And some critics say that colleges have not been able to resolve the dilemma involving teaching methods and processes, and mastery of the disciplines. Some academics have insisted that the former are unnecessary; that a teacher needs but to master his subject to become knowledgeable about how to teach it.

Teachers of educational methods have also had to contend with other attacks. On one hand, their programs are criticised for producing inexperienced "experts" with a cultivated disrespect for the traditional procedures, thus graduating arrogant young sophisticates whose answer to every problem is the abolition of what used to be and the introduction of something new. On the other hand, some employers of new teachers insist that colleges are doing too little to help future teachers participate in innovative practice. These critics complain that because colleges have reacted to earlier criticism, they have become so conservative that they certify students as teachers for service in schools of today with little or no instruction or practice in the new developments that will be implemented in the schools of tomorrow. The tenor of this complaint continues: Technological advances dealing with automation—computers and other modern machines which accomplish jobs for many individuals—have been treated only incidentally or not at all in many teacher education curricula. Television, which appears to have unlimited potential for educational institutions, has been almost entirely neglected. If teachers are to meet the needs of society, and if they are to be accountable for educating tomorrow's high school students, the complaint goes, teacher education must make better use of these industrial innovations and advances in technology.

Equal-Opportunity Employment. In the early seventies, it has been common to build school staffs without prejudice as to race, creed, religion, or sex. In the fifties, on the other hand, typical high schools were dominated by males, and typical elementary schools were dominated by females. Today, the sex distribution has begun to equalize in many schools, probably because of the more educated and dedicated individuals, both male and female, who have made the teaching profession their lifetime occupation. Consequently, criticism about deficiencies in one or another category has abated. Programs in higher education are also less discriminatory in areas which at one time were dominated by either the male or the female. It seems obvious that sexism in hiring practices is beginning to disappear from our schools and colleges.

Alternatives for Consideration

The goal of this module has been to make clear that almost all aspects of education and schooling have evoked contradictory feelings from supporters with different educational theories. For the innovative systems, periods of success have been followed by periods of vitriolic attacks. Despite the presence of sacred cows in the system today, some of yesterday's "cows" have been eliminated, and more are on their way out.

A New Era. The world of the school currently teeters on the threshold of a new era. The people with a primary interest in the educational process will probably acquire the broader decision-making power that they have been demanding: teachers will help to make education policy; students clamoring to be heard will be consulted about the educative process; parents resisting increased costs for expensive innovations will be appointed to community committees to examine problem areas. The input of all concerned will be thoroughly considered, and their arguments will be given the weight they deserve as decisions are pondered. It is to be hoped that because of such changes quality education will become a goal to be achieved through mutual discussion and joint effort.

In this new era, teachers will probably no longer accept the shackles of the standard institutional organization. They will decline to serve as implementors of policies made by authorities far removed from the classroom. Rather, as active participants in the educative process, they will assume greater responsibility for creating the institutional policy which governs them. Because teachers are closer to the students, than administrators, who are remote from the scene of daily activities, teachers should be able to create a classroom that will be more responsive to student needs. Perhaps they may be able to open up the structure to a whole range of innovative ideas, which may bring about reform.

Fantini's Model. One breathtaking concept to conjure with in this regard is the possible dissolution of the school as we have known it, and the consequent creation of a whole new institution. This change has been the theme and prophecy of some of the more revolutionary critics of the sixties. Fantini summarizes the direction of this change as follows:[9]

	Traditional	**Reformed**
Center of control	Professional dominance	The public, the community as partners with the professional
Role of Parent Organizations	To interpret the school to the community, for public relations	To participate as active agents in matters substantive to the educational process

[9] Mario Fantini, *The Reform of Urban Schools* (Washington, D.C.: National Education Association, 1970), pp. 39–40.

	Traditional	**Reformed**
Bureaucracy	Centralized authority, limiting flexibility and initiative to the professional at the individual school level	Decentralized decision making allowing for maximum local, lay, and professional initiative and flexibility, with central authority concentrating on technical assistance, long-range planning and system-wide coordination
Educational Objectives	Emphasis on grade level performance basic skills, cognitive (intellectual) achievement	Emphasis on both *cognitive* and *affective* (feeling) development. Humanistically oriented objectives—e.g., identity, connectedness, powerlessness
Curriculum Relevance	Determined by needs of the disciplines (physical sciences, social sciences)	Determined by needs of society, groups, the individual
Test of Professional Efficiency and Promotion	Emphasis on credentials and systematized advancement through the system	Emphasis on performances with students and with parent-community participants
Institutional Philosophy	Negative self-fulfilling prophecy; student failure blamed on learner and his background	Positive self-fulfilling prophecy; no student failures, only program failures; accountable to learner and community
Basic Learning Unit	Classroom, credentialized teacher, school building	The community, various agents as teachers, including other students and paraprofessionals

The critics who favor these changes see a crucial mass of educational consumers (students and parents) for whom the public schools are obsolete and no longer a viable choice. The consumers with a stake in education have suffered a loss of confidence, and as a result have become alienated. Inevitably, they have retaliated by attacking the school as being a nineteenth-century institution which purports to deal with problems new to the twentieth century. In some of their attacks they have been joined by business, industry, and concerned governmental officials.

In the judgment of critics such as Fantini, the schools as they presently function cannot meet the challenge of contemporary public education. The established school is neither equipped for, nor desirous of, becoming the major instrument in today's society for solving social ills and simultaneously attempting to provide for the manpower needs of an advanced technological society. According to this view, the assumptions underlying our contemporary schools, based as they are on archaic notions of man and his environment, cannot accommodate the drastic changes regarding the concepts of man which typify the twentieth century.

Attempts at Traditional Reforms. Schoolmen have responded to the attacks of radical critics, who call for the abolition of an allegedly obsolete institution, in a familiar way: As in times past, they have resorted to the "add-on" strategy. While working within the framework of the traditional structure, they have added on layers of extras, in order to meet the needs of pupils and to quiet critics. Thus, vocational education, special education, adult education, and early childhood education have been tacked on to the school curriculum—almost self-sustaining appendages, with no bloodline connections to the central corpus.

In their efforts to explain and cope with problems caused by the seeming inability of schools to educate the children of the poor, educators coined such phrases as "culturally deprived" and "culturally disadvantaged" to describe children not brought up in the mainstream of American culture. Soon these terms became pejorative. They implied that something was wrong with the learner; his cultural background had not prepared him for school. If he did not learn, it was not the school's fault. Give him the proper cultural background, then the schools would teach him. Educators then invented new programs, for example, Head Start and Upward Bound, which, added on to the existing program, would, it was hoped, repair the pupil's cultural faults and make him ready to learn. Indeed, most of the federal programs of intervention that were financed to support the application of remedies to distressful situations were attempts "to get learners to adjust to schools rather than the other way around."[10] So the "revolutionary" compensatory programs (such as Head Start and Upward Bound) which were set in motion to help solve unique problems, turned out, after implementation, to be not so revolutionary after all. They became appendages to the standard system—new layers applied to the outmoded framework—and were conducted outside the regular system. The "Federal seed money made available to public education in the 1960s was new money which probably should have been used in new ways to explore more effective ways to use the old money."[11] Instead, the critics contend, it supplied neither a revised foundation nor a changed model, but fundamentally more of the same kind of effort to secure adaptation for the old system. Schools continued to prepare children for "rural, spacious living, and to deliver old easy answers even though the questions have changed."[12] Consequently, the critics were not surprised when the compensatory programs failed.

The Alternative-School Movement. The activists among the radical critics have implemented their demands for a new structure and process by establishing new schools. These establishments, called *alternative* schools, appear to follow no particular pattern; each school is different from another, and each is different from the traditional school. In recent years, however, some alternative schools have been established as part of the regular school system, or have been subsumed under the protective mantle of the local school district.

The founders of the alternative schools represent a wide spectrum of philosophical and political beliefs, and the school locations range from storefronts in the ghetto to more prepossessing locations in rural areas. Generally, all of these schools are based on the assumption that they are ultimately accountable to the children who attend, and to their parents. Most of them are in the progressive tradition, although a few are very conservative. As a rule, faculties of alternative schools profess no allegiance to specific bodies of knowledge, nor to sets of bureaucratic rules. Their aim is to foster self-respect and a sense of community

[10] Ibid., p. 10.
[11] Ibid., p. 12.
[12] Ibid., p. 7.

through processes of shared decision making in which students assume a major role in determining the nature and direction of their own learning. They refuse to force ideas, however sound, on students. Instead, their goals, unlike those of the teachers of traditional schools, are not to do something *for* or *to* pupils, but to do something *with* pupils.

The next decade may very well see a conflict between those who endorse the existence of an alternative-school movement outside of the traditional school, and those proponents of the same kinds of change who want to work from within the system. Many within the system are also seeking alternative solutions. They too object to the "facelessness" of big institutions, the "tracking" and "grouping" to increase quantitative achievement, and the regimentation which is a part of the age-grade system. They too resist the propensity for schools to train for passive consumerism; they resent the repeated failure to transmit basic skills; and they resent the failure of some educators to recognize the existence of plural values among those to be educated. Like the proponents of the "outside" alternative schools, they desire a school characterized by relatively informal, unregimented, nonauthoritarian, person-to-person human relationships. But they want to create such schools within present school systems.

Whether the "inside" forces or the "outside" forces are successful, it appears likely that the new times and the new critics may succeed in bringing about a new realignment of participants in public education. The critics consider the changes already made to be gains promising richer yields for all:

1. For learners, a school system responsive to their needs, resonant with their personal style, and affirmative in its expectations of them.
2. For parents, a tangible grasp of the destiny of their children and the beginnings of richer meaning for their own lives.
3. For professionals, surcease from an increasingly negative community climate and, even more positively, new allies in their task.[13]

At present there is little hard data to indicate what changes the future will bring. Some signs indicate that perhaps a new wave of educational conservatism may upend the hopes of Fantini and his friends. It will be interesting to see what really develops.

SUGGESTED READING

Callahan, Raymond E. *Education and the Cult of Efficiency.* Chicago: University of Chicago Press, 1962.

Crary, Ryland W. *Humanizing the School.* New York: Alfred A. Knopf, Inc., 1969.

Cremin, Lawrence A. *The Transformation of the School.* New York: Alfred A. Knopf, Inc., 1961.

Dropkin, Stan, Ernest Schwarcz, and Harold Full. *Contemporary American Education: An Anthology of Issues, Problems, and Challenges.* New York: Macmillan Publishing Co., Inc., 1975.

[13] Ibid., p. 13.

Friedenberg, Edgar Z. *Coming of Age in America.* New York: Random House, Inc., 1965.

Goodman, Paul. *Compulsory Mis-Education.* New York: Random House, Inc., 1970.

Heath, Robert W., Ed. *New Curricula.* New York: Harper & Row, Publishers, 1964.

Illich, Ivan. *Deschooling Society.* New York: Harper & Row, Publishers, 1971.

Postman, Neil, and Charles Weingartner, *Teaching As a Subversive Activity.* New York: Delacorte Press, 1969.

Rickover, Hyman G. *American Education: A National Failure.* New York: E. P. Dutton & Co., Inc., 1963.

Silberman, Charles E. *Crisis in the Classroom.* New York: Random House, Inc., 1970.

Tanner, Daniel. *Secondary Education—Perspectives and Prospects.* New York: Macmillan Publishing Co., Inc., 1972.

POST TEST

1. (*Circle one.*) Of the following, the area that has received the least criticism is
   a. teacher competency.
   b. emphasis of school programs.
   c. the provision of increased opportunities for schooling;
   d. school building and facilities.
   e. administration.

2. Identify, as the critics have done, the characteristics listed below by labeling each with a (P) for Progressive or a (T) for Traditional education:
   a. Subject-centered program. _____
   b. Focus of class is child's own problems. _____
   c. Failure of mastery of skills in a grade results in repetition of the grade. _____
   d. Emphasis on memorization of facts. _____
   e. Child's own rate and style of learning are considered. _____

3. (*Circle one.*) In the development and implementation of a goals- and objective-setting process, the following groups should be actively involved:
   a. staff.
   b. local taxpayers.
   c. state government officials.
   d. students.
   e. local board members.
   f. state board of education members.
   g. administrators.
   h. all of above.
   i. a,b,c,d,e, of above.
   j. a,b,d,e,g, of above.

4. Some disadvantages of large and small high schools are listed below. Label each properly for a large (L), or a small (S), high school:
   a. Lacks financial support for a comprehensive program in curriculum. _____

    b. Graduates are placed in an inferior competitive position.   _____

    c. Greater opportunity for anonymity.   _____

5. (*Circle one.*) The critics of the competency of the teaching staff contend that
    a. too many poorly trained teachers are permitted to remain too long in their positions in one system.
    b. teachers are rigid and authoritarian.
    c. teachers show a lack of dedication to, and an interest in, the community they serve.
    d. teachers place too much emphasis on grades and thus destroy the students' thirst for knowledge.
    e. a,c,d, of above.
    f. all of above.

6. (*Circle one.*) The increase in teacher militancy was brought about because
    a. there was a decrease in job availability.
    b. teachers' roles were threatened by parental aides in schools.
    c. the student population was declining.
    d. teachers felt their right of tenure was in jeopardy.
    e. the social and economic status of teachers was threatened.
    f. a,c,d,e, of above.
    g. all of above.
    h. a,b,d, of above.

7. (*Circle one.*) The NEA has made more significant educational studies on a national level than any other single agency in America. True or False.

8. (*Circle one.*) Economic determinism and collective bargaining are basic tenets of the AFT, which believes in the strike as a weapon to gain an end. True or False

9. (*Circle one.*) The National Association of Secondary School Principals has indicated that the most functional high school has approximately two thousand students in a four-year program. True or False

10. (*Circle one.*) Some necessary changes in teacher education programs are
    a. more practice in using inquiry and discovery techniques.
    b. increased use of advances in technological machinery.
    c. more instruction on specific roles that exclude male or female candidates.
    d. more opportunity to observe the implementation of potential innovations of industry.
    e. a,b,d, of above.
    f. all of above.

11. According to Fantini's summary of the direction of change, label the following statements True or False:
    a. In the traditional school, the curriculum was determined by the needs of society, groups, and the individual._____
    b. In the reformed school, the institutional philosophy will be positive and self-fulfilling, with no student failure._____

    c. In the reformed school, the center of control will be the public and the professional._____
    d. In the reformed school, the test of professional efficiency will be based on credentials and systematized advancement through the system._____
    e. In the traditional school, the role of parent organizations was to participate as active agents in matters substantive to the educational process._____

12. (*Circle one.*) Schoolmen in past eras have responded to attacks of radical critics calling for abolition of obsolete institutions by
    a. using the "add-on" strategy.
    b. adding layers of extras within the framework of the traditional curriculum.
    c. adding new programs for unique problems, like Head Start, Upward Bound, etc.
    d. faulting the child's environment and the parents.
    e. a,b,d, of above.
    f. all of above.
    g. a,b,c, of above.

13. (*Circle one.*) The tenets of philosophy upon which some current alternative schools are based are
    a. accountability to children who attend, and their parents.
    b. no allegiance to specific bodies of knowledge.
    c. no bureaucratic rules.
    d. respect for self and for community.
    e. share decision making regarding nature and direction of learning.
    f. a,b,e, of above.
    g. all of above.

14. (*Circle one.*) Accreditation agencies *today*
    a. are more strict on grade requirements.
    b. classify secondary schools by actual pupil progress.
    c. are less important to students.
    d. are the final authority on school population requirements.
    e. maintain that all secondary schools are of high caliber.
    f. are not as important for college admission as in the past;
    g. all of above.
    h. b and d, of above.
    i. c and f, of above.
    j. none of above.

Aims in Education

Leo Charles Daley

Jersey City State College

module 3

Nature of Aims in Education / Development and Significance of Aims / Philosophical Basis of Education Aims / Conflicting Viewpoints / Aims and Problems of Education / Present and Future Outlook

RATIONALE

The foundation upon which the educational enterprise rests is a philosophy that emphasizes those values productive of a good life. The interrelationships between the meaning and limits of human existence and the educational activities considered essential to the production of a worthwhile life are enormously important. These relationships determine the aims and priority attributed to the aims in every educational activity. This module examines this complex problem. Nothing can be of more importance to a professional in education.

Every educational activity begins with a statement of aims and continues with an underlying assumption of value priorities. Each day the teacher in a classroom acts consistent with a set of educational principles. The administration of a school system evaluates the educational enterprise on its success or failure in achieving the important aims of education. Professional conferences dealing with education operate on a set of assumptions to guide the deliberations toward the ideal. Nothing then could be more relevant for the professional educator than a careful study of the nature, development, and statement of aims in education. This is the first step in the educational process. Decisions regarding the aims in education depend upon the kind of person the schools hope to produce. These aims are derived from a philosophical conception of human excellence and individual happiness. They are designed therefore to have the utmost impact upon the life of the individual student. Obviously, any statement of aims includes more than a bland statement of an idealistic educator. The accepted aims of a school or of an individual professional educator will change the lives of individual students. In a wider sense, the society in which we live—the community, the nation, the global community, are affected by the priorities in educational purposes we give in our schools.

As you study this module keep in mind the fact that it has always been important for a professional educator to consider the purposes of education. Today however, this problem takes on an urgency that tends to dwarf the problems of past educators. Science provides humanity with information on the control and alteration of life. It is possible theoretically to prolong life in an increasingly industrialized society which sells comfort at the expense of future generations who will suffer from the contamination of the air and the seas. The behavior of thousands can be managed and manipulated by employing technologically sophisticated means unknown in the past. Rapidly increasing technological innovations affect issues that are decided upon the basis of value judgments. When these values are translated into public policy, they involve the schools. The school becomes both the agent of society and the hope of society. In a nation dedicated to the ideals of democracy its schools must consider the implications of these issues in the formulation of its aims. The professional educator feels with intense acuteness that the problems of educational aims have a dimension exceeding curricular techniques.

The crucial issues of our day are not susceptible to the therapy of an easy meliorism that assumes an optimism confident of inevitable progress. When we look beyond our nation at the countries of the earth, many of whom suffer intensely from economic uncertainty and political instability, mass poverty and mass illiteracy, injustice and criminal violence, we realize that this is a world capable of destroying itself. In stating the aims in education one recognizes that the role of the school in modern times must be examined against the magnitude of the social problems that beset society and the human community.

We do not assume that the schools are the only institution responsible and capable of resolving the myriad problems that beset us today. However, it is one of the more important agencies in the community. It occupies more of the student's time each day of the week than any other institution of society except the family. What the schools aim at and achieve will have important consequences for the human community. How else can one justify public support of this institution? In this module we will examine the role the school plays in society. It is important that a professional educator understand the effect of educational aims on the community as well as on the individual student.

The Tenth Amendment of the American Constitution declares that anything not specifically mentioned in the Constitution is delegated to the authority of each state. This in effect creates fifty individual school systems, with the federal government assigned a limited role. The federal government participates only on the basis of the "general welfare" phrase in the preamble to the Constitution. This decentralization permits the states to develop aims that meet local needs, and protects the local educational system from a remote bureaucracy that could enforce policies detrimental to local interests. Of course there are disadvantages in the local control of education in matters of financing, equality, and quality education. However, professional educators ought to be capable of predicting with accuracy the effects on education of the different aims which arise from a variety of values, philosophies, and policies. The study of this module will assist you in this matter.

As you study this module, it may appear that the stress is upon the formulation of an ideal in education that is inconsistent with the realities of economics and politics. It is true, unfortunately, that in some places educational plans are formulated more to save money than to advance education. It happens that some educational aims are light-years removed from any ideal consistent with a rational philosophy. However, in examining the purpose of education one does achieve insight in identifying the irrational, the limiting, and the self-defeating aspects of any educational program that is designed at the expense of human welfare. As one studies the conflicting positions on the purpose and role of the school, he builds a theoretical foundation valuable in analyzing and evaluating the operations of the schools. The struggle to provide the best possible educational experiences for every single student may then continue more effectively.

This module concludes with the almost overwhelming task of examining the future outlook of our schools. It is almost a truism to state that change is an essential condition to life. Social change will take place, and the schools as a principal institution of society will serve a different world. However, there exists a continuity. The new world will conform in many respects with the old. The problems that constrain the optimal development of contemporary education cannot be wished away. The clusters of interdependent social issues found in economics, race, environment, urbanization, population, resources, crime, health, war, and the use of power will continue, unfortunately. They will influence if not determine the shape of tomorrow. What we aim at in education today will affect future schools, whereas a different society of the future will confront simular problems, magnified or diminished as a result of our present plans and activities.

Objectives

The importance of this module is derived from the fact that all discussion of public schooling is shaped by one's view of the various aims in education. No philosopher had more influence on the shape of American public education than the philosopher, John Dewey. Dewey thought that *education,* as a word, is an abstraction. As such it has no concrete existence. It follows, theorized Dewey, that education as such has no aims of itself. It is always a person—a student, a teacher, an administrator, a politician, a citizen—who has concepts that shape his personal thinking about the purposes of education.

Upon completing your study of this module, you should be able to

1. Explain the meaning and implications of an aim as it relates to education.
2. Distinguish proximate from remote aims in education.
3. Describe the basis upon which some theorists distinguish between means and ends in education.
4. Explain why past societies stressed special aims in their schools, and the effects produced by these aims.
5. Explain how different philosophical assumptions lead to different priorities assigned to educational aims.
6. State the implications for educational policies that derive from current philosophies.
7. Explain the effect on educational aims of a position on the nature of truth, man, and values.
8. Explain the relationship between philosophical issues and the place of the school in the surrounding culture.
9. Explain the social forces that influence educational purposes.
10. Explain the important differences between Progressivist and Essentialist theorists' on educational purposes.
11. Cite some of the theories of some important modern thinkers who have influenced educational purposes.
12. Explain the important principles intrinsic to democratic values in education.
13. Explain the relationship between social problems and educational aims.
14. Identify the educational tasks confronting modern education.
15. Explain the important challenges that confront education in the future.
16. Describe the importance of critical thinking as a goal of education.

MODULE TEXT

Nature of Aims in Education

The great English philosopher of the past century, John Stuart Mill, confronted with the difficulty of implementing a public policy of universal benevolence toward all persons while preserving each person's individual freedom to act without any governmental coercion, thought that a universal, free public educational system would resolve the problem. If each school had as one of its principal aims the encouragement of benevolence, every individual would come to realize that choosing the greatest good for the majority of citizens is the only policy rationally consistent with one's own self-interest. Reflecting on the events of the past century, one wonders if Mr. Mill was somewhat unreasonably optimistic. Nevertheless, people as a rule turn to education as the panacea of most of their problem.

If we are told in a discussion that the world population will double in the next twenty-five years, creating an unbearable burden on the natural resources of the planet, someone might suggest the solution may be found if our schools would introduce compulsory courses on family planning. This solution, of course, assumes that the other 94 per cent of the world population will receive similar instruction, with similar effect. In truth, it is a rare discussion involving an important social issue that does not include some reference to education. For instance, it is believed by many that racial prejudice, religious intolerance, human greed, crime and violence, the misuse of military or police powers, and the exploitation of people can be cured if the schools provide the right courses, include the right mixture of students, and are taught by the best of teachers, who follow an ideal set of aims. As virtually every citizen has an opinion about what our schools must teach, public expectations grow.

Beyond the goals and hopes of individual parents, taxpayers, teachers, and administrators there exist the collective expectations of diverse community groups: cultural, ethnic, political, religious, economic, and patriotic organizations with demands for the establishment of specialized programs, or pressures for alloting particular prominence to the educational goals consistent with the aims unique to the group or organization. Although it may appear encouraging that so many have so much confidence in the power of education, the picture is clouded by the fact that there exists no universal agreement on the nature of the good life or the ideal society. For instance, one group might see education as the ideal means to achieve a desirable niche in the economy. Another might argue that the nature of one's occupation ought never serve as a basis for limiting the amount of one's education: that there exists no correlation between career training and life-enrichment education. Regardless of the optimism inherent in the conviction of inevitable progress and prosperity through education, despite the multiplicity of aims, and notwithstanding the conflicting philosophical viewpoints, it is essential to understand first the meaning and complexity involved in the very nature of an aim. Thus it is possible to clarify our aims. Then the first necessary step in the educational process can be productive.

Definition of Aim. An aim is an expression of direction or purpose toward some goal. When an educator declares that the purpose of formal schooling is to produce good citizenship, this person is expressing the desire that every student be educated to become an ideal member of the community. The statement assumes that the school must direct its efforts to the achievement of this goal. Hardly anyone would disagree with the aim of good citizenship. However, there is contained within the goal of good citizenship a multiplicity of aims that stem from the many fields of endeavor involved in producing a good citizen. A good citizen is expected to behave in a manner consistent with the social norms rooted in law. This expectation implies knowledge, understandings, attitudes, appreciations, and values that contain a wide variety of aims.

Remote versus Proximate Goals. The aim "good citizenship" is called a *general aim,* for it includes a number of intermediary aims necessary for its production. It may be termed a *remote aim,* for it is the ultimate goal of more imminent or proximate aims. Thus the ability to read and understand a book on the American Revolution may be a desirable *proximate aim* essential for the achievement of the *distant remote aim* of good citizenship. When one considers the diversity of skills, knowledge, attitudes, values, beliefs, and understandings necessary to transmit the volume of thoughts and behavior to succeeding generations for the continuance of civilization, one realizes the necessity of clarifying the aims in education through classifications into *general* or *particular, remote* or *proximate, distant* or *immediate.* A further distinction, ultimate or instrumental, is a matter of philosophical dispute.

Ultimate versus Instrumental Goals. Aristotle saw "happiness" as the ultimate end toward which every human activity aims. This aim may be termed the *absolute end,* with all other aims viewed as means that are desired because they may produce this ultimate, absolute end. The means serve as instruments that are more, or less, important. Within the framework of the school, certain studies promote skills useful in the everyday affairs of living. Aims designed to promote such outcomes are called *instrumental.* Any aim that transcends mere utility is referred to as *fundamental,* for it is directed toward the ultimate goals of human existence.

Dewey's Position. John Dewey objected to the foregoing distinction. The notion of an ultimate end was meaningless to him, for he saw no possible distinction between the means and the ends. The basis upon which one distinguishes a means from an end is that a means is desirable as a medium by which something is achieved, and an end is something that is desired for itself. Dewey considered each means as a temporary end in itself. According to his thinking, each end becomes the means of moving on to a further point as soon as it is achieved. This position has serious consequences for his view of education.

Within the philosophy of John Dewey no level of experience—physical, biological, or social—is assigned a superior metaphysical status. Education is construed very broadly. It is by no means restricted to formal schooling. In general, education consists in any change that takes place within a person. Specifically, education denotes the conscious and deliberate effort of some social group to shape the intellectual and emotional dispositions and behavior of its youth. The method of the educative experience is thinking. Thinking, he contended, basically is a form of experience, and experience in turn includes much more than mere knowing. According to his notion, experience involves the active process of doing and undergoing, of acting upon things in the environment and receiving the reactions to our acts. The basic aim of education, he believed, is to promote thinking, and one learns to think by connecting what is done with the consequences that follow from doing. The aims in education require a study of the individual child in connection with the conditions and institutions of his society. In formulating aims the educator should view education as a social process, because it is by participation in the activities and understandings of society that the young learn the behavior that is characteristic of an individual human being.

According to John Dewey, no aims *of* education exist. Education is an abstraction. Only individual persons who have needs can have aims. Each society insures its continuance through the education of the young. Thus education is understood as part of the ongoing life of society, for it is in society that the person thinks, acts, tests, revises, and expands his ideas, and grows. There exist aims *in* education, for education is the process of changing through the experience of thinking. It takes place within an individual who acts as a member of a group and who becomes aware of the meanings implicit in his actions. Education is therefore viewed as a social process.

Dewey considered the school per se to be a miniature ideal society. In the environment of formal education, he maintained, it becomes possible to develop individuals and to improve society. His theory of education is thus rooted in the democratic conception. This preference for democracy is not an arbitrary decision based upon social conditioning. According to his conception, any society that is concerned seriously with the quality of the cultural and material well-being of its members will organize itself democratically. Members of such a society will be free to inquire openly and to reconstruct experience in the interest of producing more humane experiences. Therefore the aims in education must include those habits consistent with democratic theory. An atmosphere of freedom is not merely a means productive of efficient learning; it is inseparable from the purposes and aims of education itself.

As a result, we may conclude that any aim pertaining to education ought to be based upon student outcomes. It should formulate precisely the way in which a student is expected to change. The expected changes involve thinking, connecting, and valuing. They include: knowing, recognizing, recalling, organizing, judging, criticizing, associating, interpreting, and generalizing. Certain aims designed to produce value changes may occur simultaneously with cognitive understanding of the material, or they may occur separately, depending upon the nature of the material. In the interest of formulating clear, precise, and unambiguous behavioral changes in values, the educator may include one or more of the following categories of goals: understanding and comprehension of the material, analysis of the meaning and consequences, tolerance and acceptance, interest, commitment, internalizations.

Development and Significance of Aims

A knowledge of the purposes ascribed to education in earlier societies is useful in understanding our present practices. Modern theories of the role and purpose of the schools did not arrive fully developed on the scene. A look at the past helps us understand how modern theory came into being. It provides us with a balanced judgment in improving our present theories because we have learned vicariously from past experiences. It enables us to obtain a deeper insight into the significance and nature of aims in education.

Educational Aims of Ancient Sumer. The mark of an educated person in the very earliest known schools of ancient Sumer was determined by the ability of a man or woman to read, write, compute, and lead a life loyal to king and state, and to be respectful to the gods. This civilization of Southern Mesopotamia, which endured for over two thousand years, developed a sophisticated system of mathematics, literature, architecture, law, and science. Although education rested in the hands of the priests of the temples, the Sumerians reorganized its power to influence the public good. Today's modern society, with its vast numbers of people interacting in complex relationships unheard of in ancient Sumer, convinces us with overwhelming certainty that the stake of society in education is vital. The social importance of education identifies the school as the important agency for the development of the capacities of the individual, with the public interest well in mind.

Hindu and Chinese Education. The social influence on formal education is very clear, after an examination of early Indian Hindu schools of the nineteenth century. In this Hindu society, moving from one caste to another was not possible. The caste a person was born in determined the *dharma* or the social rules governing him for life. An individual could improve his social status only by observing the rules of conduct throughout his entire life. Then following his death, he might be reborn *samsara* into a higher social level, or escape rebirth altogether. Thus the purpose of education was to provide moral training for obedience and self-discipline. Learning the ritual governing one's caste, and developing habits by which to limit one's desires and appetites, had greater personal significance and social value than acquiring information in mathematics and science.

In post-Confucian China, formal education was privately conducted by masters who taught small groups of boys. The aim was to produce a group of intellectuals who revered their ancestors, gave deference to the past, and behaved in a manner consonant with their station in society. Those who were ambitious for public office were required to pass rigid provincial examinations testing their ability to recall in detail the content of the Nine Classics. These Classics contained five volumes of the writings of Confucius and four Shu books written by subsequent followers of Confucius. These works stressed the view that the foundation of any good society is the disciplined individual in a disciplined family living in social harmony in a disciplined society. The purpose of education was to produce a man of character who demonstrated in his life the virtues of intelligence, courage, benevolence, and prudent judgment.

Goals of Greek Education. The value of Greek education to Western society cannot be overemphasized. It is here that many of the concepts basic to Western civilization were first formulated and developed. The conflict of social cohesion versus individual freedom as reflected in the purposes of education is particularly instructive to the modern educator attempting to function in an open, democratic society. This conflict is most clearly illustrated by the contrasting educational systems established in Sparta and Athens.

In Sparta, social cohesion was achieved by demanding absolute loyalty to the State. The individual person belonged to the State. Consequently, the aim of the Spartan educational system, like that of some modern totalitarian government, was to produce loyal patriots, disciplined warrior-servants. Athens, on the other hand, was the first democratic State. It became an inspiration to the world as the home of some of the greatest figures in human history. Here, although the state required by law that each elementary school be regulated, education remained a private matter. The purpose of formal education, in the Athenian view, was to produce a well-balanced person capable intellectually, responsible socially, and healthy physically. Intellectual speculation and critical analysis was tolerated at least during the time of Pericles. After Athens suffered a crushing military defeat, however, forces of reaction took over and we see the spectacle of Socratic execution for "corrupting" youth by teaching them to be "free thinkers."

The Stoic philosophers of Greece prepared the way intellectually for the eventual dominance of Christianity. According to the Stoics, the essential point in living is to achieve a correct state of mind as evidenced by accepting the will of the gods, carrying out the duties required of one's station in society, and controlling one's appetites and desires. Obviously, this is well suited to a society without social mobility. Stoic ideas were transformed by Christianity into the position that a person must place his duty to God above that of the State. The superiority of religious allegiance to secular political authority led to church dominance during the Middle Ages. Accordingly, in Western Europe the church held a monopoly on education. The purpose of education was to develop in the person the disposition to live a holy life to insure eternal salvation. Under church control a spirit of free inquiry and mutual examination of all ideas was deemed unnecessary in religious matters, and in a feudal society the social limitations on the common man did not encourage mass formal education.

The effects of the Reformation were momentous for education. The rejection of an absolute authority in the church and the insistence upon a private interpretation of the Bible by Protestant theorists paved the way for universal schooling. It led, in its emphasis on the individual person, to a rejection of any subservience to the absolute authority of the state as well.

Democracy's Task. The important task confronting democracy is to maintain social order and stability while preserving the liberties of the individual person against unnecessary restraints. It is apparent as we examine the relationships between society and educational aims that every society has standards of values which translate into aims in education. Schools are expected to transmit these values, for they define what the society considers to be acceptable, desirable, and good as a principle agent in the process of socialization. In a democracy the student cannot be treated as a means to some social end. A student ought not to be educated for purposes that extend beyond his own interests. Each individual person is intrinsically worthwhile. The schools must aim for the attainment of the difficult objective of social responsibility, where it is universally recognized that the preservation of one's personal dignity and rights can be achieved only through mutual cooperation in an open and free society. If the student is accepted as an end in himself, he must come to accept every other person the same way. Educating the individual person in a manner consistent with democratic goals is to educate him for purposes identical with his own interests.

These important aims in education define the role of the school as something much more important than custodians of past traditions. Schools in a democracy must recognize the constantly changing patterns of social existence. In providing students with opportunity to think, experience, and act as part of the ongoing life of society, the schools improve the quality of living for many future citizens.

Philosophical Basis of Educational Aims

There are a number of philosophical systems of thought that vary one from another because they respond differently to the perennial problems of truth, man, and values. When a philosopher takes a logical position on the question of man's nature and destiny, the possibility of truth and the origins and nature of values, there emerges a systematic view of what is significant in life, what the possibilities and limitations in life are, and what way of life seems most worthwhile for an intelligent person. The educational problem of identifying aims has its roots in a philosophical position, for what is considered most valuable in education is inextricably associated with one's position on the nature of the good life.

Some philosophers think that philosophy cannot be limited by subject matter, for its purpose consists in identifying problems and suggesting ways to handle these problems. Whereas education is not distinct from the total life situation, the philosopher is free to explain education, criticize its practice, offer solutions, and assign educational aims.

In this subsection you will study the effect of different philosophical systems on the formulation of aims and the assignment of priorities in aims. An examination of the thought of all philosophers is obviously beyond the scope of this module. For convenience we shall be content to identify the general system of philosophy in which groups of philosophers may be identified in a general way only. Then it will be possible to examine the tendencies of each system and to assess educational purposes. Differences in assigning priorities will be found to emerge from the intellectual differences which exist among the systems.

Scientific Realism. When Professor Skinner demonstrated his ability to teach pigeons to play ping pong, many realists felt that the implications of this experiment provided additional scientific evidence of the validity of the Realist position, to wit: Man is a being with a material reality that exists independent of human awareness and which behaves in a necessary, determined manner. As a functioning organic machine a human being has no freedom of action. Each act is determined by a chain of causes and effects that can be understood and controlled.

According to the Realists, the truth of a proposition depends upon the validity of the procedures employed in formulating and verifying it. Speculative propositions that are not verifiable through controlled experiences have no meaning. It follows that value judgments are never factual for they are not amenable to scientific investigation. Such statements are assertions only of personal preference, although science can determine the prevailing social opinion as to what is an acceptable standard of individual value. Therefore Scientific Realists hold that educators should be concerned with shaping the immature judgments of students in ways consistent with scientific information on physical nature and social environment.

The principal aim of education according to scientific realism is to provide human beings with the essential knowledge required to survive in nature. This knowledge may yield one the skills necessary to achieve a secure and happy life. To secure this knowledge and skill the schools must condition the environment, control and manipulate the experiences of the student, and facilitate a knowledge of science and mathematics.

Idealism. Idealism is one of the oldest philosophical systems of thought. Its origins go back to ancient India in the East, and to Plato in the West, who based their thought on the notion that reality is spiritual in nature. Although Idealists have never come to universal agreement on the nature of this reality, they do agree on assigning an importance and essential role to mental state. In their thinking, Mind, or Idea, or Spirit, is real and eternal. Reality then is rational and knowable, and truth is knowable and amenable to logical analysis. Thus, although one is free to think and choose, when one acts consistently with his spiritual nature, his behavior is good and has value. Values, of course, are eternal and unchanging, too. Something that is good today has always been, and always will be, good, for ultimately it is really an idea and so its value is eternal. When we choose something, we choose it because we subjectively judge that it is good for us. However, its value is intrinsic; our choosing it does not give it value.

Because he believes all this to be so, the Idealist believes that the aim of education is to assist in the development of an individual conscious Mind or Self. To put it more dramatically, education must contribute to the attainment of the good life of the spirit. Consequently, the aim of the teacher must be to enlarge the mental horizons, stimulate reflective thinking, encourage free moral choices, stimulate interest in the values of human civilization, and encourage desires for increasing knowledge throughout life. In short, the ultimate aim of all education is to develop the person's self-realization.

Existentialism. Existentialism is a relatively new philosophy. Although some thinkers, who are considered Existentialists, trace their origins back to the Socratic search for self-knowledge, most of them will date the beginning of Existentialism with the writings of the nineteenth-century Danish theologian, Sören Kierkegaard, and with the rise of science to a position of great importance in the nineteenth century. The new scientific movement created a spirit of pessimism in which mankind was seen as a by-product of evolution, a mere chance collection of atoms functioning in a materialistic universe. Generally philosophers came to accept the idea that metaphysical questions concerning the nature of man and the universe could never be resolved rationally. This notion was supported by the nineteenth-century tradition which assigned to *feeling* a role of extreme importance. The Romantic movement, in particular, affirmed the importance of living a life filled with movement, growth, and feeling. Add to these factors the tremendous cataclysmic events of the early twentieth century—holocaustic wars, crippling depression, and oppressive totalitarianisms—and you have the important forces that contributed to the creation of this austere philosophy.

The Existentialist thinker prefers to return to the early Greek philosophers' search for Being. Existentialists repudiate any effort to arrive at a logical or systematic method which provides a body of principles or propositions about man, truth, and value. Rather, they believe philosophy to be a way of life. It should be concerned not with abstractions but with how to live. The primary fact is that a person exists, lives, and becomes what he chooses. There are no Essences or Preconditions limiting him. For him, everything is possible. He can make life what he wills.

The act of choosing something demonstrates that life has meaning for the person. It is personal decision that puts meaning into life. Otherwise life is without meaning. Thus the meaning and value existing in life are human, free choice. In this sense the person can be said to create values. The meanings and values of things are determined by each individual person.

Further, man decides his own essence; is responsible for his own condition. He acts freely when he decides what is significant for him. Each action defines the nature of man that exists in his mind. A man is what his life shows him to be.

In stressing the primacy of existence, the Existentialist asserts the importance of the individual. This individualism is not without social responsibilty. As the person produces value, he determines the kind of community in which he is involved. The meaning in life is derived from his own actions. He is thereby responsible for what he does. When he refuses to accept responsibility for what he does, he demonstrates the fact that the action was not freely chosen, for it consists in denying the freedom it pretends to affirm. For instance, one may choose to be a thief. Yet he is responsible for this choice as for any other choice. A denial of being a thief then, consists in denying that this was chosen. The morality of the choice consists in its being made freely; hence responsibly.

In the *Apology* Socrates informed the court that no one could harm a good man. This statement is very existential. The meaning in life comes not from what happens to us but from what we ourselves do. In an existentialist sense the ancient belief that a man's character is his fate is true, for his fate is of his own making. He lives by values of his own invention in an unexplainable existence.

Existentialism cannot admit to any set of preconceived aims in education. To do so would assume that values exist independently of individual choices. However, Existentialists do believe that there must be certain guidelines to follow. The principal guideline is that education exists in order to assist individual persons to become aware—aware both of the human predicament and of the nature of his own life and existence. This awareness can be developed through self-knowledge. By stating the guidelines, the aim of education is rooted in the individual person. The school must develop free choice to develop his value thinking.

The aim of self-knowledge is of great importance to Existentialists. In their view, each person must become aware of his strengths and limitations, for such awareness is the basis of wisdom and effective living.

In order that the individual may develop his value thinking, the Existentialist's school must provide a setting in which the individual can make free choices. Because one's free acts are predicated on one's idea of what he, as a human being, ought to be, the development of an awareness of self-responsibility in choosing is valuable. Although, without doubt, the school should provide the student with the opportunity of becoming involved socially, it is the individual person, not the improvement of society, that should be the school's major concern. Consequently, Existentialists are convinced that an educator must never impose his personal aims upon the student. The school exists primarily for the development of the individual. The teacher's role is to be a guide or resource person who encourages students to become aware, to discover, to create, and to act authentically.

Therefore Existentialist educators endorse important democratic educational aims:

1. Freedom to think.
2. Freedom to inquire.
3. Freedom to disagree.
4. Freedom to choose.

Experimentalism. Experimentalism is not a separate philosophy. Rather, it is a word used to name any philosophy that stresses empirical verification of propositions. Thus, in an Experimentalist view, man can know only through experience.

Any proposition untested or untestable by sense verification is meaningless. Consequently, every problem worthy of consideration must be examined in its concrete social or behavioral setting. Pragmatism and Instrumentation are both examples of philosophies encompassed in the Experimentation view.

In Experimentalist thought, truth is something that happens to an idea. Experimentalists arrive at this conclusion through their analysis of problem solving. According to this analysis, one's thought processes begin when one *feels* a problem. In other words, thinking is problem solving. Briefly, the process works in this way: Once one has felt the existence of a problem, he formulates tentative plans of actions in his brain. These tentative plans of actions are ideas. The problem-solver then proceeds to test his tentative solutions, that is, his ideas. The ideas that he finds to be worthwhile—that is, the ideas that are productive of growth intellectually, emotionally, or socially—are solutions to the problem. (Usually one finds only one solution, although there may be many possible solutions.) Because they work, these ideas can be considered to be not only worthwhile, but also true.

What is valuable or true today is not necessarily valuable or true tomorrow, however, because in Experimentalist belief the problem-solving process always takes place in a changing society. Because of changing conditions, what is worthwhile today may be worthless in the future. Therefore, Experimentalists cannot conceive of the existence of unchanging absolutes. Because the test of any value is based on contemporary human experience, what is good today may turn out to be bad in the future.

The Experimentalists' beliefs concerning truth, values, and the fluidity of society have convinced them that the principal aim in education is to enable the pupil to adjust to an ever-changing society. According to this theory, the school is a miniature society. As each individual acts and develops, he grows and affects his society. This society in turn grows and has an influence on the individual's growth. Therefore education is a social enterprise and the school's role must be to assist the student to live intelligently by thinking effectively and cooperating socially in a free, open, democratic society.

To be effective in such a school, the educator must understand the value of democracy. In a democracy the government is committed to the cultural and material prosperity of each citizen, and so the power is vested in the citizens. In turn, the citizen is expected to take an active role in the operation of the community. Voting alone is not sufficient to carry out one's social responsibility. The citizen must also be informed about the problems and programs dealing with issues. Ideally the citizen will strive to take an active part, either as a follower or as a leader in society.

Furthermore, every citizen of a democracy must be free to choose his life's work, to develop his talents, and to do so without the restrictions and limitations of bias, prejudice, and hate. In short, he must have full opportunity to develop his full potential. The educational system in a democracy serves this aim. Any deliberate, artificial segregation in education directly violates this important objective. Therefore schools must encourage equal opportunity both through the content of the curriculum and through the organization of the school itself.

In the democracy visualized by the Experimentalists, each citizen is free to follow the dictates of his conscience. Any tyranny over the minds and spirits of citizens in a democracy is intolerable. Each person is free to worship or not, as he chooses; to speak freely as he thinks, without damage to another; and to live where and how he wishes. The only limitations over his freedom are provisions necessary to save the public from harm.

If this ideal democracy is to succeed, it is essential for education to aim at encouraging those habits of behavior that are consistent with democratic living. Consequently, the schools must encourage the development of abilities in critical evaluation. Indoctrination in which pupils are forced to accept authoritarian statements without question must not be permitted.

Furthermore, each student must come to realize that his actions have consequences for himself and others. It is necessary for the school to have rules, of course. Yet the educational aim is to develop self-discipline. Blind obedience is inconsistent with this aim. Rather, every student must realize that it is essential to cooperate with others to attain common objectives. Such cooperation is necessary if one is to be a functioning part of society. Many problems cannot be solved by an individual operating alone. Without social cooperation, the result is anarchy.

A most important objective in education is to develop in our young people skill in thinking, for thinking is the instrument by which the student solves his problems. In this context the "what" of thinking is subordinated to the "how." Therefore the educator must stress ability in gathering information, skill in testing individual and group hypotheses, and an attitude of intellectual honesty. He should encourage students to be open-minded as they search for solutions. He should also encourage habits of initiative and independent self-direction.

Ultimately, Experimentalists believe, schools exist to provide students with experiences that will enable them to lead productive and happy lives. Areas of additional aims with great enduring value are

1. Good health.
2. Vocational skills.
3. Interests and hobbies for leisure living.
4. Preparation for parenthood.
5. Ability to deal with social problems.

Conflicting Viewpoints

The vast majority of educators agree that education must aim at enriching the life of the individual student; that the school is society's principal agent for transmitting the benefits of civilization; and that, in a democracy, education must aim at the development of those values that stress the importance and worth of the individual and the desirability of mutual cooperation. Beyond these points, however, there are significant differences in educational opinion concerning educational aims and matters of educational theory.

The place of subject matter in education is one of the primary matters about which educators disagree. Many educational theorists stress the importance of the subject matter that is taught. They view students as recipients of essential information which they expect students to master in order to function effectively as individuals and citizens. According to this theory, the schools can expand the mental horizons of students by requiring them to understand and to reflect on the wealth of information that constitutes our cultural heritage. For example, they believe that a knowledge of mathematics and science is essential if the student is to be equipped for modern living. They believe that the student should learn mathematics and science whether the student likes it or not. Therefore, they insist that the school must be teacher-centered and adult-oriented, and that the task of the school should be to shape the person into an informed, rational, and intelligent adult.

Some thinkers, who may agree with many aspects of this position, consider that the cognitive aspects of education should be subordinate to the realm of values. They insist that students must understand and adopt the basic eternal values of civilization. The ultimate aim of education, they say, is to encourage the full acceptance of these social and religious values. Pupils must be encouraged to make responsible moral choices. The school achieves this end by stimulating interest in the content and values presented in the subject matter of its courses, and provides opportunities for the pupil to apply his knowledge to social and moral problems. In this manner the child gradually takes on the values of human civilization. Thus, education aims at a disciplined approach, into which is built a solid foundation of humanities, natural sciences, mathematics, and social sciences.

Many educators who subscribe to the positions just described believe that the traditional arts subjects have intrinsic value. In their view, these subjects not only contribute to the development of well-balanced individuals, they also contribute to the social survival of society, for important individual habits such as concentration, alertness, observation, and reflection are developed through practice gained in the study of the liberal arts. Because these traits contribute to a person's future success, by encouraging the intellectual development of the more intelligent youngsters in this way, the schools contribute to the well-being of society. Although these educators believe that less gifted pupils also ought to be educated in this way, and to the highest level possible for them, they suggest that when it becomes evident that these students have reached a point at which they are unable to profit by additional academic work, the schools should substitute practical subjects that will enable them to enter the working forces of the community. These subjects they consider to be vocational training rather than education as such.

According to Progressivists, the function of intelligence is to direct and guide behavior in the solving of problems. Therefore the essential aim of educators is to develop skill in thinking, and so thinking should be the method of educative experience. In this context, thinking as a form of experience is more than knowing. It includes action and reaction and takes place when one connects what one does with the consequences of one's action. Consequently, thinking always occurs in a problem situation. In such situations, when a student perceives the relationship between the problem experienced and his goals, he is energized to act. First he casts around to gather information that bears on his problem. As he gathers usable information, he formulates plans of action (ideas). He then tests out these ideas. In testing the various hypotheses or plans, he connects the consequences of his tests with his decisions. This is a fairly complex process requiring considerable skill of the learner. The progressive educator believes that it is the function of the schools to guide the student in this process. In their view, to develop the individual student's skill in this process of thinking is far more important than storing information in his brain. Therefore they maintain that the learning process must be centered upon the individual who is experiencing; it should be problem-centered rather than subject-centered.

Progressive thinkers agree that another important aim in education is to develop in students skills of democratic living. Although they believe in focusing education on the individual, they also believe that that focus must include the conditions and institutions of the society in which the individual lives and experiences. Education to them is a social process, for they see the school as part of the ongoing processes of society. Within the school each student thinks, acts, tests, and revises his ideas and participates in the activities and understanding of society, just as he does in the large society, for the school can never be separated from society. When educators attempt to divorce education from society, they inhibit learning. Because the student acts as part of a group of persons who will affect his society as he acts, education must deal with the whole person. School experiences affect his intellectual development as he develops thinking skills. They influence his emotional and social development as he interacts with others in the social situation that is the school. They contribute greatly to his skill in living effectively in a changing society.

Aims and Problems of Education

The Question of Quality Education. At the outset of our study of this problem it is wise to keep in mind that the schools are not the sole agency responsible for individual and social progress. It is unfair to blame the educational system for the entire social malaise afflicting many in our society. In a country where prestige is contingent upon the amount of money one has, where important managerial positions are awarded to conformists and manipulators more often than socially minded persons, where criminals pocket millions in profits through racketeering, it is unrealistic to expect public schools to guarantee that even a large majority of its graduates will be socially responsible, economically secure, well-adjusted citizens. Although education must aim at developing a commitment to the principles of the sacredness of the individual person, the respect for the rights of others, and the freedom of man, we realize that citizens have other inner commitments; e.g., values, religious beliefs, and so on. Yet these are the principles by which our society came to be. Many educators who are aware of the school's limitations are nevertheless in the front lines of social conflict. If their commitment to social improvement seems impossible, it still must be maintained, even in the face of unfair criticism.

A major criticism of public secondary education is based on the assumption that the schools do not provide excellent academic preparation. Often critics assume that the public school is in no way equal to such private academies as Andover, Choate, Exeter, Groton, or Hotchkiss. It is thought that making the public school identical with the rich private schools would provide their sons and daughters who attend public schools with the opportunities of the upper-class youth who attend the upper-class academies.

Experienced teachers can point out the vast difference between these two types of schools; many private schools have smaller classes, more supervision of study, less distracting environments, and are usually comprised of students who are very academically oriented. Despite the enormous differences, it should be noted that public education has succeeded in raising the public level of education above anything in past history, and that the upper level students of our better public high schools compare favorably with the products of our most prestigous preparatory schools.

One test of a democratic government is the amount and excellence of the education it is willing to provide individuals of every age group. Rather than define excellence in education as an abstraction, it may be wiser to examine it in terms of individual needs and aspirations, and in terms of its success in contributing to the development of democratic values in our society. When we do so we discover that our public school system extends to every level, from the earliest primary grade to the university graduate school. It provides programs that meet a wide variety of needs.

Frequently graduates of the public schools are the equal in academic achievement of students anywhere. But it must be admitted that some richer, smaller private schools are more successful with the academically slower pupils; this is because special attention is given to them, in smaller groups than is possible in large urban public schools. However, this extra attention is usually provided only to those capable of paying high tuition cost. The public schools are designed to meet the needs of everyone, and their limitations in this area are more often owing to a lack of finances than to a lack of proper aim, desire, or expertise.

Any school that fails to contribute significantly to the development of democratic values may be considered a failure, no matter how great the knowledge, skills, and culture of its graduates. When we examine our social scene, we may well wonder whether or not our schools have been successful in encouraging the development of democratic social values. Answers to questions such as the following are not always pleasing:

Does entrenched privilege exist anywhere unchallenged? Are our citizens universally protected from oppression by economically or politically powerful persons? Are our minorities protected from enslavement by others? Is everyone rich and poor alike, equal before the law in practice as well as in theory? Do the majority of people act out of a conviction of the intrinsic worth of each person? Are significant numbers of our citizens manipulated for the profit of some others? Do our citizens have a real say in the selection of the political candidates who will represent them?

Obviously the success of the public schools in furthering the aim of developing democratic social values has great significance for the continuance of an open and free society. The problem of excellence in education extends beyond the cognitive realms of knowledge and understanding. A well-ordered comprehension of abstract principles may leave out many significant characteristics of concrete reality in society.

The Question of Religion in Public Education. The framers of the Constitution of the United States were close to the suffering produced by religious intolerance in Europe. Therefore they designed the First Amendment to guarantee religious freedom by separating the church from the state. This amendment stipulates that the Congress may not pass laws to establish a religion, and may not legislate against the free exercise of religion. Because of this amendment, the federal government must maintain neutrality in these matters.

Public schools are restrained, therefore, from exercising any coercive measures affecting the belief or nonbelief of its students. No ceremony described as religious may be practiced in public schools. The public school must avoid giving preferential treatment to any specific religion, or even to religion in general.

However, in maintaining its neutral position, the schools must not be considered hostile toward religion. Because this is so, and because private religious education is legally protected, educators may cooperate with religious authorities to the extent that public school students are excused from class requirements to attend religious instruction or worship outside the school. It is possible for public schools to include courses in the curriculum wherein the various religions are studied. These courses must be taught only for a general understanding of religion or of specific religions, and never to indoctrinate students with religious beliefs of any kind.

Present and Future Outlook

As we enter the closing quarter of the twentieth century, we realize that we live during the most exciting, the most revolutionary, and the most rapidly changing century of human history thus far. These great changes markedly affect the role of the public school. Such factors as urbanization, technological advancement, changing moral values, and economic and international problems constantly confront our schools with new challenges.

At the beginning of the nineteenth century, the population of the United States was a little over 4 million people. The vast majority of these citizens lived in an agricultural society. In this frontier society the student's time in school was minimal, and technological skills were limited. The majority of this population derived from Northern Europe, and shared a similar culture if not the same language. Our United States today is a quite different country. We live in a mass society with over 200 million people. About three out of four Americans live in 212 urban centers. Technological progress is such that a person without specialized abilities is at a serious disadvantage in the economic market place. The concentration of vast numbers of people places a serious strain on the economic and material resources of the schools. Cultural diversity among these millions with different languages and ethnic backgrounds, and of various races, provokes additional strain on the tasks confronting educators. The brilliant developments in technology, which serve as a boon to so many people in yielding unparalleled luxury, comfort, and wealth, are also the cause of much social dysfunction and distress. Increasing automation in industry, for instance, although it provides greater wealth, also causes greater unemployment and inhumane working conditions.

Economic opportunity is seriously limited for the unskilled. This presents a problem for education. When educators aim at the development of more sophisticated academic programs, they risk setting up conditions that cause the less motivated and less able students to drop out of school in frustration. These persons are likely to become unemployable economic burdens on society. When educational programs are designed to meet the vocational needs of students, they are criticized for a variety of reasons. Many people object to the increase in expenditures for modern technical equipment. Some theorists argue that the schools are neglecting the intellectual disciplines to provide the lower classes with the type of education almost guaranteed to keep them in the lower classes. Then, too, there is the problem of employing graduates who are trained in particular vocational fields. In some fields the trade unions control the labor market for skilled tradesmen. An influx of young graduates might flood the market and create a serious shortage of jobs.

As the ability of modern man to apply the rapidly increasing discoveries of science to technology improves, the goal of maintaining human freedom is more urgent than ever before. A rapidly increasing population with progressively greater social problems demands greater government involvement in planning and in acting to remedy social ills. And although greater government involvement may do much to improve the general welfare, it may be a threat to freedom. For instance, in order to increase its efficiency in the social field the government may feel it necessary to know more about the lives of its citizens. Even if surveillance over the people may encourage intelligent planning, it also threatens the rights and liberties of the individual. Technological advances make it possible for the government to obtain and accumulate personal data about everyone, to a degree unheard of in past generations. Similarly, advances in the field of communications make it easier for any government to influence the thinking of its citizens. This represents a threat in many directions. It may be specially aimed at dissent. The right of a few to argue that the majority is wrong is an important catalytic source of social progress. If democratic goals are to continue to be upheld in the schools, educators must increase their efforts to insure the existence of a population capable of sifting through the mass of information, of analyzing and evaluating propaganda, and of proposing creative solutions to the issues of the day.

Many authors have attempted to describe man and society today. Most of them emphasize the rapid change taking place in our moral values. Many of them are concerned about the growing disparity between our scientific knowledge and our moral ideals. Civilization rests upon both knowledge and the ideal use of this knowledge. Einstein recognized this first, when he argued that our generation has the knowledge to unleash the atom but, without a change in our ideal thinking, does not have sufficient knowledge to prevent catastrophe. Even a cursory look at human society reveals universal tensions and anxieties. In our alienation we express ideal commitments to the notions of the rights of man, brotherhood, justice, life, and equality, but deny them in practice. Our social problems are compounded by these facts: crime increases enormously each year; family stability is disintegrating, with huge numbers of divorces; many of our youth fall prey to delinquency and drug addiction.

Obviously, there is a need for the teaching of morals and values. No one would suggest that our public schools are the principal or the sole agency for value education. But if our aim is to produce a thinking public capable of living harmoniously with each other, public education must include the teaching of values that are humane.

Above all it is important that our schools avoid creating the impression that moral values hold an unimportant place in human life. Students must recognize that many of the momentous decisions of life are determined by moral value judgments. No responsible person would disagree with the Kantian thought that human beings ought to be treated as persons; as ends rather than as means manipulated for the self-interest of the manipulator. Yet, if this principle were consistently followed, commercial exploitation and overt criminal activity would be significantly diminished. Recognizing that moral behavior can never be forced, educators ought to make a conscious effort to encourage this ethical aim in education.

To be consistent with this viewpoint, educators must recognize the potential damage implicit in stressing material goals exclusively. In a mass society rife with commercial huckstering in which values are totally ignored, the potential for moral debasement is prodigious. The harm to the quality of living which ensues from such huckstering cannot be underestimated. Neither can one underestimate the harm such amoral commercialism can do to the cultural values which in the past have produced human growth. As a result of misplaced faith in material goals, the economically privileged classes in general might struggle intransigeantly to maintain the untenable position of economic individualism, whereas large-scale labor unions, anxious to improve the prerogatives of their members, might hold positions productive of great harm to the mass of people.

Problems of Poverty and Education. Closely associated with the problem of values in educational aims is the seemingly overwhelming problem of educating urban youth. During the past twenty-five years, families of the rural poor have been migrating to the overcrowded slum areas of our cities. Some conception of the dimension of this problem can be seen from the fact that only 10 per cent of the pupils in urban schools in 1950 came from impoverished families. By 1970, over half of the pupils were from this background. As the minority groups of Blacks, Puerto Ricans, Mexican Americans, poor whites, and foreign children crowded into the city schools, many of the more easily educable youth fled these schools and moved with their families to the suburbs.

It is the aim of the school to encourage the development of healthy, morally responsible, rational-thinking persons capable of living materially and culturally successful lives. The achievement of this objective is inhibited by poverty, slum-living in crime-ridden areas, and feelings of despair, anxiety, fear, and hate. Poverty breeds aggression, violence, social anarchy, and educational indifference. All these contribute to school situations that produce youth who leave school unskilled, ill-educated, and unemployable. This educational failure reinforces the feelings of despair, anxiety, fear, and hate which are associated with poverty. Add these to the feelings of inferiority that are the common self-image of many persons in racial and ethnic minority groups, and the result is often hopelessness and apathy. These apathetic attitudes are passed on to the children of succeeding generations who, all too often, live without much hope and so see no sense in trying to change anything.

The dimensions of the problem of educating the urban poor are so vast that they seem to threaten the harmony of the nation, and therefore the schools cannot continue a conservative, bureaucratic, status-quo approach. Neither can one find much hope in the policies of some schools of education, which seem to believe that it is sufficient to educate middle-class teachers to serve in urban schools as evangelists of middle-class values. Artificial devices such as busing and forced numerical quotas have not proved very effective, for they touch only the tip of the iceberg. It would be wiser to take measures by which schools replace the anti-intellectual, apathetic family environment with an invigorating educational environment as early in the child's life as possible. In this program, educators should utilize accurate diagnostic techniques to identify learning problems and then provide remediation measures at the earliest possible time. Instruction should be individualized, and personalized, insofar as possible. To accomplish these goals it would be necessary to keep instructional groups small and intimate.

Despite all the factors that shape our culture—income, religion, ethnic ties, and occupations—it is still only what individuals themselves do that offers much hope for the gradual improvement of the social problems affecting the poor. The poor may help themselves out of their bondage by judicious use of political power. The accomplishment of this task will require that the schools aim at developing in the poor a sense of community commitment, and an awareness of the political machinery available to oppressed people; it will require schools to provide teachers who will deal frankly with racial and ethnic problems in an atmosphere that reflects an open democratic society. In the urban schools, educators must also aim at sustaining intensive programs of language learning and vocational skills.

The Problem of International Understanding. The problem that affects the role of the public school today, and which will continue to do so in the future, is the absence of international understanding and cooperation. In international quarrels today, all too often it is force that determines policy. In the age of potential total destruction it is imperative that nations learn to live with one another in such a way that differences can be settled through negotiations. International law must replace international anarchy. Although good reasons exist to urge one to be dubious about the achievement of this worthy ideal, we must be committed to the aim of peace, and to encourage it everywhere possible—or there will be no future for mankind. The school cannot avoid its share in this most pressing social responsibility of our times. We must acquaint our students with the issues involved, and encourage them to think through to possible resolutions. Students must realize that the proliferation of nuclear nations capable of creating unimaginable devastation is a threat to the existence of civilization.

The Problem of Overpopulation. Associated with the question of international harmony is the problem of overpopulation. The statistical increase in the number of human beings in this century affects detrimentally the stability of every society, the well-being of the individual person, and the natural resources of the earth. The population of the world at the time of Christ (about 370 million) was approximately half the size of the present population of China. It required sixteen centuries before this number reached a half billion. Today the world population is close to 4 billion people, with a projection of 6 billion by the end of this century, 25 years from now. The problem is not only starvation; it is the corollary debasement of humanity living a qualitatively inferior existence in a world of unmanageable numbers. The desirable living areas that are productive of a reasonable existence are too dense at the present time. Furthermore, as the available resources are diminished, as energy crises proliferate, economic positions will become more precarious and international competition more fierce. As the world population increases at a calamitous rate, the threat to a democratic way of life will increase proportionately.

What can the schools do? At best, educators may aim at developing an awareness of this threat to social stability and to the quality of individual living. In stressing thinking skills, education helps to some degree. We must begin somewhere to deal effectively with this problem. The public schools provide some measure of hope.

SUGGESTED READING

Brameld, Theodore. *Education for the Emerging Age.* New York: Harper & Row, Publishers, 1961.

Berman, Louise M. *New Priorities in the Curriculum.* Columbus, Ohio: Charles E. Merrill Publishers, 1968.

Dewey, John. *Experience and Education.* New York: Macmillan Publishing Co., Inc., 1958.

Mayhew, Lewis B. *Campus 1980.* New York: Delacorte Press, 1968.

Morris, Van Cleve. *Philosophy and the American School.* Boston: Houghton Mifflin Company, 1961.

Park, Joe. *Selected Readings in the Philosophy of Education.* New York: Macmillan Publishing Co., Inc., 1974.

Phenix, Philip H. *Education and the Common Good.* New York: Harper & Row, Publishers, 1961.

Scobey, Mary Margaret, and Grace Graham, Eds. *To Nurture Humaneness.* Washington, D.C.: Association for Supervision and Curriculum Development, 1970.

Ulich, Robert. *Education in Western Culture.* New York: Harcourt Brace Jovanovich, Inc., 1965.

———, *History of Educational Thought.* New York: American Book Company, 1950.

Whitehead, Alfred North. *The Aims of Education.* New York: Macmillan Publishing Co., Inc., 1929.

POST TEST

I. *Circle the correct letter in each of the following:*

1. An aim in education
   a. is a vague statement of opinion.
   b. never varies.
   c. provides universal agreement.
   d. is an expression of direction toward some goal.
   e. is all of the above.

2. The aim of good citizenship is considered
   a. a general aim.
   b. a proximate aim.
   c. a necessary aim.
   d. too vague to be meaningful.
   e. none of the above.

3. The ability to read a book with understanding may be called
   a. a general aim.

    b. an ultimate aim.
    c. a proximate aim.
    d. all of the above.
    e. none of the above.

4. According to John Dewey, an ultimate aim is
    a. necessary to define the role of the school.
    b. meaningless.
    c. a valuable guide for the teacher.
    d. necessary to encourage students.
    e. none of the above.

5. Aristotle thought that the ultimate end of every action was
    a. to attain successful living.
    b. material prosperity.
    c. happiness.
    d. life adjustment.
    e. none of the above.

6. According to John Dewey, levels of experience are
    a. important if immediately felt.
    b. unimportant to educational theory.
    c. socially determined.
    d. have no superior metaphysical status.
    e. important if nonacademic.

7. According to John Dewey, there exist
    a. no aims of education.
    b. aims in education.
    c. individuals who have aims.
    d. aims that take place within the individual.
    e. all of the above.

8. Any aim pertaining to education
    a. ought to be mandated by state school authorities.
    b. ought to be based upon student outcomes.
    c. ought to be determined without reference to pupils.
    d. all of the above.
    e. none of the above.

9. An important value to be gained in the study of educational purposes in ancient Greece is
    a. to improve cultural knowledge.
    b. to develop a knowledge of the past for its own sake.
    c. to achieve insight into the conflict between the aims of social cohesion and individual liberty.
    d. all of the above.
    e. none of the above.

10. In feudal society, limitations on the common man
    a. encouraged the need for universal education.
    b. discouraged mass formal education.

    c. made formal education unnecessary.
    d. contributed to vocational skills.
    e. none of the above.

11. The Reformation period encouraged
    a. obedience to authority.
    b. the elimination of formal education.
    e. all of the above.
    d. rights of the individual person.
    e. none of the above.

12. The important task confronting a democracy is to
    a. keep people in line.
    b. encourage anarchy.
    c. maintain individual liberty.
    d. maintain social order while preserving individual liberties.
    e. encourage dissent.

13. The important aims in education
    a. define the role of the school.
    b. recognize the changing patterns of social existence.
    c. provide opportunity to think and to experience.
    d. are part of the ongoing life of the community.
    e. all of the above.

14. The aim in education for Scientific Realists is
    a. to meet individual needs.
    b. social improvement.
    c. life adjustment.
    d. to provide essential knowledge.
    e. none of the above.

15. The aim in education for an Idealist is to
    a. develop the mind or self.
    b. help attain the life of the spirit.
    c. enlarge the mental horizons.
    d. stimulate reflective thinking.
    e. all of the above.

16. Existentialist thinkers agree that important aims include
    a. freedom to think.
    b. freedom to disagree.
    c. freedom to choose.
    d. none of the above.
    e. all of the above.

17. Existentialists think
    a. the schools must provide a setting for the person to make free choices and to develop his value thinking.
    b. the schools must be the agent for social conformity.
    c. that to encourage knowledge of essentials is the role of the school.

    d. all of the above.
    e. none of the above.

18. Truth to the Experimentalists is
    a. absolute and unchanging.
    b. unattainable.
    c. something that happens to an idea.
    d. discovered in nature.
    e. found in social settings.

19. Experimentalists think the aim in education is
    a. to develop scientific knowledge.
    b. to encourage social conformity.
    c. to encourage a thorough knowledge of science and humanities.
    d. to enable one to adjust to an ever-changing society.
    e. all of the above.

20. Democracy is an important value objective because
    a. power is vested in the citizen.
    b. the government is committed to material prosperity.
    c. the government is committed to the cultural well-being of citizens.
    d. all of the above.
    e. none of the above.

21. Additional aims productive of encouraging a happy life are
    a. good health.
    b. vocational skills.
    c. interests for leisure living.
    d. preparation for parenthood.
    e. all of the above.

22. as a rule, progressive educators
    a. consider a subject-centered school important.
    b. think that skill in thinking an essential aim in education.
    c. encourage intellectual development of the gifted through subjects.
    d. think that adult-oriented goals are essential.
    e. all of the above.

23. Schools can be considered failures
    a. when they fail to contribute to the development of democratic values.
    b. when class size exceeds 25.
    c. when academic success is average.
    d. all of the above.
    e. none of the above.

24. In matters of religion, public schools must
    a. remain hostile.
    b. indoctrinate pupils.
    c. promote religion.
    d. remain neutral.
    e. discourage participation in private religious education.

25. To improve urban education schools must
   a. replace the family environment with an educational environment.
   b. stress language learning.
   c. stress vocational skills.
   d. encourage a frank, open, democratic atmosphere.
   e. all of the above.

II. *List five important problem areas which cause serious concern in determining educational aims:*

1. _____

2. _____

3. _____

4. _____

5. _____

Organization of Schools

William A. Cuff

Montclair State College

module 4

School Systems / Governance of the Schools / Administrative and Faculty Structure / Curriculum / Organizational Modifications

RATIONALE

"Deschool society!" sounds the rallying cry of one brand of educational critic. They fear that the education establishment is bent on dehumanizing learning, perpetuating mindlessness, and fostering the social pathologies of an imperfect world. The critics' alarm would be more widespread if our schools did not produce so many resourceful, articulate critics.

American schools, serving 59 million students at a cost approaching $100 million dollars, and with a professional staff numbering nearly three million, constitute a gigantic industry. Its many units interact with one another in complex and overlapping arrangements. The content and media of instruction increase every year, and new teaching procedures raise far more questions than can be answered.

The student contemplating a teaching career may, because of an unpleasant personal experience as a student, harbor suspicions about the organization of the schools. More likely, the organization has created a neutral impression, but remains largely an enigma.

To calculate that one might join up to fight "the system" from within, and set things right, misses a point—that the teaching profession consists mainly of well-meaning people, who also have once been students. Yet, the field of education that beckons you does possess many faults, as does any other segment of society that needs the correcting influence of intelligent, enthusiastic, fresh members. And young novices can be most effective when they understand and can adequately transact with the system.

Many entering teachers eventually move into administrative roles, ranging from department head to state superintendent of schools or college president. Because leadership develops both from personal qualities and a close knowledge of the situation, future leaders especially should develop a thorough familiarity with their professional environment.

The answer to education's problems is not to throw out the system, for another would surely rise to replace it, and might be worse. A much better reply lies in the direction of a genuine understanding of our institutions. This module will try to lead the student in that direction.

Objectives

This module will treat six major aspects of the organization of American schools, which are listed on the title page of this module. Possibly you may take issue with the positioning of some of the module's parts. As you study, you are invited to reorganize the module and fill in the gaps to suit your own lines of thought. Whatever your method of study, you can expect to come to understand the manner in which our schools are organized and governed, to see the relationships among teachers and administrators, to discover the bases from which the curriculum is built, and to view some of the major recent changes in the school organization.

Upon completing your study of this module, you should be able to

1. Distinguish between public and nonpublic schools with respect to goals and operations.
2. Explain three ways in which the grades from kindergarten on are organized in American school districts.
3. Distinguish between the types of public secondary schools.
4. Describe our educational provisions for atypical youngsters.
5. Diagram the organizational structures of typical public school systems and secondary schools.
6. Compare the powers of the board of education and school administrators.
7. Describe the roles of the board of education, superintendent of schools, building principal, and supervisor.
8. State the commonly understood functions of the classroom teacher.
9. Compare the functions of the classroom teacher with those of the paraprofessional.
10. Describe the normal relationship between classroom teachers and school administrators.
11. Describe and contrast the functions of school supervisors in various types of school organizations.
12. State the principal concerns and functions of teachers' professional organizations.
13. Describe the functions of the several groups of people involved in curriculum decisions.
14. Contrast the faculty structure of elementary, intermediate, and secondary schools.
15. Describe alternatives for organizing the faculty of a secondary school.
16. Describe the criteria for high school graduation.
17. Illustrate and compare several patterns of offerings, schedules, and calendars in our public schools.
18. Describe alternative geographical distribution patterns for the schools within a community.
19. State several arguments for and against Performance Contracting.
20. Describe the economics of the Extended School Year.

School Systems

A common myth is that there is a unitary national system of education in America. The fact is that we have many formal systems of education. Each state operates its own public schools. In the privately supported sector, wealth, religion, geography, and independence have created many more systems. Alongside the traditional forms of higher education we now have public two-year community colleges across the land. Nonetheless, a casual observer sees far more similarities than differences among schools at a given level, suggesting that, speaking practically, the myth borders on truth.

Nonpublic Schools. Privately supported schools generally offer a variety of alternatives to the schools supported by public taxation, in accordance with the means and interests of their clients. Religious motives support several systems, the largest of which is the Roman Catholic. With an enrollment of nearly four million, it includes four out of every five nonpublic school children.

THE ROMAN CATHOLIC SCHOOL SYSTEM. The typical Roman Catholic elementary school draws its students and its funds from its parish. Being a parochial, that is, parish school, it is usually under the direction of the local pastor, although diocesan influence on elementary schools has increased over the years. Sunday collections (plus the fact that often the teachers are Religious who receive only a subsistence wage) have made tuition unnecessary, or at most, modest. Roman Catholic secondary schools are more frequently supported and administered through the diocese. The bishop of each Roman Catholic diocese appoints a staff of clergy to administer the high schools therein.

Roman Catholics have always been strong supporters of their schools. Not many years ago, Catholics who refused to send their children to Catholic schools committed a serious sin. Nevertheless, from 1965 to 1973 Catholic school enrollment dropped from its peak of 5.6 million, and the downward trend is continuing. This is because of an evident shift in morality, considerable decline in Religious vocations, falling birthrate, departure of Catholics from cities, and a growing inclination of Catholics to participate in the broader community. Efforts to counter rising costs with government assistance have run afoul of the Constitution's provisions for separation of Church and State, forcing the closing of many schools.

OTHER NONPUBLIC SCHOOLS. Other nonpublic schools are supported by gifts, endowments, and tuition. Their boards of trustees determine policies, but the headmaster or director frequently has a strong hand.

Nearly all privately supported secondary schools offer the same college preparatory program that constitutes the principal activity in a comprehensive public highschool curriculum. Many independent or private schools also provide prestigious fellowships, small classes, connections with reputable colleges, and unusual educational experiences—at a high cost. A substantial increase in independent schools in Northern cities and throughout the South has occurred as a result of the court-ordered dismantling of racial barriers in the nation's public school systems.

Alternative Schools. Disenchantment with conventional schools, especially among social dissidents and Blacks, has led to the establishment of *alternative* or *free* schools. Small, inexpensive, and unconventionally operated, often with a volunteer staff, these schools have occasionally achieved notable success. Because funding by means of donations and voluntary tuition provide meager support, every year many of these schools close or join with other schools. Nevertheless, the alternative school movement has stimulated alternative programs within some public high schools.

The Voucher Plan. Partly to provide support for nonpublic schools, the federal government launched an experimental *voucher plan* in 1970. In this plan, families receive a voucher in the amount of the local public school cost per child, which may be applied to the tuition at a nonpublic school (and in some cases, to another public school). The receiving school submits the voucher for payment out of public funds. Constitutional and administrative problems have impeded the implementation of the voucher plan and, of course, it has encountered strong opposition from public-school advocates.

The American K through 12 System. By the end of the nineteenth century, public and private school systems in all parts of the country had formed the twelve-grade (in some cases eleven) continuum characteristic of present-day American education. Since then, kindergarten has become nearly universal, nursery school is available to both the wealthy and the urban poor, and two years of college is within the reach of most students so inclined. In this three-quarters of a century, the twelve-year ladder has also undergone several modifications insofar as the grouping of the grades is concerned. Every plan of grade organization has persisted to some degree, in large measure because construction costs mitigate against change until other factors mandate new classroom space. In some communities the mandate for integration or a drop in enrollment has caused a shifting around of students within existing buildings, which facilitated a reorganization of the grades.

THE TRADITIONAL PLAN. The *traditional* plan, begun nearly a century ago, calls for eight years of elementary and four years of secondary schooling, and is known as the 8–4 plan. Nonpublic schools have rarely departed from this plan.

THE JUNIOR HIGH SCHOOL REORGANIZATION. The junior high school movement that began around 1900 bred the *reorganized* plan, consisting of six years of elementary and six years of secondary schooling, with several variations. Many sparsely populated areas have opted for the 6–6 plan, wherein economical considerations dictate inclusion of all the secondary-school years in a single high school. Some other communities, because of their building situation, have adopted the 6–2–4 plan. In some instances, communities that already had efficient four-year high schools and eight-year elementary schools simply segregated the seventh and eighth grades from the lower grades but left them in the same building; other communities finding themselves in need of a larger high school, moved Grades 7 and 8 into the old high school and built a brand new school for Grades 9–12.

The ideal junior high school, however, included Grades 7, 8, and 9 in a separate structure: the 6–3–3 plan. As before, the senior high school very often received priority for the new facilities, and the junior high school inherited an outmoded high school building. Even when given the choice, however, many communities retained the traditional 8–4 plan, but adopted some of the junior high school features, such as departments and activities for the upper years of their eight-grade elementary schools. About 55 per cent of the nation's 18,000 public high schools are in reorganized school districts. A few private schools have adopted the six-year high school plan, also.

THE ADVENT OF THE MIDDLE SCHOOLS. Reorganization had failed to become universal by 1960, when the middle or intermediate school came on the scene with much of the same rationalizing that supported the junior high school earlier in the century. The ideal middle school is neither elementary nor secondary, but draws grades from both in an intermediate unit having the sixth, seventh, and eighth grades, and sometimes the fifth. The *intermediate-school* plan, either 5–3–4 or 4–4–4, attempts to create a school experience quite different from either a repetition of elementary-school subjects or a premature introduction to downward-thrusted secondary-school subjects. As with the junior high school, communities have not rushed to construct new facilities just because the middle school seems to be a good idea. Yet the available opportunities for change, helped by a resurgence of the four-year high school, have produced a rapid growth for the inter-

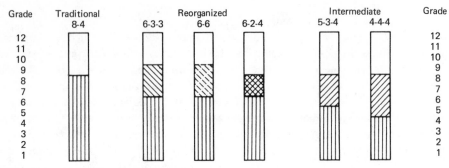

Figure 4-1 *Grade Organization Plans.*

mediate plan, to the point where, by 1971 in New Jersey, middle schools out-numbered junior high schools. The 6–2–4 plan is often grouped with the intermediate-school plan.

High Schools. Public high schools usually fall into three broad categories. The Comprehensive High School, with its diversity of program offerings ranging from the academics to agriculture, predominates. The vocational high school, offering sometimes one, more often several job-training programs, formerly occurred only in large cities; now it also thrives in other areas as a regional school, such as the county vocational high schools in some states. Technical high schools, with strong science and mathematics programs, likewise occurred in cities but have now spread to suburban and rural communities; here they have somewhat broader offerings, and often share building space with a vocational school.

Throughout the country standards for graduation from high school are much the same. Students are expected to complete 16 to 18 credits, called Carnegie Units, each representing a full year of course work on a daily-meeting basis. College admission standards are quite similar but academic subjects are specified.

Some schools seem to discriminate between the programs students have taken, and the program is inscribed on the graduation diploma. Although the number of credits is about the same, each program—academic, business, vocational, or general—has a prescribed core of subjects. Nonacademic courses often count for less credit than academic courses, even when they meet as often. Other high schools have recently moved to equalize the credits for academic and nonacademic subjects. With the encouragement of state education departments they have also begun to grant graduation credit for certain out-of-school learning experiences.

Colleges have increasingly liberalized their admission standards, particularly with respect to the courses accepted. A foreign language is no longer mandated. Some students with excellent records are being admitted after only three years of high school. Public colleges in some jurisdictions must accept any high school graduate.

The Community School Idea. The adult-education movement that got under way early in this century has recently transformed itself into the "community school." Operating under local school district officials, generally using public high school facilities, the community school offers to adults a wide variety of practical, personal interest, and academic courses, similar in many cases to those found in the high school curriculum. Classes are mostly conducted at night.

A high school equivalency program constitutes an important segment of the community school in communities where educational attainments of a significant portion of the adults are low. Basic reading, health, and English for the foreign-born have emerged as other vital courses in urban centers. Teachers recruited from the community, without regard for certification requirements, as well as members of the public school faculty, work part-time at an hourly wage in the community school. Many community school programs receive some federal and state funding.

Governance of the Schools

Public schools today feel the impact of community issues, state regulation, and national welfare. Agencies at the three levels are now forging new relationships that will reshape the operation and curriculum of schools as never before.

The Federal Government and the Schools. Under our Constitution the federal government has no powers in the governance of American schools; education is a state function. Exceptions to this include schools for the dependents of military servicemen in foreign lands, and the schools of the District of Columbia. Yet, since 1785, Congress has supported education through legislation designed to facilitate the establishment of schools in new settlements, encourage schools to provide vocational programs, improve the diet of school children, prepare older school youth for military service, and provide war veterans with educational opportunities.

The degree of federal influence leaped to new levels with the National Science Foundation Act of 1950, the Economic Opportunity Act of 1964, and the Elementary and Secondary Education Act of 1965. Using the power of the purse rather than the law, Congress has now effected substantial changes in science and other subjects, educational opportunities for the poor, and the activities of the state education departments. The United States Office of Education has moved from a rather passive role to an active leadership stance.

The federal courts have been active in remedying alleged wrongs in education, most notably by ending dual education systems in the South, and adjudicating the separateness of governmental and religious interests in the schools.

The State Role in School Governance. Under their responsibility to provide education for all, the states have established state boards of education, departments of education, and the office of state commissioner or superintendent. Although the state boards of education are appointed, some superintendents are elected. In some states a separate board of higher education, a department of higher education, and a chancellor, minister to colleges and universities.

State legislation and regulations delineate the powers and responsibilities of local school authorities. These laws and regulations are, at times, augmented by rulings from the board, the commissioner, or the courts, on issues that have been raised. For example, several state courts have recently ruled (and other cases are pending) that the legislatures must correct disparities in the funding of local schools.

State departments of education regulate the flow of state aid to the public schools. The amounts of aid vary from a bit over 10 to about 90 per cent of the local costs. The departments also enforce minimal standards for teachers, school buildings, pupil transportation, certain materials, and the curriculum. Just what the standards and the degree of enforcement are varies somewhat from state to state. A few states specify textbooks; one provides high school examinations.

The control exerted over nonpublic schools by state education departments is somewhat looser than that over public schools. Again, the degree of control varies from state to state. Some states require state certification for nonpublic school teachers; a few provide certain funds or services for nonpublic schools.

Governance in Higher Education. Usually colleges, universities, and community colleges are governed by their own boards of trustees. A board of a private institution may consist of benefactors and some alumni. Tax-supported institutions may have prominent or deserving citizens on their boards. In the first case the board is self-perpetuating; in the second, appointments are made at the state level.

Higher education institutions are, in most cases, subject to certain standards set by the state, but "diploma mills" still operate freely in a few states.

At most colleges and universities the faculty plays an active role in governance. Curriculum and personnel matters originate within the departments; faculty members may even participate in the selection of the president. College or university policies may come under the scrutiny of the faculty senate. In recent years students have been given some say in these matters. The trustees have the final decision, of course.

Running the Public Schools. By their constitutions and/or statutes, 49 states delegate to local school districts the responsibility for operating the public schools. Hawaii is the exception. The local system may be a county (as in the South), a city, a town, a village, an unincorporated community, or a region encompassing several localities. Although the local school district often conforms with a municipality, in most instances it functions quite independently from the government of that municipality. The school board answers to the state board of education, as its agent for implementing state education laws and regulations at the local level, within the framework of the state and federal constitutions.

A group of lay citizens known as the board of education, or school board, governs the local school system. No individual member of the board has the legal right to exercise operational functions within the school system; statutes give only the board as a whole, or its appointed officials, that right.

Local school board members attain office either by election or by appointment. In many cities the mayor appoints board members, subject to confirmation by the city council. In other communities, citizens elect them. Most communities attempt to keep the selection process separate from partisan politics by avoiding political recommendations and conducting school district elections at a different time of the year from regular government elections.

Members of the school board normally receive no pay, even though they often put considerable time into the work; but their out-of-pocket expenses are paid. Board members are expected to avoid conflicts of interest with school business; most often, this means they do not vote on matters where they or their families might stand to gain.

SCHOOL DISTRICT OPERATIONS. The states vary with respect to school district operational details, and within each state different types of school districts utilize different procedures, but the effects are generally similar. From one to more than twenty citizens, averaging about seven, are elected or appointed to staggered terms of several years each on the local school board.

The school board prepares an annual school budget and submits it for approval by the voters or by the city council. Some states require this approval only when new tax monies must be raised to support the schools. Rejection of the budget requires resubmission, conferring with municipal authorities, and/or referral to the state education department. Usually this process results in small fund cuts and ultimate authorization to operate.

Expenditures for capital acquisitions, such as property, construction, or major equipment, often need separate approval. To borrow money for a major project, such as the construction of a new school building costing several million dollars, the board of education must get the approval of the voters (or of the city council), and arrange to sell bonds through the finance market or a state lending agency. Both the budget and bond issues require public notice in newspapers and compliance with other state mandates. The public vote on a bond issue may occur at any time.

Approval of the budget or bond issue usually refers to the total amount. The board of education may shift funds among categories, or spend less than the sum authorized. Of course, board members interested in reappointment or re-election eventually answer to their constituents for their actions on fiscal and other matters.

The respective roles of the states and the local school districts in the area of financing the schools are constantly shifting, generally in the direction of an increase in participation by the states.

School boards meet periodically, often monthly, in open session, to carry on the business of the school district. Boards may also meet in executive session to deal with personnel or other sensitive matters, and to thrash out differences while hidden from public view. Because of this practice, the public meeting is no more than a time for recording and announcing the result. A few states prohibit these closed meetings, and citizens' groups in the other states have campaigned for the same legislation.

Although board approval is required for disbursement of funds, appointments of personnel, and approval of programs, boards of education often work out policies by which the administration executes the will of the board in many routine matters, in most cases without more than an after-the-fact report to the board. The teachers' salary schedule is an example of this kind of policy. The board adopts the schedule and the administration fixes each employee's salary accordingly, and then presents the list for official approval. The board, however, usually hears appeals from students, parents, and teachers who are dissatisfied with administrative actions. Policies of this sort permit the board to act on major issues without having to spend time on myriad individual cases.

REGIONALIZATION, CONSOLIDATION, AND DECENTRALIZATION. A regional high school district consists of several localities, each of which was originally a small, separate, K–12 school district. Unable to meet the rising costs of quality secondary education, the small districts join to become a unified district, elect a regional school board, and open a single large high school, or several high schools. The merger affects only the high school grades; the original districts continue to have their own boards of education and to operate elementary schools that feed into the secondary school(s) of the regional district.

A consolidated school district has the same origin as the regional district. However, the consolidation or centralization eliminates the original school districts entirely; this permits the larger district to provide the better programs and services to children in both elementary and secondary school grades that the individual districts could or would not provide. The single board of education that emerges operates both elementary and secondary schools, K–12.

Strong encouragement from state education departments has been instrumental in reducing the total number of school districts in the nation from 128,000 in 1930 to 18,000 by 1970. Close to one thousand districts operate no schools today, but instead send their children to nearby communities for their schooling.

On the other hand, large city school districts, although economically offering a great variety of secondary-education opportunities and other services, require massive bureaucracies which tend to become self-serving and remote from the people they serve. In 1969 the state decentralized the New York City public school system's elementary school division into 32 community school districts, each with its own elected board of education and a proportional share of city funds.

The move to decentralize large city districts has proceeded unevenly. City residents, especially those of the lower class, lack the skills in local governance that their country cousins acquired long ago. Subject to the outcomes of their poverty and other urban conditions, the residents of some community school districts stand weakly before the buffeting forces of extremism, opportunism, and politics.

Teachers' Organizations and the Schools. Strikes, jurisdictional disputes, and collective bargaining have given a new image to teachers' organizations, or, more correctly, to those general associations and unions that seek to secure appropriate compensation, benefits, and working conditions for teachers. The primary groups are the National Education Association (NEA), with well in excess of one million members, and the American Federation of Teachers (AFT), with close to 200,000. Each has active branches in every state and in many large communities. Most small communities have NEA affiliates only. In higher education, the American Association of University Professors and its campus chapters serve the same purpose although both the NEA and AFT are moving into the field. There is a lively competition among these groups for members; presently under study is a merger between NEA and AFT. Except in certain Catholic dioceses, nonpublic school teachers are generally unorganized.

Less prominent associations bear the names of school subjects or jobs, such as the National Council of Teachers of English and the American Personnel and Guidance Association, and aim to improve the teaching or service so identified. These groups also have state and sometimes county or city affiliates.

All of these organizations issue journals, newsletters, and action letters. They have annual conventions and periodic conferences, for which teachers are usually given a day or two every year to attend. Dues vary according to the services provided. For the general organizations, a member's fee often exceeds one hundred dollars for the combined local, state, and national groups. The special organizations charge a fraction of that amount. Among the services added recently are group travel and insurance.

Teachers come in closest contact with the NEA or AFT local affiliate in their school district. It is this group that negotiates salaries and other matters with the board of education, and which supports teachers' grievances, with the backing of the state and national units.

The politics of negotiation has given teachers a growing voice in school district policies that has aroused the concern of school administrators and of school boards who have their own associations.

Administrative and Faculty Structure

The professional staff of a school district performs many specialized functions, on a horizontal as well as a vertical plane. The vertical hierarchy ties the organization together, and the breadth of teacher-diversity assures appropriate services to the students. Transactions among all of these individuals make the schools work.

School Administrators. To carry out its decisions, the board of education appoints a qualified educator, usually called the superintendent of schools, or, in certain cases, the administrative or district principal. The superintendent has the responsibility of seeing that the schools operate according to policies enacted by the board of education, and of communicating to the board the information and recommendations necessary for them to act.

In many school districts there is also a school business administrator who manages funds, processes orders, and oversees such noninstructional operations as plant maintenance and utilities. New Jersey statutes provide that fiscal affairs are the province of the school board secretary, who may work independently of the superintendent if the board so desires. In some cases the offices of secretary and business manager are combined. In some jurisdictions the superintendent must act as business administrator.

The superintendent of schools of a medium-size or large school district has a central staff to bring additional expertise to certain administrative functions. He may have one or more assistant superintendents to head the different levels, or to oversee geographic areas of the school district; directors to oversee particular programs (such as special education or the computer center); and supervisors to advise the instructional staff and to coordinate programs.

Each school is under the direction of a principal, who is responsible to the superintendent (or a deputy), the school board, and the community, for its operation. Although the principal ordinarily delegates to others some of the authority to carry on certain supervisory and management functions, full responsibility for performance in these areas still rests with the principal. Except in very small schools, the principal does no regular teaching.

The relationship of the principal to the instructional program, however, involves several dimensions. One includes the bureaucratic accountability just described. Another provides for the principal's collegial relations with other educators, thus acknowledging his authority as a professional educator. A third dimension involves the rights and responsibilities of students, accentuated lately by court decisions, majority-at-eighteen laws, and sexual equalism. Traditionally, this dimension is a vital concern of any school administrator. A fourth relates to the parents of the students. The original job title, "principal teacher," and the English school title, "headmaster," emphasize the multidimensional role of the principal.

As a rule, the principal shares some administrative duties with a vice-principal

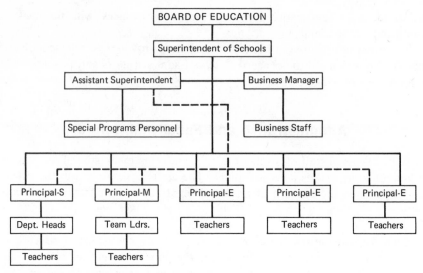

Figure 4-2 *Typical Suburban School District Organization.*

or assistant principal who occasionally teaches part-time. The principal specifies the scope of his own and his assistant's areas of operations, for example, directing the activities program, handling discipline problems, or supervising some of the teachers.

Assistance with the instructional program, in some schools, is provided by a supervisor or curriculum director. Such a person works with experienced, novice,

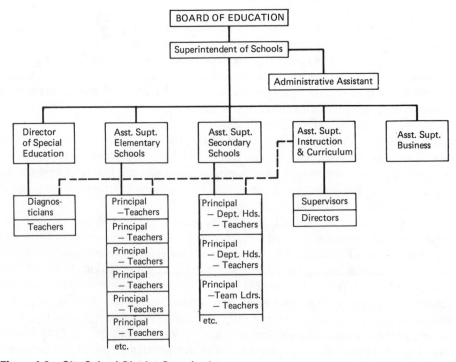

Figure 4-3 *City School District Organization.*

and student teachers individually, and with departmental and interdepartmental committees.

A department head, or chairperson, performs leadership functions within a subject area. Size of the school and of the department guide the determination, by the school board, as to the amount of responsibility, time, and extra compensation given to each department head. The department head's job may range from such trivial tasks as the distribution of textbooks, to total supervision of the department's faculty, and is related to the responsibilities assumed by other administrators and supervisors. More often than not, a department head teaches part-time.

Supervision. As in the school district, the personnel in each school fall into an organizational structure. The principal, assistants, and department heads are arranged so that every staff member knows to whom he or she is responsible. Whenever a teacher, for example, deals regularly with two or more administrators, one of them should be clearly indicated as the teacher's immediate supervisor.

IMPROVEMENT OF INSTRUCTION. The term *supervision* applies to most of the foregoing administrative positions to some degree, and represents the relationship that teachers most frequently have with their immediate superior. It refers primarily to two kinds of activity: the first is evaluation and improvement of the teaching performance of individual faculty members within the supervisor's department, school, or other assignment; the second is curriculum development.

Evaluating primarily involves probationary, or nontenured, teachers, in order to arrive at decisions on reappointment or the granting of tenure. However, tenured teachers may also be evaluated, especially in districts with merit-pay plans, or in cases where a teacher's effectiveness has been questioned. Teachers' organizations now demand better systems of evaluation and more thorough training of supervisors for the evaluation of teachers.

Improvement of teaching performance does not necessarily imply any deficiency, although it may certainly deal with this. The novice working on the acquisition of basic strategies, the professional searching for alternative approaches, and the master seeking deeper insights into the teaching-learning process are all striving for improvement. The supervisor assists each in an appropriate way, but the common ideal is for every teacher eventually to become his or her own supervisor, and for the official supervisor to become a partner or colleague.

CURRICULUM DEVELOPMENT. Curriculum development involves both the supervisor and the teachers as a group. The day has long passed when curriculum was determined by higher authority and passed down to the teachers to implement. The quality of teacher education today and the modern, evolutionary concept of curriculum logically place the authority for curriculum decisions in the teachers' hands, although the school board still has the final say. In this activity the supervisor heads a committee of teachers that evaluates old and new teaching procedures and materials, examines the content of instruction, and plans and implements innovations. Obviously these operations should proceed continuously in every department and at every grade level. The quality of the leadership has a great deal to do with the achievement of this ideal.

Committees and Committee Work. Because the required amount of labor for such activities far exceeds the capacity of the administrative staff, and better results often obtain when those who will have to carry out the decisions take part in their formulation, a considerable part of the planning and decision making in a school takes place in committees. The principal appoints, the faculty elects, or individuals volunteer to be on a committee. A steering committee may parcel out the work to the various committees.

A subject-area committee generally consists of all the teachers assigned to that subject, and often includes the entire department. In the house plan, a subject-area committee brings together teachers from the several houses. This committee works mostly on curriculum development.

Other standing committees work on such matters as scheduling, safety, assemblies, the budget, and student management. These committees review the operation in question every year, at least, and make appropriate recommendations. Membership may change from year to year.

Pro tem committees work on such problems as the report card, a school plant modification, or other problems that occasionally arise. The periodic high school evaluation requires committee participation by every faculty member. Pro tem committees disband as soon as their assigned work is completed.

An administrative cabinet, consisting of the principal and chairpersons of departments, generally, formulates executive decisions. A faculty council, usually elected, advises the principal on matters initiated by either party.

Similar committees also exist on the district level. They draw their memberships from all the schools, or from the schools at one level when the matter affects only that level.

The board of education often divides itself into committees in order to save individual members from intensive involvement in every aspect of school business, but the practice has some drawbacks.

Students and citizens sometimes serve on committees appointed by the principal, the superintendent, or the board of education. This practice varies widely. Such participation allows the public to have a much greater involvement in school affairs than is customary.

Committee decisions are nearly always recommendations to the appointer. The enduring quality of public or professional participation on committee assignments seems related to the degree of acceptance by the school authorities of the committee recommendations.

The Structure of School Faculties. Any organization of more than a handful of members ultimately separates into divisions according to some organizationally relevant criteria. This creates a pyramid-like personnel structure, which promotes coordination and communication.

HIGH SCHOOL. High school faculties most often consist of departments corresponding to the major fields of knowledge or special functions. The number of departments, however, is related to the size of the faculty, as can be seen in examining lists of departments for typical high schools. Departments usually contain from four to twenty members. Unwieldly groups that are too large, and ridiculously small groups, are avoided.

JUNIOR HIGH SCHOOL. Junior high school faculties are structured like high school faculties, but they tend to be smaller and, of course, have fewer teachers in the vocational fields. In small school districts the junior high and high school faculty departments are often joined, and teachers may shift readily from one school to the other (more often to the high school) from year to year. In certain cases, instrumental music, for example, a teacher may work in both schools simultaneously.

MIDDLE SCHOOL. Middle school faculties are frequently structured as inter-departmental teams insofar as the basic academic subject teachers are concerned, and by subject or specialty otherwise. Ordinarily, four teachers—English, social studies, mathematics, and science—form a team. As with junior high schools, middle schools tend to be smaller than high schools.

ELEMENTARY SCHOOL. Elementary school faculties tend to have less internal structure than other faculties, because of the independence of each teacher in the self-contained classroom. Sometimes grade-level or upper-lower divisions exist, but these function more for long-range planning and administrative convenience than for day-to-day instructional operations. Elementary school teachers of music, art, and physical education, and librarians and nurses often constitute a district-wide division, because there may be but one of each in a school, and oftentimes one for several schools.

SPECIAL PROGRAMS DIVISION. At the district level there is often found a special programs division, which includes diagnostic teams and special-education person-nel. Learning disabilities specialists, teachers of the handicapped, school social workers, psychologists, and consulting physicians, who see to the needs of atypical youngsters, make up this unit. Classroom instruction is often attuned to a particular handicap, requiring cooperative arrangements among neighboring schools and school districts in order to form classes of efficient size. Extra state funds partially support these programs, some of which include complete institutional care for the children.

SCHOOLS-WITHIN-A-SCHOOL. A few innovative high schools and junior high schools, and many middle schools, have developed the *house plan* or school-within-a-school. This plan is an attempt to remedy the impersonalization of the student in a large- or medium-size secondary school. A vertical house includes students and teachers in several grades, and a horizontal house takes students from a single grade. Each house in effect functions like a small high school. Ordinarily, one or the other type of house is used.

In a typical "house," an administrator, counselor, from twelve to twenty teachers, and two to four hundred students are situated in a wing or floor of the school building. Students occasionally may have to travel to other parts of the school for subjects that have to serve the entire school, but they usually remain in the house, as do the academic teachers. The design of the building bears sig-nificantly on the feasibility of the house plan.

THE DIFFERENTIATED STAFFING PATTERN. Our schools have begun to move from a monolithic to a differentiated faculty profile. Aides have been hired to perform specified tasks under teacher supervision. Teachers work in teams, per-forming somewhat different functions, according to the distribution of relative strengths among them.

Although some teaching teams operate as groups of equals, differentiated staffing provides a pyramid-like structure, with clearly distinguished leader and follower roles in the instructional situation. The team leader is a *master teacher* whose extensive experience and proven quality are capitalized on to influence strongly team activities and to guide the professional development of its junior members. *Associate teachers* assume directing roles in the teaching process and bear responsibility for student performance and behavior. *Teaching interns* plan, prescribe, and give instruction, subject to the approval of the master or an associate. *Instructional aides* support the team efforts by performing assignments that do not call for professional expertise.

Obviously, the traditional bank of identical classrooms and the lock-step curriculum have begun to depart along with the monolithic faculty organization as schools shift toward a more individualized and personally meaningful curriculum. Revamping of the instructional procedures obviously has not been done in so piecemeal a fashion as that of the major overhauling of the entire school. Because so radical a change often disturbs some teachers, confuses the public, and adds to school costs, differentiated staffing and its concomitants are taking hold quite slowly.

Curriculum

Curriculum Structure. The curriculum may be defined as the formal learning experiences arranged and conducted by the school. Generally the professional staff recommends and the board of education approves every subject or course offered in the school district. Most of the states mandate certain studies by law or regulation, and many of them require state approval for new courses.

HORIZONTAL AND VERTICAL DIMENSIONS. Comprehensive curriculum planning includes both the horizontal and vertical dimensions. Horizontally, the studies should match the readiness level of the student, provide him with personally significant options of means and goals, bear sensible relations to each other, and maintain an appropriate balance of work volume, internal diversity, and the several domains of behavior. Vertically, each area of learning should progress from unit to unit and grade to grade in a forceful, articulated manner, with provisions for differential rates of learning.

THE SOURCES OF THE CURRICULUM. The sources of the curriculum include both the individual and society. The elementary school level emphasizes tool skills and orientation to the social and intellectual environment. The secondary-school level stresses vocational preparation and the development of interests. (College-

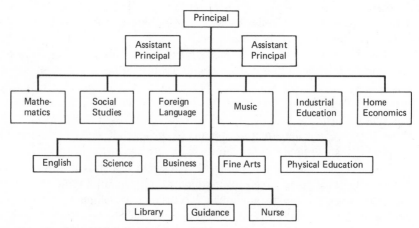

Figure 4-4 *Traditional High School Organization.*

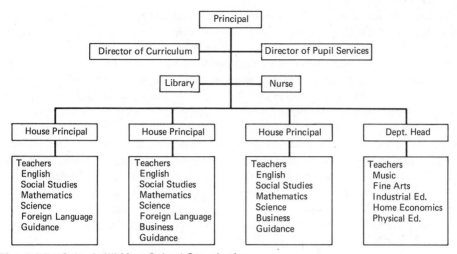

Figure 4-5 *Schools-Within-a-School Organization.*

oriented courses are considered to be prevocational.) At each level, the curriculum provides for individual growth in terms of societal expectations.

In practice, the influence of society seems to outweigh that of the individual in the design of the curriculum. Perhaps this is a vestige of Puritan days when the job of education was to exterminate the child's inborn corruption. Societal influence gained force after the excesses of the era of progressive education tagged concern for individual development as suspect or foolish. Nevertheless, today some areas of the curriculum are person-centered, and most areas are partly so.

In any event, the schools begin by dividing human experiences into a dozen or two compartments called subjects, and then programming the students through this array. To this end the content of each subject is subdivided into segments of equal length and of graded difficulty, which are then arranged as courses within the twelve-year span.

English language arts receives the greatest emphasis as a school subject, students being required to take courses every year, from reading in the first grade to the final English course in the twelfth. Some subjects, art, for instance, are required only through elementary school. Others, such as business, may not be offered until high school. The major thrust of a high school student's set of courses over the years is called his program, or course of study, which may be, for example, vocational.

Most school subjects treat the same major topics a number of times over the years, in a spiral fashion. Each revisitation takes the student to a greater depth in the major topic, provides new applications, and relates to him in a more mature way. The spiral starts with a small-content radius, and ends with a great one, with often an extension into a more specialized aspect of the subject.

THE ACTIVITIES PROGRAM. In modern times, the definition of *curriculum* has been extended to include many activities other than subject classes. Although these activities are under the direction of the faculty, they may take place both during or after the scheduled school day. They range from interest clubs based on regular school subjects, to interscholastic athletics, and even occasionally include college-type fraternities and sororities and other activities that involve substantial expenditures by the student. The student council often plays a role in the regulation of other activities. Even though their primary role is to promote the special interests and talents of the students who opt to get involved, activities also provide entertainment and other benefits to the school and community.

Initially, all activities occurred after school and were very informal. The recognition of their value resulted in the school officials scheduling them during the school day, in a special period, making participation possible for students with jobs, home responsibilities, or long bus rides home; this was also motivated by an attempt to encourage and guide the activities. However, the large number of non-participants imposed a custodial burden on the school; moreover, certain activities, such as varsity sports, did not fit within the time allotted in the scheduled day for activities. The practice declined, but intensive activities, such as the band or newspaper, moved into the regular curriculum as courses. One outcome has been that graduation credit is now given for the knowledge and considerable labor these activities entailed.

MINICOURSES. High schools have always offered courses that did not last the full year, usually in the form of one-semester advanced subjects. The most popular short course today by far is Driver Education. Since 1960, many schools have begun to offer some courses lasting only ten weeks, occasionally less, called *minicourses.*

In some schools minicourse programs have replaced certain full-year courses by providing a set of options, from which the student picks four. Some English and History Departments using this approach provide dozens of options as replacements for standard English and American History courses. Where this is so, other departments have created new short courses that dovetail with the English and history minicourses. Some after-school activities that are too superficial for year-long treatment have also been made into minicourses.

Scheduling students, teachers, and facilities for minicourses adds considerably to the administrative burden because it requires many schedules rather than a single schedule for the school year. Fortunately, the use of new electronic scheduling tools relieves this administrative burden and makes it possible to balance course sections with pupil demand. Pupils can be given most of their first choices or can alter their selections where space permits.

Curriculum Improvement. GOALS, PURPOSES, AND OBJECTIVES. The rationale of the curriculum begins with the over-all purposes of the schools as set forth in the statements of educational philosophy and the goals of the state and the school district. These statements are usually global, and provide for considerable diversity among students. Within the framework provided by the state and local district statements, each school sets up its own unique purposes. It has long been the practice of individual high schools to review and restate their purposes during the periodic evaluations for accreditation by the state and/or regional accrediting association. Other schools have undertaken to do this more frequently. Similarly, goals and purposes are drawn up for each subject and course. These goals and purposes should be based on those of the total school. They should give substance to the school's general purposes by providing more specific goals, usually as long-range behaviors for the students to learn, which, when combined, will provide the outcome sought in the school's statement of purpose.

Courses are divided into units, each of which has a set of objectives. These unit objectives are intermediate objectives, they may have little enduring value in themselves, and may be valuable only as intermediate steps toward achieving the larger purposes that are the course goals. They describe behaviors that indicate when a student has acquired the particular concepts, skills, information, and attitudes around which the unit is built.

The short-term behavioral objectives found in lesson plans constitute the elements of instruction. They form the basis for the specific activities and material used by the students. Combined, they make up the goals of the units; these in turn combine to make up the goals of the courses, which in turn combine to make up the purposes of the school and ultimately the educational aims of the district, state, and nation. Without large goals there would be no direction, but without lesson goals there would be no accomplishment.

THE HIDDEN CURRICULUM. Within the stated objectives of education can be found references to the adjustment of the child to the society of which he is a part. The official curriculum describes, to some extent, an orientation to our ways of life and work. But the typical procedures of teachers, who teach by lecture, and of the school itself, which stresses the custodial functions more than the humanistic functions, often express a narrower orientation, that makes school life bearable for adults even if it makes life unbearable for some students. By these procedures (a sort of silent language), the school attempts to force pupils to perform according to a set of contrived values.

Order, unquestioned authority, denial of human needs, and sex-role stereotypes are but a few of the socializing elements the child encounters year after year. Many of these elements are questionable. Of course, teachers need systematic ways to manage their charges under our compulsory education laws. But the school, with the acquiescence, if not strong direction, from the community, often seems bent on modeling youngsters after an institutional ideal. Lack of success in school appears to be related more strongly to failure to conform to institutional demands than to lack of intellect.

EDUCATIONAL RESEARCH AND DEVELOPMENT. An important part of curriculum improvement is educational research and development. Traditionally, education has relied upon conventional wisdom and the supposed intuitive gifts of the teacher. Since the turn of the century, investigators have devised reliable ways to measure a variety of mental characteristics and to examine various theories of human behavior. They have shattered a few myths by the application of hard data to tasks based upon intuition and have brought education to the threshold of science.

Of course, quality research takes money. The amount of support given to educational research in the past consisted largely of the donated efforts of doctoral students who were producing their dissertations. Their studies lacked concentrated effort and sophisticated techniques. With an occasional exception, neither the universities nor school authorities at any level provided funds for research. The United States Office of Education was mainly a collector and distributor of school statistics.

Since 1950, however, support of educational research has gradually increased, the sources being the federal government and private foundations. The Elementary and Secondary Education Act of 1965 not only directly supported a great increase in research activity, it also stimulated state and local school systems to create research offices and development programs. The amount of funds available for educational research and development increased more than five times from 1961 to 1971, to 2.7 million dollars. A considerable portion of these funds were aimed toward using schools to correct certain racial and economic disadvantages among the people rather than toward increasing our knowledge about learning and teaching.

It is too early to point to any massive breakthrough resulting from the numerous high-powered projects that the late infusion of support has made possible. Much of the effort has been put into improving methodologies and learning tools, and in disseminating significant research findings. Analysis of the research on racial factors in intelligence, and on compensatory programs for the poor—both of which have generated much controversy—point to the need for improving the quality of educational research.

State and federally funded educational development centers are springing up in all parts of the country. Located within the reach of every school district, the centers provide access to information in the form of seminars, specialized libraries of up-to-date books and periodicals, workshops devoted to innovative methods and other topics, and direct assistance in program development. Their impact has yet to be determined.

Scheduling. Years ago, public and private high schools unanimously adopted a six- to eight-period day. Although the Eight-Year Study (conducted forty years ago) showed that other arrangements than the standard curriculum and the routine schedule for all students produced an equally well-prepared individual, to this day high schools preponderantly follow this traditional pattern. Perhaps the tradition is difficult to break; it is certainly easier to administer the standardized school which follows a recurring pattern of daily activities and most courses have been adapted to it.

Although junior high schools adopted the same type of schedule as the high school when they were established, it was in the former that the *block-of-time* schedule first took hold. This provided for a single teacher to teach two subjects for two consecutive periods to the same group of students. The teacher often had considerable freedom to depart from the equal-time convention, and to mix the two subjects in a Core curriculum approach. Some schools even gave the equivalent

Time	Traditional Periods	Block-Time Program	Middle School Block-Time	Flexible Schedule	Time
8:30					8:30
	1	1			
9:20			Team		9:20
	2	2			
10:10		(Eng/Soc. St.)			10:10
	3	3			
11:00					11:00
	4	4	4		
11:50					11:50
	Lunch	Lunch	Lunch	Lunch	
12:40					12:40
	6	6	6		
1:30		(Sci./Math)			1:30
	7	7	Team		
2:20					2:20
		Dismissal			

Figure 4-6 *Types of Daily Schedules.*

of three periods to the time block. This idea has spotty acceptance in the junior high school today, and has never taken hold in high school.

As a rule, however, modern middle schools use the block-of-time together with team teaching and the house plan. Each team plans the use of the time block every day for its group of 75 to 150 students. The block may extend longer than three hours, and it may be segmented.

Organizational Modifications

The organization, the governance, the personnel structure, and the curriculum of school systems evolve new forms only over long periods of time. The middle school has pointed long-range planning in a new direction; increased federal spending for schools may tend to accelerate the progress toward new national standards; and new professional roles and relationships will have to emerge from the current state of flux. Minicourses introduce new studies into the curriculum every semester. These modifications, and those that follow, are evidence of a massive reorganization of American schools. The end is nowhere in sight, and turning back is out of the question.

Flexible Scheduling. Every secondary school occasionally makes scheduling adjustments for special events. Lately, learning activities that involve uncustomary time spans, off-campus visits, and the use of different school facilities for a variety of courses, have increased considerably. To facilitate these irregularities, some schools have initiated the *flexible scheduling* approach. Flexible scheduling means that instead of setting the schedule during the summer for the entire school year, the administration makes a schedule at frequent intervals, occasionally every day. Electronic data equipment has aided the production and reproduction of schedules within the available time limits.

The process starts with each teacher writing a prescription of learning activities for a week or two for each student, based on individual learning needs, and with the necessary time allocations. All the data are collected, sorted, and put into the computer, which matches the data with the availability of the student, teachers, and facilities. Of course, the teachers anticipate appropriate large-group activities, and include on the prescriptions such items as all the affected students for the period in question. Computer print-outs are distributed at, or just before, the start of the week, and the students and teachers automatically follow their new schedules. Often, one day's schedule differs substantially from the next, and a course may skip certain days.

One of the results of the introduction of the flexible schedule is that teachers have started to build more variety and creativity into their planning. But because of the complexities inherent in such flexibility, schools are changing over to this plan very cautiously.

Extending the School Year. Ever since the school year stabilized at approximately 180 days per school year, educators and the public have sought uses for school plants that are idle during the summer months. For many years, some high schools have conducted summer sessions that allowed students to remedy failing course work, and occasionally offered enrichment courses as an added attraction.

Summer schools generally carry a tuition charge, and often admit students from surrounding communities. Elementary schools are usually unused in the summer, except for an occasional community recreation program or, lately, Head Start classes. Over the years there have been many attempts to schedule schools for year-round schooling but few of these attempts have captured the imagination of the tax payer to the point of becoming popular.

Accelerating educational costs since mid-century have stimulated school leaders to try the 12-month plan to squeeze more educational use out of the school buildings. Staggering the attendance of students over the entire twelve months could, theoretically, increase the capacity of the building by 20 per cent. This attractive economy appealed especially to those communities experiencing large enrollment growth. In addition, students interested in finishing high school in three years could attend for the entire twelve months, and thus remove themselves from the school one year sooner.

The school year has been extended in other ways. One plan calls for several breaks during the year. For example, by attending for nine weeks and then skipping three weeks, the student can attain the required annual attendance, but in four cycles. The second plan is that for some of the students, the usual two-month summer vacation is taken at other times of the year. This means that one-fifth of the students are out of school at any given time; each time a group returns from vacation, a new instructional cycle begins and a new group departs for vacation.

State and federal education agencies provide support for experimentation with the year-round school, but adoption has been slow because of conflicts with family vacation habits.

Performance Contracting. A performance contract is an agreement by which one party agrees to effect a certain result for a fee from the second party. In recent years, a handful of school boards have contracted with business firms to obtain certain levels in pupil achievement in elementary school subjects. These contracts, which resulted from an effort by federal authorities to introduce performance contracting to the public schools, involved incentive subsidies.

Performance contracting is one of a number of innovations that some public officials have persuaded the schools to use in an effort to apply business methods to upgrade the quality of education. The voucher plan and removal of tenure protection for teachers are other plans that, like performance contracting, imply a distrust of the education profession. This distrust has been reciprocated by teachers and other school personnel. Educators have been less suspicious of electronic data processes, simulation, and program planning budgeting systems, innovations also based on business practices. They have been less suspicious partly because these pose little threat to teachers and partly because they appear to be workable.

A typical contract calls for the firm to raise the average score of second graders on a standardized reading test by 1.2 years in a one-year period. If a better average obtains, a bonus is paid. If achievement is less, a penalty applies. The business firm is free to use teaching machines and other tools, unlicensed teachers, unconventional reward systems, and any other reasonable means. Pre- and post-tests must be administered by an outside party. Children receive all other instruction from the regular faculty.

The Texarkana, Texas, and Gary, Indiana, school districts experimented with performance contracts a few years ago. Supporters enthusiastically publicized the rather favorable results, but subsequent investigation revealed serious misrepresentation in those evaluations. The initial enthusiasm for this innovation subsequently faded.

Educational Parks. An educational park is a clustering of all the public schools in a community, or in one part of a large city, on a single campus. The cluster also includes the school district administrative offices and other child-service agencies. It is centrally located in the community, which may mean that transportation is required for some students.

Supposedly, this arrangement makes the school district more efficient. It has the additional advantage of mixing all the racial and ethnic elements, in this way eliminating segregation in the schools.

The educational park is different from the neighborhood school pattern traditional in most American communities, where it has been customary to try whenever possible to locate at least the elementary schools within reasonable walking distance of the smallest school child. Although this traditional scattering of schools results in a few inefficiencies—for instance, failing to deliver certain services to the children—it nevertheless facilitates a close bond between the home and school. The educational park is designed to deliver all school services more efficiently, but it is remote from the neighborhoods of most children.

Creating an educational park means abandonment of existing schools at other sites, and because of the expense involved in erecting new structures, the concept has appeal only as a long-range replacement plan. Furthermore, many citizens like to have the child near home, and prefer that he mix with others in his own racial and economic group. The attractive architectural structures for educational parks have won considerably more acclaim from the school-construction industry than from parents.

SUGGESTED READING

Books

Aiken, Wilfred M. *The Story of the Eight-Year Study.* New York: Harper & Row, Publishers, 1942.

Campbell, Roald F., Luvern L. Cunningham, and Roderick F. McPhee. *The Organization and Control of American Schools.* Columbus, Ohio: Charles E. Merrill Publishers, 1965.

Chamberlain, Leo M., and Leslie W. Kindred. *The Teachers and School Organization,* 3rd Ed. Englewood Cliffs, N.J.: Prentice-Hall, Inc., 1958.

Cicourel, Aaron V., and John I. Kitsuse. *The Educational Decision Makers.* Indianapolis: Bobbs-Merrill Co., Inc., 1963.

Haubrich, Vernon F., Ed. *Freedom, Bureaucracy and Schooling.* Washington, D.C.: The Association for Supervision and Curriculum Development, 1971.

Jackson, Philip W. *Life in Classrooms.* New York: Holt, Rinehart & Winston, Inc., 1968.

Kimbrough, Ralph B., and Michael Y. Nunnery. *Education Administration: An Introduction.* New York: Macmillan Publishing Co., Inc., 1976.

Lewis, Leonard J., and A. J. Loveridge. *The Management of Education.* New York: Praeger Publishers, Inc., 1965.

Miller, Van, George R. Madden, and James B. Kincheloe. *The Public Administration of American Public Schools.* New York: Macmillan Publishing Co., Inc., 1972.

Olivero, James E., Ed. *Educational Manpower; From Aides to Differentiated Staff Patterns, Bold New Venture.* Bloomington, Ind.: Indiana University Press, 1970.

Wynn, Dale R. *Organization of Public Schools.* Washington, D.C.: Center for Applied Research, 1964.

Periodicals

American Teacher. (Journal of the American Federation of Teachers.)

The Bulletin of the National Association of Secondary School Principals.

Educational Leadership. (Journal of the Association for Supervision and Curriculum Development.)

The National Elementary Principal.

The New Schools Exchange Newsletter. (A journal on alternative schools.)

The New York Times. (See the Annual Education Review, January 16, 1974, the Education page each Sunday, and *The New York Times Index.*)

Phi Delta Kappan. (See the special issue on alternative schools, March 1973.)

Research in Education. (The ERIC monthly catalogue.)

Today's Education. (Journal of the National Education Association.)

POST TEST

Circle the correct letter in each of the following.

1. Education is a legal responsibility of the government of
   a. the United States.
   b. each state.
   c. every community.
   d. every county.

2. Roman Catholic schools in this country get their funds mostly from
   a. parish collections and tuition.
   b. Rome.
   c. public taxation.
   d. endowments.

3. "Community schools" serve mostly
   a. preschoolers.
   b. elementary school children.
   c. high school youth.
   d. adults.

4. The number of American school children who attend nonpublic schools is approximately
   a. 2 per cent.
   b. 10 per cent.
   c. 30 per cent.
   d. 50 per cent.

5. A current trend among high schools regarding credit for academic and non-academic courses has been to make the credits
   a. more equal.
   b. greater for academic subjects than for nonacademic.
   c. greater for nonacademic subjects than for academic.
   d. nonexistent.

6. The number of Carnegie Units traditionally required for high school graduation is about
   a. 4   **b.** 8   **c.** 16   **d.** 24

7. The voucher plan provides credit for
   a. summer school course work.
   b. nonpublic school tuition.
   c. graduate study.
   d. new school buildings.

8. A middle school would most likely be found in a school district in which the grade organization plan is
   a. 8–4   **b.** 6–3–3   **c.** 5–3–4   **d.** 6–6

9. Nonpublic high schools appeal to some families because, compared with public high schools, nonpublic schools usually are
   a. less expensive.
   b. more exclusive.
   c. more democratic.
   d. more academically challenging.

10. Vocational and technical high schools are generally not a part of a
   a. large city school district.
   b. suburban school district.
   c. regional school district.
   d. county school system.

11. Federal fiscal support for education has traditionally been provided for
   a. teacher salaries and supplies.
   b. school buildings.
   c. vocational education.
   d. general school funding.

12. Since 1960, the level of federal spending for public education has
   a. risen.
   b. remained the same.
   c. fallen.
   d. shown no discernible trend.

13. State education laws and regulations usually do not apply to
   a. teacher qualifications.
   b. school buildings.
   c. state financial aid.
   d. final examinations.

14. Which of the following statements about school board members is true?
    a. They are elected in some communities, appointed in others.
    b. They assume various administrative responsibilities.
    c. They usually are active partisan politicians.
    d. They are encouraged to have business dealings with the school district.

15. Which of the following statements about the powers of school boards in general is false?
    a. They appoint all personnel.
    b. They always meet in open session.
    c. They authorize each expenditure.
    d. They adopt the curriculum.

16. In order to attend to the major issues and avoid spending time on hundreds of routine matters, a board of education typically adopts
    a. policies.
    b. the budget.
    c. a bond issue.
    d. executive sessions.

17. A merger of several small school districts into a single K–12 district, eliminating the original districts altogether, is known as
    a. decentralization.
    b. regionalization.
    c. consolidation.
    d. administration.

18. As a class of workers, teachers are
    a. organized into labor organizations.
    b. not professionally organized.
    c. organized into subject or service-area associations.
    d. a, c, of the above.

19. The administrative head of a local school district is the
    a. president of the school board.
    b. president of the teachers' professional organization.
    c. school business administrator.
    d. Superintendent of schools.

20. The school principal's relationship to the curriculum is influenced by
    a. the school board and superintendent.
    b. other educators in the district.
    c. students and parents.
    d. all of the above.

21. The administrative structure in a school district, optimally, is
    a. vague.
    b. in a constant state of flux.
    c. well-defined, with definite lines of authority.
    d. highly complex, with at least two superiors in direct charge of each teacher.

22. Supervision is primarily concerned with all the following except
    a. evaluation of teaching performance.
    b. improvement of teaching performance.
    c. composition of the budget.
    d. curriculum development.

23. Curriculum development nowadays usually involves
    a. administrators and supervisors only.
    b. committees of teachers, supervisors, and administrators.
    c. individual teachers only.
    d. state education department specialists.

24. Faculties organized on an interdepartmental-team basis are most often found in
    a. elementary schools.
    b. middle schools.
    c. junior high schools.
    d. high schools.

25. A horizontal house plan for a school means that
    a. the school has but one floor.
    b. several grades occur in each house.
    c. a house includes only one grade.
    d. the faculty is organized primarily by departments.

26. In the differentiated staff arrangement, a teaching intern ordinarily
    a. independently prescribes and gives instruction.
    b. guides the team's activities.
    c. performs nonprofessional services.
    d. instructs under close supervision.

27. The school curriculum in most communities appears to be influenced
    a. most strongly by societal concerns.
    b. most strongly by concern for individual student development.
    c. about evenly by societal and individual concerns.
    d. by a variety of factors, with no major determinant.

28. Minicourses usually
    a. are held after school.
    b. consume five to twenty minutes each day.
    c. last ten weeks or less.
    d. are each taught by two or more teachers.

29. A flexible schedule may change
    a. daily.
    b. every few days.
    c. weekly.
    d. at any of these frequencies.

30. Opposition to extending the school year to twelve months springs mostly from
    a. high costs.
    b. administrative problems.
    c. family vacation habits.
    d. corruption of the curriculum.

31. Performance contracting in education has recently
   a. spread rapidly throughout the nation.
   b. demonstrated highly superior results.
   c. failed to show benefits.
   d. none of the above.

32. Educational parks
   a. include all schools of the district on a single campus.
   b. are a recreation department facility.
   c. provide space for high school students' automobiles.
   d. already exist in many communities.

Legal Bases for Schools

William J. Meisner

Jersey City State College

module 5

Federal Government's Role / State's Role / Local School District's Role

RATIONALE

Education in the United States has a number of interesting features that distinguish it from educational programs elsewhere. One is that education in the United States is highly decentralized.

The Constitution of the United States makes no specific reference or provision for the support of public education, although in Amendment Ten of the Bill of Rights the implication is that the federal government has granted this right to the respective states. Legal interpretations of the Constitution as well as court-case decisions have clearly indicated that the responsibility for education rests with the states. The states in turn have delegated most of the actual function of education to the local sector; in some cases the county level and in others the municipal level. The federal government, however, continues to demonstrate its concern for quality education through the United States Office of Education and through a great amount of enabling legislation that has been passed by Congress, directed at providing sound educational programs.

Another feature of the American educational system is its provision for public educational programs from kindergarten through the college level. A third feature is that the actual day-by-day control of the system is in the hands of citizens, usually directly elected, rather than in governmental agencies or professional educators. Local boards of education form policies for the operation of local schools within the framework of the state laws regarding education. The provision of public education for all citizens, regardless of race, color, creed, or wealth, is not always found in other countries. Still another feature of the public schools in America is their nonsectarian nature. Efforts are made to develop moral and ethical codes, but no specific creed may be taught in the public schools.

Because of its highly decentralized nature, the educational system in the United States, along with the agencies that legally control it, is a complex enterprise. In this module we shall attempt to outline the legal roles played by the various sectors of government in the conduct of our nation's educational policy and practice.

All too often teachers are unaware of the complicated bureaucratic structure that governs the everyday operation of their classrooms. Who provides the money, and in what amounts? Who determines how the money will be spent? Why can certain items be purchased through federal and state funds and others cannot? Who determines policy regarding curricula, textbooks, and so on? These are matters about which the intelligent and well-prepared teacher should be informed. This module is aimed at briefly outlining the major areas of educational influence and the legal bases for that influence. This module will be divided into three parts, representing the three bases upon which our educational structure is built: (1) the federal government and its role, (2) the state legislature and its role, and (3) the local school district and its role.

An understanding of the legal bases for our educational structure, and some familiarity with its effect, will enable the teacher to better comprehend the complexities of the system, the reasons for some of the problems that occur, and an appreciation of the flexibility a system of this kind affords. This module does not include specific cases in school law which have been the result of the sometimes ambiguous role of each arm of government. The area of school law is too vast and too complex to attempt to do justice to it in such a limited amount of space. After completion of this module, students whose interest lies in the area of school law should be encouraged to probe more deeply into areas such as

1. Teacher rights and responsibilities.
2. Student rights and responsibilities.
3. Sources of the law.
4. Liability of teachers.
5. Standard of negligence.
6. Liability for pupil injury.
7. Defamation of character.
8. Corporal punishment.
9. *Loco Parentis.*

In addition to these, students might wish to read about the many other interesting and significant areas of the law that deal with education. This module should serve as a base upon which to build a reasonable knowledge of the laws that govern the teaching profession, as well as the situations that gave rise to such laws.

Objectives

Upon completing your study of this module, you should be able to

1. Identify the major roles played by the branches of government as they relate to education.
2. List specific roles of each branch of government in its conduct of the educational system.
3. Identify which branch of government has primary responsibility for financing education, and to know how far that responsibility extends.
4. List the major functions of a board of education.
5. List the role that the Supreme Court plays in educational decision making.
6. Identify the key figures in any educational structure on the district level.
7. List some general federal legislation that has affected the educational structure.
8. Describe how most state educational structures are developed.
9. Describe the characteristics and types of local school districts.
10. List the legal roles of the board of education president, board of education members, superintendent, and school principal.
11. List some of the inter-relationships between the various arms of government with regard to education.
12. Select appropriate answers in the accompanying Post Test with a maximum of three errors.

MODULE TEXT

Federal Government's Role

Education in America is considered primarily a function of the fifty states. The constitutional basis for this lies in the interpretation of the Tenth Amendment to the Constitution. This amendment states, "The powers not delegated to the United

States by the Constitution, nor prohibited by it to the States, are reserved to the States respectively, or to the people." Whereas there is no reference in the Constitution to education specifically, this amendment includes the education of the people.

Background. Although education, according to the Constitution, is in the hands of the individual states, the federal government has influenced it greatly through special programs, special legislation, and financial support. The power for Congress to do this has come, via an interpretation of the Supreme Court, from the Preamble of the United States Constitution, which states, "We the people of the United States, in Order to form a more perfect Union, establish Justice, insure domestic Tranquility, provide for the common defense, promote the general Welfare, and secure the Blessings of Liberty to ourselves and our Posterity, do ordain and establish this Constitution for the United States of America." The phrase, "promote the general Welfare," has come to be known as the *general welfare clause,* and is used as the basis for the justification of federal support of public education. Also, there is a reference to a legislative general welfare clause in Article 1, Section 8 of the Constitution.

Although the Constitution is silent on federal support to education, there was precedent for it before any specific court case was even considered. The Ordinance of 1785 provided that a section of land in every township developed from the lands between the Appalachian Mountains and the Mississippi River, approximately one thirty-sixth of the entire Northwest Territory, would be reserved for the maintenance of public schools. This was followed by the Northwest Ordinance of 1787, which encouraged "schools and the means of education" to be established firmly in all new states that were formed from this area. Despite criticism about the constitutionality of federal assistance, it appears obvious that precedent clearly indicates that the founding fathers of this country recognized the federal role in education.

Since that time a great deal of federal legislation has been passed—and upheld by the courts—to continue and expand the federal role in public education. After 1850, new states were given two to four sections in new townships by the government for educational purposes. In 1862 the Morrill Act (Land Grant College Act) was passed to provide higher educational assistance. This was later reinforced by the second Morrill Act of 1890, which provided continuing annual support for these institutions. The Hatch Act of 1887 gave federal support to vocational education. The Smith-Lever Act of 1914, regarding aid to agricultural education, the Smith-Hughes Act of 1917, dealing with vocational subjects taught in high school, The George-Deen Act of 1937, regarding distributive education, all represented federal concern for public education and the willingness on the part of the federal government to commit public funds for its support. From the close of World War II to the present, the number of federal programs developed would be too numerous to mention. Suffice it to say that the federal role in education has increased dramatically in the past twenty-five years, and the challenges to federal support of education have significantly decreased. It would appear that the recognition on the part of the Congress for the need for these programs is coupled with increasing public demand for more programs to meet the exigencies of a rapidly changing nation. This is not to say, of course, that a bureaucracy as diverse as our federal government does not build into it a labyrinth of rules and regulations that sometimes result in the frustration of the very segment it seeks to assist. In general, however, these federal educational programs have greatly assisted the development of public education in America.

The federal role in public education today can be roughly divided into four areas:

1. Decisions of the federal courts with regard to education.
2. United States Office of Education.
3. Federally controlled programs.
4. General federal aid.

Decisions of the Federal Courts. As we previously stated, this module will not delve into the intricacies of the interpretation of laws. Federal court decisions have, however, greatly expanded the scope and influence that the federal government can exert over public education within the states. Court decisions regarding such matters as discrimination, inequality of opportunity, and busing have tremendously influenced the course and character of education in America. Although the court system does operate independently of the other two branches of the government, it is obvious that the appointment of liberal or conservative or moderate judges has affected the outcome of educational decisions in the courts.

The U.S. Office of Education. The United States Office of Education was established in 1867 within the Department of the Interior. In 1939 it was made a part of the Federal Security Agency. In 1953 the Department of Health, Education, and Welfare replaced the Federal Security Agency, and the head of the new department, of which the Office of Education is a part, was made a member of the President's cabinet. The head of the United States Office of Education is called the Commissioner of Education and is appointed directly by the President.

In 1867 the Office of Education was charged with the responsibility:

To collect such statistics and facts as shall show the condition and progress of education in the several States and Territories, and to diffuse such information respecting the organization and management of schools and school systems, and methods of teaching, as shall aid the People of the United States in the establishment and maintenance of efficient school systems, and otherwise promote the cause of education throughout the country.

The scope and function of the United States Office of Education has greatly expanded since Congress gave it this initial mandate. The Office still performs some of its original functions, such as conducting research on educational practices in the United States and providing information and services to the various state agencies, but its role has been enlarged considerably. The Office has a strong, if indirect, control over local and state education authorities through its function of administering federal grants. There seems to be considerable debate among educational experts as to whether the Office of Education exercises too much or too little power over education in America. On the one hand, proponents of the "excessive power" position say that control of federal-grant money enables the Office of Education to control the direction in which educational development will progress; and, conversely, can impede progress in a direction which it does not favor. On the other hand, proponents of the "too little power" position feel that the Office of

Education is in a better position to envision national goals without local or state encumbrances, and thus should exert greater influence in implementing those goals. Regardless of the position one takes, it is obvious that the United States Office of Education is in a transitional period in which its power and influence over education in America are expanding slowly but constantly.

Federally Controlled Educational Programs. In addition to decisions made by United States courts, the operation of the Office of Education, and direct aid from the government, the federal role also extends to the operation of educational programs directly controlled by agencies within the government. The Congress still provides directly for funding in the District of Columbia, although moves in recent years are pointing toward more local control of the political and educational system of the District. The Department of the Interior controls the educational system for the trust territories in the Pacific, such as Samoa and the Marshall and Caroline Islands; it also has the responsibility for the education of the children of National Park employees. Schools on Indian reservations are controlled by the Bureau of Indian Affairs, which is an agency of the Interior Department.

The Defense Department is directly responsible for the education of military personnel in technical and vocational training in connection with military service, and also provides for the education of the dependents of military personnel on bases located throughout the world. The United States military academies of the army, navy, coast guard, and air force all come under the direct control of the Department of Defense.

General Federal Aid. The present federal role in American education is a supporting one. Access to almost limitless funds places the federal government in the most strategic position to provide resources for educational development. It can deal more equitably with the special problems that the various states, because of local concerns, are unable to cope with. There is, of course, the concern that too much fiscal support will result in too much jurisdictional influence. However, if this concern can be overcome, the federal government is in an excellent position to highlight national goals and needs and to provide the financial base that will develop quality education in America.

State's Role

In the United States, the legislature of each of the fifty states is charged with the jurisdictional leadership role in education. Unlike many countries, the United States does not have *an educational system;* it has fifty educational systems. This jurisdictional power is derived not only from the implications of the Tenth Amendment of the United States Constitution; it is also mandated in every state constitution. State legislatures, within the limits of their respective constitutions, are the chief policy makers for education within the state. The legislatures, through statutes, grant powers to state boards of education, state departments of educations, commissioners of education, and county and local boards of education. These groups, however, are not autonomous and so have only those powers that are expressly granted by the legislature. The legislative delegation of power falls generally into two categories: mandatory laws and permissive laws. Mandatory statutes, such as those concerning

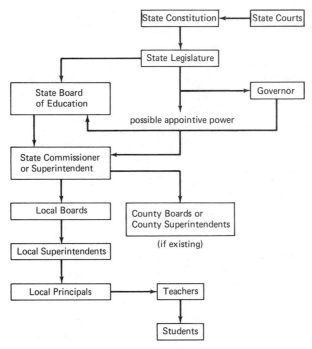

Figure 5-1 *A Model for the Structure of Public Education.*

attendance rules, retirement, tenure, and state-aid formulas, are to be followed without variation by all schools and school personnel within the state. Permissive statutes, such as those concerning school dismissal, elective course offerings, and vacation policy, allow the school districts some flexibility in arranging local programs.

A diagram of a typical state structure for public education might look like the model presented in Figure 5-1.

The State Board of Education. Despite the fact that each state educational structure has a unique character, the one common feature is a state board of education which is responsible for the over-all program for that state. State Boards generally have both regulatory and advisory functions. Their main function, however, is the formulation of educational policies for the public schools of the state. (Some states have special boards for the regulation of public colleges and universities.)

The regulatory function of the state board is important in providing uniformity and consistent operation of essential functions in the various schools within the state. The advisory function is less defined in most states. It can serve as an information organ to the legislature; it can assist local schools in analyzing and evaluating proposed projects; it can serve as an arbitrator; it can provide services such as study commissions, financial advisement certification, school redistricting, and teacher education, as well as other functions.

Members of state boards of education may be either appointed or elected. The more common method, however, is appointment by the governor of the state. Members usually serve terms of three to five years, which are staggered to provide some continuity. They serve without pay, and are usually respected citizens of the state.

State Commissioner or Superintendent. The state commissioner or superintendent is the chief school officer of the state. The main responsibility of the commissioner is to serve as the executive officer of the state board of education. It is his duty to carry out the policies set down by the board. His term varies from state to state, and he is selected in a variety of ways. Twenty-four state superintendents or commissioners are selected by state boards of education; twenty-one are elected by the people; and five are appointed by the governor. There have been a variety of arguments offered regarding how the state commissioner or superintendent should be selected. To date it seems that each state finds its method of selection adequate to the needs of the state.

The state superintendent reports his concerns regarding education in the state to the governor, the legislature, and the state board of education. As the executive officer of the state board of education, he supervises and regulates the schools of the state. Traditionally, state departments of education have delegated their responsibilities in the following areas to their chief executive officer:

1. Operational functions.
2. Regulatory functions.
3. Service functions.
4. Developmental functions.
5. Public support functions.

Operational functions include coordinating such agencies as schools for the blind; regulatory functions include such matters as teacher certification, and approval of school programs and facilities; service functions include research, advising, and consulting; developmental activities include staffing and self-improvement of the department, and attempting to improve its operational activities; public support includes public relations, and political activities with the legislature and other governmental agencies. Clearly, the role of the state commissioner or superintendent is a complicated one; it assumes a different character in each state. Essentially, however, he is to be the executive head of the state department of education; as such, with the help of his staff he regulates and supervises the public schools of the state. State departments of education are frequently granted power by the legislature, which in turn they delegate to the state commissioner.

State departments of education for the most part do not exercise strong leadership over the schools of the state. Their major role seems to lie in regulatory or operational areas. The Congress, in 1965, passed the Elementary and Secondary School Act, which was aimed at strengthening the role of the state departments. Although they have indeed been strengthened in most states, their functions still tend to be concentrated in the traditional areas of regulation and operation.

County Boards. Approximately half the state systems in the United States (26) have some form of intermediate school organization based on a county unit. (The State of New York has an intermediate system, but it is not organized on a county level.) The most significant purpose of the county organization is to coordinate the activities of the state and local levels. In states that do not have this level the state works directly with the local districts. This intermediate level of school organization is perhaps the most criticized in the entire structure. Many educational experts doubt the necessity for this level, claiming that it simply creates an additional bureaucratic channel that serves no critical need in the over-all operation of a state educational system. Admittedly, the county level in some states seems, on the surface, to perform no essential function, although in many rural states it serves to operate special-needs facilities that local districts, because of their size, cannot afford to operate.

Future Trends. Although historically the states have not exercised the leadership role that has been assigned to them by the United States Constitution and their own state constitutions, it would appear—in light of the increased number of challenges being leveled at the outmoded property-tax system of funding public schools—that this role will have to increase significantly. The Elementary and Secondary Education Act's (ESEA) Title Five which provided substantial amounts of federal funds for the strengthening of state educational agencies as well as increased public demand for more uniformity in the operation of school districts within a given state, seem to have pumped new vitality into the traditionally lethargic posture of state departments and boards of education. We can look forward in the future to seeing the state assume a much larger leadership role in the operation of public schools.

Local School District's Role

Because the jurisdictional control of education in the United States is exclusively a state function, and because the state traditionally has played a relatively minor role, the major burden for the operation of public schools has fallen to the local district. The local school district is a creation of the state, specific areas designated to carry out educational programs on a local level. Because these school districts have been created by the legislatures of various states, they vary greatly; no pattern can be observed in the nearly 24,000 districts. Some are less than a square mile in size and have thousands of students; others are hundreds of square miles in size and have only several hundred students. Approximately 50 per cent of the school districts have fewer than three hundred students.

The organizational structure in the local districts also varies greatly from state to state and from district to district. Some are strictly elementary districts, serving Grades 1–8. Students are then bused to regional secondary schools for education beyond the elementary level. Other districts include a 1–8 elementary school and also a 9–12 secondary school. Still others operate elementary schools that go through Grade 6, a junior high school that includes Grades 7,8, and 9, and a senior high school that includes Grades 10,11, and 12. The latter is more commonly known as a 6–3–3 plan. A new concept that has been used in many states is the middle school, incorporating Grades 5,6,7, and 8, thus separating early-elementary from late-elementary levels. Consolidated school districts as well as regional districts serve areas in which the student population of several school districts are combined to conserve tax dollars. Vocational and technical schools can be operated on a local, county, or even a consolidational or regional level. Other vertical plans for school organization are in operation in parts of the United States.

The Local School Board. The policy-making body of the local school district is the local board of education. It is called by a variety of titles in the various states: board of trustees, board of directors, district trustees, or board of education. This local school board is comprised of citizens of the district, either elected directly by the people or appointed by the chief executive of the political unit (mayor, manager, and so forth). School board members in almost every case are not identified with a political party when they run for election. The most important function of the local school board is to formulate policies for the operation of the schools within the local district. Their function is not to get involved in the day-to-day operation of the schools, although this frequently does occur because they are directly responsible to the voters of the district. The tradition of local control of schools in the United States is a long-standing one, and most states have fostered this concept by placing great power for the operation of the schools in the hands of the district board of education.

The local board not only represents the citizens of the district, it also is charged with the responsibility for carrying out the state laws and mandates of the state department and state board of education. In effect, board members serve two masters. They are usually elected (although some states do provide for appointed boards) for overlapping terms of from three to six years. Some of the most important duties of the local school boards are

1. Appointment of a local superintendent of schools.
2. Preparation and submission of an annual school budget, which is submitted to the voters or the appointive authority for approval.
3. Hiring top-level personnel (this may vary from district to district).
4. Appraisal of performance of personnel. (Technically, the board hires and fires teachers, administrators, and so on, although this function is generally delegated to the superintendent.)
5. Public relations with the community.

School board regular meetings must be public, and conducted at regularly scheduled times. One member of the board serves as president or chairperson, and all usually serve without compensation. The chief executive officer of the board is usually the clerk, who in most larger districts is a paid employee and who may also serve as the business administrator of the district. In some districts the superintendent performs this function. The qualifications to serve as a member of a local school board are few; usually the member must live in the district and be a registered voter.

The Local Superintendent. The local school board is charged with the responsibility of employing a professionally trained administrator to serve as the chief local school officer and carry out the policies of the local board. Generally, school boards are policy-making bodies, as we have already pointed out; their role is not intended to extend into the day-to-day operation of the schools within the district. Under ideal conditions, the board formulates the policy and then extends to the superintendent and to the principals and their staffs considerable latitude in carrying out these policies. The superintendent, as the chief executive officer of the district, usually delegates a great deal of this power to building principals who actually implement the policy of the board. It should be noted that because of the elective nature of some local school boards, and thus their responsibility to the electorate, boards and board members frequently get involved in matters that technically should be handled by the professional educators.

The quality of the educational program in a local district depends, in large measure, on the leadership provided by the superintendent. Aside from state mandated curriculum offerings, the rest of the program is the responsibility of local authorities. The superintendent generally serves as the chief public relations person between the schools and the people of the district, and it is often his duty to convince a municipality of the need for a particular program. As the chief executive officer of the district, it is his duty to recommend to the board changes in personnel and additions to existing programs, as well as supervising and maintaining his staff. Although the board nominally has the power to appoint and reappoint teachers, they usually rely on the recommendations of the superintendent. The superintendent also has the responsibility to promote the educational growth of his staff through in-service training programs. These programs are aimed at increasing the competency of staff members while they are in the employ of the local district.

One particularly important function of the local superintendent is connected with the school budget. Although the board has the responsibility for adopting the budget, it is usually the superintendent who prepares the figures and makes the recommendations for various expenditures. His expertise in the field of educational administration places him in an extremely powerful position with regard to the expenditures of public funds. After the board has adopted a budget and it is ultimately approved by the people or the governing body of the district, it is the superintendent's function to see to it that school funds are properly spent. (The superintendent also is charged with the responsibility for informing the school board of building needs and enrollment quotas.)

In addition to these many duties, the superintendent is in charge of student records, state formulas, teacher personnel records, school census figures, inventories, and insurance records—only a few of the many critical records kept by most school districts. The superintendent must also make frequent reports to the local school board, to various state agencies, to the federal government and its agencies, and to local governing units.

Because most elected and appointed school board members are not experts in the field of educational management, the superintendent must educate board members as to the needs of education within the district. In order to enlighten them and the community in general, he usually prepares position papers, pamphlets, provides journals and reports, and encourages board members to attend professional conferences and conventions.

Many school districts in the United States are quite large, and the responsibilities for managing them have become too much for one person to administer. As a result, the staff of superintendents in some districts has grown to include assistant superintendents in charge of various areas; directors of such departments as curriculum, guidance, career planning, and personnel; directors of buildings and grounds; and business managers, as well as other staff assistants and clerical personnel.

The Local Principal. Whereas the local superintendent of schools is responsible for the operation of an entire school district, the local principal is responsible for the operation of a particular school within the district. The superintendent delegates much of the responsibility granted him by the school board to his principals, who are directly responsible to him. In the larger districts this delegation of power and responsibility follows a chain of command which, although it may vary from district to district, usually runs in a straight line from the board of education to the superintendent, to the assistant superintendent and directors, to the principals.

The school principal is responsible for the total operation of his school. In larger systems he may have assistants, that is, vice principals, department chairpersons, and directors to help him, but in the last analysis, his is the final responsibility. He is charged with the educational leadership of his school. Historically the principal was a "head teacher" who was simply in charge of the records of the school. However, this role has changed considerably as the educational structure of the United States has grown. The principal should be a highly skilled person who can inspire and stimulate his teachers and staff and prompt his students to strive for educational excellence.

The local principal is concerned with all phases of the educational program. He should be constantly working with his professional staff to develop new programs, delete obsolete programs, and improve courses of study. He should also be interested in developing athletic, extra and cocurricular activities, and teacher development, as well as curriculum improvement in his school.

The supervision of teachers within the school is another important role of the principal. As it is his recommendation to the superintendent that usually determines what board action will be taken with regard to retention of staff, he must assist new teachers to develop professionally and aid experienced teachers to continue professional growth. He generally helps to stimulate teacher growth by scheduling workshops or staff meetings to discuss mutual concerns, or encourages new teachers to observe other teachers demonstrate new teaching techniques, or encourages particular staff members to attend professional meetings.

The principal is responsible for the accurate record-keeping within his jurisdiction. State and federal records may determine how much aid a district will receive, and thus require careful attention. The construction and supervision of the school schedule for teachers and students is another of the principal's mammoth tasks. The complexities of modern American life require that students be guided into advanced schooling and career planning in a carefully thought-out manner. This over-all guidance program is also the responsibility of the principal. The principal is of course charged with the task of maintaining proper school discipline and of providing an atmosphere in which the orderly process of learning can occur. He generally works jointly with his staff and subordinates to insure that each student has a school climate in which he can best develop his potential. Although teachers have a closer contact with the students in general, the principal has the over-all responsibility. He must account to the superintendent, and thus to the board, for the impact that the school has on each student.

The local role in the administration of the American educational system is an operational one. Most developments and innovations in education are the result of local initiative. The state attempts to prevent the local schools from falling below certain minimum standards but generally does not interfere greatly beyond this point. The federal influence on the local schools is so subtle that it is rarely noticeable in the total program. If any one role were to be identified as being of paramount significance in American education, then the local role would have to be so characterized.

Conclusion

Federal, state, and local governments all have a role to play in public education in the United States. The federal role is chiefly an interest in or a concern for education, and the state role is essentially that of providing an adequate educational system. The local role is an operational one, providing the framework for the day-to-day operation of the schools of the state. Frequently there is bureaucratic over-lapping of the roles, but for the most part the local level exerts the major portion of the leadership. The federal government has been concerned chiefly with equality of educational opportunity, solutions to national problems, and maintaining and preserving American ideals. The state government has been concerned with pro-moting the welfare of the state, and providing equal opportunities for education within the state. Local school districts have been concerned with meeting immediate educational needs within the district, as they see those needs. The local level, un-fortunately, is not always willing or able to see all the needs, or make the necessary provisions to meet those needs. As a result, there has been increased emphasis placed on the state and federal role in American education. The broader scope of the more diverse branches of government seem very necessary to insure that each student in each district will be afforded an equal opportunity to pursue his educa-tion to the extent that he wishes, and to have the same opportunity as every other student to achieve personal dignity. Despite the obvious drawbacks of a tripartite educational system as compared with systems in other countries, it appears that all three of the educational partners in America have a significant role to play in the furtherance of quality education in the United States.

SUGGESTED READING

Beach, Fred F., and Robert F. Will. *The State and Education, The Structure and Control of Public Education at the State Level*. Washington, D.C.: U.S. Office of Education, 1960.

Burrup, Percy E. *The Teacher and the Public School System*. New York: Harper & Row, Publishers, 1967, Chap. 3.

Campbell, Roald, F., Luvern L. Cunningham, and Roderick F. McPhee. *The Organization and Control of American Schools*. Columbus, Ohio: Charles E. Merrill Publishers, 1965, Chap. 2.

Chamberlain, Leo M., and Leslie W. Kindred. *The Teacher and School Organization*. Englewood Cliffs, N.J.: Prentice-Hall, Inc., 1966, Chap. 2.

De Young, Chris A., and Richard Winn. *American Education*. New York: McGraw-Hill Book Company, 1964, Chap. 2.

Fensch, Edwin A., and Robert E. Wilson. *The Superintendency Team*. Columbus, Ohio: Charles E. Merrill Publishers, 1964.

Hazard, William R. *Education and the Law: Cases and Materials on Public Schools*. New York: Macmillan Publishing Co., Inc., 1971.

McCloskey, Gordon. *Education and Public Understanding*. New York: Harper & Row, Publishers, 1967, Chap. 10.

McKean, Robert C., and H. H. Mills. *The Supervisor*. Washington, D.C.: Center for Applied Research and Education, Inc., 1964, Chaps. 2 and 3.

Morphet, Edgar L., Roe L. Johns, and Theodore L. Reller, *Educational Organization and Administration*. Englewood Cliffs, New Jersey: Prentice-Hall, Inc., 1967, Chap. 8.

POST TEST

1. Which amendment to the Constitution of the United States has been interpreted to give the control of education to the states?

   _____

2. Which clause of the Preamble of the U.S. Constitution has been used to justify the federal role in education?

   _____

3. The federal government influences education through which four areas?

   _____

4. Which federal office administers and oversees most of the federal government's role in American education?

   _____

5. Compared with the state and local districts' more definitive role, the federal role in education is mainly

   _____

6. The interpretation of the U.S. Constitution has given this to the state, with regard to education.

   _____

7. State legislatures have provided for these groups to supervise and set educational policy for the state.

   _____

8. Who is the top executive educational official of the state?

   _____

9. What is the primary contribution that the state makes to the local district? (The top state executive supervises the distribution of this.)

   _____

10. Approximately how many local school districts are there in the United States?

    _____

11. What is the primary role of the local board of education?

    _____

12. Boards of education on a local level are selected in two ways. What are they?

_____

13. Who is the chief executive officer of the local school board?

_____

14. Education in America is largely supported by an archaic tax. What is it?

_____

15. Who is the chief official, with over-all responsibility, in a given school?

_____

Financing Schools

Noble C. Hiebert

Ramsey, N.J.

module 6

Means of Financing Education / Budgetary Practices / Educational Plan / Expenditure Plan / Revenue Plan

RATIONALE

Money for education is often very difficult to get, primarily because many people consider the cost of education to be an expense instead of an investment. The economist Kenneth Galbraith once said, "The private economy in America is reasonably affluent, but the public economy is poverty stricken."

In the financing of education it is always assumed that the purpose of education is apparent to both those who want it and those who are willing to pay for it.

History shows that the cost of education in the early days of our country was probably the price of board and room for the teacher. Since then, however, the need for more education and the higher cost of providing it have both escalated. The level of education has risen to the point that nearly all the children of all the people are attending school while the expenditures for educational purposes have caused the schools to become the largest enterprise in most communities. Therefore, our studies shall include an examination of not only well-planned expenditure procedures, but the sources of the funds. Because the prime money-raising sources and powers rest in the hands of government, we shall also examine the different methods used to support education.

Teachers (as groups) are usually believed to have little regard for the source of the school funds, and little knowledge of the cost of anything but salaries. This module will help those entering the teaching profession to understand the processes of financial expenditure and money-procurement, so that their entry into the worka-day world, with its unionization and negotiating, will be a more knowledgeable and profitable one.

We shall explore the possible means of financing education; the plans and formats for planning expenditures; and finally, the impact of recent legislation and legal decisions that will affect the level of educational expenditures and the means and methods of raising funds.

The expenditures in any school district are based upon the educational needs. The revenue collected by the community for education becomes the source for funds to pay the bills. The legal structure of every state provides the framework upon which the financing of all schools is based.

Because the United States Constitution, by the simple omission of any reference to the subject, left the legal responsibility for education to each state, many different patterns of financing have developed among the separate states.

The fifty states have not all accepted the obligation to develop and support education with the same degree of thoroughness. The early development of the individual state school systems is a story of diversity, struggles, and dedication; the result is the present American educational format, with its extremes of centralization and decentralization. Within states the varying degrees of acceptance of responsibility for education lead not only to broad differences in their financial provision for education, but also to wide ranges of educational offerings, because of differences in each state's ability to support good programs.

Very early in American history, the federal government entered the financing picture with the Land Grant Acts of 1787, which dedicated certain parts of new state lands to education. Later on, the Smith-Hughes legislation gave support to vocational programs, largely in the field of Home Economics. Other legislation, such as the post-World War II GI bills and the National Defense Education Act, provided funds to assist schools in accelerating development in the basic fields of science, mathematics, and foreign languages. In recent years the National Elementary and Secondary Education Act has made federal funds available to local school districts for various kinds of specific projects.

Generally, because the state governments found other more important things to deal with, the cause of education and its early existence depended almost entirely upon local community interest and initiative. Each respective community, rural or urban, provided "schools" according to its desires and needs. Only in the twentieth century did society begin to take an active interest in the quality of the education being offered. The consequent state legislative acts demonstrated the desire of state government to provide and assure at least a minimum education for all its people.

Objectives

Upon completing your study of this module, you should be able to

1. Describe the basic historical pattern of educational finance in the United States.
2. Describe your own state's pattern of school finance and give some basic facts about its development.
3. Cite and define the most frequently used sources of funds for financing education.
4. Show some understanding of the separate roles of federal, state, and local governments in providing funds for public education.
5. Describe a format for an accountable expenditure plan for public schools.
6. Give an example of an educational plan and translate the plan into the dollar requirements for financing it.
7. Name and briefly describe the most important recent court decisions that affect school financing.
8. Show how the quality of education is related to the amount of money provided.
9. Give the rationale for the premise that the "control of education" is closely related to the source of funds to support it.
10. Give a brief definition for the PPBES (Program, Planning, Budgeting, and Evaluation System).
11. Describe what a regressive tax is and give some examples. Also a non-regressive tax.
12. Cite advantages and disadvantages of the local control of education.
13. Describe the basic provisions of the following court cases: The *Serrano* v. *Priest* decision (California); The *Cahill* v. *Robinson* (Botter) decision (New Jersey).
14. Explain how these decisions might affect educational finance legislation in your home state.
15. Discuss the theory of dedicated taxes.
16. Outline the process of budget preparation.
17. Describe the role of the teacher in budget preparation.

MODULE TEXT

Expenditures for education have generally been considered good and worthwhile investments instead of just necessary expenses. Experience has shown that a good education usually costs more money than a mediocre education, and that the best-educated people tend to produce many times the amount of money annually than was required to educate them.

But we know that the need for more advanced education and the cost to provide it have both risen dramatically. Therefore, our task will be (1) to understand the arts and skills necessary to produce good educational plans; (2) to learn the possible sources for raising the funds in order to prepare good revenue plans, and (3) to learn about spending these funds prudently in order to prepare a sound expenditure plan.

Means of Financing Education

School revenue is a very important area in the study of school finance. In the early days of our country and our economy, financing education was relatively simple. Today, with our complex revenue system and the various demands made upon it by the many departments of local, state, and national governments, it becomes of great importance that schools be able to tap resources that are not already drained by other agencies.

State Taxing Sources. State sources of revenue encompass a multiplicity of taxes, fees, and levies. The most widely used taxes for state funds are the personal income tax and the sales tax.

THE SALES TAX. The sales tax is an extremely important source of revenue for state governments in funding education. In 1969, the sales taxes levied by 45 states produced 30 per cent of their total state revenue.

The primary advantages of a sales tax are

1. It is relatively easy to collect.
2. It is considered a relatively "painless" tax, because the collections are only a few cents at a time and are usually a part of a purchase that an individual is committed to make.

The disadvantages of the sales tax are

1. A sales tax on all goods taxes the poor man for the necessities of life at the same rate that it taxes the rich man. Economists call this a "regressive tendency." It is partially overcome in many states by exempting food, medicine, and clothing from the sales tax.
2. The enactment of a sales tax may affect the location of large shopping centers. This is true where a bordering state has a lower sales-tax rate or perhaps no sales tax.

Although the sales tax is often said to be a way in which the tax load can be well spread throughout the state, it usually falls far short of this promise. Because most states tax only the sale of tangible (physical) property, Mr. Jones, who earns $5,000 a year, must pay the same amount of taxes on food, clothing, furniture, and other necessities for himself and his family as does Mr. Smith, who earns $50,000 a year.

Many states ignore a seemingly logical source for funds in the form of a sales tax on services. A tax on garbage collection, electricity, and other utilities could bring in a sizable tax income, and possibly relieve the tax load on food and clothing.

THE PERSONAL INCOME TAX. The personal income tax is the largest single source of income for the federal government. Forty-one states, as of 1970, also levy income taxes, although their tax bases and rate structures vary widely.

The following are major advantages of the personal income tax.

1. It is the tax most directly related to the individual's ability to pay—his personal income.
2. It can be adjusted, through the use of exemptions or credits, to take into account special circumstances, for instance, the illness of a taxpayer or a member of his family, unusual business expenses, and so forth.
3. It is easy to collect through payroll deductions.
4. The income from this tax increases and decreases, according to the earning power of the taxpayer.
5. It permits a larger share of the tax burden to be adjusted to the size of the family, through the exemption system. It results in equal treatment of individuals and households with equal income, a characteristic that grows in importance as the margin between people's incomes and their consumer expenditures widens, and as family homesteads become increasingly less indicative of the owner's taxpaying ability.

These are the major disadvantages of the personal income tax.

1. The income from this tax usually decreases at a faster rate when the economy recedes than does income from other tax sources.
2. Because of the many ways people find to escape paying their just share of tax on their income, the costs of administering the tax become significant.
3. An income tax is politically unpopular. Because such a tax must be paid at specific times, the taxpayer does not visualize what he is buying (services) for this money and therefore resents having to pay it.

A good example of the political climate accompanying the attempts to introduce a personal income tax occurred recently in the state of New Jersey. Governor Brendan Byrne in 1974 put the entire weight of his office and whatever political clout he could muster to enact personal income tax legislation to finance education, but the state legislators, who had to answer to the local voter, refused to support him.

CORPORATION INCOME TAX. The corporate income tax is a tax upon the profits of business corporations, and can be very lucrative. There is much discussion as to its fairness, because the individuals who hold stock in the company pay income tax upon the money they receive in dividends. The corporations (or rather the individuals who run them) contend that this represents double taxation.

Politically this tax is not popular among lawmakers. Largely because of the influence of corporation lobbyists the rate and structure of corporate taxes vary greatly from state to state. Corporation tax rates in bordering states may differ by as much as 2 to 3 per cent. Some states try to avoid such taxes, or to keep them very low in order to attract businesses with high property-tax income potential; others set high tax rates for corporations and businesses to reimburse the state for services required by large industry (roads, police protection, traffic control, and fire protection).

SEVERANCE TAXES. Severance taxes are levied on minerals and oil, but are not a major revenue-producing source of taxation, particularly in states with limited mineral and oil resources. In mineral-rich states strong industry lobbies in the legislature often prevent the levying of such taxes.

EXCISE TAXES. Excise taxes are taxes on such items as motor fuel, tobacco, and alcoholic beverages. They produce substantial revenue for most state governments; however, they generally are not used as a direct source for funds to support education.

OTHER STATE TAXES. In recent years, state-run lotteries are being used to raise funds for governmental expenses. Taxes on liquor, para-mutual betting at race tracks, and tobacco products, all good revenue sources, have an unusual origin. Taxes on these "vices" were first imposed for the primary (and clearly stated) purpose of helping to regulate or curtail them because alcohol and tobacco were considered detrimental to the health of the user and betting was considered immoral. It is ironic that the revenue from these sources has now become such an integral part of state income that the morality issue has long since been lost in most states. Instead, governments tend to create attractive establishments for greater patronage by the public so that tax incomes will be greater.

Local Taxing Sources. The local sources for tax revenues are often limited by the extent to which such sources are being utilized by the state and federal governments.

THE PROPERTY TAX. In every state of the Union, certain or all of the local school units levy a tax on general property to help support part of their programs. This practice seems to have been justified through the nineteenth century and much of the twentieth because it proved to be a reliable source of revenue for local schools and other local governmental agencies. Furthermore, the property tax usually remained available to the local authorities because the demands of state and federal governments could be met by other and better taxing methods. Also, the property tax continued in favor for so many years because (1) it is a direct tax —the collection and payment involve only one transaction between the governmental agency and the property owner; (2) most people understand its purposes and know how tax rates are determined; (3) it is a highly visible tax—the taxpayer knows exactly what services his tax dollars are paying for; (4) until recent years it was understood that a man's home was a good indication of his wealth, therefore a tax on a man's real estate property would be the fairest way to tax according to the individual's ability to pay.

The property tax has recently begun to fall into disfavor. What seemed to be advantages early in its existence have, today, turned into disadvantages. For example, some citizens have found that funds invested in other ventures are more profitable than funds invested in the purchase of real estate, which is subject to the local property tax. This trend has made the property tax increasingly unfair. The man or woman who owns nothing but the roof over his head is taxed on his home at the same rate as his neighbor, who may, in addition to his house, have many holdings of wealth in other ventures. When a method of taxation places heavier proportionate burdens upon the "have nots" than it does on the "haves," it is a *regressive tax* and is judged to be a negative influence upon the economic health of the community.

Another shortcoming of the property tax involves the frequent inequalities in the assessment local governments make upon real estate property. The word *assessment* is used to describe the determined value of property for taxing purposes. All too often assessed values do not keep pace with the changing property values; consequently, one property owner may pay a lower tax than his neighbor, even though both properties have the same potential market value. For example, Mr. Jones purchased his house in 1940 for $20,000, and he is still paying his taxes at a rate based upon the original $20,000 purchase price. But Mr. Smith, his next door neighbor, who purchased a similar house in 1970 for $50,000, must pay his taxes at the rate applied to the $50,000 purchase price. The two houses are identical, and have the same 1970 value, yet Mr. Smith has to pay two and a half times as much in property taxes as Mr. Jones.

In order to eliminate such inequalities, at least one state, New Jersey, by statute, requires each of its communities to assess all real estate at 100 per cent of its market value. Ideally, this is a fair and just procedure, but it has proved to be almost impossible to enforce for the purpose of equalizing school financing structure throughout the state. In New Jersey, the basis for the decision of the Superior Court in 1972 was that the school finance system was unconstitutional because it violated a section of the state constitution requiring the state legislature "to provide for the maintenance and support of a thorough and efficient system of free public schools." In each case brought before the state courts the primary premise for the decision was that the present tax structure causes inequality of educational opportunity in New Jersey communities because of their various levels of wealth.

Provisions such as those of the equal protection clause in the California constitution and the requirement for a uniform system of public education in the New Jersey constitution are found in the constitutions on statutes in almost every state.

Assessments are usually adjusted in local communities by recording the property sales during a calendar year and then applying the percentage of market value increase to the assessment figure of these properties. Periodically, city governments hire professional firms to reassess all properties in a community, but this practice is too costly for regular application.

The use of the property tax as a primary source of funds for financing schools has recently come under attack by the courts. The 1971 California Supreme Court decision in *Serrano* v. *Priest* opened a new era in American school financing. In this historic case the court ruled that the traditional taxing patterns for financing public schools were not legal under the California State Constitution; therefore the court ordered that major revisions in the methods of financing public schools be made. Basically, the ruling contended, the system for financing schools in California violated the provision in the California Constitution that every child in the state must be granted an equally good education. Later, in the *Robinson* v. *Cahill* case in New Jersey, Judge Botter made a similar finding and ordered the state legislature to make major changes in its school financing structure. In 1974 the State of Connecticut was faced with a similar decision; for instance, the courts of Connecticut followed California's lead in declaring the real property tax an unequitable and unconstitutional method of financing public schools. These decisions seem to accept the theory that the quality of educational opportunity can be better justified by the money spent for schooling than by the results of pupil-performance tests. By 1975, the opinions expressed by the courts in the Serrano and other cases had affected the programs for financing education in most states.

The various court decisions have generally agreed on several basic principles:

1. The public education of a child shall not depend on wealth other than that of the state as a whole.
2. Taxes levied for school purposes must generate the same funds for support of schools in poor districts as they do in wealthy districts.
3. Although the courts generally agreed that the property tax usually discriminates against the poor, none of the decisions requires its elimination in favor of other forms of taxation.

OTHER LOCAL TAXING SOURCES. Over the past few years, an increasing number of states have authorized local governments to levy nonproperty taxes as a means of securing added revenues. Today many cities, counties, and even school districts levy almost the same kinds of taxes that are levied by the states. In addition to sales taxes on income from gasoline, alcoholic beverages, cigarettes and tobacco, amusements, and motor vehicles, for example, the State of Pennsylvania permits local school districts to assess taxes on coal, oil, and other minerals found within their borders. Several of the larger Pennsylvania cities now levy direct taxes on payrolls to provide governmental revenues.

Budgetary Practices

The budgetary practices now used in schools are patterned after those of business and industrial corporations. At first these practices were incorporated into governmental bodies, and their use in the second decade of the century gradually spread through the respective governmental levels—state, country, and municipal —to school districts. It was natural, of course, that it was in the large cities, where schools rapidly became big businesses, that sophisticated budgeting was first used.

In 1927 several writers about public school finance, Engelhardt and Engelhardt, Arthur B. Moehlman and others set forth the theory of the budget as a functional approach to scientific management of school receipts and expenditures. In his book Moehlman outlined in detail the procedure in the development of a school budget for a large city and showed the completed budget as well as the various steps in its preparation. Budget formats developed in almost as many forms as there were states, because many state legislatures set their own particular methods of monetary control by mandating specific methods of accounting. Finally, in 1957, the U.S. Office of Education, with the cooperation of five major educational associations, developed a financial accounting manual for the guidance of local and state school systems in the United States. This manual served to standardize school accounting and budgeting methods and its format has been almost universally adopted by all states. This format is described in more detail in the section of the module on the expenditure plan.

Figure 6-1 *The Budget Triangle.*

Assuming that the function of the board of education is of a legislative nature, and that that of the superintendent of schools is executive, we can begin to delineate their respective functions in preparing school budgets.

The preparation of the budget plan, including the detailed estimates, is generally considered to be the job of the superintendent of schools. The determination of broad policies for the school, and the final decision on moneys to be raised and expended, must be that of the board of education.

The preparation of the budget consists of the formulation of three plans: (1) the educational plan, which describes the proposed school program and the board policies that govern and control it; (2) the expenditure plan, which translates the program into dollar costs; and (3) the revenue plan, which describes the plan to raise the dollars necessary to finance the proposed program. These three plans are closely interrelated and are sometimes described as the parts of an equilateral triangle.

The Educational Plan

The educational plan is the most important part of the budget-planning process, for it represents the proposals for the fulfillment of the aims and objectives of the school system. And it is the most difficult to determine because of the many variables and influences which affect the budgetary decision-making process.

In preparing the educational plan the superintendent finds himself faced with many questions:

1. What services of the school should be increased next year?
2. Should the school provide more guidance services, or should it put more emphasis on more and better facilities and instructional media for teachers?
3. Should more emphasis be put on expensive programs such as driver education, or should the social science offerings be increased instead?
4. Should the school provide preschool and special education classes?
5. To what extent should the pupils be offered extracurricular activities at the possible expense of some academic offering?

These and countless other questions must be answered in preparing the educational proposal for consideration by the board of education.

What Does the Plan Show? The plan will show the organizational pattern under which the school is to operate the following school year, for example, K–6, 7–8, 9–12; K–6, 7–9, 10–12; or K–5, 6–8, 9–12. The selection of the organizational plan is usually guided by either a philosophical motive or the pressures for more efficient use of available classroom space, or both. A philosophical motive might be described as follows:

Change from the junior high school organization (7–8–9) to the middle school pattern (6–7–8). The "older" junior high school pattern established a version of the high school, with modifications as appropriate for preadolescent students. The increase in sophistication, the growth in knowledge, and the earlier maturation of children in the 12–14 age bracket in this decade of the twentieth century point to the need for modification of organization. Introducing the more fluid, flexible, and departmentalized pattern of middle school organization appears justified.

A "pressure" motive could be described as follows:

In the coming year, the facilities used by the junior high school will be severely overtaxed. For various reasons this enrollment has grown faster than other levels of our organization. The crunch can be relieved by moving the very large Grade 9 to the high school building, where space is available, and replacing the students with the smaller group currently in Grade 6.

This move will bring about a new pattern, consisting of Grades 6–7–8 in one building, to be known as the middle school.

The plan will also indicate the number of pupils expected, as well as recommended class sizes and groupings. There are several ways to make predictions of future school population figures; the method used would depend largely upon conditions existing within a community at the time of budget planning. For example, a town with ample land available for building houses must not only consider what happens to the population already in the community (is it stable, or are people constantly moving in and out?), but must also consider the number and kind of houses that will be erected on the available lands. Another town, where there is little or no prospect of new homes being built, must determine whether its people tend to stay in the community (even though their children have grown up and left home); they must also consider whether the high cost of living in the town might tend to cause the exodus of older people, to be replaced by younger families with school-age children.

The plan must indicate the recommended number of classrooms needed to house the school population.

The plan must indicate the number of teachers, specialists, supervisors, and administrators needed to provide an efficient educational process. Also, important consideration must be given to the number of staff members needed to keep the classrooms clean, warm, and in good repair.

The plan must outline the educational program offerings proposed. Changes, additions, or dropping of courses should be explained in the plan because they will be a vital part of the later budgetary picture. The extent of extracurricular offerings for students must be outlined, as well as the kinds of interscholastic sports programs.

Who Is Involved in Preparing the Plan? No matter how complex the problems of defining and delineating an efficient and justifiable educational plan, the superintendent should utilize all resources available to him in preparing it. These resources include school faculty, staff members, parents, and other members of the community. The input from classroom personnel tends to be the grass roots variety, which gives the superintendent views of the program from the standpoint of the people who deal directly with the children. Teacher contributions usually come from discussions with the school principal, who has helped them establish goals and objectives for their class. Contacts with the parents and other interested members of the community will tend to give added direction to the kinds and extent of programs the community will support.

With the input from all these sources, the educational plan, when finally presented to the board of education, will have a support base which will help it to survive intense scrutiny and withstand negative opposition. The input from the potential applicator (the classroom teacher) will have contributed a reality to the requests, which will reduce the risks of vulnerability resulting from excessive theory. The input from the primary source of school revenue, the taxpayer, who represents the expressed desires of citizens, will supply the imagination-to-grow-on. The final synthesis, screened through the judgment of the superintendent and district administrators, will provide a defensible compromise position. This application of sound reasoning, supported by evidence from research, should provide the board and the voting citizens with sufficient direction, and should culminate in their agreement that the educational plan is a good combination of "blue-sky" dreams and dollar reality.

It is a good strategy to present an educational plan to the board of education for enough in advance to allow its members to consider the merits of educational planning and decide upon program offerings before the controlling and distracting element of funding and taxes is brought up. Such an approach often results in enhancing the educational aspects in budget-planning discussions, and diminishes the importance of those aspects dealing with the availability or unavailability of funds.

In order that you may better understand the components of an educational plan, a typical table of contents and excerpts from the expository text of the plan, as presented to a board of education by a superintendent of schools, has been included in this module. The table of contents indicates the areas of discussion in an educational plan, and the excerpts show how the presentation to the board is made.

The Table of Contents
An Educational Plan for Budget Year 19— to 19—

Introduction

The prologue to the budget is provided annually to the board of education for the purposes of enlarging upon and explaining educational projects and proposals included in the budget. The prologue, hopefully, serves the added purpose of communicating to the board the state of progress in various projects that have been carried on. The prologue shall also provide a basis for board of education consideration of new and advanced pilot projects that are related to school functions and must be considered in the appropriation of funds. . . .

Testing Program

For the past twelve months considerable emphasis has been given to the development of a more feasible and effective means of assessing the quality of instructional programs in the schools. A portion of this assessment program is the use of a series of evaluative tests.

In the spring of 19— the Educational Records Bureau was engaged to do an evaluation of the existing testing program and also was asked to make recommendations for changes and additions. Those suggested changes which the Superintendent and the staff felt would enhance the program have been recommended within this budget and funds are included for these purposes. Also, at the same time the school guidance personnel assisted in the development of a diagnostic testing program and methods of utilizing test results by principals and teachers to bring about improved evaluative instructional techniques. The Educational Records Bureau's suggestions, plus the one year of experience under this program, have resulted in budgetary recommendations that will provide individual continuing test records for each student *in the elementary school* (K–8). Such test records will be available to principals and classroom teachers before the beginning of each school year to assist in fashioning programs and teaching methods that better fit the needs of the individual student.

On the secondary level (9–12), validated tests are being recommended for certain academic areas. In some departments where such tests are not available, it is planned to place more emphasis on well-constructed teacher-made tests that may in time serve as reasonable, validated bench marks for judgment of teaching quality and student-learning progress. Funds for workshops to train teachers in the techniques of good test-making are included in this budget.

Hopefully, this program, when fully developed, will give the administration a more effective means for judging instructional improvement and a better measuring stick for reporting progress toward excellence within the school system.

Summary

Funds included in this budget for the project (purchase of tests, testing materials, and cost of automatic scoring), are

(Acct. No. 250.03)	High School	$3,378
(Acct. No. 250.03)	Elementary (Grades K–8)	9,635
(Acct. No. 213.17)	Cost of teacher workshops	1,500
	Total cost	$14,513

Elementary Guidance

The addition of a broader testing program now makes more data available than ever before to principals and teachers for improvement in instruction. These added services will require coordination and supervision as well as added administration time. In order to have someone to give full attention to the administration of the testing program so that it can be of greater value to teachers and principals in learning how to better utilize test data, your Superintendent recommends that the Board of Education authorize the establishment of the Position of Director of Testing for Grades K thru 8.

If the recommendation to add one full-time person to the guidance staff in the Middle School receives approval, then the above recommendation can be carried out without any further addition of personnel. The functions could be carried out by a member of the present Middle School guidance staff on a half-time testing and half-time guidance basis.

Vocational Education

Greater attention must be given to the fulfillment of the broader needs for students at the High School level. Academic preparation may be of prime importance to many, but some experience in the work world for the majority of these students can certainly be of great positive educational value. For others, the academic experiences in the High School are only bases for vocational or vocational preparatory programs. Broad opportunities must be provided for both groups. . . .

Continuation of the Idea Bank

This budget includes a proposal for a continuation of the Idea Bank for the next school year. The following paragraph, which was used in the original idea bank proposal to explain to the Board of Education its basic philosophy, is reproduced here to again give a simple background explanation of the program.

> Historically, principals are charged with the obligation of utmost stewardship in planning and developing educational programs within their schools. However, it is realistic to assume that ideas developed ahead of time for budgetary purposes do not always include all of the needs that arise during the teaching season. Therefore, the funds requested under contingency in the #240 account are designed to be an "idea bank" to be used for purchasing materials that are needed when teachers find that the development of a new idea needs funds not provided for in the current budget. Inclusion of these funds would tend to relieve teachers of the apprehension and inhibition that comes from the realization: "I didn't include this in my budget; therefore, I must wait another year before I can develop this idea in my classroom," and hopefully would encourage greater creativity in teaching for the classroom. Your Superintendent feels that this idea will stimulate classroom teachers to seek out and develop new ideas at a much greater pace than is now apparent.

Again, it is the feeling of the Administration and the staff that the Idea Bank has proved to be productive in development of new ideas and program procedures within the classroom and has directly benefitted programs for students. The programs and materials approved have invariably been those that can be immediately implemented and can have almost an immediate beneficial effect upon the classroom teaching. The following include some examples of projects already under way this year.

1. The upgraded primary classes have been experimenting with different sets of diagnostic materials which permit teachers to be more efficient in discovering and evaluating children's learning problems. The results of such evaluation and diagnosis will serve to give guidance and direction in filling the needs of these immature students. Idea Bank funds were used to purchase these materials.

2. The school kindergartens are experimenting with a set of materials specifically developed to implement an individualized approach to the discovery of reading for youngsters at an early age. This idea coincides with the present kindergarten philosophy to begin teaching reading to children as soon as they are ready to read. Through the Idea Bank funds it was possible to purchase these materials, and the program is already functioning.

3. High School Course in Advanced Chemistry and Physics.

Although it is very early to evaluate the benefits students may derive by participation in this new, advanced Honors course, the teacher evaluation at the present time seems to indicate that the contents of the course should prove particularly helpful to those who are planning to pursue science studies in college. The comments of the science department chairman are as follows:

> The course certainly seems to be a very worthwhile addition to the curriculum. It provides the superior science student with a level of study that will allow him to compete with science students from other high schools that offer similar courses. Some neighboring high schools offer a full second-year course in chemistry and/or physics. At the present time our half-year course will be evaluated to determine whether future curricula, particularly when we have more classroom space, should offer these Honors courses on a full-year basis.

4. Science in the Middle School.

Science books and materials have been purchased for the seventh and eighth grades in the Middle School to bring about a better continuity with the Elementary SCIS Program. Funds for this project were made available through the Idea Bank.

5. The Talented-Pupil Program.

The talented-pupil program in the elementary schools (Grades 1–5) has given individual consideration to the needs of talented students, and requires new materials. It was possible to use funds from the Idea Bank to purchase these materials for immediate use.

The above résumés represent some of the results of the Idea Bank philosophy, and on the strength of these illustrations and on prior experiences, a continuation of this program is recommended and funds are included in the budget proposal for this purpose.

Reviewing these examples should illustrate the several basic aims of this superintendent in presenting these topics to his board of education. He wanted to inform the board of education that

1. Plans are being made and things are being done to improve instruction.
2. Evaluation of educational progress is a regular and ongoing process in the district. It is a well-planned operation, which supplies the kinds of information needed upon which to base educational decisions (accountability).
3. The students at the upper and lower ends of the continuum are not being ignored. The talented-pupil program described, which provides for the upper-level group, reveals the amount of attention lavished by the staff on individualization of instructional planning. It serves to alleviate fears that all students are treated as though they are identical.
4. The elements of creativity, professional growth, and action research are being fostered in the district. The Idea-Bank concept and the implementation of proposals that have already taken place reveal that staff support and participation are positive.
5. Vocational education programs have also been updated. In this upper-middle-class community the needs of all the children are being attended to. Courses have been broadened and program offerings have been modified to keep pace with the changes and demands evident in contemporary society.

Expenditure Plan

After full consideration of the plan for education in the school system, the costs of the proposal must be determined. The board of education must ask the community to provide the dollars to finance the educational plan and therefore must have a detailed translation of this plan in terms of dollar costs.

To enable board members and the public to better understand what they are paying for, a pattern of budget categories has been devised. In this way those who decide can better determine how to set priorities in considering programs for the final expenditure budget.

It must be assumed that there will always be limitations to the amount of funds that can be raised in a community for the purposes of good education. Therefore those programs that are judged to have the most promise of success in improving the educational process, and those that show promise of fulfilling the urgent learning needs of children will be considered first. Staff members may at times find it difficult to understand why a particular program proposal has not been included in the immediate plan, but if priorities have been made on the basis of professional judgment, teachers should be able to get answers from their supervisors.

A financial manual for school budget accounting has been prepared by the U.S. Department of Health, Education, and Welfare. This manual provides descriptions of the detailed categories for budget accounting.

The major divisions of this format are

1. Expenditures for operation.
2. Expenditures for capital purchases.
3. Expenditures for new buildings and major additions.

Expenditures for Operation. The working divisions of school expenditures for operation according to the manual follow.

ADMINISTRATION. This account consists of those activities that relate to the general system-wide regulation and direction of the affairs of the school district. All expenses relating to the functions of the office of the superintendent of schools and the business office of the school system are listed in this section. Legal fees paid by the system and public relations expenses incurred by the board of education are some of the details included.

INSTRUCTION. The instruction account consists of those activities dealing directly with the teaching of students or improving the quality of teaching. All salaries of instructional personnel, including classroom teachers, school principals, specialists, and supervisors must be listed here. Also to be included are books and magazines for the classroom and the library; audiovisual materials (not including equipment); and teaching supplies. Funds for this account usually make up 60 per cent or more of the entire operations budget.

ATTENDANCE. Those services that are required to improve and control attendance of pupils in school.

HEALTH SERVICES. These are charges for activities in the field of physical and mental health that are not for direct instruction. Salaries and expenses for nurses, doctors, and psychiatrists are included.

PUPIL TRANSPORTATION. These services consist of those activities that have as their purpose the transportation of pupils to and from school and on trips for co-curricular activities. Many states provide reimbursement to communities for varying portions of the transportation expenditures. However, minimum distances from the school are usually set by state statutes, to regulate the extent of reimbursement costs.

OPERATION OF PLANT. Operation of the plant consists of the housekeeping activities concerned with keeping the school buildings open, clean, and warm. Salaries for custodial personnel to do this work are charged to this account. Some of the expenses included are cleaning, heating, lighting, power, moving furniture, and caring for grounds.

MAINTENANCE OF PLANT. Maintenance of plant consists of those activities concerned with keeping the school properties in good repair and good order. Repairs and replacement of furniture and equipment are usually in this category.

FIXED CHARGES. These are charges that are usually at a fixed rate and of a recurring nature: for example, premium costs for all types of insurance; costs for rental of land and buildings; pension and employee retirement expenses; and tuition costs for pupils sent to other communities.

FOOD SERVICES. Any expenses for running food services in the school that are not covered by receipts from sales are recorded in this account.

STUDENT-BODY ACTIVITIES. Student-body activities include the costs for activities run directly for pupils, such as interscholastic athletics, entertainments, publications, clubs, and music activities. Usually the extent of such activities is determined in accord with the wishes and needs of the students and the willingness of the taxpayer to pay for it. Often gate receipts from activities will offset a considerable portion of the expenditures. The account also includes salaries for coaches and sponsors to supervise youth activities, as well as costs of the supplies necessary to carry on the programs.

Expenditures for Capital Purchases. CAPITAL OUTLAY. Expenditures for capital outlay are usually for land or existing buildings, adding to or remodeling buildings, or the purchase of furniture and equipment needed for the facilities constructed. Costs for improvement of school sites may also be listed in this account.

Expenditures for New Buildings and Major Additions. DEBT SERVICE. Debt service is the account that budgets funds to pay principal and interest on debts. Usually such debts have been incurred by selling bonds to raise money for major construction and site purchase.

Authorization for funds to build new school buildings or major additions must still be obtained in many states through public referendum. In other states the decisions for new building expenditures rest entirely in the hands of the local board of education.

Usually payments for large expenditures are raised by tax funds under long-term debt service programs which permit boards of education to repay loans for sums so large that they could not very well be raised through one year's taxation.

Programmed Budgeting. The foregoing format of accounting gives a pattern for listing school expenditures for services and materials by descriptive category. In contrast, recent procedures have been developed to provide a financial story of each program carried on in the school. This system is called Planned Program Budgeting System (PPBS). Programmed budgeting provides details for planning, assessing, and implementing costs of programs that a school system may offer to reach its stated objectives.

This new system is a management process that allows school personnel responsible for managing and budgeting a program to define goals for their programs and describe anticipated results. In this way all those who design programs are also involved in determination of program costs. This kind of involvement by school personnel often enhances support for the budget and probably makes the participants more sensitive to the complete school-cost factors of which their program is a small part.

To implement programmed budgeting first requires identification of the program (that is, mathematics, trade and industrial occupations, library, and so on), and a determination of the operational relationships that exist among the activities. A district may wish to plan and manage its educational programs by discipline: Grades K–12 (mathematics, language arts, and so on) or by time span (elementary, middle or junior high school, and senior high school). Whatever program approach is selected by the community must fit into the approved budgetary accounting pattern prescribed by the state.

The State of New Jersey, although not mandating a standard programming structure for use by all New Jersey school districts, did design a suggested format to indicate the types of information it would need from school districts for computing state aid. This state format was developed from the experiences of the several pilot school districts which had run experimental programs. The New Jersey format is presented as Figure 6-2.

Generally, programmed budgeting has not been widely adapted because its basic patterns are complex and therefore difficult to carry out. In many instances the smaller school districts lack the necessary personnel to implement the programming approach.

The United States Department of Health, Education, and Welfare has recently (1973), in cooperation with nine cosponsoring educational organizations, revised its 1957 *Financial Accounting Handbook (II)*. This revision has been designed to introduce and implement the procedures for programmed cost accounting at the

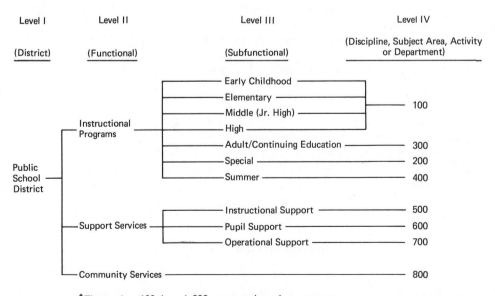

*The numbers 100 through 800 represent the various programs.

Figure 6-2 *New Jersey Department of Education Public School Districts—Program Structure.*

local and intermediate levels, so eventually the cost of individual programs can be identified and measured.

It should not be assumed that programmed budgeting is another plan to curtail expenditures or to facilitate the retrenchment of programs. It is concerned with the effectiveness of the various ways in which the school can organize to achieve stated goals and objectives. It is aimed at securing the optimum results by allocating the school's resources to the more productive programs and denying them to the less productive ones. Programmed budgeting has been criticized because it seems to accentuate efficiency at the expense of quality education, but with careful use by reasonable practitioners there seems to be no reason why programmed budgeting should have anything other than a beneficial effect on education.

Revenue Plan

After completion of the budgetary plan for dollars needed to provide the educational program desired by the board of education and the staff, consideration must be given to a plan to provide the funds. In order to do this, the board must decide upon, and then study the available sources of revenue; the board must then outline a plan that will support its educational plan. A good revenue plan will usually include the following:

1. State aid for education includes *Formula aid:* The amount of aid is usually determined by a formula established by state law; usually considered are such factors as community ability and/or willingness to pay its share for education. *Transportation aid:* Most states reimburse communities for a portion of the moneys spent for transporting students to and from school.
2. Tuition income includes moneys received from other school districts whose children attend the local schools.
3. Local property taxes have traditionally been the largest contributor to the support of local schools. However, in recent years the state governmental bodies are beginning to assume a greater portion of the burden of school support.

The clamor for greater state involvement in financing education to lessen the impact upon local property owners continues to increase. The effect of this point of view has been felt in many legislative bodies of the fifty states, and has accelerated the trend of shifting the major burdens of school financing from the local level to the state level.

SUGGESTED READING

Broudy, Harry S. *The Real World of the Public Schools.* New York: Harcourt Brace Jovanovich, Inc., 1972.

Burrup, Percy E. *Financing Education in a Climate of Change.* Boston: Allyn & Bacon, Inc., 1974.

Candoli, Carl I., et al. *School Business Administration: A Planning Approach.* Boston: Allyn & Bacon, Inc., 1973.

Committee on Educational Finance. *The Challenge of Change in School Finance.* Washington, D.C.: National Education Association, 1967.

Committee on Educational Finance. *A Time for Priorities: Financing the Schools for the 70's.* Washington, D.C.: National Education Association, 1970.

Garvue, Robert J. *Modern Public School Finance.* New York: Macmillan Publishing Co., Inc., 1969.

Johns, Roe L., et al. *Economic Factors Affecting the Financing of Education.* Gainesville, Fla.: National Educational Finance Project, 1970.

Johns, Roe L., et al. *Financing Education.* Columbus, Ohio: Charles E. Merrill Publishers, 1972.

Miller, Van, George R. Madden, and James B. Kincheloe. *The Public Administration of American School Systems.* New York: Macmillan Publishing Co., Inc., 1972.

National Education Association. *What Everyone Should Know About Financing Our Schools.* Washington, D.C.: The Association, 1966.

Wise, Arthur A. *Rich Schools, Poor Schools: The Promise of Equal Educational Opportunity.* Chicago: University of Chicago Press, 1969.

POST TEST

MULTIPLE CHOICE *Circle the correct letter in each of the following:*

1. Compared to a person with less education, the more highly educated person tends to earn
   a. less money.   **b.** more money.   **c.** as much money.

2. Teachers (as a group) are usually considered to have _____ regard for the source of school support funds.
   a. no.   **b.** little.   **c.** much.

3. The state governments get their responsibility for providing educational opportunity from the federal government by
   a. omission.   **b.** statute.   **c.** presidential mandate.

4. The government provides funds for education through the Smith-Hughes Act for
   a. remedial reading.   **b.** vocational education.   **c.** American history.

5. Good education generally costs _____ mediocre education.
   a. less than.   **b.** more than.   **c.** the same as.

6. The last major underutilized revenue source for most states is the
   a. sales tax.   **b.** property tax.   **c.** income tax.

7. Every state in the Union uses the _____ tax to raise a portion of revenue for schools.
   a. income.   **b.** sales.   **c.** property.

8. The use of the _____ tax for school revenues has recently fallen into disfavor.
   a. income.   **b.** sales.   **c.** property.

9. The function of the board of education is _____ in nature.
   a. legislative.　　**b.** executive.　　**c.** judicial.

10. The function of the superintendent of schools is by nature
    a. legislative.　　**b.** executive.　　**c.** judicial.

Completion *Fill in the blank with the appropriate word.*

11. The preparation of the budget proposal is the primary responsibility of the

    _____

12. The school budget should be divided into the following three parts:

    a. _____

    b. _____

    c. _____

13. The National Defense Education Act provided funds to assist schools in accelerating development in the basic fields of

    a. _____

    b. _____

    c. _____

14. The National Elementary and Secondary Education Act made funds available to local school districts for _____

15. Name two recent court cases in which the decisions have had a direct effect upon the philosophy of financing education.

    a. _____

    b. _____

16. Name the primary advantages of a sales tax.

    a. _____

    b. _____

17. Name two basic disadvantages of a sales tax.

    a. _____

    b. _____

18. The largest single source of income for the federal government is _____

    _____

19. Name the major advantages of a personal income tax.

    a. _____

    b. _____

    c. _____

20. Name the major disadvantages of the personal income tax.

a. _____

b. _____

c. _____

21. The use of property tax as a source of revenue is usually reserved for the

_____ government.

General Curriculum

George A. Finchum

East Tennessee State University

module 7

RATIONALE

The curriculum is the heart of the school; if there were no curriculum, there would be no reason for having schools at all. For that reason it is essential that prospective teachers gain an excellent understanding of what the curriculum is, how the curriculum is built, curriculum theory, and curriculum problems. Consequently this module has been designed to introduce you to the concepts necessary for an understanding of curriculum in general. Upon completing it you should be familiar with basic curriculum theory and practice, and be able to think clearly about the curriculum and the problems educators face when attempting to design a curriculum that will best serve their communities.

Objectives

In this module we shall consider briefly concepts about curriculum in general. Upon completion of this module, you should be able to

1. Write a comprehensive definition of *curriculum.*
2. List at least five of the seven factors or agencies identified as having influence on curriculum in American schools.
3. Recognize a basic concept about the *subject-centered curriculum.*
4. List and define the four basic concepts of curriculum: *scope, sequence, articulation,* and *balance.*
5. Indicate six specific extra-curricular activities as being a recognized part of the school's formal curriculum.
6. Recognize three basic considerations for *general education.*
7. Identify *the* current trend in grade placement for "exploratory education."
8. Identify the current grade placement for initiating "specialized education."
9. Match six concepts of Career Education with the age group and/or grade placement suggested by the U.S. Office of Education.

MODULE TEXT

The term *curriculum* has been used with several different connotations in the past, and some confusion has resulted in communication because of the consequent ambiguities. Some people, for example, have used the term to refer to the subjects that are offered by a school. When asked "What is your school curriculum?" they respond with, "I have algebra, English, history, French, biology, and P.E." Others refer to the *select sequence* or *track* for which they are scheduled when they respond with, "I'm in the college preparatory program, or the business program, or the general program." Sometimes the reference is to the courses within a particular subject field: "Our science curriculum and our language arts curriculum are very sound." Another reference to curriculum pertains to specialized professional schools: "I am a student in the two-year-curriculum in nursing."

Definition of Curriculum

As it is most commonly used by educators today, *the term curriculum encompasses all the learning experiences that have been planned by, and are under the direction of, the school.* This definition is broader than the definitions described in the preceding paragraph, all of which were commonly accepted earlier in this century. However, our definition is less comprehensive than the definition which holds that the curriculum includes all the experiences the pupil has while he is enrolled in school, whether the experiences are planned by the school or not. The unplanned agenda that makes up such a large part of every pupil's life is not part of the curriculum per se.

In this module we shall accept the "experiences selected by the school" as our frame of reference for the word *curriculum.* We do recognize that many unplanned experiences produce learning, for instance the social skills pupils learn in the school are incidental to their classroom and extraclass activities. But, as we define it, the curriculum includes only those learning experiences to which the school intends to expose its pupils, and which will contribute positively to their development.

Misleading Perspective. You will notice that this definition of curriculum begins with "experiences," continues with "planning by the school," specifies supervision by school authorities, and mentions not at all the subjects that are taught. Unfortunately, there is a tendency on the part of teachers and administrators to focus on texts and pupil schedules, and to think almost solely in terms of subject matter and so lose sight of the experiences for which the subject matter was selected. Subtly, the emphasis is shifted, and almost unwittingly teachers find themselves teaching for thoroughness of recall of knowledge rather than for understanding, appreciation, skill, desirable attitudes and ideals, development in thinking, problem solving (including the application of learning to real problems), and other higher mental faculties.

This change in perspective among school personnel is so gradual and so subtle that this precautionary alert to students entering the profession cannot be overstressed. As one thinks of how the school is organized, it is easy to see how the change of emphasis occurs. During the planning, representative teachers are selected to serve on curriculum-planning or curriculum-modification committees as subject-matter specialists. When general goals for the school are proposed in committee, each teacher specialist looks into his own discipline to discover the experiences that can contribute to the realization of the goals. It is at this point after the curriculum has been proposed and adopted, that direction is lost and problems occur. The majority of teachers not present to hear the discussions which preceded the adoption of goals, or to agree upon activities and experiences, are presented only with the results of the planning meetings that were concerned the "what," and therefore are deprived of the opportunity to explore the "why." They teach history because it has been prescribed by the committee; they teach literature because the curriculum now requires it. Unfortunately, under these circumstances, what the curriculum committee planned as an exciting and timely exposure to an area of knowledge emerges as an academic, and perhaps dull, presentation of an accumulation of knowledge.

Factors Influencing Curriculum

In modern times, the curriculum has been influenced by numerous forces: committees appointed by national organizations, by political parties with educational platforms, and by local groups of concerned citizen groups. Because education in this country is viewed as the way to solve all social problems, every group with a conviction or an ax to grind has had recourse to the schools. Naturally, requests made by some of the groups have been in conflict with the requests of others. The following factors or agencies have probably had the most influence on the curriculum in American schools:

1. State laws and regulations specify the parameters within which the schools must function. In some states, the prescriptions are specific and numerous and thus inhibit the freedom of curriculum action of the schools. State textbook-adoption committees, for example, exist in some states to select the texts used in every grade, in every school, and every subject. Similarly prescribed state examinations, like the Regents examinations in New York, very greatly influence local curriculum plans. In other states, the laws and mandates are few, permitting much latitude in interpretation by the schools.
2. Studies supported by the federal government, or by national organizations such as the National Education Association, and the learned societies in each discipline, have been used as resources by local districts. The recent curriculum revolution, resulting in the "new math," "new science," and so on, came to pass largely through the activity of the learned societies combined with financial support from the Department of Health, Education, and Welfare.
3. Local citizens groups may influence the schools in adverse ways. Those emphasizing the conservatism of tradition have sometimes operated as deterrents to change because of their desire to retain the admired features of previous eras. Sometimes special-interest groups work to control curriculum planning through petitions to boards of education to adopt certain policies or actions, or through petitions and personal contacts with teachers to urge elimination or inclusion of certain units of instruction. Citizens of a liberal orientation have just as often pressured for more openness of the school campus and more flexibility of curriculum organization.
4. Regional accrediting agencies established near the turn of the century have provided standards and procedures to follow in evaluating school curriculums for the purpose of improving them. Because of the standardization of procedures, some schools have been deterred from taking curriculum action which appeared enlightened and defensible in consideration of their local goals and resources. Other communities have been motivated to change for the better because of the threat to their reputation were accreditation to be denied.

5. Textbook authors and their publishers, by selecting certain topics to write about and certain units to include in their texts, have an impact on the people who select curriculum activities. The expenditure of large sums by publishing houses on research and then on the production of curriculum aids makes some material readily available and other material scarce. The highly sophisticated advertising and public relations campaigns used by some companies to protect their investment has sometimes resulted in the national popularization of curriculum activities which proved of little worth on the local level after they were adopted by gullible purchasers.

6. Standardized testing programs exert influence because schools choosing to use such tests must of course include in their curriculums the material upon which the test is based. As a consequence, the action of the local decision makers on what activities are appropriate for their local students is often very much predetermined by the decision of those who are engaged in developing evaluative instruments for a much wider audience. Moreover, school personnel working at the local level frequently examine tests to discover what is considered important by the test designer. The fact that the latter is preoccupied with a national clientele often is not taken into consideration.

7. American foreign policy and international commitment and relationships cause some groups to agitate for curriculum changes. For instance, the launching of the first space vehicle by the Soviet Union triggered a demand for excellence in the sciences and mathematics areas that led to wholesale changes in the offerings of most American schools.

Curriculum Designs

There are two basic approaches to curriculum design: subject-centered and student-centered. The subject-centered curriculum is the oldest and one of the most widely used types of curriculum organizations in American schools. Its history can be traced to the liberal arts of the ancient world: the *trivium,* composed of grammar, rhetoric, and logic; and the *quadrivium,* composed of arithmetic, geometry, astronomy, and music. In time the *trivium* was expanded to include history and literature, and the *quadrivium* eventually included algebra, trigonometry, geography, botany, zoology, physics, and chemistry. The subject-matter curriculum is distinctive in that all subjects are taught as separate disciplines or courses. Scope and sequence are readily identifiable in curriculums that follow this approach. Subject-centered curriculums range from those in which courses are taught completely independent from one another to modified versions which call for integration of knowledge; the latter are known as correlated or fused programs. In all variations, however, the emphasis is on the subject matter, and the organization of the courses is determined by the nature of the subject matter.

More attention is given to the utilization of the knowledge in the student-centered curriculum. In the subject matter studied, its application to the solution of current and future problems, and the needs and interests of the pupils involved in the learning, are the points of concern and the goals to be achieved. The Core and the Activity curriculums, to be discussed later on, exemplify the application of this orientation in the schools.

Curriculum Organization

Either one or the other of the two basic approaches described in the preceding section—subject-centered or student-centered—is the foundation of all curriculum changes made to date. As a matter of fact, a running battle has been waged between the proponents of educational theories supporting each concept, to such an extent that "educational history becomes a series of actions and reactions in which successive movements or factions rebel against their predecessors."[1]

So long as there are differences of opinion about the purposes of American secondary education, the tendency to shift back and forth between the basic approaches will continue. But even if this were not true, divergent theories about learning would necessitate utilizing different methods of presentation and organization of the program in order to achieve the purposes of schooling. For example, the subject-centered school of thought endorses teaching the concept of democracy by means of lucid explanations; the student-centered theory of learning, however, urges limiting the explication to a minimum and using many opportunities to practice the democratic processes until they are mastered. According to the former school of thought, mastery can be demonstrated by means of a paper and pencil test; according to the latter theory, one can only test mastery of the concept by observing the pupil's daily behavior and interaction. A decision on which theory is best hinges on judgments concerning the efficacy and efficiency of each approach. The older subject-matter tradition places heavy emphasis on the material to be learned; the student-centered theory has emphasized the needs, problems, and desires of students. Contemporary thinking seems to be in favor of balancing the two concepts.

The Subject-Centered Curriculum. Supporters of the subject-centered curriculum believe that the subjects taught in school are the heritage of man; they have been thoroughly investigated and classified, and must be transmitted to the young so that they can pursue "the good life." They believe that the essential knowledge in our civilization must be presented for mastery so that the mistakes of the past can be avoided and the accumulated genius of history can be made to contribute to the continued advancement of civilization.

The offering of subjects in the school with this tradition is based on several beliefs and assumptions:

1. The belief that the major role of the school is to transmit the cultural heritage from generation to generation.
2. The assumption that each subject has an internal order which can be presented in sequence from simple to complex.
3. The assumption that once this internal order is mastered the student will have the capacity for dealing with the culture as he encounters it.
4. The belief that mastery of the subject matter is helped by an authoritarian atmosphere and is hindered by a democratic atmosphere.

[1] Leonard H. Clark, Raymond L. Klein, and John B. Burks, *The American Secondary School Curriculum*, 2nd Ed. (New York: Macmillan Publishing Co., Inc., 1972), p. 607.

5. The belief that history supports this type of curriculum because it has been the favorite form of organization throughout the ages.
6. The belief that the most effective and efficient way to teach is the expository method—that is, talking, lecturing, writing, and reading.
7. The belief that professional educators have the capacity for selecting the most important aspects of each subject to focus upon, and can do so without consulting students or parents before the students appear in school.
8. The belief that the content of the subjects is universally true and accurate, and hence is not affected by the local or individual situation.
9. The belief that each subject can be taught by itself, as a compartmented entity separate from all other subjects, and with little reference to what is happening outside the classroom.
10. The belief that drill, memorization, and absorption are necessary to establish content in students' minds.[2]

The Student-Centered Curriculum. One of the concepts stressed by the progressive education movement (from about 1900 until 1955) was the necessity for placing emphasis upon the learner rather than upon the subject matter, and thus, upon selecting content to meet the needs and interests of youth. Although subject matter would still be included in the curriculum, the basis for selection would be different. Individual differences, societal changes, community influences, and relevance of subject matter became criteria for selection. The gap between where an individual student was and where he ought to be or wanted to be—defined as *need*—became the value base for selecting subject matter.

During those years, many types of curriculum plans were tried. Some featured the culture, and others featured problems, process, or structure. If the student-centered curriculum is considered as one end of a continuum, and the traditional subject-centered curriculum is established as the other end, the major variations that enjoyed some degree of popularity fall somewhere between the two. (Figure 7-1.)

The Correlated Curriculum. The first step on the continuum away from the segmented and tightly compartmentalized learning became known as the Correlated curriculum. In this movement toward integration of learning, the departmental organization was retained but bridges were built among some subjects; thereafter, subjects were not studied in total isolation from each other. The chronological

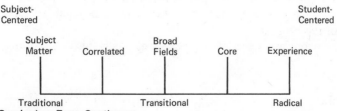

Figure 7-1 *Curriculum Type Continuum.*

[2] Albert I. Oliver, *Curriculum Improvement* (New York: Dodd, Mead, & Co., 1971), p. 308.

paralleling of American history and American literature by two or more teachers is one example of correlation. In this scheme, the literature of the era being studied in the history class might become the subject of study in the English class; and the essay assignment given in the history class might be used as a writing sample in the English class. The major contributions of this kind of curriculum arrangement were cited: provides additional insights about the period studied; saves time because one assignment satisfies double requirements; and gives students a sense of the relatedness of various fields of knowledge.

The Broad-Fields Curriculum. The next, more advanced, step—the Broad-Fields curriculum—consisted of the combining or "fusing" of two or more related subjects. The new course, broader than either of the single components in the merger, promoted better understanding of the total subject matter. Combining zoology with botany and anatomy and coming up with a subject called biology was one of the earliest attempts at merging subjects into a "fused" broad field courses. Other hybrid courses were general science, resulting from the merging of chemistry, biology, physics, and geology; and the American Problems course, the result of combining government, sociology, and economics. Some junior high schools expanded the Broad-Fields curriculum into a block-of-time approach. They appointed teachers to teach English and social studies to one class of students for a double period of time daily. They also combined mathematics and general science and provided one teacher for that block of time.

The Broad-Fields curriculum, by using broad areas of subject matter, enabled the teacher in the elementary schools to organize the day around five or six subjects, such as language arts and social studies, rather than around nine to fifteen subjects, such as writing, reading, spelling, geography, history, and so on. In cutting down on compartmentalization, the teacher was enabled to deal with the child's problems of personal and social living on a broader basis. The double-period assignment for teachers in the junior high block of time diminished by half the number of students faced in any day. Each teacher, consequently, was provided with more time in which to know each student better, and could therefore more easily meet the student's revealed needs.

The Core Curriculum. The Core curriculum featured larger blocks of time for meeting during the school day, and almost completely abandoned the division of knowledge by traditional subject lines. Whereas the other curriculum modifications maintained subject or disciplinary integrity in their correlating and merging, the Core curriculum began with the problems and concerns of youth and society, and utilized only that subject matter needed to solve a problem or meet the broader purposes of the program.

The following are some of the goals and distinguishing features of the Core curriculum:

1. Growth toward the capacity to function as an effective citizen in a democracy was the goal of all instruction.
2. Problem solving was the basic class activity, with the process of solving more important than the solution.

Period	Mon	Tues	Wed	Thurs	Fri
1	Math	Math	Math	Math	Math
2	Home Arts	Sci	Sci	Sci	Sci
3	Home Arts	Music	Typing	Music	Typing
4	Core	Core	Core	Core	Core
5	Core	Core	Core	Core	Core
6	Core	Core	Core	Core	Core
7	P.E.	P.E.	P.E.	P.E.	P.E.

Figure 7-2   *Typical Daily Schedule for Ninth Grade.*

3. Any subject matter could be used to help solve a personal or social problem in any class, no matter from what subject it was drawn.
4. Students and teachers cooperated in planning class activities, and scheduled the skills to be taught when the need was felt by the student.
5. A block of time, consisting of two or three class periods, was scheduled for each Core session.
6. Teachers were able to attend to the guidance aspects of their responsibilities because the greater length of time spent in each class allowed them to get to know their students better.
7. Students were grouped for classes in a heterogeneous fashion. Problem-solving methods of learning enabled each student to find a role to play, one in which he could make a contribution and could practice the skill of surviving in the established democratic atmosphere.

The Core block of time was devoted to the general education aspects of the curriculum; it did not consume the entire day. And because more time was devoted to general education in the early years of secondary school, the Core block was longest in the seventh and eighth grades. As the student progressed toward graduation, less time was allocated to the Core and more to specialized areas of interest or career needs.

Figure 7-2 illustrates a typical daily schedule in the ninth grade; Figure 7-3 shows the pattern of diminishing length of time for the Core block of time in the upper secondary grades.

The daily schedule in subsequent years would follow a plan more like the plan in Figure 7-3.

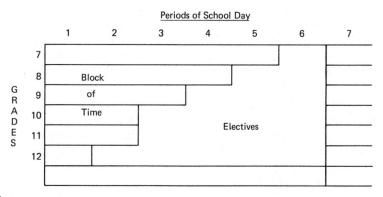

Figure 7-3

The Experience Curriculum.   The end of the continuum is the revolutionary, unstructured experience-centered curriculum. In this curriculum the teacher is concerned with the growth and development of individual pupils rather than with preconceived ideas of what the mythical "average pupil" should know at a certain grade level.

The features of this curriculum, identified as the "Activity curriculum" by Smith, Stanley, and Shores, are

1. The interests and purposes of students determine what is taught, when it is taught, and the order in which it is learned.
2. The program is not planned in advance. Since the interests of the student determine the educational program, it is impossible to determine before the arrival of the student the content of the course.
3. Cooperative planning by teacher and student is featured.
4. Problem-solving is the dominant method of teaching and learning.
5. Teachers must have a broad general education, with specialized training in adolescent development, guidance, and special methods of teaching.
6. Time-blocks should be available, but not planned in advance.
7. Grouping of students will be based upon student interest, not age and grade, and consequently grade designations can be eliminated.[3]

The following outline presents the contrast between the two extreme positions on the curriculum continuum:

Subject-Centered Curriculum	*Experience Curriculum*
1. Centered on subjects.	1. Centered in learners.
2. Emphasis upon teaching subject matter.	2. Emphasis upon promoting the all-around growth of learners.
3. Subject matter selected and organized before the teaching situation begins.	3. Subject matter selected and organized cooperatively by all learners during the learning situation.
4. Controlled by teacher.	4. Controlled and directed cooperatively by learners and teachers.
5. Emphasis upon teaching facts; imparting information that requires knowledge for its own sake or for possible future use.	5. Emphasis upon meanings that will be used immediately, in improving living.
6. Emphasis upon teaching specific habits and skills as separate and isolated aspects of learning.	6. Emphasis upon building habits and skills as integral parts of larger experiences.
7. Emphasis upon uniformity of exposures to learning situations and, insofar as possible, uniformity of learning results.	7. Emphasis upon variability in exposures to learning situations and variability in the results expected and achieved.
8. Education is considered to be schooling.	8. Education considered as a continuous, intelligent process of growth.

[3] B. Othanel Smith, William O. Stanley, and J. Harlan Shores, *Fundamentals of Curriculum Development* (Harcourt Brace Jovanovich, Inc., 1957), pp. 270–291.

Four Basic Concepts

Scope and Sequence. To understand curriculum, two very basic concepts are of primary importance. *Scope* refers to the "what" of the curriculum, and *sequence* refers to the "when." Before considering any of the other elements, competent educators must know what they expect to teach—or perhaps what they expect the students to learn. And they should have some knowledge of when they want these concepts to be learned, or when according to psychological studies, they are most commonly learned by any given student. To direct learning activities without having considered scope and sequence, is an example of poor, or at best lazy, instruction.

The extent of man's knowledge has increased so rapidly in the past two decades that not even the most able scholar is able to assimilate all the knowledge in his discipline in a lifetime. Therefore, selecting those segments of our heritage that will constitute the "what" of the curriculum has become a demanding imperative. In considering the scope of the curriculum, planners must consider not only what subjects to offer but also what parts of each subject to single out for focus.

Nor is initial attention to curriculum scope sufficient. As times change, as new information emerges to meet new conditions, the knowledge that was considered to be most worth knowing may lose its relevancy and be replaced by information or knowledge of greater worth. The task of the curriculum builder is to examine the various subjects constantly, regularly, and systematically so as to determine what knowledge is currently of the greatest worth. In this examination he uses criteria and a priority system based on suitability for the particular population and locality.

These criteria and priorities should stem from the district's philosophy of education and educational goals. Thus the curriculum content selected for districts whose educational goal is the recall of vast amounts of knowledge will probably encourage memorization and quotation; and districts that seek to develop inquiring, problem-solving minds will be likely select problem-solving and inquiry-oriented activities.

Once the subject matter to be included is decided upon, its placement becomes important. In determining what shall precede what, and what shall follow what, curriculum workers must depend heavily upon the psychology of learning. Thus, in arithmetic, for example, addition must precede multiplication; and, because of what psychologists of learning tell us concerning the optimum time for learning particular concepts and skills, the introduction to fractions must be postponed to a later grade.

Curriculum planners, in general, make use of considerations such as the following to arrive at decisions concerning sequence:

1. Chronological considerations: Using a time-line approach, placing Colonial history before twentieth-century American history; eighteenth-century novelists and poets before contemporary writers.
2. Geographical expansion: Starting with the known neighborhood in Grade 1 and moving to foreign countries in Grade 6 geography study.
3. Considerations of logic: Prerequisites for subsequent study are taught first; addition before multiplication, French I before French II, and so on.

4. Considerations of difficulty: Proceeding from simple to complex, from concrete to abstract.
5. Matters of maturation: Attending to growth rules established by psychologists and using them as aids to determine the timing.
6. Rules of readiness: Content should be introduced only when the pupils show that they are physically, intellectually, and emotionally mature enough, and that they have already had the necessary background.
7. Factors of immediacy: Presenting information near the time it will be used; teaching about liability insurance when students are ready to get drivers' licenses.[4]

Articulation and Balance. Two additional concepts that should be understood are articulation and balance. *Articulation* is the term used to indicate the educator's concern for developing a working relationship between the *scope* and *sequence* from grade to grade—kindergarten through Grade 12 and beyond. Many teachers teach without regard to what the teacher before them has attempted to teach, or what the teacher in the next year plans to teach. Attempting to make a smooth progression from one grade to the next, without gaps or unnecessary repetition, is called *vertical articulation.* When departmentalization exists, some teachers do not concern themselves at all with the activities their pupils experience in other teachers' classes. Attempting to correlate what is taught in different fields at the same grade level is called *horizontal articulation.*

Articulation has been improved in many schools by fostering cooperation among teachers of a common subject. For instance, teachers of American History in Grades 5, 6, and 11, working together as a committee, easily recognize when the same history is repeated three times. Time can be saved and interest in the course preserved by designating a particular era for each grade level to focus upon. Where this kind of articulation takes place, Early American History is scheduled for Grade 5; in-depth coverage of the development of the country, from 1789 to the emergence of the nation as a world power at the beginning of the twentieth century, is reserved for Grade 8; and study in depth of the nation as a world power is scheduled for Grade 11. Social studies, particularly history, appears to take on increased relevance for the youth in senior high schools where articulation has been well planned.

Balance refers to the inclusion of appropriate amounts of time in the curriculum for *all* the disciplines, that is, an overwhelming amount of time is not allotted to one of the subject areas at the expense of all the others. An example is the increasing attention to the language arts in most American elementary schools. This has reached a point in some schools where more than one-half of any given day is allotted to this area. In some cases language arts is the subject of study for as much as three hours of the school day; some two to three hours are then left for all other elements of the curriculum: mathematics, science, social studies, art, music, and physical education. Such a curriculum is out of balance. In systems where balance is maintained, the total amount of time available is blocked out by the teacher and curriculum coordinators, and then they—along with their students—develop a

[4] Oliver, *op. cit.,* Pp. 267–281.

program in which the time is divided equitably among all educational areas of the curriculum.

Extracurricular Activities

Is participation in the Junior ROTC in a high school part of curriculum? Is going on a weekend field trip to the state capital a formal part of the curriculum? When the students build a replica of a pioneer fort to exhibit at the school's social studies fair, is this a part of their curriculum? When an athlete plays tennis or some other sport on the varsity team at an away-from-home event, is he involved in a part of the school's curriculum? Is participation in the school band, orchestra, or organized dance team a part of the formal curriculum? And if a student attends an optional assembly program wherein the ministers of various denominations explain the significance of Christmas as viewed by their parishioners, is he involved in formal curriculum activity? The answer to all the questions is "Yes." Remember, if the school provides the learning experience for the students, it is considered to be curriculum.

General Education

General education is the vast area of any school program that includes those understandings, skills, and attitudes which every student is expected to learn. General education is based on three considerations: (1) the psychological needs of students at various stages of development; (2) the demands of the community and society in which the school exists; and (3) the influences of leaders in the recognized disciplines.

The "common-learnings program" refers to that portion of the total curriculum that seeks to prepare all students to live in a democratic society. It accommodates future lawyers, soldiers, housewives, and laborers, and, without reference to their potential careers, arranges for them to mingle, learn, and interact as citizens of a community. In order to develop the traits and understandings adult citizens must have in common to sustain a democracy—despite their personal differences—the common-learnings curriculum concentrates on teaching pupils to live in community with others and to participate cooperatively with them for the good of the whole. Such topics as home management, personal relationships, health, aesthetic values, and concepts concerning democracy and government, are the focus of its thrust.

General education should not be confused with liberal education. The connotation of the latter term is more academic, and often deals primarily with the humanities; it does not include such utilitarian studies as driver training, home and family relations, life adjustment, or industrial arts. And although general education does encompass many aspects of the liberal arts disciplines, the intention in general education is usually practical—more immediately applicable than liberal arts subjects, which, at the secondary level, are usually academic prerequisites for further course work at the college level.

The emphasis on general education decreases as one progresses from the elementary school through the high school. Four fifths of a student's time may be devoted to general education in the early years of the junior high school, but by the twelfth grade general education may make up only one fifth, or even less, of his program. When the guidance program operates effectively, it is possible to identify individual purposes and goals early, thereby allowing pupils to focus increasingly on specialized programs.

Exploratory Education

Junior high school education was introduced on the theory that the curriculum should help youth in the selection of their life's work. This theory specified that before pupils began specialized study in preparation for their adult careers, they should have an opportunity to explore, sample, and then try out a variety of curricular offerings. As a consequence, most junior high schools introduced "exploratory education" programs designed to allow pupils to explore the curriculum and discover in what directions their inclinations lay. To achieve this, they offered a rich menu of elective courses from which pupils might choose their semester-length courses. In addition, many junior high schools arranged cycle courses, or sequences, in which pupils sampled different subject areas every six to nine weeks. For example, a language course might be first six weeks of French, then a second six weeks of Spanish, and so on. Successful junior high school faculties, in the true spirit of exploration, resorted to a number of subterfuges to avoid laying upon this exploratory program the cold hand of the bureaucratic Carnegie Unit. Their goal was to keep the curriculum flexible, to prevent offerings from being frozen into a format with a rigid, prescribed structure.

Specialized Education

Specialized education includes the subject matter that individual students may want to learn for their own particular reasons. Its primary function is to provide for individual differences among students and to give each a chance to develop in the way he sees fit. College preparatory students, business-oriented students, or trade or agriculture students all elect the courses that best prepare them to advance the next step toward their ultimate career goal. In most schools, elective courses and special organizational provisions within the structure of the program of studies are the principal means of implementing specialized education. As a rule, specialized education does not begin until the secondary grades.

The program that is kept most flexible (so that students with interests in one track can also take courses offered in other tracks) is probably the most desirable.

Career Education

The newest development in curriculum for American education in the 1970s is Career Education. The President, and his appointed officials in the U.S. Office of Education, have identified Career Education as necessary to meet the needs of all youth in the last quarter of the twentieth century. One pattern for Career Education includes the following:

Grades K–6:	Career Awareness.
Grades 7–10:	Career Exploration.
Ages 17–24:	The World of Work.
Grades 11–12:	Job Entry Level—Vocational, Pretechnical, College Prep.
Grades 13–14:	Specialized Jobs—Post-Secondary Technical Training.
Grades 15–16:	Technical Jobs.
Grades 17 +:	Professional Jobs.

Career occupational clusters identified by the U.S. Office of Education are

1. Agribusiness and Natural Resources.
2. Business and Office Procedures.
3. Health Occupations.
4. Public Service.
5. Environment.
6. Communication and Media.
7. Hospitality and Recreation.
8. Manufacturing.
9. Marketing and Distribution.
10. Marine Science.
11. Personnel Services.
12. Construction.
13. Transportation.
14. Consumer and Homemaking Education.
15. Fine Arts and the Humanities.

The concerns of the U.S. Office of Education that led to its sponsoring research into this area of career development were (1) that many students who graduated from high school still lacked the necessary skills for gaining employment; and (2) the emerging fact that technological developments would force most employees to change jobs at least five times in the course of a career.

The foregoing design, which the career researchers are continuing to develop, exposes each child to the opportunities extant in a multitude of careers. Although the focus is narrowed to just one career to be studied in depth at the eleventh grade level, the broad coverage suited to many careers of the earlier years is intended to acquaint the student with options for when and if the time to change jobs arrives.

The major concern of the individual teacher is the inclusion of career-related concepts into the units selected for study in the classroom. Instead of treating each subject in the curriculum as a structured discipline, the teacher is encouraged to explore and mine the subject for knowledge to apply to as many occupations as possible, and to accentuate its utility and relevance for a future career.

The Curriculum Process

Although improving the curriculum has been going on in the schools of this country for a long time, it is only recently that educators have given much attention to the process of improving it.

In this module we have made several references to the ways in which curriculum changes were made in former years. They were fairly perfunctory, autocratic, or incidental actions. Prior to 1920, the periodic revision of the Course of Study appeared to satisfy the expectations of those who identified that document with the curriculum. When the chief administrator of the school district determined that the curriculum needed to be improved, he assembled several persons whom he believed to have competency in writing; he then indicated the areas of his concern and requested that they produce new documents for printing and circulation, to serve as teachers' guides until the next revision.

In those days the authority for curriculum planning, and the responsibility for periodic modifications of school offerings, rested squarely with the superintendent. The in-put from teachers, parents, and students was minimal, indeed. Generally, teachers were not asked what instructional problems needed attention, nor what the needs of the students might be. Decisions pertaining to these matters, based pretty much on individual opinions, were made at the upper administrative level, and were provided to the group engaged in rewriting the curriculum, for inclusion in the published document. For teachers on the school staff, the resulting revised document set forth the precise ground to be covered in each subject for each grade level. In many cases, the expectation was that supervisors would visit classes to make sure that deviations from the written guide were few in number and modest in degree.

Before judging this procedure too harshly, and condemning it as autocratic and repressive, consider the times and the status of the teaching profession of that era. In the past fifty years, many things have changed in addition to philosophical positions of administrators, the architecture of school buildings, and the amount of financial support for the secondary schools. Probably the most influential change has been the increase of collegiate training required for those who wish to qualify as certified teachers in the secondary school. In the early days of the century, the local school administrator was the most highly educated person on the school staff, perhaps even in the whole community. For no other member of the teaching staff was the college degree a prerequisite for service. Consequently, the entire staff looked to this educational leader as the most qualified person to make decisions, and the community accepted his appointment of Course of Study revisers with trust.

Curriculum Understanding. Nowadays the school assumes the responsibility for developing attitudes and cultivating appreciations as well as cognitive learning. In its new content the experiences for which the school accepts responsibility may occur in school buses, cafeterias, and corridors as well as in the classroom. Let us look at some of the changes that accompany this broadened view of curriculum.

1. The course of study (fully described on page 178) is no longer intended to be a step by step compendium of classroom activity, although some teachers still revere it and try to follow it point by point. Instead it is intended to be a guide that will furnish assistance to competent professionals without inhibiting their efforts to make intelligent contribution of their own.

2. Curriculum planning is considered to be an ongoing process which constantly focuses, in a broken-front fashion, on the experiences offered by the school. Nevertheless, some teachers still consider curriculum modification to be a discrete act with a beginning and an ending. Teachers of this sort look for and expect to find

the "quiet pond" school, where no one rocks the boat and no ripples disturb the serenity of the waters, and where every ten years revisions are made and implemented in an expeditious manner. They refuse to accept the concept that a dynamic curriculum, one responsive to social, intellectual, and cultural changes of all sorts, can never be treated as a static entity; that when one facet is brought up to date, the time has arrived for starting on the next facet.

3. Laymen increasingly are being incorporated into curriculum planning. As they consider matters in which the expertise of members of the community can be helpful, school leaders are inviting participation by these laymen.

Pupils, too, are being relied upon to make contributions—formally, as members of curriculum committees, and informally in classrooms and school activities. As the recipients-to-be of the benefits the curriculum is designed to yield, it is expected that students will offer cues concerning the desirability of action to be taken, or modifications of actions in progress.

4. Teachers are expected, encouraged, and/or required to become involved in the curriculum process in various ways. The verbs in the immediately foregoing sentence describe the situation in different communities, as teachers currently report it. Some teachers, especially those in large districts, report feelings of resentment because it appears that, as in the old days, changes are being forced upon them. The resentment stems from the fact that in most cases they have been provided with no opportunity to participate in the deliberations substantiating he change. Because individual teachers are so far removed from the district central office, and because each teacher is just one of many members of a large staff, each functions in an atmosphere of isolation. In their minds, the superintendent or his curriculum coordinator still autocratically pulls the strings, and the supervisor still downgrades teachers for lack of fidelity to the course of study.

Attitudes of this sort sometimes are discovered among teachers working in small districts. There is usually not so much justification for these teachers' resentment as there may be for those serving in monolithic bureaucratic systems. In the smaller unit, each teacher must assume more personal responsibility for district attitudes about curriculum because the source of decision making is less remote from the daily scene of activity, and consequently more available for influencing. Frequently, the exclusion from decision-making activities, when it occurs, is the result of lack of interest by the resentful teacher. Content to drift along, unwilling to sacrifice the time or effort necessary for committee meetings, unwilling to volunteer (and serving only with reluctance when appointed), such teachers feel it their prerogative to complain about the decisions arrived at. Obviously, they have failed to grasp the significance of the curriculum process and hence are guilty of disservice to their profession.

The present expectation in all good school districts is that teachers will work in group planning; will involve themselves—at different levels and to differing degrees—in the improvement tasks that the school undertakes; will make decisions about the curriculum within their own classrooms; will participate in experimenting with and evaluating innovations; and will write, edit, or develop teaching units or plot guidelines for particular courses, in accordance with their individual talents.

It is almost universally accepted by educators today that the real curriculum of the school goes into operation when the teacher closes the door of the classroom. Here, where teachers and students live together five or six hours per day, where individual differences emerge and individual interests are noted, teachers are free to respond creatively—and innovate imaginatively—in order to achieve specific goals. This professional behavior constitutes the curriculum planning each teacher does on his own, in the privacy of his classroom. Publicly, he participates at another level, and engages in cooperative planning with other teachers.

It is expected that the experiences teachers have in their classrooms will be discussed in small, informal group meetings and in more formal faculty meetings, and that experimental efforts will be shared. Out of this sharing may come helpful hints, or answers to bothersome problems which have been a source of bewilderment for other teachers in the past.

Action at the School Level. One of the advantages of the individual school serving as a curriculum-planning unit lies in the face-to-face contact possible in a small group. Another advantage is that those individuals who are to be involved in the implementation of the change are involved in the discussion and decision making about the change.

In the individual school planning procedure the principal or his designate acts as the educational leader, but much of the actual curriculum planning is done by the teachers who not only serve on committees and attend meetings of several kinds, but also do much of the research and writing for new curriculum proposals.

Central office personnel come to the school to act as advisors in the curriculum building process. They are actually staff consultants to the principal whose line of authority is traced directly to the superintendent. If this curriculum planning procedure is to succeed, it is essential that the school be blessed with good human relations free from adversary relationships between administration and staff and other tensions. For this reason educational leaders should attempt to build the following attitudes in themselves and all other participants in the curriculum-change process.

1. Tolerance of feelings of dissatisfaction expressed by others. Everyone who strives for excellence in his work experiences, from time to time, periods of dissatisfaction with his work. These feelings are legitimate and usually temporary; they need not lead to complaining of a negative sort, nor to taking positions inimical to the success of the group effort. Curriculum builders generally seek to learn the causes of these dissatisfactions, and then encourage each other to channel their feelings constructively into productive activity to bring about appropriate changes. Some new members of the profession reveal a propensity for overreacting to what they hear, and for magnifying the negative comments made in periods of dissatisfaction. Some young professionals have been so misled by legitimate complaints that they have developed into chronic gripers and pessimistic gossips of gloom. They pass on to their peers every uncomplimentary expression heard, moreover, they fail to see the improvements effected by the original complainer, and the consequent change of attitude in the more supportive and affirmative teachers.
2. Willingness to contribute suggestions toward the solution of a problem, whether general or specific. Some staff members hold themselves aloof from group discussions, either because they feel inferior or because they feel

superior. Sometimes the latter are reluctant to divulge their special techniques, fearing that the others will catch up, thus diminishing their own "advantage." New teachers, who are more apt to fall into the "insecure" category, must remind themselves that in group dynamics, the mantle of leadership often falls upon the shoulders of the person who asks a question or requests clarification of a point under discussion. Although the inquirer asks because he wants to know, the wording used or the response given may be enough to start the group in the direction leading to a solution.

3. Willingness to work with others. The human relations involved in becoming a member of a faculty are worthy of considerable attention from neophytes. As small fish in a big pond, first-year teachers must remember that their lack of status and service precludes their being in a position of special privilege, a position they may have enjoyed as senior students on a college campus. On the other hand, some senior members of the staff with recognized status on a faculty may abuse the canons of good relations and be guilty of unprofessional offenses. Resolving dilemmas resulting from hurt feelings, avoiding feuds, fending off pressure to join one faculty faction or another, and all the while displaying a willingness and capacity for teamwork for the good of the cause, calls for concentrated effort.

4. Open-mindedness about new educational decisions and practices. There is so little that is absolutely known in education that any teacher acts presumptuously who clings to ideas merely because they are supported by tradition. Mature teachers who refuse to entertain suggestions to innovate, and new teachers who have illusions about the excellence of their teaching ability, contribute to the retardation of faculty progress. All teachers do not accept a new concept with the same degree of alacrity. Some welcome and feel comfortable in experimental situations; others are interested, but prefer to "wait and see" before acting. Some teachers may actively oppose an innovative idea, and carry on a debate in defense of their position. So long as the positions taken are open to compromise, so long as entrenchment around the cause of tradition and tranquility are avoided, and so long as new proposals do not generate saboteurs, the cause of progress need not be threatened.

5. Willingness to do homework, that is, reading professional literature. Teachers who join a faculty merely because there is a job opening usually fail to develop this trait of the true professional. For them, the off-the-top-of-the-head responses to problems old and new suffice. In his reading, the true professional gravitates toward books, periodicals, and topics with educational overtones. When confronted with a problem, he uses resources intelligently to find the answers.

The general committees may focus upon

1. Evaluation of the existing curriculum to see whether it is the best, or in what ways it might better serve the interests, needs, and abilities of the students in the schools; or
2. Revision of the existing curriculum undertaken as a result of prior evaluation; or

3. Development of the curriculum in those areas in which it provides for only one kind of student (the average student), in order to accommodate the slow- or fast-learning student; or

4. Study of problems relating to the school program, such as marking procedures, reporting to parents, assigning of homework, or the giving of tests, all of which have an effect upon the curriculum; or

5. Research into current practices and trends to provide authoritative information regarding educational development; or

6. Survey of the role of the teacher to formulate plans for equitable assignments and cogent staff utilization; or

7. Investigation of local problems peculiar to the school or district, such as delinquency, drop outs, advanced placement, cooperative programs, and so forth.

All these committees are intended to serve as recommending agencies to the district central curriculum council or to the school principals' council, so that conclusions can be circulated in the widest fashion possible for the guidance of the entire staff.

SUGGESTED READING

Association for Supervision and Curriculum Development. *What Are the Sources of the Curriculum? A Symposium.* Washington, D.C.: National Education Association, 1962.

Clark, Leonard H., Raymond L. Klein, and John B. Burks. *The American Secondary School Curriculum,* 2nd Ed. New York: Macmillan Publishing Co., Inc., 1972.

Doll, Ronald C. *Curriculum Improvement: Decision-Making and Process.* 2nd Ed. Boston: Allyn & Bacon, Inc., 1970.

Goodlad, John I. *School, Curriculum, and the Individual.* Waltham, Mass: Ginn/ Blaisdell, 1966.

———, *School Curriculum Reform in the United States.* New York: Fund for Advancement of Education, 1964.

——— et al. *The Changing School Curriculum.* New York: Fund for the Advancement of Education, 1966.

Hoyt, Kenneth B., et al. *Career Education: What It Is and How to Do It.* Salt Lake City, Utah: Olympus Publishing Company, 1972.

Johnson, James A., et al. *Introduction to the Foundations of American Education.* 2nd Ed. Boston: Allyn & Bacon, Inc., 1973.

Kneller, George F., Ed. *Foundations of Education.* 3rd Ed. New York: John Wiley & Sons, Inc., 1971.

Saylor, J. Galen, Ed. *The School of the Future: Now.* Washington, D.C.: Association for Supervision and Curriculum Development, 1972.

Tanner, Daniel, and Laurel Tanner. *Curriculum Development: Theory Into Practice.* New York: Macmillan Publishing Co., Inc., 1975.

Van Til, William. *Education: A Beginning,* 2nd Ed. Boston: Houghton Mifflin Company, 1974.

Wilson, L. Craig. *The Open Access Curriculum.* Boston: Allyn & Bacon, Inc., 1971.

POST TEST

DEFINITIONS

A. Curriculum can be defined as

_____

_____

B. List and define the four basic concepts of curriculum

  1. _____ :

  2. _____ :

  3. _____ :

  4. _____ :

MULTIPLE CHOICE

A. (*Circle one.*) The "subject-matter curriculum" is unique in that
  1. it usually merges related subjects into a Core course.
  2. scope and sequence are more readily identifiable than in any other design.
  3. it requires the use of team teaching and differentiated staffing.
  4. student needs take precedence over content-analysis.
  5. it is the most recent means of curriculum organization in American schools.

B. (*Circle three*) Three of the following considerations are basic to the concept of "general education."
  1. The vocational goals of a majority of the students at a given time.
  2. The psychological needs of students at various ages of development.
  3. The influence of leaders in recognized disciplines.
  4. The teachers frequently explore new content—concepts and generalizations.
  5. The demands of the community and society in which the school exists.

C. (*Circle one.*) The current trends is to encourage "exploratory education" in the
  1. primary school.
  2. elementary school.
  3. junior high school.
  4. senior high school.
  5. junior college.

D. (*Circle one.*) "Specialized education" is a basic objective of the
  1. primary school.
  2. elementary school.
  3. middle school.
  4. junior high school.
  5. Comprehensive High School.

MATCHING *In the following, match the Career-Education concepts with grade placement.*

_____**A.** K–6 (elementary grades).

_____**B.** 7–10 (Jr.H.S. and H.S. freshman and sophomores)

_____**C.** 11–12 (H.S. juniors and seniors).

_____**D.** 13–14 (junior college, technical schools, and college freshman and sophomores.

_____**E.** 15–16 (college juniors and seniors).

_____**F.** 17 + (college and technical school graduates).

1. Career Entry.

2. Technical Careers.

3. Specialized Careers.

4. Career Awareness.

5. Professional Careers.

6. Career Exploration.

RECOGNITION *Below are six extracurricular activities. According to your definition of* curriculum, *check those which you believe would be a formal part of the curriculum of a public school.*

_____**1.** The student is a volunteer cadet in the Junior ROTC program.

_____**2.** The student participates in the school band at ball games, parades, and at musical festivities.

_____**3.** The student goes on a class-sponsored field trip to visit the state capital over the weekend.

_____**4.** The student plays tennis for the varsity team at other schools and in regional and/or state tournaments.

_____**5.** The student attends an optional assembly program wherein the ministers of various denominations explain the significance of Christmas to their churches.

_____**6.** The student prepares, at home, a replica of a pioneer fort to exhibit at the school's social studies fair sponsored by the PTA event.

Elementary and Secondary School Curriculum

George A. Finchum

East Tennessee State University

module 8

Elementary School Curriculum / Organizational Patterns / Programs / Individually Guided Education / Ten Reasonable Expectations / Secondary School Curriculum / General Objectives / General Terms and Nomenclature / The Subject Fields / Three Proposals

RATIONALE

In Module 7 you learned something about the curriculum and curriculum theory in general. The purpose of this module is to add to your understanding of the curriculum concepts explained in Module 7, by describing the current elementary and secondary school curriculums and major proposals for revising them. It should give you insight into the ways educators have attempted to apply curriculum principles to both elementary and secondary schools, and the direction the schools' development may take in the future.

Objectives

Specifically at the completion of your study of this module you should be able to do the following:

FOR THE ELEMENTARY SCHOOL
1. List the seven basic areas of the elementary school curriculum.
2. Identify the most typical organization for the American elementary school.
3. List the five primary divisions of the language arts component of elementary curriculum.
4. Describe the importance of *reading* in the elementary school curriculum.
5. List six social sciences from which social studies concepts, skills, and understandings have been chosen for the school curriculum.
6. Identify *the* basic trend in social studies education.
7. List the primary group that has promoted "new math," and two of three agencies promoting the "new science" for elementary schools.
8. Identify the four subject areas in an elementary school that are usually taught by area specialists.
9. List the four basic components of Individually Guided Education (IGE).
10. List the four learning modes for IGE.
11. List six of Goodlad's "Ten Reasonable Expectations" for the American elementary school.

FOR THE SECONDARY SCHOOL
1. List the seven Cardinal Principles of Education as defined in 1918.
2. List seven new objectives as stated by the White House Conference in 1955.
3. Identify the grade levels found in the American high school.
4. Recognize the three tracks in the Comprehensive High School.
5. Identify the subject area most frequently taught in high schools.
6. List five electives in the Language Arts Program.
7. Explain why organized athletics is *not* a basic element of the health and physical education curriculum.
8. Identify the most frequently taught Social Studies course in high schools.
9. Identify the subjects taught in junior high-level Social Studies courses.

10. List five Social Studies electives in the high school.
11. List the four most frequently offered Mathematics courses for Grades 9–12.
12. List the four most frequently offered Science courses for Grades 9–12.
13. List three study groups responsible for the "new science" curriculums for Biology, Geology, and Physics.
14. List five Music Education courses in high schools.
15. List five Business Education courses in high schools.
16. Identify Office Education as the new two- or three-credit course in business education.
17. List five areas of study in Industrial Arts Education.
18. List five areas of study in Home Economics Education.
19. Recognize the three most traditional courses in foreign languages.
20. Recognize the three basic trends in Foreign Language Education.
21. List four areas in Art courses.
22. List four areas in Agriculture courses.
23. List six broad areas of Vocational Education in American high schools.
24. List three of the primary areas of Distributive Education.
25. List eight or more of Conant's 21 Recommendations.
26. List five recommendations made in the Trump plan.
27. Discuss the percentage breakdown for the amount of time recommended by the Trump plan for independent study, small-group instruction, and large-group instruction.

MODULE TEXT

Part I: The Elementary School Curriculum

American elementary schools, for the purposes of this module, are defined as follows:

1. K–6 organization: the school includes kindergarten and Grades 1 through 6; this is the most common American elementary school.
2. K–4 organization: the school includes levels through Grade 4 and is usually followed by a *middle school.*
3. Middle school includes intermediate Grades 5 and 6, and Grades 7 and 8 from the junior high school.
4. Primary school usually includes kindergarten through Grade 3.
5. Nongraded, or multiunit school is an elementary school and may include the same years as in the foregoing, K–6; but the students progress at a rate—faster or slower—determined by their own abilities and application.
6. K–8 organization: the traditional eight-grade elementary school. In recent years, the upper grades have been termed *middle* or *junior high school* grades.

Programs

An elementary school curriculum includes such elements as (1) language arts, (2) social studies, (3) mathematics, (4) science, (5) art, (6) music, and

(7) physical education. Other areas sometimes included in the elementary curriculums are (1) industrial arts, (2) foreign language, and (3) special emphasis on career awareness.

Language Arts. The study of English and language arts includes approximately one-half of the teaching day in a typical elementary school. This subject area includes reading, writing, speaking, spelling, listening, language structure and usage, literature, and many other related areas. It is generally believed that language arts are basic to the further pursuit of any of the other disciplines.

The skills of communication are the primary objectives of elementary education almost anywhere in the world. In the United States, the language arts generally include the study of the English language in a variety of ways. In the order of how strongly they are stressed, five of the ways are

READING. The reading class may be the single most important period of instruction in American elementary schools. Indeed, unless students can read, they are not likely to succeed in most other areas of the curriculum. The techniques used by the teacher to teach reading include (1) word recognition, (2) oral reading, (3) silent reading, (4) whole word versus syllables, and (5) a general nongraded approach. Individualization is found more often in reading programs than in any other subject area in the elementary school classroom. Table 8-1 indicates the reason for this.

An analysis of the data in Table 8-1 dramatizes the difficult problem associated with providing the same instruction for all children at a given level, even in the first year. Annually thereafter, the task of teaching reading increases in difficulty, as does the task of teaching all the other subjects in the curriculum. Because of this, a wide variety of individualized reading programs have been introduced and are meeting with varying degrees of success.

SPELLING. Spelling correlates highly with writing and reading. Two recognized areas are (1) formal instruction versus incidental, and (2) phonics versus word-recognition instruction. Spelling correctly must become a concern for all teachers, not just for teachers of language arts. In addition, the concern must be exercised at all times during the school day, not only when the schedule calls for spelling.

WRITING. In the primary grades, emphasis is on the technique of printing. Throughout the school there has been a decrease in emphasis on cursive writing or script-writing styles. The objective seems to be legibility and speed. Composition is usually taught from Grade 3 up.

SPEAKING. The "show and tell" activity continues to provide the basic opportunity for students to "learn" to speak before a group. Individual reports are, of course, used throughout the grades.

Table 8-1

AGE	GRADE	RANGE OF READING ABILITY BY GRADE LEVELS	RANGE IN YEARS
6	1	$0-2\frac{1}{2}$	$2\frac{1}{2}$
7	2	$\frac{1}{2}-3\frac{1}{2}$	3
8	3	$1-5$	4
9	4	$1\frac{1}{2}-6\frac{1}{2}$	5
10	5	$2-8$	6
11	6	$2\frac{1}{2}-9\frac{1}{2}$	7

LISTENING. Very little formal instruction is provided in this skill. Evidently teachers seem to expect that learning how to listen will just happen. Note-taking—a skill related to listening—is almost totally absent from the elementary classroom.

In the sixties there was a trend to improve the language arts by increasing the amount of time allotted to it in the daily schedule. As a result, over-all balance in the total curriculum was lost. Fortunately, this trend is being reversed in the seventies, but the language arts remain the largest single block of time in the general elementary school program.

Social Studies. The social studies are those facts, concepts, and generalizations, and the attitudes, skills, and values derived from the social sciences for study and development in American schools. The social studies include the broadest range of absolute knowledge in the world of man. The social studies relate to man's existence (history); how he came to be what he is (anthropology); how he makes a living (economics); how he relates to other human beings (sociology); how he learns and why he behaves as he does (psychology); how he organizes his thoughts (philosophy); how he governs himself (political science); and how he relates to the environment in which he finds himself—both its effect on him and his effect on it (geography).

In most elementary schools the social studies have a recognized place in the curriculum only from Grade 4 upward. Recently, the social studies have departed quite radically from the older and more specialized pattern of organization centered on the various disciplines in each grade. In these new programs the curriculum consists of sequence of integrated themes that introduce the pupils to all of the social studies. From Grade 1 through Grade 6, students are increasingly being introduced to *all* the social studies around a wide variety of integrated themes. A typical, but by no means universal, sequence for social studies at the grade/year level concept follows.

1. Grade 1– Home and School.
2. Grade 2– Community.
3. Grade 3– States.
4. Grade 4– Regions.
5. Grade 5– The United States.
6. Grade 6– Other Nations.

In this scheme, Grades 1 and 2 are laden with sociological concepts; geography and anthropology are important in Grades 3 and 4; history and geography of the United States are the basic areas of content for Grade 5; the geography and history of other of the world's nations are the most predominant themes in Grade 6. Economics and government (political science) are increasingly important in the elementary school social studies.

Mathematics. Arithmetic, or *numbers,* as it may be termed in the primary grades, is more nearly standardized than any other area in the elementary-school curriculum. The major issue in recent years has been the programs developed by the School Mathematics Study Groups (SMSG) and other federally funded projects. Begun after the funding of the National Science Foundation (1950), and continued with the National Defense Education Act (NDEA) of 1958, the "new math" programs called for emphasis on concepts and processes rather than on memorization of tables and answers. Some schools have kept the "old math," but most implemented the newer programs in the sixties. Whereas drill had been a basic technique in previous years, the efforts were now on numerical concept development. Presently, there are signs that indicate that the schools may be moving toward a position midway between these two extremes.

Science. Science used to be the poor relative in the elementary curriculum. With the advent of the National Science Foundation (1950), the flight of the Russian Sputnik I (1957) [and the subsequent increased funding for science educators under the National Defense Education Act (1958)], the Elementary and Secondary Education Act (1965) and subsequent amendments, science has forged ahead to a high place in many American elementary schools.

In the elementary school, science had almost always been "general" in nature, and, according to some critics, did not possess a logically organized sequence. Several elementary science projects funded by the NSF and NDEA have attempted to change this. Some of the more notable projects are

1. Elementary Science Study (ESS), Education Development Center, Inc.,
2. Science Curriculum Improvement Study (SCIS), University of California.
3. Elementary School Science Project (ESSP), University of Illinois.

Some of the more frequent elementary-school science themes are

1. Living Things.
2. Earth and Universe.
3. Forms of Energy.
4. The Seasons.

Art. Art in the elementary school may be taught by all teachers as an integrated subject, or it may be taught by an art teacher-specialist. The art teacher may "float" from room to room on a regular schedule, or she may have a base room to which the students may come.

In an elementary-level art class, the experiences, usually termed *manipulative activities,* include

1. Painting (easel, finger, water).
2. Drawing (chalk, crayon, pencil).
3. Modeling (clay, papier-mâché).
4. Construction (cardboard, puppets, wood).
5. Crafts (jewelry, leather work, mosaics).
6. Weaving.
7. Printing.
8. Cutting and Tearing.

In addition to prescribed activities, the teacher of art encourages creative (inward) emotional and intellectual activities of a wide variety.

Music. Music is usually taught by a teacher-specialist in the elementary school. The music teacher may "float" from one room to another, or she may have a special room. In systems with several small schools, the music teacher may serve in more than one school. Included in a variety of aesthetic activities are

1. Listening (records, radio, TV).
2. Singing.
3. Playing instruments.
4. Reading notes and composing.
5. Rhythm.
6. Biographies of musicians.
7. Musical programs for parents and community.

Health, Safety, and Physical Education. These three areas are treated as one subject in most schools. In some, the regular teacher of the self-contained classroom is responsible for the program. Since former President Dwight Eisenhower instituted the President's Physical Fitness Program, the trend has been toward hiring a specialist staff member to be responsible for health and physical education in each school. In systems with several small schools, a teacher may go to several schools to offer a special program in physical education.

The average program is about fifteen minutes of daily exercise followed by a varying amount of time for games and sport activities. Calisthenics are important, but attention is also given to dancing, activity games, and even school camping activities—which may be correlated with the science program.

The safety patrol is used both as a protective activity and as a teaching device, focusing the attention of all students on traffic safety, the primary element of safety education in the American elementary school.

Foreign Languages. The federal support of two study groups, Foreign Languages in Elementary Schools (FLES) and the Foreign Languages Program (FLP) of the Modern Languages Association, has resulted in an increase in language study in Grades 3 through 6 throughout the nation. The languages studied by children without a second language are (1) Spanish, (2) French, (3) German, (4) Russian, (5) Italian, and (6) Latin. Increasingly the various native American Indian languages are being studied, as are Chinese and Hebrew.

Teachers of foreign languages usually "float" from room to room, because relatively few teachers in self-contained classrooms teach a foreign language as a part of an ongoing program. Exceptions are the New York City schools with large numbers of Puerto Rican children, and in schools in southern Florida, New Mexico, Arizona, Texas, and California, where Spanish is the first language of many children. In many schools in these and other areas, English may be taught as a second, or foreign, language. English is sometimes successfully taught as a foreign language to Black children throughout the nation, and to white children with special dialects, such as those in Southern Appalachia.

Individually Guided Education

Complete individualization of instruction for the elementary schools was the ultimate aim of the educators who developed Individually Guided Education (IGE) at the University of Wisconsin, and for the Institute for Development of

Educational Activities, Inc. (I|D|E|A), a division of the Kettering Foundation, in Dayton, Ohio, in the late sixties and early seventies. IGE is a model for the elementary school of the future. It is an in-service program that leads to an individualized program at the elementary-school level. The IGE system includes four basic components:

1. A standard learning cycle, with pretesting, behavioral objectives, multiage grouping, and diversified learning activities.
2. A special decision-making structure, with multiunit organization, team-teaching, and differentiated staffing.[1]
3. Home-school communications—the establishment of stronger ties.
4. League linkages—the establishment of strong ties with a number of geographically close schools involved in the program.

IGE is a means of organizing a school and does not require an actual change in the curriculum. Change comes in the means of delivery; the more common elements are

1. Use of behavioral objectives.
2. Use of Learning Activity Packages (LAPS) or Unit Activity Packages (UNIPACS).
3. Use of four learning modes:
   a. Independent study.
   b. One-to-one instruction.
   c. Small-group instruction.
   d. Large-group instruction.

Ten Reasonable Expectations

Dr. John Goodlad and several of his associates at the University of California at Los Angeles published a list of "Ten Reasonable Expectations" for the American elementary school in 1970.[2] Because they seem to sum up the reconstructed elementary school of the future, these expectations are given here:

(1) Classroom practices should be guided by rather clearly discernible educational objectives which, in turn, should reflect larger school-wide and system-wide agreement on school functions.

(2) Classroom instruction, particularly in the early years, should be guided by emphasis on "learning how to learn."

(3) The subject matter employed to teach children how to learn should evidence considerable intrinsic appeal for pupils.

(4) The golden age of instructional materials is almost everywhere evident in the schools.

[1] Herbert J. Klausmeier, et al., *Individually Guided Education in the Multiunit Elementary School—Guidelines for Implementation* (Madison, Wis.: Wisconsin Department of Public Instruction, 1970), p. 15.

[2] From *Looking Behind the Classroom Door* by John E. Goodlad, M. Frances Klein and Associates. © 1974 by Wadsworth Publishing Company, Inc., Belmont, California 94002. Reprinted by permission of the publisher, Charles A. Jones Publishing Company.

(5) Today's schools pay considerable attention to and make substantial provision for individual differences among students.

(6) Today's teachers make rather substantial use of basic principles of learning and instruction.

(7) Today's classrooms should be laboratories in group dynamics and productive human interaction.

(8) One should find flexible standards of evaluation, with increasing attention to the actual performance of children, rather than comparison with grade, age, or group norms in today's classrooms.

(9) One should expect to find comparable flexibility in determining both the appropriate settings for learning and the most appropriate persons to participate in instructional activities.

(10) One should reasonably expect to find the traditional reading and listening activities of the primary years considerably expanded and enriched, not only by more vibrant attention to mathematics, but also by considerable attention to the natural and social sciences and, perhaps, to a lesser degree, the arts.

Activities

Develop a Questionnaire on one or more of the subject-area disciplines identified in this module as currently being taught in the elementary school. You might construct a separate section to inquire about the ten reasonable expectations identified by Goodlad and his associates. Visit an elementary school and determine (1) the nature of subject(s) in that school, and (2) whether or not, or to what degree, this school meets Goodlad's reasonable expectations.

General Objectives of Secondary Education

With the advent of the twentieth century, the public high school emerged in the United States as a uniquely American institution. Before the 1920s the purpose of secondary education seemed to be solely to prepare youth for higher education. Even for those who were not expected to continue their education beyond the high school years, college preparatory education was considered to be the best possible preparation for life in our society.

With the report of the Commission on the Reorganization of Secondary Education (NEA) in 1918, the purposes of American secondary education provided a new direction for the high school. The famous Seven Cardinal Principles of secondary education offered by the Commission maintain that secondary education should include all of these major areas:

1. Health.
2. Command of fundamental processes.
3. Worthy home membership.
4. Vocation.
5. Citizenship.
6. Worthy use of leisure.
7. Ethical character.

In subsequent years, several other lists of objectives have been developed by various groups. By 1955, the fourteen objectives offered by the White House

Conference on Education stated that the secondary school in America should provide a program that would develop

1. Fundamental skills of communication, arithmetic, and mathematics.
2. Appreciation for our democratic heritage.
3. Civic rights and responsibilities.
4. Respect and appreciation for human values.
5. Ability to think and evaluate constructively.
6. Effective work habits and self-discipline.
7. Social competency.
8. Ethical behavior.
9. Intellectual curiosity.
10. Aesthetic appreciation.
11. Physical and mental health.
12. Wise use of time.
13. Understanding of the physical world.
14. Awareness of our relationship with the world community.

In today's world, a sound secondary school curriculum is more important than ever before, and perhaps more difficult to achieve. The schools must provide for students with a greater variety of abilities, more diversified interests, and more divergent goals than ever before. Schools must provide opportunities for students to become proficient in established areas of knowledge that have increased in complexity, and in new areas that are only now emerging. Students must have a curriculum that will not only acquaint them with their cultural heritage and prepare them for a job or profession, but one that also will enable them, as adults, to solve the many problems that will confront their nation in a world grown small. In addition, this curriculum must equip students to resolve the many everyday personal problems associated with growing and maturing in their social milieu.

The universal education movement (1920–1960)—which has taken many districts all the way to the threshold of the individualized class, the alternate school, or the nongraded school—is the creative force responsible for the shape of the curriculum in the schools of the 1970's. Many individuals have challenged the concept of universal, free secondary education. Some have argued against compulsory attendance, urging that the "compulsory age" be lowered so that nonachieving, nonmotivated, uninterested, or disruptive students can be eliminated. Others have been in favor of no public secondary school whatever. They believe that secondary education should be the responsibility of the home, the professions, and business and industrial interests. Their proposal is that it should be conducted in private or parochial schools, and through apprenticeships.

One rather large segment of society, although endorsing public education, has resented and resisted the schools' concern with food services, health services, safety education, transportation services, and so on. They feel that these matters fall outside of the domain of the school and are distractions from the real goals of education. This group identifies the appropriate objectives of the school as being solely intellectual in nature, and they urge the elimination of vocational courses, sports, social activities, and guidance activities.

The majority of supporters of today's schools, on the other hand, consider students to be individuals with important social and emotional needs that cannot be divorced from intellectual development. They believe that the future of the country rests upon the abilities of young people—of every degree of mental ability, from every conceivable kind of background, with every sort of interest—who must be as well-prepared as possible for the task they will inherit. In their view, secondary education should provide

1. For the development of each personality to the fullest realization of inborn capacities.
2. For the maximum development of each student's intellect.
3. For development of good citizenship on the part of students.
4. For the development of understanding and knowledge about life that will lead to good physical and mental health.
5. For the moral development of its students.
6. Education in family living.
7. Educational experiences that will help students equip themselves with the skills, knowledge, understandings, and attitudes necessary for earning their own living.
8. Help for students so that they can live an enriched, enjoyable life.

As these objectives are meshed with those of the White House Conference, a broad base emerges upon which the rationale for sound curriculum judgments can be established.

General Terms and Nomenclature

In our study of the secondary curriculum, it will be necessary to understand the following terms:

1. *Junior High School:* A school that includes Grades 7, 8, and 9. For this module, Grades 7 and 8 are treated as a separate entity known as the *Junior School.*
2. *High School:* The high school grades are considered to be Grades 9, 10, 11, and 12. The elementary school, comprising Grades 1–8, prepares students for this school.
3. *Senior High School:* The senior high grades are 10, 11, and 12. Junior high graduates are promoted to this type of school.
4. *Unit:* One year of study in a class for five days per week, meeting one hour per day; one-half unit would be one semester of such work. A semester equals one-half year.
5. *Credit:* Award granted for completed units. One Carnegie Unit of credit is awarded for completing 180 classes in sessions lasting 40 minutes minimum.
6. *Track:* Separation of students into program compartments, based upon their measured ability or career plans. The most common are
   a. *General:* After completing a number of basic requirements students elect courses with no particular vocational goal or educational aim in mind.

b. *Vocational:* Students complete the basic requirements and then select those courses (units) that will prepare them for a specific vocation or job.

c. *Academic:* Students complete the basic requirements and elect a program geared to prepare them for college entrance.

7. *Instructional Unit:* Related portions of subject matter which are organized around a central theme. Units generally transcend subject-matter lines when used in a fused type curriculum.

8. *Course of Study:* A plan developed for use by teachers to help guide and direct the learning experiences of students. It is a planned arrangement of materials and activities in a particular subject, listing topics, units, resources, texts, and sometimes the potential sequence of presentation. In some schools this is a prescriptive document, and the expectation is that it will be followed in minute detail. In most schools today, it is used as a guide, relied upon when helpful, ignored when of little value. The guide serves to protect the continuity of learning experiences for pupils at each grade level, and to indicate the scope and sequence of the minimum essentials in each subject. Some Course of Study guides also include suggested experiences suitable for faster-learning and slower-learning students.

State Curriculum Guides are developed and offered by some state departments of education to all schools within their jurisdiction. They are generally broad in scope, and they outline desirable objectives, content, and methods for particular subjects. As resource books for local districts, state guides provide help in dealing with major educational problems that have arisen because of social change in the community, state, or nation.

Curriculum guides developed at the district or school level may represent a cooperative enterprise in which educators and citizens work together in committees to develop goals and procedures. They may also be the work of educators working alone. Usually cross-district representation is sought by the committee responsible for production of the guide, to help insure wide acceptance and endorsement of the product. Committee membership is drawn from every school in the district and each grade and/or each subject in a school; each committee is expected to function as a team. Experience has shown that only when there has been this grass-roots participation in the planning and the writing have documents of this sort been utilized by the classroom teachers for whom they were intended.

9. *Program of Studies:* Complete list of the subjects offered by a school.

10. *Constants:* Courses that are required of all students in the school, or all students in a particular track. Sometimes constants are referred to as the *common learnings* or the *general education curriculum.*

11. *Variables:* Elective courses that students may choose to take because of their special interest, need, or preparation.

12. *Educational Program:* A synonym for curriculum which encompasses three basic elements: (1) the program of studies, (2) the program of activities, and (3) the program of guidance.

13. *Curriculum Development:* A continuous process of planning a program to meet the needs of the pupils of a school. Pupils differ from one another, environments are never alike, and times and conditions change. These factors require that the process of planning be viewed developmentally, as

constantly ongoing, rather than as a one-time event, the results of which, upon completion, will remain static.

The Subject Fields

In the order of reported enrollment in a recent year, the following subject areas are discussed individually in this module:

1. English.
2. Health and Physical Education.
3. Social Studies.
4. Mathematics.
5. Science.
6. Music.
7. Business Education.
8. Industrial Arts.
9. Home Economics.
10. Foreign Languages.
11. Art.
12. Agriculture.
13. Vocational Trade and Industrial Education.
14. Distributive Education.

English. Of all the subjects offered in the American secondary school, English is the most frequently taken. Usually, students are enrolled in every grade, seven through twelve, and earn four or more credits for units completed in high school. Credits earned before Grade 9 satisfy the prerequisites for admission to high school. Credits earned in Grades 9–12 are prerequisites for admission to college and are classified as Carnegie Units.

English in Grades 7 and 8 is both a continuation of the language arts skill begun in the elementary grades and an introduction to the appreciation of literature. Speech and reading courses are frequently found in the junior school. Remedial English and/or reading is a common offering because of, among other things, the amount of federal funds available for this.

Grade 9 English usually includes a continuing emphasis on grammar and writing, with some study of literature in general. Grade 10 is the first year where the amount of time alloted for literature probably exceeds that allotted for grammar. American literature, with only limited time for language arts-skill development—usually in the form of a research paper—is the general theme of Grade 11. This concentration correlates with American history in the social studies for the same grade. English Literature is the most common subject for Grade 12; however, there is a distinct trend to provide a number of elective alternatives in both Grades 11 and 12, for example, (1) Business English, (2) Composition, (3) Journalism, (4) Creative Writing, (5) World Literature, (6) Mythology, (7) Speech, and (8) Dramatics.

In many schools students take some language arts subjects *in addition* to English—particularly Speech, Drama, and Journalism.

A note concerning the school librarian: Most librarians were originally certificated as English teachers and, although serving as resource persons for all teachers, they still probably serve best in the field of English-Language Arts.

Safety, Health and Physical Education. Health and Physical Education become separate subjects in Grades 7 and 8. There may also be an increase in organized athletics, although athletics does *not* generally replace an organized Health and Physical Education program.

Health is frequently a separate, required unit in high schools—but generally for only one semester. The course includes instruction in such areas as nutrition, dental care, sex education, and drug-abuse education. The latter is more likely to be taught by health teachers than social studies teachers, even though social problems are involved.

Physical Education may be required each of the four years of high school, or it may be required for no more than two years, but it is usually a required subject. The major activities in most Physical Education Programs are (1) games, sports, athletics; (2) rhythmic activities in general; (3) aquatic activities; (4) gymnastics, track, and field; (5) camping; (6) body-building activities; and (7) intramural athletics.

Two basic criticisms of the Physical Education Program have been that (1) classes have often contained too many students, and that (2) an excessive emphasis has sometimes been placed on athletics. Actually, organized athletics should be only a small part of a complete Health and Physical Education Program.

Safety education is not generally a separate subject in most secondary schools, except for the semester course in Driver Education found in almost all high schools in the nation. First aid and related topics are usually a part of the Health course.

Social Studies. More than perhaps any other subject, the seventh grade social studies courses varies from state to state and from school to school. Some possible offerings are

1. A continuation of the integrated social studies approach found in Grades 1 through 6.
2. A year's study of an introduction to World Geography.
3. A year's study of the state (history, geography, and government).
4. A regional study of Latin America, the Eastern Hemisphere, the Southern Hemisphere, and so on.
5. A course in Civics.

Whereas Grade 7 is a hodge-podge, there is almost unanimous agreement throughout the fifty states that a study of United States history, with emphasis on the middle period (1789–1900) is the most logical course for Grade 8.

At least one course and as many as three may be required in American high school social studies. The most frequently required courses are American History (Grades 11 or 12), American Government (Grade 12), and Economics (Grades 9–12). The most frequent offerings by grade level are

1. Grade 9: Civics and/or World Geography; Economics.
2. Grade 10: World History; or Ancient and Medieval History.
3. Grade 11: American History; or Modern History.
4. Grade 12: American Government and/or Problems of Democracy.

Senior high electives may include (1) Sociology, (2) Psychology, (3) State History, (4) International Relations, (5) Regional History, (6) Anthropology, (7) Current Events, and (8) Honors or Advanced Placement courses. There are literally scores of other possibilities. Perhaps the social studies provide the widest choice of courses of all disciplines in the American high school. In order to provide a wider variety, many schools have initiated minicourses (usually for six to nine weeks) in an ever widening number of topics. Economics is treated as a social studies course in many schools—perhaps most. In some states, such as Tennessee, it is a requirement. Economics could be considered a course in Business Education, and in some areas it is.

The teacher who aspires to teach the social studies in contemporary high schools should prepare himself in at least two of the identified subject areas. It is recommended that he major in the broad field of social studies in order to better serve the students with whom he will be working.

Mathematics. The "new math" developments (described in the module on the elementary education curriculum) continued into the Mathematics courses of the secondary grades. Grades 7 and 8 usually include units on (1) fractions, (2) decimals, (3) per cent, and (4) graphs. Although "General Math" is the most common name for the course in junior school, it should be kept in mind that algebra is frequently introduced at this level.

One unit in mathematics is required in most American high schools. To meet this need in a Comprehensive High School, Grade 9 usually has two distinct course offerings in mathematics: (1) General Math—per cent, ratio, proportion, graphs, insurance, banking, investing, consumer buying, and taxation—is usually a terminal course; and (2) Algebra—factoring, powers and roots, polynominals, fractional expressions, quadratic equations in one variable, linear equations in three variables— is usually a course for introducing the students to concepts in higher mathematics.

Grades 10 through 12 include courses involving concepts in higher mathematics as found in (1) Advanced General Mathematics; (2) Algebra I, II, III, IV; (3) Geometry—Plane and Solid; (4) Trigonometry; and (5) Advanced High School or College Mathematics.

Science. "General Science" is usually the name given to science courses for Grades 7 and 8. Federal agencies (such as the National Science Foundation) and legislation (such as the National Defense Education Act) have funded several programs in the field of science for the junior school-age student. Some of the better known are

1. Intermediate Science Curriculum Study (ISCS), Florida State University.
    a. Grade 7: Energy, its Forms and Characteristics and Measurement and Operational Definitions.
    b. Grade 8: Matter and its Composition; Model Building.
    c. Grade 9: Designed to synthesize and extend investigative experiences.
2. Introductory Physical Science (IPS) (Education Development Center, Inc.).
3. Biological Science Curriculum Study (BSCS), Biology for Junior School.
4. Earth Science Curriculum Project (ESCP), Earth Science (Geology) for Junior School.
5. Secondary School Science Project (SSSP), Physical Science for Junior School.

Many factors have contributed to the improvement of the science curriculum in American high schools. In 1959, James B. Conant, former president of Harvard University, completed his survey of the American high schools with a recommendation that every high school student should take at least one course in science. In addition, NSF and NDEA made funds available for the implementation of innovative programs, to purchase materials and equipment, and to pay for retraining programs for science teachers, in order to acquaint them with new methodologies. All of these factors have led to the improvement of the science curriculum in American high schools. The traditional offerings have been

1. Grade 9: General Science.
2. Grade 10: Biology.
3. Grade 11: Chemistry or Physics.
4. Grade 12: Physics or Chemistry.

The following curriculum projects for Grades 10 through 12 have met with the most success.

1. Biological Sciences Curriculum Study (BSCS), designed for the average to above-average student:
   a. Biological Science: Molecules to Man (Blue Version), molecular, biochemical, evolutionary approach.
   b. High School Biology: (BSCS Green Version), ecological, evolutionary approach.
   c. Biological Science: An Inquiry into Life (Yellow Version), cellular, biochemical, evolutionary approach.
2. Chemical Educational Materials Study (CHEM Study), University of California. This is chemistry for both the college-bound and terminal student, with emphasis on the techniques used by chemists in studying chemistry.
3. Chemical Bond Approach (CBA), Earlham College. This is the concept of the chemical bond-atomic structure and chemical equilibrium, which focuses "the making and breaking of ties between atoms in chemistry."
4. Physical Sciences Study Group (PSSG), Educational Development Center, Newton, Mass. This is physics for the college-bound and terminal students, and is based on increased laboratory work with considerably less absolute theory than in previous courses. Like many other projects funded by the government, the PSSG has texts, teacher aids, examinations, films, equipment, and tests. It has four major parts:

   a. The Universe.
   b. Optics and Waves.
   c. Mechanics.
   d. Electricity.

Electives in high school science may include

1. Applied Science.
2. Physiology.
3. Electricity—Radio.
4. Geology.
5. Aeronautics and Aviation.
6. Advanced Biology.
7. Advanced Chemistry.
8. Advanced Physics.
9. Advanced General Science.
10. Botany.
11. Zoology.
12. Physiology.

Music. As in the case of the other subject areas, music is a popular offering in Grades 7 and 8—both for aesthetics and as an exploratory field for a possible future career. Music in the high school is almost always an elective. Contemporary titles indicate the wide range of course offerings and musical activities, which have resulted in relatively high enrollments:

1. General Music.
2. Music Appreciation.
3. Band.
4. Orchestra.
5. Instrumental Classes, especially Piano.
6. Choir.
7. Glee Club.
8. Radio Music.
9. Music Festivals and Contests.

Music activity remains one of the oldest, and most often sanctioned, of the so-called extracurricular activities.

Business Education. With increasing frequency, General Business and Typing are found in the junior schools as a part of exploratory or Career Education offerings. General Business topics include (1) banking, (2) business economics, (3) business management, and (4) business organization.

Increased emphasis on Career Education has resulted in an increase in the number of students enrolled in Business Education courses in American high schools. The most frequent offerings are

1. Grade 9: Business Math, Commercial Geography.
2. Grade 10: General Business (Introduction).
3. Grade 11: Typing I; Shorthand I, Accounting I, Business English I, and Business Principles.
4. Grade 12: Typing II, Shorthand II, Business English II, Office Practices, Office Management, Consumer Education, Retail Selling.

Although these courses have been indicated for specific grade levels, students from any level in the senior high grades may be enrolled in them, many in two or even three at one time. There has been a general decline in traditional bookkeeping courses in favor of accounting, and an increase in Office Education and Distributive Education. With a background requirement of at least one year of typewriting and one year of shorthand, the office education course is usually taught at the eleventh grade level for two units of credit, or at the twelfth grade level for three units of credit. Activities include

1. Business English.
2. Business Math.
3. Business Law (legal forms).
4. Record Keeping.
5. Office Machines.
6. Filing.

7. Typewriting (advanced).
8. Shorthand (advanced).
9. Job Application (practice interviews, and so on).
10. Simulation (the classroom becomes a model office).

For students who wish to take both junior and senior Office Education, the senior year may be completed by an *internship,* which consists of one hour in the classroom and from two to four hours in an office, with full employee benefits.

Industrial Arts and Technology (Nonvocational). Industrial Arts Education is a major area of exploration in American junior high schools. Grades 7 and 8 are usually given an overview of several areas such as (1) Woodworking, (2) Plastics, (3) Electronics, (4) Metalworking, (5) Drafting and Graphic arts, and (6) Automobile and Motorcycle Mechanics. Industrial Arts I, II, III, and IV, may be found in the high school. In the larger Comprehensive High Schools, special courses are available in a wide variety of courses:

1. Shop courses: Woodworking, Metallurgy, Electronics, Plastics, Auto Mechanics, Transportation (Ground Power, Navigation, and Aeronautics).
2. Mechanical Drawing and Drafting; Pre-Engineering.
3. Printing: Graphic Arts, Bookbinding, Photography.
4. Crafts: Leather, Jewelry, Metal, Ceramics, Textiles, Wood, Weaving.
5. Job Orientation and Career Education.

Home Economics. The Smith-Hughes Act of 1917 gave Home Economics its impetus in American high schools. Initially open to students of both sexes, it eventually became a course almost solely for girls. It was sometimes required for them, but generally it remained an elective. Recently, Home Economics has again become a course for both boys and girls, particularly with increasing emphasis on such units as Bachelor Survival.

Other themes for Home Economics I and II (sometimes III and IV) include

1. Home Management: Cooking, Sewing, Housekeeping, Canning, Home Sanitation.
2. Family Management; Preparation for Marriage.
3. Housing and Interior Decorating.
4. Social and Community Relations and Activities.
5. Child Development; Health and Home Nursing.
6. Consumer Education.
7. Sex Education.

Foreign Languages. Foreign language instruction may begin in the junior school years as an exploratory subject, or it may be a continuation of study begun in the elementary-school years. In the past, it was common to find the four-year sequence of foreign language in American high schools. The leading courses were Spanish, French, and Latin. In time, the sequence in most schools dropped to two years, and even though Conant and others have recommended the restoration of a three- or four-year sequence, it has not generally been accepted.

Three basic trends should be noted:

1. Foreign languages are being offered in the elementary school; this, in effect, has restored the sequence to three, four, or more years.
2. The study of Latin has declined in favor of the modern tongues.
3. The traditional Modern Languages courses in Spanish, French, and German are giving way to courses in Russian, Chinese, Japanese, Hebrew, Arabic, Portuguese, Swedish, Greek, Polish, Norwegian, Italian, African languages (such as Swahili), and, in many schools in the American West, the native American Indian languages.

Art. As a constant in the exploratory phase of the junior school curriculum, art is offered to either seventh or eighth graders. In some schools it is required both years; it includes units that sample a wide variety of art topics: (1) painting, (2) drawing, (3) modeling, (4) weaving, (5) construction, (6) crafts, and other creative units. It is in the junior school grades that the student may choose to major or minor in Art in high school. Beginning with Grade 9 and continuing through the senior high school grades, Art is offered as an elective to all students. Only a few secondary schools offer four full years of Art, with the general program being a minimum of one semester (one-half unit) and a maximum of two credits. Consequently, students from any given level in high school may work with others from any one or all other levels.

Unlike many elementary school Art programs, the secondary program is ordinarily found in a large room especially designed for the subject. Two trends are noteworthy:

1. Direct participation as opposed to appreciation and viewing classes.
2. Commercial emphasis, that is, posters, layouts, illustrations, cartooning, designing, and graphic aids of all kinds.

Agriculture. During the past quarter century Agriculture as a curriculum area has decreased markedly in the seventh and eighth grades. Occasionally it is offered in a rural school as an elective. Even in high schools, Agricultural Education is usually found only in the rural institutions. Students may pursue Agriculture from one to four years; the general program is three years. General Agriculture includes (1) Animal Husbandry, (2) Farm Forestry, (3) Gardening, (4) Horticulture, and (5) Landscape Gardening. Advanced classes include such topics as agriculture shop and farm mechanics.

Vocational Trades and Industrial Education. Vocational Education in American secondary schools began with the advent of the industrial revolution in the nineteenth century. Industrial and Trade High Schools were established in a number of cities. This module is limited to a study of Vocational Education in the Comprehensive High School. Six broad areas have been identified as the basis for vocational programs that may include an internship:

1. Office Occupations.
2. Distributive Education.
3. Trade and Industrial Education.
4. Technical Education.
5. Agricultural Education.
6. Health Occupations Education.

A basic element of a good vocational trade and industrial education program is the internship or work experience, which is the primary difference between a Vocational and an Industrial Arts course. A few of the more frequently offered Vocational courses are

1. Air-conditioning.
2. Airplane Mechanics.
3. Auto Mechanics.
4. Bricklaying.
5. Cabinetmaking.
6. Carpentry.
7. Cosmetology.
8. Deisel Mechanics.
9. Drafting.
10. Electricity.
11. Food Trades.
12. Machine Shop.
13. Needle Trades.
14. Nursing.
15. Other Health Occupations.
16. Painting and Decorating.
17. Plumbing and Pipefitting.
18. Printing Occupations.
19. Radio and Television.
20. Restaurant Trades.
21. Sales.
22. Sheetmetal and Welding.

Two recurring issues in Vocational Education have been
1. The snobbishness of those in the precollege academic track rather than in the Vocational program.
2. Counselor's placing academically weak students in the vocational classes when they should be assigned to the general track.

Distributive Education. The "newest" separate subject area in most secondary schools, Distributive Education, is now found in most American high schools. Distributive Education (DE), first funded by the George-Deen Act (1936), is usually established as a two-year course. Distributive Education I provides a student with an introduction to the world of retailing—marketing, sales promotion, salesmanship, and advertising. There is the possibility of a work-study unit for older students.

Distributive Education II is a continuation of the first year, and includes retailing, marketing, sales promotion, salesmanship, and advertising, but with greater depth in marketing and advertising. In addition, students are required to work approximately three hours per day in an area of retailing or wholesaling. The Distributive Education Club of America (DECA) is a part of the program for working students who may not be able to become members of other clubs offered by the school. The DECA provides the DE student with the opportunity to have a greater role in school organization.

Three Proposals

In contemporary American education, no study of the secondary element would be complete without a brief survey of the work of two highly respected educators, who made their respective proposals in 1959 and 1961, and of the 1973 recommendations of the National Commission on the Reform of Secondary Education.

The American High School Today. James B. Conant, former president of Harvard University, and diplomat, published his widely lauded study of *The American High School Today* in 1959.[3] Conant's proposals focused on the comprehensive high school, with three objectives:

1. A general education for all future citizens.
2. A good elective program for those who wish to use their skills immediately upon graduation.
3. A good program for those who plan to prepare for their ultimate profession in a college or university.

The major portion of Conant's study centers on 21 basic recommendations; briefly, they are as follows:

1. Establish a counseling system, with one full-time counselor for each 250 to 300 pupils.
2. Provide individualized programs for each student, but eliminate tracks.
3. Require nine units for all students: English, four years; Social Studies, three or four years; Mathematics, one year; and Science, one year.
4. Eliminate homogeneous grouping, particularly in required courses; courses should include students with a wide range of ability.
5. Provide a record of courses taken, as a supplement to the high school diploma.
6. Require English Composition for approximately half the time in English courses.
7. Provide diversified programs for the development of marketable skills, to include Typing, Office Machines, Home Economics, Distributive Education, Vocational Agriculture, and some technical courses.
8. Give special consideration to slow readers.
9. Require at least fifteen hours of homework in special programs for the academically talented.
10. Provide Advanced Placement courses for the top 3 per cent.
11. Make an annual academic inventory for the upper 15 per cent of all students.
12. Organize the school day into not less than six periods, not counting Physical Education.
13. Require prerequisites for advanced academic courses, including a *C* average in the subject area to be studied.
14. Eliminate ranking students in class according to their average of grades in all subjects.
15. Publish an academic honors list, but do not rank students.
16. Establish Developmental Reading Programs for the more able students.
17. Establish summer schools: for the repeating of courses by slower students and for curriculum broadening for more able students. (No speed-up programs were recommended.)
18. Extend Foreign Language Programs to include a third or fourth year.

[3] James B. Conant, *The American High School Today: A First Report to Interested Citizens* (New York: McGraw-Hill Book Company, 1959), p. 73.

19. Require that Science be taken by all students for at least one year.
20. Establish the homeroom as a continuous unit for the four years that a student is in high school; this would provide the recommended guidance and counseling unit.
21. Require twelfth-grade Social Studies in Economics or Problems of Democracy/American Government; the students would be heterogeneously grouped for this class.[4]

The Trump Plan. J. Lloyd Trump and Dorsey Baynham outlined the requirements for better staff utilization in American secondary schools at a time of serious teacher shortage.[5] *Focus on Change: A Guide to Better Schools* implied a number of curriculum changes within five general area recommendations.

TEAM TEACHING. The most generally accepted recommendation was team teaching. As defined by Trump, three or four teachers working together in either similar areas or in a variety of fields at a given level were bound to provide a better program for the students they taught. Specific curricular implications were expected to be made in the concepts of articulation and balance.

INDEPENDENT STUDY. Independent study was recommended for up to 40 per cent of a student's day. This would certainly require a much wider variety of instructional materials and more equipment than in the past. In addition, it would encourage the study of topics not usually found in a traditional scope and sequence.

ABILITY GROUPING. Ability grouping was approved and recommended by Trump and his associates, who saw nothing wrong with the concept.

DIFFERENTIATED STAFFING. Differentiated staffing patterns would include team leaders, regular teachers, and teacher assistants. Teacher assistants would include staff specialists, community consultants, general aides, and clerks. In addition, universities and colleges would be encouraged to place students in their teacher training programs in the schools, to assist and to gain orientation to teaching.

FLEXIBILITY. The key word in the Trump pronouncements was *Flexibility*. He recommended that the self-contained classroom of thirty students be abolished. In its place he recommended team teaching designed to provide up to 40 per cent of the time for large-group instruction (150 or more students); 40 per cent for independent study; and 20 per cent for small-group instruction (about 15 students).

National Commission on the Reform of Secondary Education. During the sixties, critics of education were seriously critical of secondary education: First, they said, it was not relevant to the needs and lives of its clientele, and second, it had become a joyless mind-killing prison. As a result, numerous attempts have been made to establish alternative modes of secondary education that would be more useful and more beneficial to adolescents in the real world.

Because of this great wave of criticism, and because of the belief that secondary education would be faced by extraordinary new problems in the last quarter of the century, a National Commission on the Reform of Secondary Education was formed under the sponsorship of the Charles F. Kettering Foundation.

[4] Ibid., pp. 41–76.
[5] J. Lloyd Trump and Dorsey Baynham, *Focus on Change: Guide to Better Schools* (Chicago: Rand McNally & Co., 1961), p. 147.

After a period of considerable study, which included a series of panels and monthly hearings in various parts of the nation, on-site visits to schools, and discussions with pupils, teachers, and administrators, the Commission issued its report.[6] Although the report contains little that is earth shaking, it does show some of the directions secondary education may take in the near future. These include, among other things, a more open schooling, alternative educational paths during secondary school years, an increased emphasis on the practical and career aspects of education, and increased emphasis on global education. In the succeeding paragraphs we will discuss some of the recommendations that are particularly pertinent to this module.

The Commission felt that the time had come for an extensive reorganization of secondary education. Consequently, they proposed a re-examination of the goals, that is, the longrange results of secondary education. The goals they suggest are learner-centered, and are in two categories: Content goals, which are the "general skills that students must acquire if they are to function at a level that is personally and socially rewarding," and "process goals, which are the individual abilities and attitudes influenced by the procedures, environment and activities of the school." Following are the goals for secondary education that the Commission recommends.

Content Goals
  Achievement of Communications Skills
  Achievement of Computation Skills
  Attainment of Proficiency in Critical and Objective Thinking
  Acquisition of Occupational Competence
  Clear Perception of Nature and Environment
  Development of Economic Understanding
  Acceptance of Responsibility for Citizenship
Process Goals
  Knowledge of Self
  Appreciation of Others
  Ability to Adjust to Change
  Respect for Law and Authority
  Clarification of Values
  Appreciation of the Achievements of Man.

The Commission also recommends that every school and its subordinate departments formulate a statement on goals and develop performance criteria for students. The community as a whole, they say, should formulate the goals for secondary education.

The curriculum, according to the report, must be drastically overhauled. A revised curriculum would eliminate busywork and bias. It would also provide opportunities for pupils "to take full advantage of career opportunities in their communities." In Grades 8 through 10 students should explore "a variety of career clusters"; in Grades 11 and 12 they should have opportunities to learn "the hard skills in a career area of their choice." Suitable vocational guidance and job placement should be provided. The curriculum should also be expanded to include truly global education.

[6] The National Commission on the Reform of Secondary Education, *The Reform of Secondary Education* (New York: McGraw-Hill Book Company, 1973).

Global education, in the perspective of a curriculum for both college preparatory and non-college-bound students, is concerned with scientific, ecological, and economic issues which affect everyone. These include questions of war and peace, interdependency of natural resources, climate control, the use of the sea bed, the population issue, and other concerns where national positions are not necessarily controlled by inherited, prescientific, political positions.[7]

What they seek in global education is "basic international literacy" and basic understanding of the historical, geographic, economic, and political truths that such literacy involves.

The curriculum the Commission envisages cannot be taught adequately with the present school offerings and school organization. For one thing, many pupils are kept in school when they would rather not be there. Therefore the Commission recommends that schooling not be compulsory after age fourteen or Grade 8. This provision would, they say, free the schools to do a more adequate job with pupils who want to go to school. All instruction should be performance-based and individualized. Instead of a single institution providing secondary schooling, there should be many alternatives funded by the school boards. Furthermore, schools should give students credit for work experience, and chances to substitute examinations for classwork. Secondary learning then would take place not only in traditional and alternative schools, but also in work experiences, social experiences, volunteer agency experiences, community experiences, individual study, study via the television and other media, and so on. Under this kind of program students would be able to drop out and then return to formal schooling almost at will—even if in the meantime they have become older than most secondary students. In fact, education from K–14 at public expense would be a person's right at anytime during his life.

These recommendations, if carried out, would necessitate a much more open and flexible school program. Many signs indicate that secondary education may move in this direction, Commission recommendations or no!

Activities

1. Prepare a checklist for the fourteen secondary school subject areas identified in this module, with appropriate subdivisions for each grade for each subject. Visit both a junior and a senior high school and determine the scope and sequence of course titles. (If possible, this should be a group project.) When the visit has been completed, compare the curriculum of that school with those typical curriculums identified in the module.

2. Develop a questionnaire based on Conant's 21 recommendations. Visit a Comprehensive High School and determine the degree to which these recommendations have been implemented.

3. (Optional.) If there is a secondary school in your area that has team teaching as part of its over-all pattern of organization, visit this school and determine the degree to which the Trump plan has been implemented, or to what degree the Trump recommendations influenced the school in its organization.

[7] Ibid., p. 64.

SUGGESTED READING

Association for Supervision and Curriculum Development. *What are the Sources of the Curriculum? A Symposium.* Washington, D.C.: National Education Association, 1962.

Doll, Ronald C. *Curriculum Improvement: Decision-Making and Process,* 2nd Ed. Boston: Allyn & Bacon, Inc., 1970.

Goodlad, John I. *School, Curriculum, and the Individual.* Waltham, Mass: Ginn/ Blaisdell, 1966.

———— *School Curriculum Reform in the United States.* New York: Fund for Advancement of Education, 1964.

———— et al. *The Changing School Curriculum.* New York: Fund for the Advancement of Education, 1966.

Johnson, James A., et al. *Introduction to the Foundations of American Education,* 2nd Ed. Boston: Allyn & Bacon, Inc., 1973.

Margolin, Edythe. *Young Children: Their Curriculum and Learning Processes.* New York: Macmillan Publishing Co., Inc., 1976.

Palardy, J. Michael. *Elementary School Curriculum: An Anthology of Trends and Challenges.* New York: Macmillan Publishing Co., Inc., 1971.

Rodgers, Frederick A. *Curriculum and Instruction in the Elementary School.* New York: Macmillan Publishing Co., Inc., 1975.

Saylor, J. Galen, Ed. *The School of the Future: Now.* Washington, D.C.: Association for Supervision and Curriculum Development, 1972.

Tanner, Daniel, and Laurel Tanner, *Curriculum Development: Theory Into Practice.* New York: Macmillan Publishing Co., Inc., 1975.

Van Til, William. *Education: A Beginning,* 2nd. Ed. Boston: Houghton Mifflin Company, 1974.

Wilson, L. Craig. *The Open Access Curriculum.* Boston: Allyn & Bacon, Inc., 1971.

Wright, Betty A., Louie T. Camp, William K. Stosberg, and Babette Fleming. *Elementary School Curriculum: Better Teaching Now.* New York: Macmillan Publishing Co., Inc., 1971.

On the Secondary School Curriculum

Alexander, William M., Ed. *The Changing High School Curriculum: Readings,* 2nd Ed. New York: Holt, Rinehart & Winston, Inc., 1972.

Bechner, Weldon, and Joe D. Cornett. *The Secondary School Curriculum: Content and Structure.* Scranton, Pa.: Intext Educational Publishers, 1972.

Conant, James B. *The American High School Today* New York: McGraw-Hill Book Company, 1959.

Haas, Glen, Joseph Bondi, and Jon Wiles. *Curriculum Planning: A New Approach.* Boston: Allyn & Bacon, Inc., 1974.

Inlow, Gail M. *The Emergent in Curriculum,* 2nd Ed. New York: John Wiley & Sons, Inc., 1973.

Johnson, Harold T. *Foundations of Curriculum,* Columbus, Ohio: Charles E. Merrill Publishers, 1968.

Koopman, G. Robert. *Curriculum Development,* New York: The Center for Applied Research in Education, Inc., 1966.

Tanner, Daniel. *Secondary Education: Perspectives and Prospects*. New York: Macmillan Publishing Co., Inc., 1972.

Trump, J. Lloyd, and Dorsey Baynham. *Focus on Change: A Guide to Better Schools*. Chicago: Rand McNally & Co., 1961.

Trump, J. Lloyd, and Delmas F. Miller. *Secondary School Curriculum Improvement: Challenges, Humanism, Accountability*. Boston: Allyn & Bacon, Inc., 1973.

Van Til, William, Ed. *Curriculum: Quest for Relevance*. 2nd Ed. Boston: Houghton Mifflin Company, 1974.

POST TEST

Part I: The Elementary School

MULTIPLE CHOICE

A. (*Circle one.*) The most typical elementary school organization in the United States is

1. K–3   **2.** K–6   **3.** K–8   **4.** 5–8   **5.** nongraded

B. (*Circle one.*) Which of the following best delineates the position of *reading* in the elementary curriculum?

1. Reading is perhaps the most important period of instruction in schools.

2. Student-ability spread declines as the children progress through school.

3. Individualization is harder to accomplish in reading than in any other area.

4. all of the above.

5. none of the above.

C. (*Circle One.*) The basic trend in social studies education is toward

1. major emphasis on geography and history.

2. major emphasis on the behavioral sciences.

3. Integrated Social Studies.

4. postponing the study of social studies to the middle grades.

5. combining social studies with the language arts into a Core curriculum.

D. (*Circle one.*) All of the following agencies supported the "new science" except one. Which supported the development of "new math?"

1. ESS.   **2.** ESSP.   **3.** SCIS.   **4.** BSCS.   **5.** SMSG.

LISTING

A. List five agencies, factors, or forces that may influence curriculum in the American school:

1. _____   **2.** _____

3. _____   **4.** _____

5. _____

B. List the seven basic areas of the elementary school curriculum:

1. _____   **2.** _____   **3.** _____   **4.** _____

5. _____   **6.** _____   **7.** _____

C. List the five primary divisions of the language arts component:

1. _____ **2.** _____ **3.** _____ **4.** _____ **5.** _____

D. List six social sciences from which the social studies are derived:

1. _____ **2.** _____ **3.** _____

4. _____ **5.** _____ **6.** _____

E. List two groups that have been instrumental in the development of the "new science" in elementary school curriculums:

1. _____ **2.** _____

F. List four subjects usually taught by an area specialist in elementary schools:

1. _____ **2.** _____ **3.** _____ **4.** _____

G. List the four basic components of Individually Guided Education (IGE):

1. _____ **2.** _____

3. _____ **4.** _____

H. List the four learning modes of IGE:

1. _____ **2.** _____

3. _____ **4.** _____

I. List six of Goodlad's "Ten Reasonable Expectations" concerning the American elementary school:

1. _____

2. _____

3. _____

4. _____

5. _____

6. _____

Part II: The Secondary School

MULTIPLE CHOICE (*Circle one.*)

A. The term *high school* should be used to indicate grades
    1. 7–9.   **2.** 10–12.   **3.** 7–12.   **4.** 9–12.   **5.** 9–14.

B. The recognized *tracks* in the Comprehensive High School are
    1. General, Vocational, Aesthetic.
    2. Academic, Aesthetic, General.
    3. Academic, General, Vocational.
    4. Academic, Exploratory, General.
    5. General, Exploratory, Specialized.

C. The subject most frequently taught in high schools is
1. social studies.
2. English.
3. science.
4. mathematics.
5. art and music.

D. All of the following are part of the health and physical education curriculum. Which *one* is least important in the over-all program for this area?
1. organized athletics.
2. calisthentics.
3. gymnastics, field and track.
4. intramural athletics.
5. a separate course in health.

E. The most frequently taught social studies course in high schools is
1. Economics.
2. Government.
3. World Geography.
4. World History.
5. American History.

F. Grade 7 social studies may include any one of the following. Which is *least* likely to occur at this level?
1. State Geography and History.
2. Geography.
3. Civics.
4. Integrated Social Studies.
5. American History.

G. A new Business Education course, taught for two or three credits in Grades 11 and 12, is
1. Office Practice.
2. Office Machines.
3. Office Education.
4. Accounting.
5. Consumer Education.

H. Which one of the following lists includes the three traditional foreign language courses in the American high school?
1. Latin, French, German.
2. French, Spanish, Latin.
3. German, French, Greek.
4. Greek, Latin, Spanish.

I. Which one of the following is *not* given as a trend in foreign language instruction?
1. The decline in the teaching of American Indian languages in high schools.
2. The decline in the teaching of Latin.
3. An increasing in the number of Modern Language courses.
4. Offering foreign languages to junior high or elementary schools.

J. The percentage of time recommended for *large group: small group: independent study,* respectively, in the Trump Plan was
1. 20:60:20. 2. 40:40:20. 3. 20:40:40. 4. 40:20:40. 5. 60:20:20.

LISTING

A. List the Seven Cardinal Principles of education stated in 1918:

1. _____ 2. _____

3. _____ 4. _____

5. _____ 6. _____

7. _____

B. List seven of the fourteen new objectives stated by the White House Conference on Education in 1955:

1. _____   2. _____

3. _____   4. _____

5. _____   6. _____

7. _____

C. List five elective courses in the Language Arts Program:

1. _____   2. _____   3. _____

4. _____   5. _____

D. List five social studies electives in the American high school.

1. _____   2. _____   3. _____

4. _____   5. _____

E. List the four most frequently offered mathematics courses for Grades 9–12:

1. _____   2. _____   3. _____   4. _____

F. List the four most frequently offered science courses for Grades 9–12:

1. _____   2. _____   3. _____   4. _____

G. List three study groups that have promoted the "new science" curriculums for Biology, Geology, and Physics:

1. _____

2. _____

3. _____

H. List five Music electives in high schools:

1. _____   2. _____   3. _____

4. _____   5. _____

I. List five Business Education electives in high schools:

1. _____   2. _____   3. _____

4. _____   5. _____

J. List five areas of Industrial Arts Education:

1. _____   2. _____   3. _____

4. _____   5. _____

K. List five areas in Home Economics Education:

1. _____   2. _____   3. _____

4. _____   5. _____

L. List four areas of Art Education:

1. _____ 2. _____ 3. _____ 4. _____

M. List four areas of Agricultural Education:

1. _____ 2. _____ 3. _____ 4. _____

N. List six *broad areas* of Vocational Education:

1. _____ 2. _____ 3. _____

4. _____ 5. _____ 6. _____

O. List three primary areas of Distributive Education:

1. _____ 2. _____ 3. _____

P. List eight of Conant's 21 Recommendations:

1. _____
2. _____
3. _____
4. _____
5. _____
6. _____
7. _____
8. _____

Q. List five recommendations made in the Trump plan:

1. _____
2. _____
3. _____
4. _____
5. _____

The Community and Schools

William A. Liggitt

Jersey City State College

module 9

Definition of Community / Some Intangible Community Forces Affecting the School / Community Influences on the School / Aims and Purposes Related to Community / Community Investment in Education / The School and Other Social Institutions / The Teacher and the Community

RATIONALE

This module is designed to help the beginning student in education to appreciate and understand the multifaceted relationships of the school to the general Community.

The school, church, and family are three major social institutions in the community. Consequently, a part of this module is directed toward understanding both the historic and the current role of the church and the family in the educative process; how these roles impinge on, overlap, and interact with the school's role. We have considered briefly, also, the teacher and the community, particularly the interrelated responsibility of teacher and parent for the child's education, and some views of the community on the status of teachers. The plan in writing this module has been to provide some definitions of the community, church, and family; to show how the school was significantly shaped by historical forces; to emphasize how currently changing values and constructs continue to influence schools; and how schools respond to the community. Although there is some material on the teacher and the community, the chief focus in this module is on how the school fits into and is related to the general social system herein defined as the *community*. Some of the concepts about the community noted in this module are drawn from basic sociological texts on the community and family. Sociologists and other professional social scientists use generic terms for community and family analysis, and make very limited use of any school applications that would make the analysis more meaningful to a beginning education student. We have introduced some of these sociological concepts, with appropriate illustrations of their application to education, not to make the module more difficult but to alert the beginning student in education that professional education is an applied social science, to be studied at a graduate and upper-undergraduate level. In the process of becoming a master educator, the professional educator should by all means have some basic social science courses pertaining to community and family.

Your goal in studying this module should be to acquire an understanding of some of the dimensions of school-community relations; and of the importance of the teacher in these relationships; and to gain a degree of sensitivity as to how the public relates to the public school.

Objectives

Upon completing your study of this module, you should be able to
1. Define and cite examples of two contrasting types of communities, and describe how the nature of the community affects the school.
2. Recognize two specific ways of analyzing a community.
3. Identify basic criteria for defining a community.
4. Recall three intangible community factors that influence the school program.
5. Classify four major methods by which the community at large influences the school.

6. Distinguish three major social forces in society that impact on the school.
7. Cite three major changes in value patterns that influence the school.
8. Recognize two major changes in the purposes of schools between the seventeenth and twentieth centuries.
9. State two major functions of schools in any society.
10. Recognize three school functions that have a significant bearing on school discipline.
11. Compare the public's economic investment in the public schools to investments in other services.
12. Relate the compulsory education requirement to the essential purpose of education.
13. Cite the principle on which a school activity in the moral and spiritual area is illegal.
14. Recognize three basic moral values in which American people believe.
15. Contrast the role of the church and the school in the education of children and youth.
16. State two recent changes in family life that affect the educational responsibility of the school.
17. Analyze how confusion and conflict in family-member roles change the school's program.
18. Distinguish between values in lower-class neighborhoods and values in middle-class neighborhoods.
19. Describe the importance of school board membership in political life.
20. List three community organizations that have direct liaison with the public schools.
21. Distinguish between the responsibility of the family and the responsibility of the school for the education of the child.
22. Define the ages during which a child's personality is most influenced.
23. Interpret how changes in the American family since World War II have brought new responsibilities to the schools.
24. Relate two factors in the urban family pattern that weaken the family's capacity to transmit values and attitudes.
25. Define the term *in loco parentis.*
26. Identify three community attitudes about the status of teachers in the community that emerge from the history of public education.
27. Cite two factors that make it difficult for the teacher to be the "parent" in the classroom.
28. Give two reasons why teachers should live in the community in which they teach.
29. Describe how teachers use community lay leaders in the instructional program.
30. Identify the principal elements in the social system known as *community.*
31. Define cognitive, secular, urbanization, affective, sectarian, interpersonal, lower class, and middle class.

MODULE TEXT

To a student entering professional education, it is important to appreciate the special relationships that exist between the community and the school, and to understand the more or less central position of the public school in the community. As a beginning point in understanding how the school as a social institution interacts with other institutions, some definitions and explanation of the meaning of community would be helpful.

Definition of Community

A sociologist might define a community as a configuration of land, with people, culture, and a structural pattern of human relations within this geographic area. Communities are formed when varying interests of families and individuals merge for purposes of protection, preservation of culture, sharing of basic service institutions, and participation in religious, educational, business, political, social, and other common activities. Every community has an historic past. The public school or the public school system, historically, has been the mandated institution through which the community fulfills its legal obligations to provide education for its children and youth.

Consequently, a look at the community—its past, present, and future—provides a reference point for determining community expectations with respect to education. The community may be studied from a variety of angles—each with its own relevance. The traditional approach places emphasis on such factors as physical size, location, population, composition of population, economic status, housing, the character and adequacy of service agencies, that is, churches, libraries, and stores, as well as the social, economic, and political structure, and its functions and values. The authors of *Educational Administration in a Changing Community*[1] defined with great clarity and insight the concept of a community as a *social system*.

In this light, the community is a complex of forms of behavior structurally and functionally related. It is made up of numbers of people, each occupying a recognized position of status with an appropriate and usually predictable mode of behavior. . . . The broad outlines of a community as a social system include a number of principal elements:

positions—(male, female, parent, businessman, boy scout leader)

roles—(role of teacher, parent, child, policeman, minister)

institutions—(i.e., positions in high school dance, PTA meeting, luncheon club, garden club)

institutional areas—(i.e., positions in family, church, school, business, politics, government).

The authors also make the following points. It is more realistic to identify a series of community levels ranging all the way from the family to the nation. The

---

[1] American Association of School Administrators, Thirty-Seventh Yearbook (Washington, D.C.: The Association, 1959), pp. 48 ff.

boundaries of the community depend upon the nature of the interest and activities. In this age of rapid and continuous communications, the trend is toward the development of a series of communities transcending the traditional local community. One consequence is that the existence of various levels means that activities at one level begin to impinge upon other activities at other levels.

In a community with well-defined physical boundaries, economic self-sufficiency, a homogeneous population with a common heritage, beliefs, and values, the school may occupy a position of special prominence and esteem. The community's educational aspirations and goals are clearly stated and amply reflected in the school's program of studies. A *Gemeinschaft* society, where the community is self-sufficient and persons have a strong sense of community identity, usually produces strong, stable well-integrated institutions, and the school receives "good marks" for its contribution to the community. In contrast, the *Gesellschaft* type of society is marked by a division of labor, with great specialization of functions and a general lack of community identity. The inhabitants—sometimes even next door neighbors—are not acquainted with each other, and there is a high interdependence with other communities, even for basic necessities. In such a society, the roles of institutions and leaders are ambiguous, and often uncongenial or unlearned. The school in the *Gesellschaft* society, caught in conflict between community levels, is often undervalued, severely criticized, and given failing grades for its inability to be a positive vital affirmative force in a chaotic disorganized community.[2]

It is essential that the teacher understand that the school is not independent of other social institutions. The purposes, programs, and outcomes of instruction depend to a large extent on the community and the publics that it serves. The public school system in America was created by the state, with significant support from the church and the family. In a sense, the public school began as a supplement to the education services rendered by the church and the home, and in one hundred and fifty years has become the major educational institution in the community.

Some Intangible Community Forces Affecting the School

It is possible through community study to understand a great deal about how a school relates to a specific community. No institution in a social system is completely free of the norms of the total system. In this context, the authors of AASA's Thirty-seventh Yearbook[3] (*Education Administration in a Changing Community*) suggest three intangible factors for study: the force of beliefs, the force of tradition, the force of aspiration.

BELIEFS. To some extent, say the authors, a community is what people believe it is. The optimist sees it as constantly improving; the pessimist, as falling apart. If people think of their community as a place where cooperation is difficult to obtain, it will be. People behave in terms of their beliefs. In all communities, despite variations in kind and degree, there are many shared or common beliefs.

[2] For a brief discussion of *Gemeinschaft* and *Gesellschaft* societies, see the American Association of School Administrators, *Educational Administration in a Changing Community*, op. cit.; and for a fuller discussion, see Logan Wilson and William L. Kolbe, *Sociological Analysis* (New York: Harcourt Brace Jovanovich, Inc., 1949), Chap. 2.

[3] American Association of School Administrators, op. cit., Chap. 8.

These provide a core of unity without which community life would not be possible. These shared or common beliefs exist with reference to schools in the community and play a significant part in the nature and quality of instruction.

TRADITION. Tradition lends stability and predictability to behavior. It influences relationships among groups and often determines the services that community agencies render. School services and programs depend more often than not on the force of tradition.

ASPIRATION. The force of aspiration is a major factor in determining what schools shall do and how they shall do it. Community action is a product of what it has and is, and what it wants and desires. Aspiration may take the form of quantity, with emphasis on more schooling and a variety of programs, and/or quality, with emphasis on college preparatory programs. To a great extent, community processes and decisions grow out of the beliefs, concepts, interests, traditions, and aspirations of the community. The school, as a major social institution in the community, is subject to these community processes.

Community Influences on the School

The educational goals of the school—what is to be taught, and how—reflect and are influenced by the traditions and values of the community. These values are expressed by school board members, community leaders, and civic groups in the larger community.

In his book *Curriculum Improvements,*[4] Dr. Ronald Doll points out that the school curriculum may be significantly affected both by influences from society at large and by influences within the immediate community. The society at large, says Doll, affects the school in four major ways: (1) by inhibiting change through the power of *tradition;* (2) by speeding *change,* which stems in turn from broader social and cultural changes; (3) by creating problems which result from value conflicts within our society; and (4) by applying pressures that originate in major segments of American society and culture. Several traditional forces in society play a major role in shaping educational goals. Public schools are organized and administered under state laws. Hence, legal authority is a traditional guideline for establishing goals and objectives and programs in the public schools. Laws, once enacted, are not easily changed. In a dynamic, rapidly changing culture, a school program that is offered because of a legal requirement could easily become an anachronism.

The public schools originated from the Judeo-Christian tradition, with its notions of morality and property rights. These traditions tend to have a stabilizing influence on the school. Psychologically, people tend to resist change. Community viewpoints about the nature and function of education are often fixed and unyielding. These opinions are oftentimes a major force in maintaining traditional programs and traditional methods of teaching in the schools.

Despite tradition, society is constantly changing. One can expect the school to change as new forces are felt in the community. For example, in 1961, it was re-

---

[4] Ronald Doll, *Curriculum Improvement: Decision Making and Process,* 2nd Ed. (Boston: Allyn & Bacon, Inc., 1970), Chap. 3.

ported in the National Society for the Study of Education's Sixtieth Yearbook[5] that about 20 per cent of Americans were moving every year. Five per cent moved from one county to another, and not more than 15 to 20 per cent spent their entire lives in the same county. There has been a marked movement from Puerto Rico to the larger cities of the United States, so much so, that schools have been pressured into introducing bilingual education in the early grades and into employing bilingual teachers at all levels. Doll has identified three changes in American society that deserve mention as having significant impact on the schools:

1. Production and communication of knowledge.
2. Shift from political and social passivity to intense feeling about political and social concerns.
3. Rapid social movements which include integration of the races, population mobility, and movement of people from lower socio-economic to higher socio-economic status.[6]

With respect to knowledge per se, it is evident that the storage, retrieval, and communication of knowledge is becoming a major industry, one that promises to materially shape the future of the American school.

In the sixties, and continuing into the seventies, Americans, young and old, began to have intense feelings about social and political concerns, and the number of individuals who became actively involved in social issues grew dramatically in the sixties. This phenomenon creates pressure on the school for education in what psychologists call the *affective domain* of learning. As a result of this active involvement and concern on public questions, it became more important than ever before to emphasize education that focuses on feelings and emotion. We have already mentioned some facts about population mobility. Continued movement of people toward cities, and the countermovement to the suburbs; social distance between new and old residents; and the problem of communication between the "new" and "old" culture—often within the radius of a few city blocks—all contribute to accelerating the changes in school goals and programs.

Value patterns and, more specifically, value conflicts, affect the nature and program of the school. The degree of social control the community has over the individual and business, the "new morality," and the effects of the mass media are but three areas to which the school is particularly sensitive. Organizations representing big business and big labor, and groups concerned with religious, social, and family patterns and mores, are deeply interested in what is taught in school and how it is taught. These groups and organizations often provide instructional materials—films, books, pamphlets—as well as speakers to explain to students their particular viewpoints.

Because of their interest in having their value system and orientation reflected in the school curriculum, there is almost always pressure to introduce new subjects and to change the content of existing courses. Moreover, in recent years, the federal government provided large-scale funding for limited and specific curriculum

---

[5] Nelson B. Henry, ed., *Social Forces Influencing American Education,* The Sixtieth Yearbook of the National Society for the Study of Education, Part II (Chicago: University of Chicago Press, 1961).

[6] Doll, op. cit., pp. 70–71.

projects in science, mathematics, and social studies. These projects, which were conducted under the auspices of various universities, were generally designed to develop new content and new teaching method for both elementary and high school levels. Many of the federally funded projects involved the energies and the attention of scholars in the disciplines. Mathematicians, physicists, biologists, historians, sociologists, and economists were invited to examine the content of their respective disciplines and to give consultant advice on how, and to what extent, concepts from their discipline might be introduced into the public school curriculum.

Influences within the local community are likely to be the immediate and visible locus for making decisions about the school. Nearly all school controversies are a result of conflicts within the immediate community. The conflicts are often exacerbated by state and/or federal government policies. Community groups are particularly sensitive to issues in areas such as sex education, religion, driver training, Darwinian theory, student dress, athletics, and school busing.

Aims and Purposes Related to Community

The general aims, purposes, and objectives of American public education have always reflected the interests and needs of the general community, and when the aims and programs were changed or modified, it was because of community demand. In Colonial times, the overriding aim of education at all levels was to enable students to read and understand the Bible, to gain salvation, and to spread the Gospel. The Massachusetts law of 1642 encouraged education so that all may "read and understand the principles of religion and the capital laws of the country."[7]

During the nineteenth century and the early twentieth century, in addition to the religious motive, American schools were directed toward developing a common language, instilling patriotism and sense of unity, and providing technical and agricultural training. With the development of secondary schools, efforts were made primarily by committees of the National Education Association (NEA) to establish more precisely the goals of secondary education. Lists of objectives were prepared by NEA and other groups in 1918, 1920, 1937, 1938, and 1952. The 1938 statement of objectives by the Educational Policies Commission of the National Education Association, summarized in *Purposes of Education in American Democracy,* best illustrates the influences and aspirations of the American Community with respect to education.[8]

The Objectives of Self-realization

The Inquiring Mind. The educated person has an appetite for learning.
Speech. The educated person can speak the mother tongue clearly.
Reading. The educated person reads the mother tongue efficiently.
Writing. The educated person writes the mother tongue effectively.
Number. The educated person solves problems of counting and calculating.
Sight and Hearing. The educated person is skilled in listening and observing.

[7] James A. Johnson, et al., *Introduction to Foundations of Education* (Boston: Allyn & Bacon, Inc., 1973), pp. 294–295.
[8] Ibid., pp. 297–298.

Health and Knowledge. The educated person understands the basic facts concerning health and disease.

Health Habits. The educated person protects his own health and that of his dependents.

Public Health. The educated person works to improve the health of the community.

Recreation. The educated person is participant and spectator in many sports and other pastimes.

Intellectual Interests. The educated person has mental resources for the use of leisure.

Esthetic Interests. The educated person appreciates beauty.

Character. The educated person gives responsible direction to his own life.

The Objectives of Human Relationships

Respect for Humanity. The educated person puts human relationships first.

Friendships. The educated person enjoys the rich, sincere, and varied social life.

Cooperation. The educated person can work and play with others.

Courtesy. The educated person observes the amenities of social behavior.

Appreciation of the Home. The educated person appreciates the family as a social institution.

Conservation of the Home. The educated person conserves family ideals.

Homemaking. The educated person is skilled in homemaking.

Democracy in the Home. The educated person maintains democratic family relations.

The Objectives of Economic Efficiency

Work. The educated producer knows the satisfaction of good workmanship.

Occupational Information. The educated producer understands the requirement and opportunities for various jobs.

Occupational Choice. The educated person has selected his occupation.

Occupational Efficiency. The educated producer succeeds in his chosen vocation.

Occupational Adjustment. The educated producer maintains and improves his own efficiency.

Occupational Appreciation. The educated producer appreciates the social value of his work.

Personal Economics. The educated consumer plans the economics of his own life.

Consumer Judgment. The educated consumer develops standards for guiding his expenditures.

Efficiency in Buying. The educated consumer is an informed and skillful buyer.

Consumer Protection. The educated consumer takes appropriate measures to safeguard his interests.

The Objectives of Civil Responsibility

Social Justice. The educated citizen is sensitive to the disparities of human circumstance.

Social Activity. The educated citizen acts to correct unsatisfactory conditions.

Social Understanding. The educated citizen seeks to understand social structure and processes.

Critical Judgment. The educated citizen has defenses against propaganda.

Tolerance. The educated citizen respects honest differences of opinion.

Conservation. The educated citizen has a regard for the nation's resources.

Social Application of Science. The educated citizen measures scientific advance by its contribution to the general welfare.

World Citizenship. The educated citizen is a cooperating member of the world community.

Law Observance. The educated citizen respects the law.

Economic Literacy. The educated citizen is economically literate.

Political Citizenship. The educated citizen acts upon an unswerving loyalty to democratic ideals.[9]

Under the heading "Major Functions of Schools and Constraints on Students" William G. Spady concludes that, as a general principle, in nearly all Western societies schools are expected to play a major role in preparing the young to assume adult roles and responsibilities.[10] If this conclusion is correct, then schools have two general functions:

1. Instruction: Engagement in activities that increase the information base; cognitive skills, such as literary, computational, and conceptual; physical skills, such as manual abilities.
2. Socialization: Developing in the child the expectations, attitudes, values, and beliefs that enable him to interact compatibly with others in his society, and to utilize his cognitive and physical skills in effective (socially approved) ways.

Emil Durkheim argues that socialization is the most important function of the public school in any "modern society."[11] To a beginning student of education, or, for that matter, an advanced student, three other functions of schools, as set forth in the National Society for the Study of Education's Seventy-Third Yearbook, may be of interest. In addition to instruction and socialization, school systems typically perform at least three other functions:

1. Custody: Through compulsory education laws, schools have custody of children for a specified period of time.
2. Certification: Schools certify the completion of an instructional program and acquisition of certain competencies through the issuance of a diploma.
3. Selection: Schools, through establishing a course of standards and programs of study for different types of students, operate a selection system that separates young people into distinguishable groups.

One of the more critical problems in today's school system is the problem of discipline. Those who work in professional education recognize that functions relating to custody control, certification, and selection have a direct bearing on student unrest, and might be a beginning point in the examination of discipline policies.

Community Investment in Education

The public school is one of the major social institutions of the community, and one in which the entire community has a large economic and social investment.

[9] Ibid., pp. 297–298.

[10] C. Wayne Gordon, ed., *Uses of the Sociology of Education,* Seventy-Third Yearbook of The National Society for the Study of Education, Part II (Chicago: University of Chicago Press, 1974), Chap. 3.

[11] Emil Durkheim, *Moral Education: A Study in the Theory of the Sociology of Education* (New York: The Free Press, 1961).

The taxpayers, parents, businessmen, and various institutions, such as churches, businesses, and public and private agencies, are deeply concerned with the nature and functioning of the public schools.

Economic Investment. Education is nearly always the single largest expenditure in the community's budget. It is not unusual to find 50 to 70 per cent of local tax revenues being spent on public education. In states that give major state support to local education, school systems receive 50 to 80 per cent of their budget for instruction from the state. With these economic facts in mind, one must expect the community as a whole to take an active role in the community's educational system. A recent U.S. Office of Education study[12] points up in a dramatic fashion the economic investment of the nation in education at all levels:

Education may now be considered the nation's largest enterprise in terms of the number of people involved and the number of dollars expended . . . The number of students, teachers, and administrators combined now totals more than 62 million . . . In a country of 210 million people with expenditures for education during the 1973–74 school year expected to total an all time high of about $96.7 billion, education will be the principal occupation of 30% of the population. The total expenditures for education (for 1973–74) are expected to approach 8% of the Gross National Product.

This economic investment is a result of the public's belief that the state should establish and maintain a broad system of educational opportunities for its citizens, and that children through the age of sixteen must be educated. Nearly all fifty states have compulsory education laws. Most of the laws were adopted before 1900. Most states require students to attend school through the age of sixteen. The public, for a number of reasons, is now questioning the efficiency of compulsory school attendance above the age of fourteen. The opinion of the National Commission on the Reform of Secondary Education, as advanced by B. Frank Brown, Chairman,[13] suggests that the nation does not need laws that force adolescents to go to school. Brown says "it needs schools and school-related programs that make adolescents wish to come, and if the high school is to escape its outmoded role as a custodial institution, the states must no longer try to force adolescents to attend." It is difficult to assess how much of the current criticism, and the examination of compulsory attendance above the age of fourteen, is related to the tremendous costs of maintaining a compulsory system through the secondary school. It is certain, however, that while the public continues to participate in supporting the schools economically, the nature, value, and results of schools will receive even closer scrutiny.

Social Investment. The community is committed by public policy, often expressed in the state's Constitution, to maintain a school system. R. Freeman Butts, in an article in *The Nation* entitled "Assault on a Great Idea,"[14] succinctly and eloquently phrased the social investment that Americans have in their schools.

A public school serves a public purpose rather than a private one. It is not maintained for the personal advantage or private gain of the teacher, the proprietor, or the

---

[12] "Washington Report," *Phi Delta Kappan*, **44**:280–81, December 1973.
[13] Ibid., p. 229.
[14] *The Nation*, April 30, 1973. Reprinted in *Phi Delta Kappan* **45**:240 (Dec. 1973).

board of managers; nor does it exist simply for the enjoyment and happiness, or advancement of the individual student or his parents. It may, indeed it should, enhance the vocational competence, or upward social mobility or personal development of individuals, but if that were all a school attempted, the job could be done as well by a private school catering to particular jobs, or careers, or leisure time enjoyment . . .

Rather the prime purpose of the public school is to serve the general welfare of a democratic society, by assuring that the knowledge and understanding necessary to exercise the responsibilities are not only made available but actively inculcated. Achieving a sense of community is the essential purpose of public education. This work cannot be left to the vagaries of individual parents, or small groups of like minded parents, or particular interest groups, or religious sects, or private enterprisers or cultural specialists . . .

Butts goes on to point out that the convergence and mutual reinforcement of so many forces—political, social, economic, racial, religious, and intellectual—makes the search for "alternatives" to public schools beguiling, but Americans should not lose sight of the fact that the public school as a social institution has been a basic component of democratic American society.[15]

Furthermore the community has an economic and social investment in the public school. It is involved economically because of its contribution of a significant portion of its tax dollars to support the system. It is also involved because it has implicitly, if not explicitly, defined the educational goals and programs that it expects will help its citizens achieve a sense of community and guide its children into the type of adulthood specified by the parameters of American society.

The School and Other Social Institutions

In this section, we shall examine the school in relation to other social institutions in the community. Three primary social agencies in the community have educational responsibilities—the school, the church, and the family. Unfortunately, there is no rule-of-thumb, no precise way to delineate the educational responsibilities of each of these institutions.

The School and the Church. Historically, in Western Europe the church was the responsible agency for transmitting the cultural heritage and inculcating moral and spiritual values. Instruction was in Latin. Consequently it established schools at churches and monasteries. Education in the church school focused on the training of priests to carry on the teachings of the church. Similarly the American public school in its earliest inception had a distinctly unique sectarian purpose. The sole purpose of the elementary school in the Colonial period (1600–1750) predating the Constitution was to enable the child to read the Bible and to "Know the will of the Heavenly Father." The earliest secondary schools were established to insure a supply of learned ministers. E. H. Bolmeier,[16] in an article entitled "Legality and Propriety of Religious Instruction in the Public Schools," points

---

[15] Ibid.

[16] E. H. Bolmeier, "Legality and Propriety of Religious Instruction in the Public Schools," in William H. Lucio, Ed., *Readings in American Education* (Glenview, Ill.: Scott, Foresman and Company, 1963), pp. 204–205.

out that the unity of the religious purpose in the early Colonial school was natural and feasible. This community, which resembled a "religious republic," represented a single religious faith. Consequently, there was no conflict about the nature of instruction to be provided, nor was there any overlapping between the school and the church—one being the natural complement of the other. As communities became more heterogeneous in religious outlook, legislation was enacted to provide for freedom of religious worship. Gradually the emphasis in the schools shifted away from teaching religious thought and turned toward meeting the economic and social needs of the community. This change in the character of the school, which took place over a period of one hundred years, is known as the *secularization of the American schools.*

Nearly every state Constitution now contains provisions for separation of church and state. The majority of the state constitutional provisions prohibit use of state funds for sectarian purposes, and many others prohibit religious instruction in the school. For the purpose of preserving freedom of religious worship while providing compulsory schooling for all the children, the people, through constitutional and statutory means, have attempted to define the limitations on religious activities in public school programs. A review of interpretations of state courts and the United States Supreme Court pertaining to religious activities and influences in the public school show that any instruction or related activity in the public school that involves sectarian influences is illegal. The principle is that any activity that aids one or more religious sects, or that prefers one religious doctrine to another, is illegal.

It does not require much imagination to think of community situations in which these two major social institutions, the church and the school, might oppose each other in their zeal for educating the children and youth. Whether or not conflict develops and, how it is resolved if it does, depends very much on the nature of the community and its leaders. A community with one large denomination, Catholic, Protestant, or Jewish, may have fewer conflicts than a community with more evenly balanced denominations. In some communities with a diversity of religious perspectives, efforts are made to define church activities vis-à-vis school activities through church-school coordinating councils. Although it has been clearly established that the public school must be secular, and that as a secular institution it has a legitimate educational function and service to perform, a number of groups within the general population continue to criticize the public school as a "Godless" institution. Many people still believe that secular education that is completely divorced from the church is not the most desirable education for their children. As a consequence, major denominations support and maintain a system of private education in which teaching in secular subjects and religious subjects are conducted in the name of the Church. In large cities, it is not unusual to find 30 to 50 per cent of the children receiving all their education through religious schools. These church schools are supported by parents (who, incidentally, also pay taxes to support public schools) by other church members, and by church officials, some of whom contribute their teaching services without charge to the church school.

There are some individuals who prefer public schools but who insist that not only is it legal and proper for the public school to teach about religion, but that it can be done without injection of sectarianism or indoctrination of specific religious beliefs. However, most schools offer a moral- and spiritual-values course that includes such elements as development of human personality, moral responsibility, devotion to truth, and respect for excellence and brotherhood.

The Educational Policies Commission, in its publication *Moral and Spiritual Values in the Public Schools,*[17] summarized the values of American society in the realm of moral and spiritual ideals. The Commission was an official body of the National Education Association, and the statement represents an official position of the organized teaching profession, that is, members of the National Education Association. To use the language of the report, this statement was prepared "To help clarify the moral and spiritual values upon which the American people as a whole have agreed to manage their individual lives and their corporate activities including their public school." The reader will note that many of these values find political expression in the Constitution and Bill of Rights, and can also be identified in the creeds of major religious groups. The Commission defined ten basic values:

1. *Human Personality: The Basic Value.* This value is fundamental to all that follow. The basic moral and spiritual value in American life is the supreme importance of the individual personality. In educational terms, this value requires a school system which, by making freely available the common heritage of human associations and human culture, opens to every child the opportunity to grow to his full physical, intellectual, moral, and spiritual nature.

2. *Moral Responsibility.* If the individual personality is supreme, each person should feel responsible for the consequences of his own conduct. Moral responsibility and self-discipline are marks of maturity. Good schools will help children to grow up by providing a judicious balance between protective authority, on the one hand, and delegation of responsibility on the other hand. Toward the end of adolescence, the individual should have acquired a large measure of self-reliance tempered by social conscience.

3. *Institutions As the Servants of Man.* If the individual personality is supreme, and institutions are the servants of the people, domestic, cultural, and political institutions are not in themselves suitable objects of veneration except insofar as they contribute to the moral and spiritual values of human life. One of the major functions of education is to encourage a continuing appraisal of the suitability of existing institutions to the current and prospective needs of the people.

4. *Common Consent.* If the individual personality is supreme, mutual consent is better than violence. Voluntary cooperation, contrary to the idea of survival of the fittest, is essential to all forms of life. This element of the American system of values calls for an educational program which gives many opportunities for friendly cooperation.

5. *Devotion to Truth.* If the individual personality is supreme, the human mind should be liberated by access to information and opinion. In terms of human history, the rights of man to speak his mind, to worship according to conscience and training, and to have access to knowledge and divergent opinions are recent achievements. Intellectual freedom is to be prized. The public schools should provide young people with experiences in the

---

[17] Educational Policies Commission, *Moral and Spiritual Values in the Public Schools* (Washington, D.C.: National Education Association, 1951).

processes of seeking truth, of comparing opinions, and of appealing to reason on controverted questions.

6. *Respect for Excellence.* If the individual personality is supreme, excellence in mind, character, and creative ability should be fostered. Every man is entitled to equal rights before the Civil law; every man should be governed equally by moral standards. Our society, more than any other, should prize every kind of genuine worth. In terms of education, this value means a careful inventory of all the useful abilities of all young people, and the stimulation and recognition of achievement of excellence in every sphere of life.

7. *Moral Equality.* If the individual personality is supreme, all persons should be judged by the same moral standards. There is no more clearly defined element in the American system of values than the profound conviction that no man has a moral and inborn right to injure, persecute, dominate, or exploit others. In terms of the school, a spirit should be developed which is keenly resentful of all injustice, ruthlessness, special privilege, denial of opportunity, persecution, and servility.

8. *Brotherhood.* If the individual personality is supreme, the concept of brotherhood should take precedence over selfish interest. The public school should be regarded as an agency for increasing the learner's usefulness to the entire society, as well as a road for individual success. Such a school will be consistent in fostering participation in a variety of humane and constructive activities and at the same time applaud and encourage every effort to achieve self-reliance and self-respect.

9. *Pursuit of Happiness.* If the individual personality is supreme, each person should have the greatest possible opportunity for the pursuit of happiness, provided only that such activities do not substantially interfere with similar opportunities of others. Lasting happiness is not merely excitement and material comforts. It is derived largely from deep personal resources and from the affection and respect of others. The school, therefore, should give a large place to those type of activities that satisfy spiritual needs and inspire the noblest achievement.

10. *Spiritual Enrichment.* If the individual personality is supreme, each person should be offered the emotional and spiritual experiences which transcend the materialistic aspects of life. Moral values have consequences chiefly in social relationships. Spiritual values, however, take effect mainly in terms of inner emotions and sentiments. The entire outlook of many people is deeply affected by these spiritual feelings. A good school will extend full recognition of the arts as a means for expressing and evoking the inner life of the spirit.[18]

These basic moral and spiritual values represent goal statements and guidelines for developing educational programs and appropriate teaching methods. In spite of continuing protests about the "secular" American school, it is obvious from the Commission's report that the organized teaching profession supports the integration of moral and spiritual values into all aspects of the school's curriculum, and that the American school has a significant role to play in assisting children and youth to

[18] Ibid.

develop an appropriate value system for living in the United States of America. It is equally clear that both the public school and the church have educational functions and services to render to the community. The degree to which these services and functions are clearly defined, understood, and mutually accepted will in large measures determine the quality of educational services rendered by church and school.

The School, the Family, and Neighborhood. It is more difficult to define how the family's responsibilities for educating the children and youth relate to the school than it is to define the church's responsibilities. The Constitution, statutes, and court decisions have been instrumental in defining educational relationships between the church and the school. The family is responsible by law to have its children educated. For this purpose, each State through its local school districts provides a public school. The family, however, may send its children to private school or have its children tutored or educated by any other means acceptable to state authorities. The fact is that most children in the United States are educated in a formal school, either private or public, through elementary, junior, and senior high school, or through the age of sixteen.

THE FAMILY. The family is a universal institution in society. It varies in specific form and function from one society to another, and even from one group to another in the same society, but it exists in some variation everywhere and among all people. It is generally accepted that the family is the most important conditioner of the child's personality. Most children learn the conventional practices and standards of American life in the home. The young infant is nurtured in the home. Development of muscular and motor skills, and patterns for the foundations of interests, values, and attitudes are fairly well fixed before the child enters school. It is generally believed that the child's basic personality is formed in the home and neighborhood environment. The family is, as Hilda Taba has described it, the "nexus" in the shaping of personality and character, and the most potent influence in inducting young people into the culture.[19] Both the Church and the school, as the major social agencies concerned with the education of children and youth, must have a broad appreciation of the impact of the home and neighborhood on the personality development and its implication for school aims and programs.

Before World War II, the model American family might have been characterized as two parents; two to four children; one or two sets of grandparents. The family lived in a single-family dwelling and the grandparents lived nearby. Each day, the father went to work; the mother remained at home to take care of the house and to be there when children arrived from school. In this model, the family usually had their meals together and spent much time in common activities. It was in this stable, homogeneous environment that values and attitudes, and ways of thinking and knowing were passed on from one generation to another. The school's function was relatively simple in that it concentrated on the development of cognitive skills and understandings. In permanent communities with stable populations, this old-fashioned family was able to transmit principles, rules of conduct, and standards that were re-enforced by the extended family and the community school.

[19] Hilda Taba, "Changes in Family Life and the High School Program," in William H. Lucio, Ed., *Readings in American Education,* p. 225. Originally *High School Journal* **42**:302–306, May 1959.

Changes in family patterns and family life styles in the past twenty-five years have diminished the family's educational influence and have brought new responsibilities to the schools. Hilda Taba has pointed out that the urbanization of the family and increasing mobility are two critical factors that necessitate a re-examination of the school curriculum.[20] Urbanization results in family members being separated in work and leisure. Often, both the husband and wife work. Leisure is so planned that children are involved in organized community recreation leagues and their parents engage in their own leisure and business activities. Taba comments that "this leaves family unity dependent on somewhat fragile ties of affection and personal relations both pursued in a fairly limited interpersonal contact." Children from such homes find that they spend much of their time anonymously, not known by any adult—except of course the adults that they came in contact with at school. This change in family life style is of much significance to the school, if only because it compels teachers to concentrate more on the total needs of the student rather than solely on intellectual development. Increasing mobility is another factor. It is said that in California seven out of ten families change houses every year. Mobility dissolves the extended family structure, that is, grandparents and older aunts and uncles no longer live in the same neighborhood. Friendships are disrupted, and after so many moves both children and adults find that they have formed no lasting friendships, only acquaintances. In the words of Taba, "the urban mobile family pattern creates a social distance between generations and therefore weakens the capacity of the family to transmit values, codes of behavior, and attitudes." To these two factors must be added the confusion or conflict in the roles of family members. The role of the wife as homemaker and the responsibility of the husband as the sole family support are typical of the kind of questions being debated within modern families.

This brief review of the changing nature of the family suggests that the family's power to provide appropriate value education and the socializing of its children is diminishing. In recent years, the American school has faced this problem by introducing courses on family, family relations, and sex education, and by emphasizing the basic values in our culture through the study of art, music, and literature.

The Neighborhood. With family life in transition, neighborhood influences play an important educational role. A homogeneous neighborhood, one in which most families have similar customs, values, and behaviors, tends to re-enforce the value patterns of individual families. A school in such a neighborhood reflects and re-enforces the educational influences of the family and the community. On the other hand, in a heterogeneous neighborhood with a diversity of patterns and/or disorganized family life, the school must exert extra efforts to meet the educational needs of the student.

Sociologists sometimes refer to the home and neighborhood as the primary group for influencing the mental, emotional, and physical growth of the individual. Some interesting studies of these influences show that:

a lower class environment, in general, favors "more gratification and easier outlet for children's organically based drives"—rage expressions, aggressive behavior and sex expressions. The middle-class neighborhood mores restrict physical aggressions to patterned forms, either rule-controlled contests or subtleties of posture or gesture. . . .

[20] Ibid., pp. 226–227.

Among the upper class "good form" in manners, taste, and accomplishments outweigh overtly expressed competitive ambitions.[21]

There is little doubt that class status as determined by the home and the neighborhood is a potent, significant force in the education of American young people. Perhaps because it originates within the primary group, class status may be a more powerful educative influence than the school.

Cox and Mercer, commenting on family and neighborhood, observed

that irregular employment in a slum area makes hunger, cold and sickness experiences to be dreaded and compensated for. Hence the neighborhood tolerates acts and attitudes that shook the prudent and responsible bourgeoisie. Children running loose, violence and disorder in the crowded home, narrow loyalties to leaders and institutions, all these complicated and inconsistent phenomena have survival values within some neighborhood frames of reference. Many questions that are matters for individual decision in the middle class neighborhood are economically resolved among the poor. For example, a woman's place is more likely to be where she can help with the family budget. Children more frequently care for themselves. The sacredness of private property is little esteemed among the propertyless. Law enforcement officers are often resented as representative of middle class standards."[22]

If the school is to function effectively in the context of family and neighborhood, it is apparent that teacher and administrator must be thoroughly knowledgeable and sensitive to family structures and values and to the value patterns of the neighborhood. These values are always reflected in the school, visibly demonstrated by student behavior patterns and general school climate. Community values are brought to the attention of school administrators by neighborhood meetings, and sometimes through public confrontations with parent groups. Schools are social agencies, organized and maintained by the public to serve social needs. It is imperative therefore that professional teachers have a clear sense of the social needs and that teachers give adequate relevant responses to the community's values and educational aspirations.

The School and Politics. An analysis of community values as expressed in family structures and neighborhood influences provides insight into political, ethnic, and parental forces that influence the school. Schools are governed by local school boards whose members are usually elected by the voters in the community served by the school. Large cities sometimes have appointed school board members. In either case, school board membership is generally considered to be a prestigious civic responsibility; and it is often the means by which an individual enters into politics. From a post on the school board, an ambitious politician may seek the office of mayor, state assemblyman or senator. Because schools are administered under state laws, the school board member is, in one sense, an agent of the state, and it is his responsibility to enforce the state statutes. The board member

[21] Allison Davis and Robert J. Havighurst, *Father of the Man* (Boston: Houghton Mifflin Company, 1947), pp. 17–29, in William H. Lucio, Ed., op. cit., p. 223.
[22] Philip L. Cox and Blaine Mercer, *Education in Democracy* (New York: McGraw-Hill Book Company, 1961), pp. 62–63, also in William H. Lucio, Ed., op. cit., pp. 223–224.

is also the voice of the local community; it is his function to insure that the school serves the community well.

State laws generally establish minimum standards for teacher certification, salaries, pensions, and other benefits. Most states require communities to establish and support a "thorough and efficient" school system, and prescribe general instructional areas that are to be made available in the schools. School boards usually have the authority to establish higher standards than those mandated by the state, may introduce additional courses of study as requested by the community, and may of course pay higher salaries than state minimums, provided the local community is willing to support a higher quality school system than that required by the state. It has been said that the only direct voice that a taxpayer has on his taxes is a vote on the school budget, and/or a vote for school board candidates. No one enjoys paying taxes. Consequently, when school budgets are voted down, or when school board candidates are defeated, it is usually difficult to say whether the community opposes quality education or is simply protesting payment of taxes. Board members who successfully unite community forces in support of quality schools not only make a significant contribution to the local community but also capitalize on their achievements to secure political office at other levels. Schools are so important to the community that community groups will support board members for other political office if indeed they are satisfied with the school system.

Ethnic and parental groups are among the more visible groups that have a direct interest in school programs and their outcomes. Parents are organized in local school councils known as Parent-Teacher Associations (PTA) or Parent-Teachers Organizations (PTO). Through this means, parents learn a great deal about what happens in the school, come to appreciate and support school programs, and also make their wishes known with respect to improvements in the school. In many communities, the PTA or the PTO is the most direct link between the school and community and is often the means through which parent volunteers materially assist professional school personnel in the school program. In recent years, ethnic and minority groups have insisted that the schools be much more sensitive and responsive to their special needs. School officials have organized community councils, citizen advisory committees, and community leader boards as a means of encouraging an input of ideas, and feedback on the schools from the community. These councils represent community leaders who are not only interested in the school programs; they have a broader interest—that of improving the quality of life in the city. These groups look to the school to be a major force in improving the quality of life in the city.

So far, we have examined the school as a major social agency, and in its relation to the church, to the family, and to the general neighborhood. The school is an agency supported by tax dollars to serve the particular needs of the community; and its programs and teaching methods are shaped by the community's values as expressed through the church, the family, and other community institutions. Forces in the larger community and pressures in the local community shape what is taught in the school. And, at the center of these various pressures is the classroom teacher. Daily, for 180 days, the teacher sees students in order to provide instruction according to the goals and objectives of the school. It is therefore important that teachers understand the nature of the community, its values and aspirations, and how the teacher can relate most effectively to the community.

The Teacher and the Community

From the community viewpoint, the teacher is the most important person in the school system. Parents expect much from the teachers of their children. In the elementary years, the teacher is responsible for teaching the basic skills of reading, writing, and arithmetic, and for providing formal instruction in the various subject areas. Parents expect their children to be successful in school and when they are not, more often than not, the teacher and the school are criticized. The school, in many homes, is a prime topic of conversation and a factor in many family decisions. Parents expect high school teachers and counselors to assist their teenagers in making decisions about what courses to take, what jobs to aspire to, and what schools to attend after high school. The teacher is viewed as having the same authority over the child as the parent, during the time that the child is in school or is on the way to or from school. The legal term *in loco parentis* describes this relationship in which the teacher is indeed the "parent" in the classroom. Although it is established by law that the school does exercise some parental authority, this concept provides the basis for potential conflict between the community and the school. Some of the most controversial school issues at the local community level revolve around the school's authority versus the authority of the parent. The changing nature of the community, from homogeneous to heterogeneous, the shift in family values, that is, the question of family roles, and the law—now operable in many states—that gives the child adult status at age 18, are but some of the factors that complicate and obfuscate the relationship between the teacher and the community.

Historically, the teacher, like the preacher, was the best-educated person in the community. He or she was a person of moral virtue, skilled in the communication arts, and dedicated to serving one's fellow human beings without thought of recompense. Teachers who taught in the secondary schools in the early 1900s were often persons who were interested in law or medicine, and who chose to use their knowledge and talents to teach biology, history, political science, and other subjects as a means of financing their legal or medical education. (There are currently many lawyers, doctors, and men and women in important private and public positions who have had a stint of public school teaching.) As a consequence of this historical pattern, several attitudes are obvious. The teacher is expected to be a person of some intellectual and cultural attainments, one who exhibits and practices moral principles that are a cut above the prevailing practices in the community. Because teachers usually have a nine- or ten-month contract, and because many people have the notion that teaching is a stepping stone to a career in business, industry, or government, in the eyes of the community the teacher is considered a part-time employee. Teacher organizations in the past twenty-five years have made much progress in advancing the concept that teaching is a full-time profession, comparable to law, medicine, and science, but old notions die slowly. The fact is that many persons in other professions have achieved their goal by using teaching as a stepping stone, and that more than a few teachers view their occupation as a part-time job to supplement the family income. Regardless of the ethics of this attitude, the attitudinal patterns suggest some real problems when the teacher is expected to be the "parent" in the classroom.

Sometimes, depending upon the nature of the community, the teacher is viewed as a hired hand or as a political appointee. The hired-hand concept is inimical to the view that teaching is a profession. According to this concept, the employee performs services as directed by the manager or the boss, according to a specific job description. Not much is expected from the employee with respect to innovation and change, planning, evaluating, analyzing—activities usually associated with managerial or professional functions. It is understood that the teacher works for the community and for the parent, and is given specific direction on what is to be taught and how it is to be taught. During the probationary period, and even after tenure is awarded (awarding of tenure prevents arbitrary dismissal) the hired-hand concept not only determines how the teacher relates to the community, but it is fundamental to defining the nature of service rendered by the teacher.

The notion that teaching is a political job stems partly from the idea that the school is a community institution that renders a social service to the community, and that the teacher is a community employee. According to this view, the teacher, like the policeman and fireman, holds a job supported by community tax dollars and therefore is subject to the employment and personnel policies and practices as established through local political processes. Teachers, as well as police and firemen, have in recent years established significant job rights through Civil Service Codes and Union Contracts. However, where the community attitude is that jobs supported from tax funds are subject to the political process, this significantly affects how the teacher relates to the community, and what the community expects of the teacher.

The requirement that teachers live in the community in which they are employed is one of its more publicized expectations. It may be argued that a teacher will make a richer contribution to the school by living in the community. This argument has much to recommend it, especially if the community is desperately short of talented community leaders. The quality of community life as reflected in its schools, churches, service organizations, and governmental services is very much dependent upon good leadership. In this sense the teacher, by becoming actively involved, can make a substantial contribution toward maintaining and improving the community. A teacher involved in the Little League, Scouting, and working with Garden, Rotary, and Business and Professional Women Clubs will undoubtedly be sensitive to community leaders' aspirations for the community and the school system, more so than a teacher who is uninvolved and who chooses to live outside the local community.

Living in the community may be more important if the teacher is not a native of the town or the area in which he or she is employed. In many small communities, the teacher who was not educated and reared in the neighborhood is viewed as a stranger, an outsider who must be looked at very carefully before being accepted into the general community life. To live in the community and to be involved in community processes is certainly one way to hasten community acceptance, and to convince the community that you should be teaching their children. In large metropolitan areas, the notion of requiring teachers to live in the community is still alive, but in many cases the state courts have declared such a requirement illegal. Because the school is a state institution, one is likely to find that states are more concerned about whether their employees are residents of the state than whether they reside in a particular community.

The view that teaching is a political job is anathema to many who support the concept of teaching as one of the professions. It is understandable that financially hard-pressed citizens like to see their tax dollars paid to public service employees who live in, and spend their money in, the community; and who will, in addition, render other services to the community. In heavily populated metropolitan areas, where community lines are blurred insofar as services and functions are concerned, the arguments for requiring teachers to live in the community are somewhat specious. A teaching job should not be political in the sense that it is subject to the vagaries of elective politics, but there are some who believe that teachers who are either born and reared in the neighborhood, or who have some traditional social connections (through parents, grandparents, and so on) should have first preference for jobs. A good argument for this policy is that the teacher relationship to child and to parent is a personal and social relationship, one that transcends the mere imparting of knowledge to students. It is important to parents and to the community that the teachers to be employed are those in whom they can put their faith and confidence.

So far, we have described some community views on the status of the teacher in the social order. These attitudes exist to some degree in all communities, and they influence the extent to which teachers use community resources in their teaching. Educational theory and practice support and encourage instructional activities that involve community leaders and resources within the area. It is common practice in many schools to invite community leaders, for example, agency heads, to speak to classes and to assembly groups on subjects that are relevant to the students' studies. Service organizations and public-oriented groups, such as the League of Women Voters and the Urban League, provide the school with speakers and materials, written and visual, on their particular fields of interest. Parent-teacher organizations are organized to provide direct and continuous interaction between teachers and community leaders. Most communities expect to interact with the school in some way beyond the formal legal mechanism of the school board. Teachers with insight about the many, and multifaceted, relationships of the school and the community will not only strengthen their classroom teaching but will guarantee community acceptance of themselves as respected professionals, and will probably receive a full measure of social and economic support for their school.

SUGGESTED READING

American Association of School Administrators. *Educational Administration in a Changing Community*. Thirty-Seventh Yearbook. Washington, D.C.: The Association, 1959.

Association for Supervision and Curriculum Development. *Forces Affecting American Education*. Washington, D.C.: The Association, 1953.

Fantini, Mario, Marilyn Gittell, and Richard Magat. *Community Control and the Urban School*. New York: Praeger Publishers, 1970.

Gordon, C. Wayne, Ed. *Uses of the Sociology of Education*. The Seventy-Third Yearbook of the National Society for the Study of Education, Part II. Chicago: University of Chicago Press, 1974.

Havighurst, Robert J., Ed. *Metropolitanism: Its Challenge to Education*. The Sixty-

Seventh Yearbook of the National Society for the Study of Education, Part I. Chicago: University of Chicago Press, 1968.

Henry, Nelson B., Ed. *Social Forces Influencing American Education.* The Sixtieth Yearbook of the National Society for the Study of Education, Part II. Chicago: University of Chicago Press, 1961.

Katzman, Martin T. *The Political Economy of Urban Schools.* Cambridge, Mass.: Harvard University Press, 1971.

Levin, Henry M., Ed. *Community Control of Schools.* Washington, D.C.: Brookings Institution, 1970.

Lutz, Frank W., Ed. *Toward Improved Urban Education.* Worthington, Ohio: Charles A. Jones Publishing Co., 1970.

Pounds, Ralph L., and James R. Bryner. *The School in American Society,* 3rd Ed. New York: Macmillan Publishing Co., Inc., 1973.

Yeager, William A. *School-Community Relations* New York: Holt, Rinehart & Winston, Inc., 1951, Chaps. 1–6.

POST TEST

MULTIPLE CHOICE   *Circle the correct letter in each of the following:*

1. Which one of the following best describes a model *Gesellschaft* type society?
   a. A community with well-defined physical boundaries, economic, self-sufficiency, a homogeneous population with common heritage and beliefs.
   b. A community in which there is a high interdependence with other communities even for basic necessities, and the inhabitants are not generally acquainted with each other.
   c. A community with well-defined cultural boundaries, economically specialized, and with a homogeneous population.
   d. A society that is characterized by a rural, middle class set of values and well-defined historical traditions.

2. Which one of the following best describes the nature of a school in a model *Gemeinschaft* society?
   a. The school's objectives will be clearly stated and accurately reflect the community's educational aspirations.
   b. The school's objectives may be clearly stated but will most likely be severely criticized by different community factions.
   c. The school program will be but one of many programs that contribute to the community.
   d. The school program will have major support from special-interest groups within the community.

3. Which two of the following represent major approaches to community analysis for the purpose of understanding the school? (*Circle two.*)
   a. Examination of general features such as physical size, location, population, economic status, and housing.

    b. Analysis of intangible factors such as beliefs, traditions, and aspirations.

    c. Review of statements of public and private agencies on community social needs.

    d. Evaluation of community tax structure, juvenile delinquency rate, and divorce rates.

4. Which set of criteria might best be used in formulating a scientific definition of a community?

    a. A configuration of land, people, and culture, and with a structural pattern of human relations within a given area.

    b. Precise physical boundaries, a well-defined cultural area inhabited by people of varying backgrounds.

    c. Well-marked physical and cultural pattern; a set of historical traditions.

    d. An area with a historic past; a homogeneous group of social, economic, and religious institutions.

5. Which one of the following sets of factors would be most likely to have the most substantial broad-range influence on the school program?

    a. Community beliefs, traditions, aspirations.

    b. Community tax structure, location, history.

    c. Community population, family structure, religious beliefs.

    d. Community transportation patterns, mobility, congruence.

6. Society at large influences the school by inhibiting and creating change. Circle the two factors that you believe tend to inhibit change.

    a. legal authority.

    b. Judeo-Christian ethic.

    c. population mobility.

    d. knowledge explosion.

7. Which one of the following changes in American society would probably have the least impact on the public school?

    a. production and communication of knowledge.

    b. shift from passive to active feeling about political and social issues.

    c. rapid social movements.

    d. emphasis on mass transportation.

8. Schools are particularly sensitive to changes in community values. Which one of the following would be likely to have the least impact on the school?

    a. extensive use of mass media for leisure activities.

    b. changes in relationships of sexes.

    c. emphasis on social control over individual and business.

    d. decline in church attendance.

9. Which statement best describes a major change in the purposes of the school between the seventeenth century and the twentieth century?

    a. The schools shifted from religious purpose to development of a common language, technical training, and broad potentialities of the individual.

    b. The schools shifted from an emphasis on reading and writing to teaching of moral and spiritual values.

    c. The schools shifted from religious purpose to emphasis on sex education, driver training, athletics.

    d. The schools shifted from an emphasis on secular instruction to an emphasis on sectarian subjects.

10. A school has two major functions in any society. Circle the two functions that best represent general school functions.

    a. instruction.

    b. socialization.

    c. individualization.

    d. vocational training.

11. The American school performs three specialized functions: custodial, certifying, and selectivity. These functions would be likely to have most significance in which of the following school problems?

    a. student unrest.

    b. drop out rate.

    c. teaching sex education.

    d. busing.

12. Which figure best represents the percentage of local taxes generally paid for support of public schools?

    a. 20–30%.   **b.** 40–50%.   **c.** 50–60%.   **d.** 70–80%.

13. Total expenditures for education in 1973–74 was what per cent of the Gross National Product?

    a. 7–8%.   **b.** 10–12%.   **c.** 14–16%.   **d.** 18–20%.

14. According to R. Freeman Butts, achieving a sense of community is one of the prime purposes of the public school. Which one of the following ideas is justified by this purpose?

    a. compulsory education.

    b. freedom to choose an alternative school.

    c. bilingual education.

    d. no required subjects.

15. Which one of the following principles is most basic in deciding whether a school activity in the moral and spiritual area is illegal?

    a. An activity that aids one or more religious sects or prefers one religious doctrine to another.

    b. An activity that provides for religious instruction on a release-time basis.

    c. An activity that aids all religious sects without discrimination.

    d. An activity that includes formal instruction in the major world religions.

16. Which one of the following moral and spiritual values is basic to all of the other three values?

    a. moral responsibility.

    b. devotion to truth.

    c. human personality.

    d. respect for excellence.

17. Which one statement best describes the current educational role of the public school and church as defined by the State?
    a. The school is a secular institution that transmits the cultural heritage and integrates moral and spiritual teaching into the curriculum. The church is responsible for sectarian education.
    b. The school is a secular institution that provides instruction in cognitive domain and leaves teaching of moral and spiritual values to the church.
    c. The church is society's chief agent for providing both secular and sectarian instruction. The public school is a supplemental educational agent.
    d. The church and school are mutually and equally responsible for the education of the youth.

18. Which of the following changes in family patterns have created new demands on the school's program. (*Circle two.*)
    a. urbanization.
    b. mobility.
    c. leisure time pattern.
    d. rising standard of living.

19. Conflict in parental roles has diminished the family's ability to provide education in which of the following areas? (*Circle two.*)
    a. value education.   c. socialization.
    b. basic skills.   d. individualization.

20. Which one of the following behavior patterns is ordinarily associated with what sociologists call "lower class" environment?
    a. physical aggressions in patterned forms—order in the home.
    b. extreme-rage expressions, agressive behavior, disorder in the home.
    c. accepted form in manners, taste, and accomplishments.
    d. respect for property and law-enforcement officers.

21. Who of the following is more likely to be directly connected to the political structure of the community?
    a. president of parent-teachers organization.
    b. president of school board.
    c. superintendent of schools.
    d. president of Rotary Club.

22. Which of the following community organizations are directly interested in the public schools? (*Circle two.*)
    a. Parent-Teachers Association.
    b. Joint Civic Club.
    c. Garden Club.
    d. Boosters Club.

23. Which statement best defines the family's responsibility for education?
    a. the family is responsible by law to see that the child is educated.
    b. the family is responsible for educating the child through the age of twelve.
    c. the family is responsible for the education of the child until the child enters first grade.
    d. the family is responsible for educating the child in a public school.

24. The child's basic personality and character is shaped primarily
   a. in the home and neighborhood. **c.** in the neighborhood and school.
   b. in the home and school. **d.** in the church and school.

25. Which of the following changes in family life have had the most impact on the school curriculum?
   a. urbanization and mobility.
   b. parental roles and mobility.
   c. parental roles and increased leisure.
   d. birth rates and economic dependency.

26. Which of the following factors in the urban family pattern has weakened the family's capacity to transmit values and attitudes. (*Circle two.*)
   a. increased frequency of divorce.
   b. increased family income.
   c. conflict in role of family members.
   d. decreased church attendance.

27. The term *in loco parentis* means
   a. exercising the same authority as a parent.
   b. authorization to belong to a parents' club.
   c. prohibition on exercising parental authority.
   d. recognition of emotional instability of parents.

28. Which of the following best represent historic community attitudes toward teachers? (*Circle two.*)
   a. an intellectual leader. **c.** a professional.
   b. a part-time employee. **d.** an upper-class person.

29. (*Circle two.*) The teacher's ability to substitute as the parent authority in the classroom is restricted by
   a. not residing in the community.
   b. viewing teaching as a part-time job.
   c. a lack of academic qualifications.
   d. the teacher's ambition to be a community leader.

30. (*Circle two.*) A reasonable professional argument can be made for requiring teachers to live in the community where they teach on the basis that
   a. the community is in need of talented community leaders.
   b. the teacher should spend his money in the community that provides employment.
   c. the teacher is more likely to be accepted by the community.
   d. the teacher should faithfully observe the regulations of the board of education.

31. (*Circle one.*) In today's schools, community leaders
   a. are often invited into the classroom to present information on certain subjects.
   b. must often be excluded from participating in the formal school program.
   c. must often be utilized as experts to be consulted chiefly by the teacher.
   d. must generally be ignored by the school on the basis that they have nothing to contribute to the program.

32. Which one of the following groups of factors is most comprehensive in defining a community?
   a. land, people, pattern of human relations.
   b. family, church, school.
   c. size, location, service agencies.
   d. industries, population, family structure.

33. Which two of the following contain a term that is not parallel to the other two terms?
   a. cognitive, affective, interconnective.
   b. secular, urbanized, clerical.
   c. lower class, middle class, upper class.
   d. individualization, socialization, democratization.

Moral Values and Schools

M. J. McLaughlin

Providence College

module 10

Colonial Background / State Systems Established / Educators Meet on National Level / Federal Government Influence / Values—Moral and Spiritual

RATIONALE

In this module we will develop a brief historical background of education in this country in order to promote an understanding of the movement in education which is away from a theocratic school toward what might be called a *democratic-theistic school*. Democratic-theism implies that democracy becomes a religion within the culture. The ultimate would, therefore, be a federally controlled system of education. Democracy would become an all-imposing faith in which all people must believe. Instead of democracy becoming democratic, it would inevitably become authoritarian. Therefore it is to the students advantage to get a glimpse of education in history's movement.

Another part of the module will be concerned with values: moral and spiritual values permeate the reading. The whole concept of a free, democratic system of education is based on a Judeo-Christian concept of philosophy. In Colonial times, it was much easier for a teacher to bring into the classroom his moral and spiritual values. However, in this era of education in which the population is composed of multicultural, multireligious backgrounds, the teacher must be careful in expounding his philosophical concepts. Imposing his values on pupils may be considered unethical (and illegal, in some areas). It is hoped then, that this module will give some glimmer of direction to the future teacher regarding the imposition of his values on his pupils.

In order to present the module as an integrated unit, consideration of democracy and authoritarianism is merged with the treatment of central control versus decentralization; and moral and spiritual values are combined with the concept of quality education for all.

The Objectives for the module should be used to stimulate further study regarding educational history and educational philosophy. This module is not intended to give easy answers; it is intended to raise questions, especially questions regarding the future of education and cultural trends in this country.

Objectives

After you have studied and learned the information in this module, you should be able to

1. Describe how the education of the Colonial period of our country was directly related to religion.
2. State the three powers of local school committees established in the early 1800's.
3. Give at least three steps in the democratization of schools and the shift of control from local to state government.
4. Explain the functions of the three committees established by the National Education Association in the 1890s, and state the three important results effected by these committees.

5. State and briefly explain the Seven Cardinal Principles of secondary education established in 1918.
6. Name two federal acts that were passed in the mid 1800s and explain how they affected schools.
7. Explain how the "equalization" bill and the various "title" schemes steered the control of education away from the local government.
8. Give the full title names and explain briefly each of the following innovative projects: IGE, MUS-E, MATCH, CAM.
9. Differentiate between values and morals.
10. Show, by example, how discipline problems often have a relationship to the moral values of teachers and students.

MODULE TEXT

Colonial Background

At the time of the founding of the American colonies, education was offered by the local communities, which had been established on a theocratic form of government. The church had set up its own school for the children in the community. The basic text included the *primer,* which cited various readings from the Bible. (The word *church* is used because the original thirteen colonies were in most instances founded on Anglo-Saxon Protestant religions, and the religious sects set up the civil governing bodies; thereby, theocratic governments came into being in the colonies.)

Generally, the church hired a person to teach the youth of the parish. In many cases the teacher was an indentured servant who had some educational background, particularly in Biblical studies. Within a short time after seminaries had sprung up throughout the Colonies, students from these seminaries were hired to teach. Harvard College in the Massachusetts Bay Colony, a Congregational seminary; and Brown University in the Rhode Island and Providence Plantations colony, a Baptist seminary (originally called Rhode Island College) supplied many teachers for the Northeast. The point is that in Colonial history, education had to be a local concern.

The concept of localizing education became so entrenched in the colonist's thinking that it had its influence on the framers of the Constitution. One must remember that the men who participated in the forming of the Constitution were born in the Colonies and many of them were products of two generations in colonial living. The history of the era shows that the feeling toward the mother country, England, had diminished somewhat since the first emigrees one hundred years before had begun a new culture in the wilderness. There were a number of Loyalists in the Colonies, to be sure, but understandably they were in the minority. Because of this prevailing feeling of support for local independence, the framers of the Constitution jealously guarded the right to self-governance and continued the practice of educating their own children in their own way.

Philosophy of Education of the Founding Fathers. The leaders of the American Revolution formed a definite philosophy of education in connection with their policies of government. It was the destiny of America, they felt, to separate from the Old World and to establish a government based on new principles. They began with the principle that human life is capable of the greatest improvement, and that the function of government is to effect this improvement by helping to secure for the people the enjoyment of their natural rights. They concluded with the belief that the practices of governments should conform to the natural law, and that chief among man's natural rights were security of life, person, and property; the privilege of pursuing one's personal happiness; and the exercise of liberty or self-direction.

Conflicting Theories Concerning Educational Practice. The leaders agreed that education is the principal means by which governments can procure the welfare of the people. But they held very diverse views respecting the details of an educational system. In general they appear to have fallen into two groups with regard to the fundamental principles of educational organization and practice. One group believed that government and its educational system should be highly centralized, and that people should be prepared for citizenship by being carefully taught in a particular system of ideas. The other group, whose view prevailed, held that that government governs best which governs least; that individuals and localities should manage their own affairs insofar as possible; and that the central government, instead of indoctrinating its citizens with a system of ideas, should make it possible for them to cultivate their minds, and should encourage them to think and speak freely on matters of government.

During the Colonial expansion, many religious sects entered the existing Colonies. Because of the influence of more than one religion, movements by various groups advocated a different type of educational structure, especially for financing the community schools. For instance, a movement in the Southern Colonies, called *Multiple Establishment,* created a central treasury from which each religious sect could draw sums of money to operate its school. It did not take the New England Colonies long to follow suit, and, in Article III of the Massachusetts Constitution of 1780, provisions were made to grant subsidies to support, financially, teachers in parish schools.

State Systems Established

The constitution of the United States does not mention education, and so the Tenth Amendment automatically reserved that right to state control.

A number of movements started in the early 1800s for free nonsectarian schools. The theocratic type of government no longer existed, so another type of educational system had to be devised. Eventually, state educational systems were proposed and passed.

Jefferson's Proposals. As a member of a committee to revise the legal code of Virginia, Thomas Jefferson drew up a group of bills which indirectly affected the course of education. He was the author of a bill separating church and state in Virginia. He drew up three bills for the establishment of a state system of public schools which was to include elementary schools in every locality, secondary schools in every section, and a state university. The elementary schools were to be locally controlled and supported and were to be open to all children without charge. The secondary schools and the university were to be built out of state funds and principally supported by tuition fees. A system of state scholarships was intended to provide for the secondary and college education of poor boys of exceptional talent.

Movements Toward Local Control. Jefferson frequently asserted his belief that popular education was the business of the state and vital to its welfare, but his plan for county schools was never adopted. George Washington was much attracted to the idea of a national university which would afford to all children opportunities for intellectual culture, and enable young men from all parts of the country to come into contact with each other and so effect the unity of the country. He donated funds and selected a site in the capital city for the national university, but Congress refused to charter the institution. Colonial developments had created a situation (pertaining to these and other efforts) favorable to local control of lower schools, and private and state control of colleges and universities.

State legislatures enacted laws making education mandatory for the local cities and towns. Not only did the states contribute financially toward education, they mandated that the local communities establish their own governing boards called *school committees*. These committees were empowered to build schools, hire and dismiss teachers, set curriculum standards, and generally adhere to the laws concerning education proposed by the state. The state was all-powerful. However, the local community through its legalized school committee exerted some influence on the direction of education. For example, during the early period of the Industrial Revolution in the early 1800s, youth, before the age of 15, were permitted to work in the various business houses, mills, and so on. The local communities petitioned the state legislature to enact a compulsory school-attendance law. The states complied, and statutory enactments advocated by school committees were inaugurated.

Role of Immigration. Another step on the road to democratizing education was the great influx of immigrants from disparate nations and cultural groups.

Although Americanization occurred in countless ways outside the classroom, a special burden rested upon the common school, for it was the one institution that reached most of the young. As Tyack points out,

German farmers who had retained their language and customs for centuries when trans-planted to Russia became Americanized in one generation when they settled in South Dakota. Children of parents who spoke a babel of tongues in the iron mines of the Mesabi Range were taught meticulously correct English in the Minnesota grammar and high schools.[1]

Naturally, assimilation of ethnic groups proceeded at different rates in different environments, and immigrants adapted to Americans more often only reluctantly and in a superficial manner. Americanization normally meant discarding old customs and values. Hence, successful assimilation often disrupted families and

---

[1] David B. Tyack, Ed., *Turning Points in American Educational History* (Waltham, Mass.: Ginn/Blaisdell, 1967), p. 228.

sowed doubt and discord between the generations. The job of the school became the creation of a national feeling, a unity of thought and action, and the conversion process by which one ceased being a European and became an American. The fear was that the new population would develop into a network of clans, "congregating without coalescing and condemned to contiguity without sympathy."[2] Deliberate effort would be required in order to avert the national disaster, but if the young were assimilated, the resisting older members of the family could be reached through them.

"The process of uprooting and transplantation awoke immigrants to their own distinctiveness; for the 'first time they learned what it meant to be 'Italian' or 'Polish' by living in a land where their mores were not self-evident and unquestioned. And in turn, Americans were forced to define their own values more self-consciously in the process of teaching them to the newcomers. In the textbooks American heroes and history were glorified often at the cost of other nations. The English language taught in the schools was largely prescriptive, its grammar artificial and usage canonical as if to build barriers against foreign corruptions."[3] Often the most ardent Americanizers in the schools were teachers who came from second- or third-generation immigrant families.

Until the first quarter of the twentieth century, hope ran high that the schools could unify the nation and that the hybrid people would be stronger than the native stock. Where deemed necessary, children were instructed that they must change their ways and not emulate their parents. The public school in many cases became a wedge between children and their parents. Parents, in turn, chagrined by the disintegration of the family ties and the erosion of respect for foreign folkways by the children, became ambivalent about the schools. They hoped that schools would open the doors of opportunity for their children. And although they learned from the knowledge the children acquired and brought home, they resented the dissolution of respect and the developing unmanageable attitudes.

Ridicule became a help in the process of Americanizing. Group pressure prevented children caught in the conflict of cultures from conforming to the expectations of the home as opposed to the example of their peers and school teachers. They learned quickly.

The common school had a tremendous impact upon the newcomer, but the immigrant also made an imprint upon the school. The teacher in the urban ghetto classroom learned that he could not take familiar skills and attitudes for granted; now it became essential to take over a whole realm of new duties formerly performed by the family. Teachers often gave children baths, taught them manners, proper dress, and names for familiar objects.

Teachers were trained to believe that the school should start from scratch in implanting "correct" ideas and behavior; the childrens' backgrounds and environments were not to be trusted. The community expected the school to be policeman as well as parent-surrogate, to be responsible for what happened outside of school as well as inside.

Creating a State System. From the time of the Revolution on, substantial numbers of Americans supposed that the free citizen was the uniform man, that

---

[2] Ibid, p. 229.
[3] Ibid, p. 229.

diversity somehow endangered the promise of American life because it threatened cohesiveness. Others saw a "free society as a place where it was safe to be unpopular, comfortable to be different. The common school in successive decades expressed both points of view in differing degrees, seeking to strike the precarious balance of ordered liberty. The task of Americanizing the immigrant posed, in all its complexity, the problem of unity within diversity."[4]

Local communities were concerned about the need for an enlightened citizenry, and in order to have a school system that could cater to a heterogeneous population, concluded that the schools would have to have trained professional teachers. It was a short step to instituting teacher-training programs, and thus were founded "teacher training colleges" and/or "normal schools." The training institutions issued diplomas to those who successfully completed the course work. The important point here to consider is that the state now controlled the educational background of the teachers. Although the local school boards had some control over the schools, the state had jurisdiction over the learning process within the schools! Two of the outstanding leaders in the movement toward preparation of teachers and the creation of training schools were Horace Mann and Henry Barnard. They hoped to introduce systems to relace the chaos—actual or potential —which they had witnessed. In their pursuit of school unification and efficiency, in order to help to unify the country, they advocated standardized textbooks and curriculum, the grading of classes, and the improvement of supervision of teachers, all of whom would be trained and certified. To a large extent, they succeeded in standardizing public education during the latter half of the nineteenth century; at least, they succeeded in the larger towns and cities of the North and West.

The strengthening of the states' role in education opened many interesting avenues. Some states attempted to accredit high schools, using either the faculty of the state university or special state boards to visit high schools; accreditation, once granted, allowed principals to recommend students for admission to the state university without examination.

Various associations on national levels were organized and members from state departments of education, local school systems, and colleges and universities throughout the country joined and attended meetings. National conferences and workshops explored the new developments in research that were going on at that time in education. As a result, wider educational horizons were sought by local groups. State departments expanded roles to include advocating the ladder system, credits for high school graduation (the Carnegie System), curriculum changes (and the state department's hiring of subject-matter experts who could be called upon by local schools to help in curriculum planning), homogeneous grouping, and heterogeneous grouping. In other words, the state departments of education became the focal points that determined the action and policies of local school committees, school administrators, and teachers.

Educators Meet on National Level

In the 1890's the National Education Association established three important committees which were to have a lasting impact on the educational scene: The

---

[4] *Ibid.,* p. 234.

Committee of Fifteen, The Committee of Ten, and The Committee of Thirteen. The Committee of Fifteen met in 1893 to study the problems and issues in elementary education. The result of their report was the establishment of a blueprint for an eight-year elementary curriculum. The emphasis was on content, which, of course, ignored individuality.

The Committee of Ten. The Committee of Ten on Secondary School Studies was appointed in 1892. Six of the ten members of this committee were college presidents, one was the United States Commissioner of Education, two were public high school principals, and one was a private school headmaster. The chairman was Charles Eliot, president of Harvard University. With authority in both university and school circles, the Committee hoped that its report would cause the colleges to modify their admission requirements and the high schools to change their programs. They took an Olympian view of their task: to select and arrange academic content and provide a model of excellence. They considered themselves experts in education, that is, in the imparting of knowledge and the development of intellectual power.

In their report they fulfilled the mandate given them by the National Council of Education: To develop secondary school programs by considering the proper limits of each subject, the best methods of instruction, the most desirable allotment of time for the subject, and the best methods of testing the pupil's attainments therein. Although the report recognized that the secondary school was terminal, nevertheless it set up a curriculum which was precollege oriented. The Committee of Thirteen proposed that a number of *constants* be required of all college entrants. The constants would include four units in foreign languages, two units in math, two units in English, one in history, and one in science.

At least three points emerge as important from this consideration of the foregoing committee reports. One is that the reports were accepted as standard operating procedure by all systems throughout the country for almost sixty years. (See Conant's report on *The American High School*.)[5] Another point is that for the first time, on a national basis, consideration was given to the subject-matter content constituting the curriculum. The third point to consider is that such compliance at the local level with the conclusions reached by a national committee appears to confirm the drift toward centralization. In the decentralized system, democratic participation and voluntary implementation inhibit the influence of authoritarian pronouncements and autocratic considerations. Have the schools since that period in our history continued the drift toward centralization? Are we closer to it today than ever before?

The Seven Cardinal Principles. Another important commission that has had an effect on education was The National Education Association's Commission for the Reorganization of Secondary Education. This commission proposed that

1. Every boy should be encouraged to remain in school until he reached his eighteenth birthday.
2. Education should be of a kind that develops in the individual qualities that will enable him to live in society with advantage to himself and to society.

[5] James B. Conant, *The American High School* (New York: McGraw-Hill Book Company, 1959).

The spirit of social reform called *progressivism,* which by the second decade of the twentieth century had become a considerable force, was applied to secondary education by the Commission in its celebrated report entitled *The Cardinal Principles of Secondary Education* published in 1918. The slogan of these reformers—social efficiency—indicated a profound shift in the burden of proof in decisions about the high school curriculum. Not only were the old liberal-arts disciplines—the classics and mathematics—placed under seige, but the modern subjects, which had been shoehorned into the college preparatory curriculum only a generation before, were being considered outmoded. Now, deciding what to teach would require assessment of individual and social needs. The new source of power in education would determine what schools could do to meet these needs.

Following are the seven major areas of the educational objectives which this National Education Association (NEA) Commission considered to be, and named the Cardinal Principles

1. *Health of the Student* (Health). The general well-being of the child at birth makes survival possible, and throughout life makes life enjoyable.
2. *Worthy Home Membership* (Human Companionship). Man needs more than physical necessities. He has to have mental contact with those with whom he lives. This mental contact is first supplied by the family, which is the primary social unit.
3. *Vocational Preparation* (Economic Security). If man is to continue in good health and in the enjoyment of life, he must at least have food, clothing and shelter. This is economic security. . . . the possession of certain essentials of life.
4. *Citizenship* (Civic Security). Man should possess a solid knowledge of the government under which he lives. He should work to sustain that government. Government is the social agency created by man to assure himself of the right to own property, and the right to life, liberty and the pursuit of happiness. Government is man's protection against the injustice, greed, envy and attack by others.
5. *Wise Use of Leisure Time* (Leisure Time). Man needs time to rest from the pressure of his labors. He has to have time that he can call his own—to relax his body and mind.
6. *Development of the Fundamental Processes* (Education). Man must learn to write, read and figure. These are the bases for acquiring further knowledge. Man, living in society, must learn of the past achievements of that society. He must develop his own abilities in order to be a contributing member of society.
7. *Ethical Character* (Divine Security). Perfection of self is the end to be sought (Humanism). Man must live by moral principles.

Although it is difficult to demonstrate the precise impact of this report by pointing to curriculum listings subsequent to 1918, it does seem clear that the Cardinal Principles both reflected and shaped a growing consensus among schoolmen on the broad purpose of secondary education. They also appear to have accelerated the thinking about the curriculum in terms of experience instead of simply the subjects to be offered.

Federal Government Influence

Historical Background. The federal government also exerted an influence on education in this country in many ways. In 1836 the Federal treasury had a surplus fund. Each state was given some of the money, which was to be deposited in local banks throughout the states. The interest accrued from those deposits was to be annually applied to the support of public schools in the several towns and cities throughout the state. The Congressional act was called, "An Act to Regulate the Deposits of Public Money."

Shortly after this Act, the first United States Commissioner of Education, Henry Barnard, was appointed. The Department of Education was created "for the purpose of collecting such statistics and facts as shall show the condition and progress of education in the several States and Territories, and of diffusing such information respecting the organization and management of schools and school systems, and methods of teaching as shall aid the people of the United States in the establishment and maintenance of efficient school systems, and otherwise promote the cause of education throughout the country."

Many federal acts were passed in this era, but perhaps the most powerful incentive for founding state universities came in the form of the Morrill Act. By its provisions each state was granted 30,000 acres of public land (or equivalent in scrip) for each of its congressmen, the proceeds to be devoted to the establishment of colleges of agriculture and mechanic arts.

Current Trends. From this brief historical background of American education, one can see the trends which have been set many years ago. One question the scholars might consider is, How far away from local control can an educational system with a democratic frame of reference go? To complete state control? To complete national control?

Naturally, the more remote the control of education, the more the democratic influence by the local community diminishes. At present, each state exerts a tremendous influence on its schools. State supervisors of the various subject matter areas may enter any school within the state to evaluate the subject matter program. If the school is not conforming to the state code, then the state may threaten to eliminate its financial appropriation to that system. Many states have some sort of "equalization" bill, which attempts to pour money into educational systems that have difficulty in reaching state financial standings. Usually "equalizing" is computed on a per capita basis. There are other state "aids" to education, but to be eligible, the community must conform to certain alternate rules and regulations imposed by a State Department of Education.

The trend toward a national system has quickened its pace. The series of elementary-secondary "title" schemes which came out of Washington during the sixties has had a powerful impact on local educational systems. The general procedure is for the local system to apply for them through its state department, then to Washington, to fund a particular project within the system. The eventual permission for the funding comes from Washington, which has sanctioned the project according to certain stipulations enunciated by Washington!

Other areas of federal intercession in education are the recent Supreme Court decisions and Congressional enactments which mandate school integration throughout the country. If a system refuses to comply, the federal government will deny all future funding to that system. This has been a controversial issue for almost a quarter of a century.

Without question, the influence of the federal government in education has increased considerably in recent years. Although it still lines up as a distant third to the state and local agencies, considerable agitation for more assistance and more leadership by that sector is currently in vogue as an outgrowth of the social change currently taking place in the urban areas. Through programs dealing with the training of teachers in workshops for "retooling" for "new math" and "new science" courses, the federal influence has been exerted upon the staff of the schools. Through financial support for the reform movements dealing with the curriculum, the federal influence has been extended into most of the classrooms in most of the schools in the country. Through grants made to the states, such as the Title V funds of 1965, which released $25 million to state departments for research and projects aimed at improving effectiveness of supervision at the state level, the federal influence has been exerted at the system level.

State versus Federal Funding and Control. State and local funds, however, continue to be the basic source of revenue for elementary and secondary education, with less than 8 per cent coming from the federal government. Regarding personnel and instructional policies, it is the local district that wields the influence. Regarding the larger issues, such as teacher certification, length of school year, and the quality of lunches, it is the state that prevails.

Many citizens concerned about the inequities in quality of education among the states have called for more federal control. They contend that

1. A population explosion following World War II has placed an educational burden on communities and states, which they are financially unable to carry.
2. The geographical mobility of people today is such that living and educational standards in some of the wealthier states are lowered by the migration of people from poor states; therefore wealthy states should share in financing schools in the poorer states to protect themselves from this influx of poorly educated migrants.
3. The ideal of equalization of educational opportunity demands that wealth be taxed where it is and distributed to the states and localities in proportion to their educational need, their financial ability, and their effort to support schools.
4. Draft rejections in World War II were in direct proportion to the quality of educational programs in the various states; therefore, in order to remain militarily strong, federal support of schools is necessary.
5. The forms of wealth have become so diversified that only tax machinery on the national level can tap these sources of wealth in a fair manner.
6. To train a jet pilot costs ten times the amount needed to educate a physician, engineer, teacher, or scientist. Professional people are as vital to national defense as are military personnel; therefore, the federal government should contribute a more equitable share to help finance the preparation of professionals.

Another large group of citizens are opposed to federal participation in support of public schools because

1. Increasing federal aid would "produce the sickening cadence of the goose step." In other words, centralization of power, sometimes a prelude to totalitarianism, would be encouraged by federal support of public schools.

2. If federal funds were given the public schools for growth, private education would be interfered with.
3. Too much of the money that is collected through taxes from the states by the federal treasury goes to overhead costs.
4. Federal support of schools would constitute a serious encroachment upon states' rights.
5. States do not need assistance; they can pay for their own schools. Rich states should not be taxed to support schools in poor states.

At present, the issue appears to be not whether federal funds will be used for education but how much, for what purposes, and with what kinds of control. The process of competitive bidding, which is currently favored as the medium by which grants are made, seems to reward novel proposals and extravagant rhetoric designed and presented by experienced public relations workers. The poorer districts most in need of the financial help offered are not always in a position to employ this kind of personnel.

At the school-district level, there remains no doubt in most districts that something will have to be done to share the financial burden of schools, which has become excessive. Because education is a state and national responsibility as well as a local one, and because the training machinery is vastly superior in the larger schools, the amplification of dependence upon federal resources for growth and survival appears almost a foregone conclusion. The amount of authority and direct control over the schools which will be surrendered in return for the fiscal support will have to be closely watched. The social ferment, the extremely volatile problems of urban education, the question of support for religious/private schools, and the unpredictability of national and international affairs in the decade ahead all militate against a static relationship.

Teacher Education Centers. A more recent federal implication concerns Teacher Education Centers. Four of these centers were established by federal funding, in Texas, California, Rhode Island, and Washington, D.C. Educators from each state were selected to be on a committee which was to participate in establishing the education center in that state. A representative from the HEW office of Education in Washington was present at each planning meeting. Because Teacher Education Centers were of comparatively recent origin, the (Department of Health, Education, and Welfare) representatives offered many guides and guidelines to the planning committee.

Eventually, the Centers were established, and they are now functioning. Most of them are composed of two main divisions: Information and Alternate Learning. The Information Center handles requests for all types of educational planning and research. ERIC[6] files are used extensively. For example, if an educator wants information about a research project, or wants research done, the Information Center will complete the request and issue it to the educator. It is also the link to U.S. Office of Education and other national, regional, and local sources of new and validated educational products and programs.

[6] Education Resources Information Center. These centers collect, file, and disseminate educational information, research, materials, and the like. There are centers for teaching various disciplines, teacher education, and so on.

The Alternate Learning Center handles mostly the innovative projects that are going on in the community or throughout the country. These projects are demonstrated to administrators or to in-service groups of teachers. Some of the projects available are

INDIVIDUALLY GUIDED EDUCATION AND THE MULTIUNIT ELEMENTARY SCHOOL. This is a system of education and instruction developed by the University of Wisconsin's Research and Development Center for Cognitive Learning. It is designed to produce higher educational achievement through adequate provision for differences among students in rate of learning, learning style, and other characteristics. Included in the Individually Guided Education (IGE) system is an extensive organizational model for instruction and administration in schools and districts; it is known as the multiunit elementary school (MUS-E).

EFFECTIVE QUESTIONING—ELEMENTARY LEVEL. This autoinstructional teacher-training package contains (1) a Teacher Handbook, including self-evaluation forms, (2) a Coordinator Handbook, (3) eleven 16mm instructional and model films, and (4) a textbook that gives detailed research findings on the Minicourse instructional model. Its prime use is for elementary teachers interested in the intermediate grades, and it is likely to be found more effective with experienced in-service teachers than with teacher trainees.

The model involves the following activities: (1) studying the teaching skill of effective questioning, and viewing a filmed sequence which shows several expert teachers using these skills in microteaching situations; (2) planning, conducting, video-recording and self-evaluating a microteaching lesson; and (3) revising the lesson, reteaching, video-recording, and again, self-evaluation.

MATCH (MATERIALS AND ACTIVITIES FOR TEACHERS AND CHILDREN) BOX. Match Boxes are self-contained, multimedia kits designed to enable elementary school teachers and children to learn and communicate predominately through nonverbal means. They stress the child's involvement and responsibility for his own learning. Each kit is designed for a class of approximately thirty students to use daily for approximately an hour for two to three weeks, after which it can be circulated to another class.

A typical kit, weighing from 40 to 100 pounds, contains photographs, films, pictures, recordings, and models which can be handled and used by individual students and by a small group of students. "The City" to name only one, is intended to show how a city changes, the importance of the neighborhoods, and the variety of city sounds.

CAM—COMPUTER-BASED ACHIEVEMENT MONITORING. This educational project is an instructional management system providing relevant data for use by teachers. It consists of three major components. First, techniques are provided to assist teachers in developing objectives and related test materials in mathematics, science, social studies, reading and English. Second, a computer-based achievement monitoring system has been devised to monitor student performance on specified objectives. Third, techniques have been developed to assist teaching teams in identifying instructional strengths and weaknesses.

The system is designed for use in classrooms that are group-paced, individualized, multigraded and so forth. It has been found to be most successful when teachers are committed to objective-based instruction. The teacher center supplies at cost user manuals, audiovisual presentations, training workshops, student and coordinator's brochures and arranges demonstration visits to sites al-

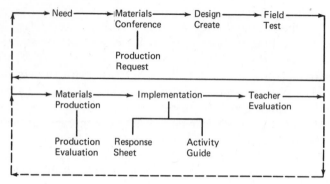

Figure 10-1 *A Systems Approach to Instructional Materials Design.*

ready implementing CAM for those teachers and administrators contemplating the use of it for their schools.

THE SYSTEM. The systems approach begins with an individual student need. This need is written into a behavioral objective which also lists the concept or skill to be learned; the pre-entry requirements, if any; whether the program is child- or teacher-directed and child- or teacher-corrected; and the perceptual modality the activity should emphasize. Material is then designed and created to meet this need. The material is field-tested with the student, evaluated, revised if necessary, and then incorporated into the class program.

The foregoing examples are used to demonstrate the type and quality of projects available at the Alternate Learning Centers. What may be gleaned from these examples is that each project emphasizes learning and knowing, but in a pragmatic sense.

Values—Moral and Spiritual

If learning and knowing are the principal school activities of youth, then valuing is certainly the next most important thing a younster does in school. But how much is valuing taught? And are moral and spiritual values taught? We shall first define *values,* and then consider moral and spiritual values.

Definitions. A value involves choice. "How should I think about this situation?" "What side of the discussion should I be on?" "What conduct is proper for this activity?" "What vocation should I select?" "What pathway should society select?"

Value selection and value judgment are used in all phases of living. The teacher in a classroom uses value selection at all times. Pupils are constantly admonished concerning the "golden rule," "cheating," "correct behavior." Valuing is involved with character building and differs from drive, which is concerned with achievement and competition.

Moral is derived from the Latin *mos, moris,* which means custom or manner. The culture of the society has established what it considers proper conduct or custom. Societal moral questions are involved in conduct because the society has established proper codes of conduct for all its citizens.

Moral concepts determine the expected behavior patterns of all members of a culture. Thus, to act in a moral way means to act in conformity to group standards of conduct, and thus win social approval and acceptance by the group.

Ethical behavior is a more inclusive concept. It applies to human conduct generally rather than to that of any particular cultural group. A moral person may conform to the standards of his particular group, but these standards may not be the accepted standards of people in other groups. A thief may be considered moral by the gang with which he is identified because he behaves in accordance with the mores of the gang. Society, however, would not judge his conduct to be ethical.

Now, once a moral code has been expounded, it takes on a *value*. Therefore, in almost every phase of the teaching-learning process, a moral value permeates the educational environment. Moral values emanate from the teacher in his endeavor to teach. A pupil either accepts the values implicit in the teaching and curriculum or rejects them because they are in conflict with the values he has learned at home or elsewhere, and elects to follow the values of his social class or group.

Usually each culture has a hierarchy of values that indicate what that society holds dear. Two of the striking things about American society is the diversity of values, and the rapid changes in American values.

To a greater or lesser degree, the cultural patterns brought by the immigrants to this New World have stuck to their descendants; and so we find that the diverse ethnic backgrounds of the American people have created a diversity of value patterns in American society. "In addition, changes in values have been hurried by the rapid technological advances of the last century and the rapid shifting in other aspects of our society, such as employment, the advent of suburban living and the distribution of wealth. Changes in values have also been encouraged by the utilitarian and pragmatic philosophies of life held by many Americans."[7]

Changing Controls in American Society. Early Americans prided themselves on their rugged individualism and on their desire for, and ability to thrive on, as little interference from government as possible. Of late, evidences of increased government interference have multiplied at a rapid rate, with zoning laws, building codes, minimum wage laws, motor vehicle laws, forms of taxation, and so on.[8]

In addition, other agencies such as trade and labor unions, professional organizations, large corporations, veterans' groups, and property owners' groups have begun to exert increasingly greater control over the behavior of many people. Despite the resistance of some of the individual members of these groups, it is no longer possible, for example, for the individual wage earner to bargain for himself with management nor for the individual worker to demand salary payments which satisfy his personal purposes.

Peer groups also now exercise more control than they formerly did. The type of house in which one lives, the style of clothes that one wears, even the activities (such as recreation) one wishes to pursue are at least somewhat influenced by the pressures and propinquity of the group in which one lives. Since people are less isolated than they were in the days of more difficult travel and communication, these pressures are greater than ever before.

UNREST AND CONFUSION. Rejection of some of the commonly held values, traditions, and institutions is partly responsible for the seething unrest in large seg-

---

[7] Leonard H. Clark, Raymond L. Klein, and John B. Burks, *The American Secondary School Curriculum,* 2nd Ed. (New York: Macmillan Publishing Co., Inc., 1972), p. 100.
[8] Ibid., p. 101.

ments of the population. Militants and activists of all descriptions, who have been venting their exasperation and frustration on society with demonstrations, strikes, protest marches, and the abandonment of established modes of earning a living, have effected, by their violent behavior, changes in government and industry.

When the confusion resulting from these major changes in society is added to the feeling of division experienced by citizens in groups where there is pressure to move toward the left or more toward the right, to vote for or to vote against violent demonstrations, to make change by evolution or to bring change about by revolution, the need for the school to take an active role in the building of values becomes readily apparent.

One can see how it is difficult for students to relate to this inconsistent world. Traditional values are not easily accepted, as they used to be; some students plainly reject them. But many students cannot seem to find replacements for traditional values. Students are unsure of what to do with the knowledge they find in school. Some are not sure that knowledge has any use at all. Some seem to confuse knowledge with wisdom and so adopt a life style of either chronic conformity or impulsive rebellion.

A value problem is indicated for a student if, in the absence of prior emotional disturbance, he finds it very difficult to face typical life situations, and to make choices and decisions; or if he typically makes choices without being aware that some alternatives may be more worthy than others. Another indication is if he does not behave in ways that are consistent with his choices and preferences—that is, if there is a gap "between his creeds and his deeds."

Teaching of Values. Teachers have at least three main alternatives in dealing with value development in their classroom. They can[9]

1. Do nothing.
2. Transmit a pre-existing set of values.
3. Help students find their own values.

DO-NOTHING APPROACH. Some teachers feel that value development is the domain of the family and the church, and they try to stay away from the area. Others elect to follow the do-nothing route because they themselves are frankly unsure about which way to turn. Still others refrain because of a conviction that values result from a trial-and-error interaction with life, and that there is nothing the school can do to accelerate the value-building process.

The error made by teachers with these attitudes can be traced to the belief that it is possible to "do nothing." Whenever a teacher urges a student to strive for good marks to get into college, or to get a good job, or to earn a good salary, he is unwittingly revealing a commitment to a value structure. He is encouraging, by example, students to respond to the Protestant work ethic, a desire for material gain, in other words, to view the "good life" in a particular way. When textbooks equate Communism with autocracy and Capitalism with freedom, values are

[9] Adapted from Merrill Harmin and Sidney B. Simon, "Values," in Dwight Allen and Eli Seifman, eds., *The Teacher's Handbook* (Glenview, Ill: Scott, Foresman and Company, 1971), p. 690.

clearly suggested; and when efforts are made to improve safety measures or health records, values are the target.

The fact that parents do not teach values to their children, that some do not know how to teach them, and that the teaching in the home or the church is often ineffective places a peculiar burden upon the school. In other areas of life, when the home and community have failed or have been unable to perform effectively, the job becomes that of the school. And in the areas of values, reason also militates against the do-nothing position.

TRANSMISSION APPROACH. Those teachers who belong to the "transmitter" group believe that it is the obligation of the school to increase efforts when it becomes apparent that some students are failing to adopt the values which the faculty has accepted as right and desirable and good. Adherents of this group suggest that one or more of the following approaches be used with more zeal in order to discharge the teaching responsibility:

The Model Approach: This approach is based upon the assumption that, just as one absorbs behavior patterns by observing others in the act of performance, so one absorbs value systems by being exposed to actual demonstrations. Teachers, then, should behave in ways that reflect the values they want to transmit.

The difficulty with this approach is that in a very complex world it is impossible to avoid exposing students to models who are practicing values antithetical to those of the school. For instance, where the home and/or school are modeling economy and rational consumption of possessions, television programs or the movies may be revealing the pleasures of free-handed profligacy of resources.

The Reward and Punishment Approach: Some teachers believe that by associating the repetition of acceptable behavior with pleasure and that of its reciprocal with pain, encouragement is given to the former. For instance, they grant early recess to young students who are sitting erect at tidy desks, and deprive of play those who talk or who have messy desks; they praise students who are regular in attendance and prompt for classes, and punish those who are not regular or who are tardy.

The problem with this approach is that sometimes extenuating circumstances regarding behavior militate against effective teaching. Sometimes honest performers are penalized because their efforts fall short, and dishonest performers reap rewards. For example, a selfish or single-minded student who attends only to the task, and completes it, earns good grades; another, who is more generous and conscientious, is late because he paused to help someone in need or to discharge an important civic responsibility, and he is downgraded.

The Explanatory Approach: The explanatory approach teaches values by giving pupils reasons to encourage them to observe standards and to practice beliefs. This is a necessary approach if slavish, unthinking rote conformity to the behavior being developed is to be avoided. Unfortunately this approach fails when behavior incompatible with the value system is rewarded by attractive consequences. It makes clear what the value is, but does not make it easier to be virtuous.

The Nagging Approach: This approach is used more than any other, probably because of the misconception that it really represents each of the three foregoing approaches. Nagging is most expeditious and incisive; it specifies what is wrong, and indicates the only kind of right behavior that will be accepted.

The problem with this approach is that it frequently results in alienation. Demanding performance without explanation, enforcing compliance by strength of position and status, nagging frequently compels the young to practice the opposite kind of behavior when the nagger is no longer present.

The Manipulation Approach: Teachers use this approach when they modify the environment or control the experience so as to favor certain value outcomes. For instance, when attempting to show pupils the value of a certain action, the teacher might refrain from listing other attractive alternatives. By listing only actions that are obviously either very good or very bad, the teacher might eliminate all question and debate because the extremes offered are so obviously black and white. The suppression of the "gray" possibilities immediately predisposes the student to opt for the value offered, the one intended by the teacher.

The Liberal Arts Approach: Educators who follow this approach want students to read widely, think deeply, and experience broadly from our cultural heritage in order to discover and adopt values that have been revered and accepted as absolute truths for ages. In the view of these educators those values have served our forefathers well for ages and, in their view, shall survive to guide future generations. They assume that close study of the masterpieces (great books) of the past will convince students of the validity and importance of these traditional values and beliefs.

CLARIFYING VALUES. Teachers who are not convinced of the existence of absolute values, who view values as being relative, personal, and situational, work toward helping students clarify their own values so that they can select the values which best fit them and their environment. With his own set of values, the student can adjust himself to a changing world, and can play an intelligent role, they believe, in the way the world will change in the future.

By using the liberal arts approach to help each student to find the best values the culture has to offer, those that might be right for himself and for his environment, and by helping each student to learn skills that will enable him to continue clarifying values throughout his life, teachers hope to equip each student to function well in a changing society. The value system arrived at by their students through this process of learning and teaching should

1. Supply each individual with a sense of purpose and direction.
2. Give the group a common orientation and supply the basis for individual action and of unified collective action.
3. Serve as a basis for judging the behavior of individuals.
4. Enable the individual to know what to expect from others, and to know how to conduct himself.
5. Fix the sense of right and wrong, fair and foul, desirable and undesirable, moral and immoral.

Traditional versus Emergent Values. George Spindler views what is happening concerning the values in the American culture as a shift from the "traditional" to the "emergent," and presents the dichotomized values juxtaposed in the following list:[10]

---

[10] George D. Spindler, "Education in a Transforming American Culture," in Harold J. Carter, Ed., *Intellectual Foundations of American Education* (New York: Pitman Publishing Corp., 1965), pp. 355–362. Copyright © 1965 by Pitman Publishing Corporation. Reprinted by permission of Pitman Publishing Corporation.

Traditional Values	**Emergent Values**

Puritan morality (Respectability, thrift, self-denial, sexual constraint; a puritan is someone who can have anything he wants, as long as he doesn't enjoy it!)

Sociability (One should like people and get along well with them. Suspicion of solitary activities is characteristic.)

Work-Success ethic (Successful people worked hard to become so. Anyone can get to the top if he tries hard enough. So people who are not successful are lazy, or stupid, or both. People must work desperately and continuously to convince themselves of their worth.)

Relativistic moral attitude (Absolutes in right and wrong are questionable. Morality is what the group thinks is right. Shame, rather than guilt-oriented personality is appropriate.)

Individualism (The individual is sacred, and always more important than the group. In one extreme form, the value sanctions egocentricity, expediency, and disregard for other people's rights. In its healthier form the value sanctions independence and originality.)

Consideration for others (Everything one does should be done with regard for others and their feelings. The individual has a built-in radar that alerts him to other's feelings. Tolerance for the other person's point of view and behavior is regarded as desirable, so long as the harmony of the group is not disrupted.)

Achievement orientation (Success is a constant goal. There is no resting on past glories. If one makes $9,000 this year, he must make $10,000 next year. Coupled with the work-success ethic, this value keeps people moving, and tense.)

Hedonistic, present-time orientation (No one can tell what the future will hold, therefore one should enjoy the present—but within the limits of the well-rounded, balanced personality and group.)

Future-time orientation (the future, not the past, or even the present, is most important. There is a "pot of gold at the end of the rainbow." Time is valuable, and cannot be wasted. Present needs must be denied for satisfactions to be gained in the future.)

Conformity to the group (Implied in the other emergent values. Everything is relative to the group. Group harmony is ultimate goal. Leadership consists of group-machinery lubrication.)

In Spindler's scheme, the Traditionalist views the Emergentist as "socialistic, communistic, spineless and weak-headed or down-right immoral." The Emergentist regards the Traditionalist as "hidebound, reactionary, selfish, or neurotically compulsive." Most of what representatives of either viewpoint do may be regarded as insidious and destructive, from the point of view of the other. The conflict goes beyond groups or institutions, because individuals in our transitional society are likely to have elements of both value systems. There are few pure types. The social character of most people is split, calling for traditionalist responses in some situations and with respect to some symbols, and emergent responses in other situations.

THE VALUE CONTINUUM. Spindler hypothesizes that the attacks upon education, and the confusion and failure of nerve characterizing educators today, can be seen clearly in the light of this conflict between positions. By placing groups, institutions, and people on a continuum ranging from reactionary to liberal, it is possible to render tentative judgments about the motivation of any critic for the value rationale of his criticism. This is also applicable to the critic's views about the method necessary to rectify the situation. This continuum is illustrated in Figure

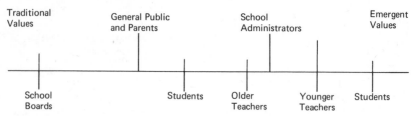

Figure 10-2 *Value Continuum Chart.*

10-2. In reproducing the value-continuum chart, the model presented by the author has been modified to satisfy the purpose of this module.[11]

Placement of the groups on the continuum are only hypothetical tendencies on norms. Individuals may, and do, vary widely from these norms. There are no "pure types" in any of the groups; yet one can expect that, as a rule, the beliefs of the majority of persons in each group will hew closely to positions indicated on the continuum.

RATIONALE FOR THE CONTINUUM. The rationale for the placement of each group on the line is important, for as the conclusions of any group change regarding the concept of value apropos the school and classroom, then the placement on the continuum may also change.

1. School boards are placed nearest the traditional end of the continuum because school boards are usually composed of persons representing the power and status quo elements of the community, as well as people in the higher age ranges. They are therefore people who have a stake in keeping things as they are, who gained their successes within the framework of the traditional value system, and consequently believe it to be good; and who, by virtue of their age, grew up and acquired their value sets during a time when American culture was presumably more tradition-oriented than it is today.
2. The general public and parent group contain many elements of varying value-predilection, and consequently cannot be realistically placed in any one position. However, the public tends to have a more conservative social philosophy than the professional education set. Also, this placement is more valid if it is viewed as describing the position of the vocal public—which criticizes the schools for not teaching fundamentals well, for eliminating report cards, and for being permissive regarding control and discipline.
3. Students are placed at two points on the continuum because it appears logical that students coming from Traditionalist families will tend toward that pole in the value line—but less rigidly than their parents; other students will tend to be closer to the opposite pole from their parents. And some students may be found at both extremes of the continuum (youth tends to be more fanatic than the aged.)
4. Older teachers may tend to hold relatively Traditionalist views, by virtue of their age and time of their childhood training. In addition, their experience with success in their profession (when goals may have been something dif-

[11] Ibid., p. 356.

ferent and when the methods and materials certainly were different) may impede their changing too radically in favor of the Emergent pole.

5. School Administrators, by virtue of their advanced training, of their exposure to contemporary philosophical ideas pertaining to theory and practice, and the community expectations concerning their leadership role, are judged to be farther along the line, toward the Emergent pole. The impact of state and federal thinking on the certification policies pertaining to administrators works to force professional educators in this category to the forefront of innovations and change.

6. Young teachers not only acquired their personal culture during a relatively Emergent-oriented period of American history, they also have been exposed to a professional education culture that has become rapidly more emergent-oriented in its value position. They, therefore, are represented by the most radical position for adults and professionals.

Using the perspectives represented by this chart, conflicts between parents and teachers, school boards and educators, parents and children, and groups within the school system can be understood as conflicts which grow out of sharp differences in values.

Spiritual Values. Spiritual values go a step further than moral values. Spiritual values are concerned with what one *thinks*. A belief in a Deity may not be directly involved in moral values. For instance, one may believe that stealing is wrong simply because it is hurtful to others, rather than because of any religious teaching. (That may be why some people feel that stealing from one's enemies is perfectly moral.) But spiritual values involve a higher principle, because of a belief in a religion, or in a religious concept. The Judeo-Christian adherence to the Ten Commandments structures the thinking of its subscribers. For instance, the act of thinking out a plan for committing larceny makes the thinker, in the Judeo-Christian sense, as guilty of committing the sin against the Seventh Commandment as the one who actually commits the act.

Spiritual values are also involved in some questions about teaching. How does one teach? The Thomist contends that there are two activities involved in the act of teaching. One is the external, which is by sensible signs. The teacher activates the senses and the intellect is then stimulated by the sense image which it receives. But man has an intelligible light of his own, and this light is internal. Whereas all teaching depends upon man's having this light, it is thus God, the giver of this light, who is the principal teacher. An analogy with a doctor is useful: The doctor works from without, and nature alone works from within, but the doctor is said to produce health. So man, too, is said to teach the truth, although he enunciates it externally while God teaches from within.

The Common Core of American Values. Since the time of the early immigrants, the American value system has been rapidly changing under the swirling forces of social change, but it still contains a central core of commonly accepted working principles. Some of the ideals of that core, as garnered by Harold Hand from the scholars who analyzed great American documents, court decisions, laws, and folkways, are

1. Human beings are of supreme and equal worth.
   a. Human life and well-being are to be valued above all material things.
   b. The dignity and worth of each person should be equally respected at all times and in all ways.
   c. The good life, however conceived, should be made equally available to all persons through equality of educational opportunity, equality at the ballot box, and equality before the law.
2. Human beings should be the architects of their own destiny.
   a. The capacity to govern wisely does not follow the contours of class, caste, family, ecclesiastical, or property lines.
   b. Repudiated are all doctrines of rule by hereditary or divine right, and rejected all forms of totalitarianism, dictatorship, and tyranny.
   c. As masters rather than instruments of the state, it is the consent of the people which gives power to the government to function, not the reverse.
3. Human well-being can best be advanced only if there is an unrestricted play of free intelligence upon all problems and difficulties. The guarantees given in the Constitution to freedom of thought, belief, speech, assembly, and press are freedoms which are not to be abrogated by any person, majority or even the government itself.
4. The law, under the constitution and as made by representatives chosen by the people which prevents the exercise of arbitrary power will regulate behavior as a self-imposed force.
5. The will of the majority will indicate the path to follow with protection for the minority. It is obligatory for those convinced that the action of the majority is inimical to democratic principles to work to change this will through persuasion, based on reason. However, it is understood that they will abide by the rule while they work to change it.
6. Ballots will be the means used in the change process, not force, and orders of the court will resolve disputes which cannot be talked out.
7. Every person has a right to worship in his own way, think his own thoughts, and speak his mind on any matter not causative of some clear and present danger to others, dress in any fashion not corruptive of public morals, seek employment in any lawful occupation of his own choosing, and domicile himself in any state of the union.[12]

These working principles are not absolute, but change with changing social circumstances. They have to be reinterpreted, reconstructed, or in some cases even abandoned, as new conditions require. In a period of pioneering, when vast virgin territory is being conquered, or in any highly individualized phase of cultural development, the individual may be left largely to himself, to work out his own destiny. Under such conditions his action may have little or no effect upon the public at large. But in a highly interdependent social system, to respect the individual by leaving him alone—as in pioneer days—may lead to evil consequences. Under these highly complex circumstances the individual may either suffer from the acts of others—over which he has no control—or he may do things himself that adversely affect other individuals. Hence, in a highly interrelated social scheme, some measure of social control may be essential to the fulfillment of these working

---

[12] Adapted pages 43–45 from *Principles of American Public Secondary Education* by Harold C. Hand, copyright © 1958 by Harcourt Brace Jovanovich, Inc., and reprinted with their permission.

principles. But some people are so accustomed to thinking in the pattern of simple community life, where formal public controls were all but absent, that it is almost impossible for them to conceive of deliberate public control and freedom and equality for the individual as being correlative terms.

Democratic Values and the Curriculum. Smith, Stanley, and Shores contend that democracy is more than a method of thinking and working together, just as it is more than a political system. As they view it, democracy is a set of moral principles, including the principle of free inquiry and deliberation by the citizen for the control of every aspect of social life. The primary business of the school is to make these principles clear, to show how they are to be used in social thought and action, and to provide experience in using them.[13]

The present school curriculum emphasizes descriptive knowledge of facts and all but neglects the moral content of the culture. In the future, curriculum planners must no longer shrink from considering questions of value; and they must not tolerate the notion that agreement on values is neither important nor feasible in a democracy.

Spiritual Values and the Curriculum. It is difficult, in our pluralistic society, to advocate that spiritual values be incorporated in the public school curriculum. The question always arises: "Which religious concept will be taught?" Even among the Judeo-Christian believers, there is contention as to which tenets of which Jewish or Christian sect, should be selected to be taught. Furthermore, there are religious (and nonreligious) groups that object to any spiritual values being offered in the curriculum. The Supreme Court of the United States therefore has disallowed any spiritual service, or the teaching of any religion, in the public schools. It should also be noted at this point that there are several recent Supreme Court decisions that caution an educator to tread softly regarding "spiritual" enunciations in a classroom. Examples of such cases are *McCollum* v. *Board of Education, Everson* v. *Board of Education,* and *Abington School District* v. *Schempp,* et al.

If spiritual values are disallowed in the public schools, are we therefore setting up a democratic theism? If so, what danger is implied? How can this be circumvented without jeopardizing the concept of separation of church and state? These questions may be the next items on the educational agenda, but once again, who will answer them: the local citizenry, the state, the national government?

Conclusion

If history does repeat itself, and history is a cycle (or circle), where is the present era on that circle? Let us assume that the history of education of the United States started in the Colonial period. The existing schools of that era were democratic in one sense and authoritarian in another sense. The teacher had to live and teach according to the dictates of the people who had hired him. This, in the sense of ultimate responsibility for education, was democratic. But the teacher had full authority to use whatever methodology he deemed necessary to impart his subject matter. The method he chose usually was the lecture and dictation, which are autocratic in nature.

[13] Ibid., pp. 146–150.

According to this view the Bible dictated the moral and spiritual atmosphere of the class. Since it was believed that every child was born bearing the effect of original sin and possessing the devil, the teacher was authorized to use the rod in order to spare the child—to spare him from damnation. In this way the child's moral and spiritual needs were taken care of.

Today's schools allow youth a wide variety of subject matter. The pupil may elect any subject on a wide scale of offerings. No longer does he have to take certain required subjects. For example, the trend today is that a foreign language is no longer required as a high school subject. Nor do colleges require language for admission. In addition, many colleges have reduced the required number of semester hours for graduation to 104.

The teacher today is encouraged to use less lecture and dictation methodology. The emphasis is increasingly on individualization. The open-class concept is here. The teacher must not only have subject matter expertise (or competency); he must know how to communicate it to the pupil. Therefore, the emphasis in schools now is on the *individual* child. This is a step beyond *child-centered*. Does this mean, then, that the individual child may demand some consideration for his moral and/or spiritual values?

But, where on the cycle is education today? We have indicated in the module a trend toward more federal funding of projects for education. Federal funds do not amount to more than 8 per cent of total state expenditure; the question is, will the American public accept more? And if it does, how much more? Whenever there is federal funding there is some type of federal control. How much federal control will the citizens accept. Ultimately, will federal control cause the elimination of local control; will the U.S. Office of Education and a bureaucratic headquarters in some central location in the nation replace the boards of education and school committees in the large cities and tiny hamlets across the country? Or, will the pendulum of school control widen further the arc of its swing and yield still more decentralization than we have functioned with in the recent past? The state of Pennsylvania has taken the "jointure" route, that is, consolidating several small school districts into single larger districts. Recommendations of the Mancuso report in New Jersey have favored the consolidation of small districts, also. In some large metropolitan areas, such as New York City, the movement has been in the opposite direction—away from centralization and toward autonomy for each neighborhood school.

As you continue your inquiry into education as a field of study, one of your tasks will be to resolve this issue in your own mind: Should this country, state, community

1. Carry on as at present?
2. Centralize totally, partially, or return to the neighborhood concept?

SUGGESTED READING

Butts, R. Freeman, and Lawrence A. Cremin. *A History of Education in American Culture.* New York: Holt, Rinehart & Winston, Inc., 1958.

Clark, Leonard H., Raymond L. Klein, and John B. Burks. *The American Secondary School Curriculum,* 2nd Ed. New York: Macmillan Publishing Co., Inc., 1972.

Dropkin, Stan, Harold Full, and Ernest Schwarcz. *Contemporary American Education,* 3rd Ed. New York: Macmillan Publishing Co., Inc., 1975.

Fenton, Edwin. *Teaching the New Social Studies in the Secondary Schools.* New York: Holt, Rinehart & Winston, Inc., 1966.

Full, Harold. *Controversy in American Education: An Anthology of Crucial Issues.* New York: Macmillan Publishing Co., Inc., 1972.

Morris, Van Cleve. *Philosophy and the American School,* Boston: Houghton Mifflin Company, 1961.

Park, Joe. *Selected Readings in the Philosophy of Education,* New York: Macmillan Publishing Co., Inc., 1974.

Rich, John Martin. *Humanistic Foundations of Education.* Worthington, Ohio: Charles A. Jones Publishing Co., 1971.

Thayer, V. T. and Martin Levit. *The Role of the School in American Society.* New York: Dodd, Mead & Co., 1966.

Ulich, Robert. *The Three Thousand Years of Educational Wisdom.* Cambridge, Mass.: Harvard University Press, 1971.

POST TEST

MULTIPLE CHOICE

1. (*Circle one.*) The first text teachers used in Colonial times was
   a. a Latin grammar.
   b. an English grammar.
   c. a reading, writing, and arithmetic text.
   d. the Bible.
   e. a Primer.

2. The cultural background that predominated in the Colonial period was
   a. Scotch-Irish.
   b. Germanic.
   c. Italian.
   d. British.
   e. Dutch.

3. The first schools in the American Colonies were under the jurisdiction of
   a. the English school system.
   b. each colony.
   c. each regional school district.

4. The Tenth Amendment of the U.S. Constitution is concerned with
   a. women's liberation.
   b. establishing a federal school system for the U.S.
   c. anything not included in the U.S. Constitution.

5. Multiple establishment meant that
   a. there were many different national groups in the country.
   b. religious groups which had schools could draw money from the central treasury to help operate their schools.

6. The first school committees were established by
    a. a state mandate to the local communities.
    b. the local community on its own initiative.

7. Compulsory attendance is a product of
    a. Colonial times.
    b. the Industrial Revolution.
    c. the twentieth century.

MATCHING

8. Select the letter in Column Two that matches with the entry in Column One:

I	II
_____Committee of Ten.	**a.** Constants for college entrance.
_____Committee of Thirteen.	**b.** Elementary education.
_____Committee of Fifteen.	**c.** Secondary education.
	d. Higher education.

MULTIPLE CHOICE

9. (*Circle one.*) "An Act to Regulate the Deposits of Public Money" was
    a. an attempt to regulate currency.
    b. an attempt by the local community to regulate school spending.
    c. an attempt by the federal government to support public schools.

10. The Morrill Act included
    a. establishing state universities.
    b. buying land from the states.
    c. establishing railroad rights.

11. Equalization means that the
    a. state attempts to equalize the cost to each community by supplementing the communities' school funds.
    b. state attempts to equalize education by training all teachers on an equal basis.
    c. federal government attempts to equalize the learning of all students by integrating neighborhoods.

12. Values are involved with
    a. how much a thing is worth.
    b. character building.
    c. an etherial thesis.

13. Morals are
    a. why we do something.   **b.** custom or manner.
    c. involved with sin.   **d.** the way one acts.

14. Discipline problems occur when
    a. a student thinks he is right.
    b. a teacher insists he is right.
    c. there is a clash of moral values between student and teacher.
    d. one's rights are abridged.

15. Spiritual values are
   a. always concerned with what society thinks is right or wrong.
   b. concerned with the Deity and the laws of the Deity as expressed in the Ten Commandments.
   c. whatever one's "spirit" drives one to do.

16. Deliberate public controls, as well as freedom and equality for the individual, must be considered as correlative principles for the school because
   a. in our highly complex society, to respect the individual by leaving him alone may lead to evil consequences.
   b. in a highly interrelated social scheme, some measure of social control is essential.
   c. in our industrialized society, the actions of the individual have little or no effect upon the public at large.
   d. a and b, of the above.
   e. a and c, of the above.

17. In Harold Hand's summation of the American Core of values, the majority
   a. will be prevented from the exercise of arbitrary power by the law as made by the people's representatives.
   b. are obliged to work to change the actions that are inimical to democratic principles, but they must abide by the rules while they do it.
   c. must abide by the orders of the court.
   d. consents that the people are masters rather than instruments of the state; they give power to the government, not the reverse.
   e. all of the above.
   f. a, c, and d, of the above.

18. On Spindler's Value Continuum, school administrators tend toward the Emergent (liberal) end because they are
   a. ambitious and wish to make a name for themselves.
   b. better paid and have more power.
   c. required by certification regulations to have advanced training and are exposed to contemporary philosophical ideas on theory and practice.
   d. forced to come into contact, on an intimate level, with politicians, who influence them to espouse liberal causes.

19. It is helpful for all teachers to keep the Value Continuum in mind as they work in a community because it
   a. equips them to form an accurate perspective on criticisms they hear.
   b. forestalls the feeling of shock if the critical comment appears to be coming from the appropriate direction.
   c. reminds them that the search for a critic-less community is fruitless.
   d. establishes a sequence for them to follow in order to diminish the opposition when they have innovations of their own to propose.
   e. all of the above.

MATCHING

20. Record the letter key to Spindler's statements in the appropriate place—to fit under the headings of Traditional or Emergent values.

    a. Respectability, thrift, self-denial.
    b. Work desperately and continuously to convince themselves of their worth.
    c. The individual is sacred.
    d. One should like people and get along with them.
    e. The individual is always more important than the group.
    f. Suspicion of solitary activities is characteristic.
    g. Absolutes in right and wrong are questionable.
    h. Tolerance for the other person's point of view . . . so long as the harmony of the group is not disrupted.
    i. The future, not the past or even the present, is most important.
    j. No one can tell what the future will hold; therefore one should enjoy the present.

Traditional: _____ _____ _____ _____ _____

Emergent: _____ _____ _____ _____ _____

MULTIPLE CHOICE

21. (*Circle One.*) Teachers who use the Do-Nothing Approach to value development in the classroom do so because they
    a. believe that value teaching is the domain of the family.
    b. are unsure themselves about what is right.
    c. are convinced that the best way to build a set of values is by trial and error.
    d. all of the above.
    e. none of the above.

22. A value problem is indicated for a student if
    a. he follows the traditional value pattern.
    b. in the absence of prior emotional disturbance, he finds it very difficult to face typical situations.
    c. he does not behave in ways that are consistent with his choices.
    d. he replaces some of the old values with values recently acquired.
    e. b, d, of the above.
    f. b, c, of the above.

23. The establishment and financing of Teacher Education Centers reflects
    a. an increase of interest in innovations by local-level citizens.
    b. a move by county agencies to contribute their share to the cost of education.
    c. action by the states to discharge responsibilities given them by the U.S. Constitution.
    d. further involvement of the federal government in education, reaching into the local systems.

24. Supporters of federal financing of education agree that
    a. inequities in ability to finance educational efforts require federal action.
    b. population mobility makes federal help a necessity.
    c. it is cheaper for the federal authorities to collect and distribute moneys.
    d. federal support encourages centralization of power.
    e. private and parochial education will grow strong.
    f. a, b, c, d, of the above.
    g. a, d, e, of the above.

Planning a Career

Gerhard K. Haukebo

Moorhead State College

Larry W. Jones

Moorhead State College

module 11

The Teaching License / Salaries and How They Are Established / Teacher Supply and Demand / Organizations for Teachers / Research: Action and Academic / Graduate Study / In-Service Study / Promotion Opportunities / Challenge of Teaching—Geographical Considerations / Additional Information

RATIONALE

The decision to enter teaching is not an easy one to make, nor should it be made lightly. A great number of factors need to be considered, and it is not always easy to get the necessary information. Students tend to have a view of teaching based on personal experiences as a pupil. Usually this view is very incomplete— often glorified, and often distorted.

Some questions about teaching can be answered only after teaching experiences. Will I like teaching? Will I be able to do well in it? Will I have discipline problems? Will children learn from me? Will I find it satisfying? This module contains some ideas and suggestions for obtaining this helpful experience before final decisions are made concerning a career in teaching.

Other kinds of information are needed in order to make a wise decision. This module deals with nine areas of concern to teachers; each subject is explained only in general terms. It must be stressed that this information is only a beginning. It will merely introduce some topics. You will need to expand your investigation, and to relate it to your region and to the changing times.

The questions in the Post Test have been grouped essentially in the same pattern as the Activities for ease in referring to appropriate pages to check the accuracy of your responses.

Objectives

Upon completing your study of this module, you should be able to

1. Explain what is meant by an "approved program" approach to teacher education.
2. Cite the responsibility of your college and your state in the matter of licensing teachers.
3. State one decided advantage to completing an NCATE approved program.
4. Name three sources from which you can get additional information about teacher certification.
5. State three principles which apply to salary schedules in terms of compensation for teaching level, amount of training, and length of experience.
6. List four elements of teacher welfare.
7. Identify the level of government at which most salary schedules are determined.
8. Describe the direction of the current national school-enrollment curve.
9. Describe the projected school enrollment for the balance of this century based upon U.S. Bureau of the Census "modest growth" projections.
10. State what is currently happening to the number and percentage of U.S. college graduates who are preparing for teaching.
11. List at least three sources from which current data about teacher supply and demand is available.

12. List three reasons why teachers need to organize.
13. Name the two major national teacher organizations and at least five good reasons for belonging to one of them.
14. Verbalize at least two reasons why a research component should be included in a teacher education program.
15. List the three basic types of educational research.
16. Select the type of research that is most appropriate for the classroom teacher.
17. Indicate whether or not a research component is included in the professional education sequence at your institution.
18. List the admission requirements for graduate school at two institutions in which you are interested.
19. List the three commonly offered advanced degrees and the amount of time required to complete each of them.
20. Verbalize how earning an advanced degree will affect your salary as a classroom teacher.
21. Identify the three major sources of in-service training.
22. List two advantages to having in-service activities conducted by a college or university.
23. List two advantages to having in-service activities conducted by a local school district.
24. List two reasons why it might be desirable to have a professional organization involved in in-service training.
25. Provide a verbal rationale as to why a certificated teacher should be involved in in-service activities.
26. List at least three positions to which a classroom teacher may be promoted and retain teaching responsibilities.
27. List at least three administrative positions at the building level to which one may be promoted, and the usual requirements of each position.
28. List at least three administrative positions in a central office of a school district to which one may be promoted, and the common requirements of each.
29. Identify two other types of positions, not included under teaching or administration, to which one may aspire.
30. List five elements or characteristics in which schools differ.
31. Identify five kinds of educational positions other than regular classroom teachers.
32. Cite three areas of educational employment opportunities in addition to U.S. public schools.

MODULE TEXT

The Teaching License

If you decide in favor of a teaching career in public education, you will need to earn a license. A license, or teaching certificate, is typically issued upon recommendation of a college or university through what is known as an *approved-*

program approach. That is, institutions that prepare teachers develop academic and experiential programs which they believe will prepare a person for a beginning in teaching. These preparatory programs are reviewed by the state, and if they are considered effective, balanced, cohesive, and well-grounded, the program is approved. Subsequently, the college need only endorse candidates as having successfully completed the program, then the state issues a provisional or probationary certificate. Many other terms are used for the initial certificate, such as *temporory, limited, initial*. These adjectives are intended to suggest that your initial license is short-term, renewable only upon satisfactory performance or additional training, or even both.

Thus the licensing of teachers is considered a responsibility of the state. Many states have adopted certification requirements through what is called *performance-based teacher education* (PBTE), or *competency-based teacher education* (CBTE).(Some consider the former a subset of the latter; others consider the two terms synonymous.) PBTE is an outgrowth of public concern regarding accountability for the educational tax dollar. The concept suggests that a prospective teacher must demonstrate certain skills and competencies before being endorsed by the college. In this form of program, college courses are not necessarily major components of the training program. Rather the college must identify the competencies prospective teachers must develop, procedures for teaching them, and methods of evaluation by which to ensure their presence. This learning may take place in instructional modules, minicourses, laboratories, or in internship experiences.

Any renewal of an initial license becomes a matter of direct communication between a teacher and the appropriate state agency. The college is involved only in the initial license endorsement in any certification program.

Of some interest, even concern to you, may be the matter of where your teaching is valid. Certainly, it qualifies you to teach in the state in which you were prepared. However, there has been a need for a workable plan to allow qualified teachers freedom of movement across state lines. A national accreditation agency, NCATE (National Council for the Accreditation of Teacher Education) offers some opportunity for reciprocity. That is, if the program you complete is NCATE-accredited, you will find that it will be accepted in a majority of states. (An estimated three out of four teachers prepared in our country graduate from NCATE-accredited programs.)

There are several places where you can find out about requirements for certification in your state and in other states. First of all, the college placement office is likely to have manuals and directories which outline requirements in the various states. Secondly, the college library should have the same information as well as references which treat accreditation generally. Third, you can write to the department of education in the state of your interest. Finally, a college catalogue will list programs leading to certification and will specify what kinds of accreditation exists for the program.

A teaching certificate entitles you to teach certain subjects at certain levels. What these are the certificate will indicate. Usually the certificate is renewable upon the grounds of satisfactory teaching experience, additional training, or some evidence of professional growth. The teaching certificate may also be revoked. Reasons for revocation and procedures for doing so vary, but generally they relate to stated standards of ethics, conduct, and professional performance.

Salaries and How They Are Established

Teachers have increasingly organized their efforts to obtain teacher welfare benefits. These include the many elements which go into economic well-being and conditions of employment. The matters of salary, fringe benefits, tenure, and retirement are of particular interest to prospective teachers.

Concerning salary, there are sizeable differences across our country, and indeed between school districts within the same regions. Salaries are essentially a matter of local determination. The wealth of a school district and the public attitude toward education are two important factors that bear on salaries. That is to say, there must be both capacity to support salaries and interest in doing so.

Although salaries do differ widely, several principles apply to most salary guides. These principles begin with the idea that starting salaries are equal within a district regardless of the level of teaching. For example, a beginning kindergarten teacher and a beginning senior high teacher would receive the same salary. Secondly, a teacher advances in salary in direct ratio to experience and, also, as a direct result of additional training. A teacher usually receives an increase after each year of experience, and as advanced training is completed, moves to a new salary lane. Table 11-1 presents a hypothetical salary guide illustrating these principles.

In addition to the basic salary allowed by the salary schedule, many teachers receive additional compensation for extra duties or for special summer work. They are paid extra for coaching, directing a play, supervising extracurricular activities, or for other similar duties.

Not apparent from the sample salary schedule are the fringe benefits which

Table 11-1 Hypothetical Salary Schedule

Level of Training	BA	BA & 15	BA & 30	MA	MA + 15	MA + 30	Doctorate
1	8,000	8,250	8,500	8,750	9,000	9,250	9,500
2	8,300	8,550	8,800	9,150	9,400	9,650	10,000
3	8,600	8,850	9,100	9,550	9,800	10,050	10,500
4	8,900	9,150	9,400	9,950	10,200	10,450	11,000
5	9,200	9,450	9,700	10,350	10,600	10,850	11,500
6	9,500	9,750	10,000	10,750	11,000	11,250	12,000
7	9,800	10,050	10,300	11,150	11,400	11,650	12,500
8	10,100	10,350	10,600	11,550	11,800	12,050	13,000
9	10,400	10,650	10,900	11,950	12.200	12,450	13,500
10	10,700	10,950	11,200	12,350	12,600	12,850	14,000
11	11,000	11,250	11,500	12,750	13,000	13,250	14,500
12	11,300	11,550	11,800	13,150	13,400	13,650	15,000
13	11,600	11,850	12,100	13,550	13,800	14,050	15,500

Years of Experience

(The amounts used are not intended to be representative of actual salaries nor to represent typical dollar differences for training and experience.)

are a part of teacher compensation. Again, the variety and extent of these benefits are a matter of local school district agreements, but they generally include payment toward a retirement fund, group life insurance, and medical and hospitalization insurance.

Another aspect of teacher welfare relates to tenure. Nearly all states have some legislation that regulates the continuance of a teacher's contract. Typically, a teacher must be employed for a probationary period, often three years, before achieving tenure. Tenure means that a person's job status is protected. Tenure is no absolute guarantee of a job, however, it does require certain prescribed procedures before dismissal is legal. These procedures usually include written notice, charges or reasons in writing, and the right to a hearing, as safeguards to the teacher.

The elements of teacher welfare are stipulated in the teacher contract, the legal document binding upon both the teacher and the school district. The contract, in turn, is the product of the collective bargaining negotiations that have taken place between representatives of the recognized or elected teacher group and the school board. Each teacher signs a contract when initially agreeing to accept a position, and each year subsequently, when agreeing to remain in the district.

Teacher Supply and Demand

The decade of the seventies saw a shift in the supply and demand for teachers. There had been a general shortage of teachers in our country since World War II, and now, for the first time, considerable publicity has been given to the oversupply of teachers. It is important to take a closer look at the matter before you, as a prospective teacher, make a final decision about teaching as a career choice. Future school enrollment and the supply of teachers are two elements warranting investigation.

The element that can be predicted for a length of time with relative accuracy is school population. The elementary school enrollment for the next six years is known because those children are already born. Current infants will be first graders in six years. In twelve years, nearly all of those elementary school children will be in Grades 7–12. This prediction of school enrollment in the elementary schools for the next six years and in the secondary schools for the next twelve years will undoubtedly prove correct. School enrollment figures assuming moderate rates of growth have been projected beyond the twelve-year period, until the turn of the century. (See Figure 11-1.) These projections cannot presume accuracy, of course, but they do give a reasonable estimate of enrollment. At any rate, the 1980s should see an upswing in school enrollment and a parallel increase in the need for teachers.

What about the number of students who are training for teaching? A 1973 report from the National Education Association projects a drop in the number of college students entering teaching, and also a drop in terms of the percentage of college graduates going into teaching. (See Tables 11-2 and 11-3.)

However there is, without question, an over-all surplus. The report just cited also projects supply and demand through 1976. Although the percentage of oversupply appears to decline, the surplus continues. (See Table 11-3.)

What these tables do not reveal is the fact that demand for teachers at some

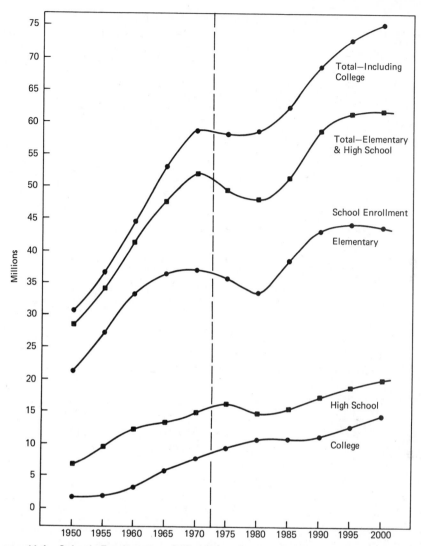

Figure 11-1 *School Enrollments, 1950–2000.* [*The Education Professions, 1971–1972,* Part 1—The Need for Teachers in Our Schools and Colleges (Washington, D.C.: U.S. Department of Health, Education and Welfare, December 1972.)]

grade levels and in some subject areas is greater than others. For example, one study in the early 1970s described shortages in three important categories of classroom teachers; that is, male elementary teachers, Black and Chicano teachers, and bilingual teachers. In addition, the study reported that shortages led to unmet needs for reading specialists, remedial mathematics teachers, industrial arts teachers, vocational education teachers, and science teachers. Of course the supply and demand picture changes each year and varies with regions of the country. One important influence is the health of the economy and the public interest in adequately staffed schools. In times of depression or recession, pressures to reduce staff develop with resultant decreased need for teachers. Conversely, in times of prosperity, there is increased support for quality education and reduced pupil-teacher ratios.

Table 11-2 Numbers of Graduates Prepared to Teach and Total Graduates Receiving the Bachelor's and First Professional Degree

YEAR	GRADUATES COMPLETING PREPARATION TO ENTER TEACHING	TOTAL GRADUATES RECEIVING BACHELOR'S AND FIRST PROFESSIONAL DEGREE	TEACHER EDUCATION GRADUATES AS PERCENT OF TOTAL GRADUATES
1	2	3	4
1971	313,558	877,676	35.0
1972	324,099	903,000*	35.9
1973	312,725	958,000*	32.6
1974	295,550	990,000*	29.9
1975	252,775	1,047,000*	24.1
1976	219,400	1,100,000*	19.9

* Projections: Adapted from NEA Research Memo 1973–8, NEA, June 1973.

A second important influence on supply and demand is the nature of federal government support. If emphasis is made on some special aspect of education, by the federal government, opportunities in that aspect become greater. Recent national priorities have dealt with programs for minority groups, for exceptional students—physically handicapped, learning disabled, retarded, or gifted—with early childhood education, and with reading instruction. No one should elect to go into a particular teaching area simply because of greater demand. However, a personal program of teacher training, which recognizes both national concerns and personal interests, might be planned. It is a truism that there will always be a demand for good teachers. It is also true that through careful planning of your preparation program, you can enhance your employment opportunities.

A primary source of information about teacher supply and demand is the college placement office. A representative of that office will be able to provide current data, describe qualities, special training, or other characteristics currently in demand, and list academic subjects or combinations of subjects particularly sought. A second source of information is the college counseling center. Often career counseling is one of the missions of that center and information about projected needs in various fields may be kept on file. Third, a college academic advisor may have helpful information or suggest still other sources of information.

In addition, there are a host of organizations and agencies that may be helpful in getting current information. The National Education Association and the Ameri-

Table 11-3 Supply and Demand for Beginning Teachers in Public Schools, 1972 to 1976

SESSION	SUPPLY OF BE-GINNING TEACHERS	DEMAND FOR BE-GINNING TEACHERS	DIFFERENCE	SUPPLY AS PER-CENT OF DEMAND
1	2	3	4	5
1972–73	243,200	132,100	111,100	184.1
1973–74	234,550	111,300	123,250	210.7
1974–75	221,675	110,400	111,275	200.8
1975–76	189,575	102,500	87,075	185.0
1976–77	164,550	115,100	49,450	143.0

Estimated data adapted from NEA Research Memo 1973–8, NEA, June 1973.

can Federation of Teachers and their affiliated state-level organizations are vitally interested in statistics on supply and demand. The U.S. Office of Education frequently publishes reports on the national picture. State departments also issue reports. State employment services deal with teachers along with all other fields. Thus, there are many sources from which a person can receive data—current and applicable to a geographic area.

Organizations for Teachers

There is a growing recognition by professional educators of the need for teachers to organize. First of all, it is increasingly important in this sociological era for some group to exert political influence at the national and state levels on matters of importance to education. Organizations such as the U.S. Chamber of Commerce, and the National School Boards Association are interested in public education but they do not represent the viewpoints of professional educators on governmental decisions.

In addition to political influence, it is recognized that teachers need to be organized in order to negotiate matters important to education, such as teacher welfare, salaries, academic freedoms, and contracts.

Teacher organizations consequently are expressing increased interest in influencing the selection of future teachers, the nature of preservice and in-service training, the rights and responsibilities of teachers, and the maintaining of professional standards by all members of the profession.

Because you should be interested in the teacher organizations that intend to play such a significant role in education, it is important that you know something about them.

Nationally, teachers are represented by two organizations, the American Federation of Teachers and the National Education Association. The major purpose of both groups is to improve the teaching profession and thereby improve education in America.

The National Education Association has about one and a quarter million members. Its officially stated purpose is "to elevate the character and advance the interests of the profession of teaching and to promote the cause of education in the United States." Recently adopted goals are: "an independent, united teaching profession; professional excellence; economic security for all educators; adequate financing for public education; human and civil rights for all educators and children; and leadership in solving social problems." An elaborate system of representative governance allows for grass-roots influence on the organization. Publications of the organization contribute to professional growth, curriculum development, and research findings.

In addition to being the larger organization, the NEA is older, having celebrated its centennial in 1957.

The American Federation of Teachers, a younger organization, was founded in 1916 and is currently affiliated with the American Federation of Labor-Congress of Industrial Organizations. Its current membership of one-quarter million is nationwide, although historically its membership was predominantly from metropolitan areas and the Northeast. As stated in its constitution, its objectives are fivefold. "(1) To bring the association of teachers into relations of mutual assistance and cooperation; (2) to obtain for them all the rights to which they are entitled; (3) to raise the standards of the teaching profession by securing the conditions essential to the best professional service; (4) to promote such a democratization of the schools as will enable them to better equip their pupils to take their places in the industrial, social, and political life of the community; and (5) to promote the welfare of the childhood of the nation by providing progressively better educational opportunity for all." The AFT offers conventions, conferences, and publications on legislative happenings as they concern teachers, as well as publications of various sorts.

Both organizations offer benefits to members, such as group buying services, credit unions, legal aid, insurance, and vacation tours. Both have organizations at the state level which specifically focus on school financing and on teacher licensure. Affiliated local organizations are also a feature of both groups.

At the local level, there has often been particularly keen competition for membership. Because teacher welfare negotiations are primarily conducted within each school district, the organization with the larger membership locally has majority, or even sole, responsibility for the negotiations. In school districts where the local chapters are of relatively equal size, the competition has sometimes become bitter. Unfortunately, the battle between teacher groups diverts energies from the more productive pursuit of solving educational problems. Therefore, many educational leaders of both groups are speaking out for discussion and action toward merging.

Research: Action and Academic

It has been said that research has established itself as a primary vehicle by which change is promoted and effected in education. If we accept this as a valid premise, then it is not difficult to understand why change is so difficult to bring about in education. Because virtually no teacher preparation institutions include any work in either conducting or interpreting research at the undergraduate level, it is the rare teacher that can function competently in these areas.

There are a number of federally funded research and development centers and regional educational laboratories that annually produce and disseminate curriculum materials and training modules designed for teachers in the public schools. Their efforts, however, are rarely tried out and even less frequently adopted. One of the primary reasons for this is the fact that only a small percentage of practicing teachers regularly read any research journals. Time is certainly a factor here, but another is the lack of training to assist in understanding the implications of what is written. This inability to understand in turn causes feelings of anxiety about and even hostility toward anything remotely related to research in any form. The net outcome is that a vast majority of teachers remain uninformed about new developments in education, and their students suffer as a result.

Educational research projects can be classified into three basic types: (1) descriptive research, (2) historical research, and (3) experimental research. Each of the foregoing types has a unique focus which distinguishes it from the others.

Descriptive research has a distinctive thrust, and is research in its broadest sense. Its purpose is to systematically describe the facts and characteristics of a given population or area of interest. Within the definition are encompassed such subtopics as developmental, case or field study, correlational, causal-comparative, quasi-experimental, and action research. Our primary interest is *action research* because it is the type most serviceable for teachers. As a subdefinition, its purpose can be said to be that of developing new skills or approaches to the solving of problems that will have direct application to the classroom setting. To carry out action research in the classroom the teacher goes through a fairly well-defined series of steps.

1. Define the problem or goal.
2. Review the related literature.
3. State testable hypotheses as clearly as possible.
4. Arrange the setting and establish the procedures and conditions.
5. Determine the means of acquiring feedback.
6. Analyze the data and evaluate the outcomes.

Historical research has as its purpose the systematic and objective reconstruction of the past. This is accomplished by the process of collecting, evaluating, verifying, and synthesizing evidence to establish facts and reach defensible conclusions. Most often this is done in relation to hypotheses that have been formulated. Insofar as the classroom teacher is concerned, except for those that may have occasion to write a thesis requiring this approach, it would be only rarely employed.

Experimental research is the most sophisticated of the three types discussed. Its function is to investigate possible cause-effect relationships brought about by exposing one or more experimental groups to one or more treatment conditions. The results are then compared with the results of one or more control groups that did not receive the treatment. Ordinarily, the beginning classroom teacher would have limited exposure to this level of research and would probably focus to a greater extent upon action research.

It has been found, then, that most undergraduate teacher education programs do not include a research component, and consequently there is general misunderstanding on the part of many classroom teachers concerning the application of educational research findings. The fact that change is so difficult to bring about in education has been attributed by many to this lack of training in conducting research and in using research findings in the classroom.

Although there are numerous kinds of research, the classroom teacher need not necessarily acquire expertise in any or all of them. Instead, what is needed is an overview, and an understanding of the various types. If, for teachers, one were to be emphasized over the other, it would probably be wise to focus upon action research.

The ultimate beneficiaries of an increased understanding of research and its implications for the classroom would be the students, because the teacher would have some basis for making systematic judgments about competing curriculums and methods of teaching. Eventually, a knowledge of research techniques may be the most significant factor in improving education.

Graduate Study

Subsequent to completing an undergraduate degree and receiving certification, the prospective teacher faces a choice. At that time, he or she must decide whether to accept a teaching position or pursue a program of graduate studies. Eventually, even the majority of those who decide to seek employment immediately will, in all likelihood, complete a sequence of graduate work.

When a graduate program is decided upon, this precipitates some additional decisions. Some of the questions to ask oneself are the following:

1. What curriculum should I pursue? Should my advanced studies be in a subject-matter area, in professional education, or in some combination of the two?
2. How should it be related to my immediate and long-range career choices? To certification requirements for various positions within a school system?
3. What type of institutions should I consider? Are some programs clearly superior to others?
4. What is the cost of obtaining a graduate education? Does it seem within my financial capacity to pursue such an undertaking? How can costs be minimized?
5. Can a program of graduate studies be undertaken on a part-time basis? During summers only?
6. What are the entrance requirements of the various institutions that offer graduate work?
7. What types of certificates and degrees can be obtained through graduate study?

The first question to consider, then, is that of what curriculum to pursue. Those whose preparation is at the elementary level usually undertake advanced study in professional education. The content of these programs usually includes work in the areas of curriculum development and instructional analysis, as well as in methods of teaching elementary school subjects.

Candidates whose undergraduate work prepared them for teaching in a secondary school ordinarily have academic majors and minors. For them the decision is somewhat more complex. They must choose between continuing to pursue their chosen academic major, taking up a study of the area of professional education, or a combination of the two.

If the decision is to undertake advanced study in professional education, the content of the program often includes work in the areas of curriculum development and instructional analysis, as well as methods of teaching secondary school subjects. A graduate student making this choice usually gains a broad overview of the educational process at the secondary level.

In all cases, it is important to relate the question of what curriculum to pursue to both immediate and long-range career choices. For example, if one aspires to become a school administrator, the academic requirements for this position should be thoroughly investigated prior to making the initial decision regarding the content of any program of graduate studies. Failure to follow such a procedure could ultimately lead to either (1) the necessity for completing additional years of academic study, or (2) abandonment of a hoped-for career choice. Because neither prospect is desirable, one should be acutely aware of the importance of initial decisions.

It is undoubtedly true that, in all fields, qualitative differences exist between institutions offering graduate work. Some pragmatic considerations for the prospective student to weigh are (1) tuition cost, (2) location, and (3) admission requirements. Although some of the prestigious private universities can offer an excellent graduate education, this fact makes little difference to the student who cannot afford to attend. The state-supported colleges and universities cost much less for tuition and, in many instances, provide outstanding programs.

Location is directly related to total cost. One of the realities to consider when contemplating attending an institution located some distance away is the high cost of moving. If a family and furniture are to be included, expenses rise exponentially. One way to avoid the cost of establishing a new residence is to attend graduate school during the summer month only. Numerous institutions of higher education have extensive summer programs where, during three or four summers of study, one can earn a Master's degree and, at the same time, keep his teaching position.

When a program of graduate studies is being considered, the entrance requirements of the various institutions should be investigated. Although the standards for admission may vary widely from school to school, in almost all cases they do exist. The criteria established by most institutions include the following: (1) the undergraduate grade-point average—usually a 300/400 is a minimum standard, and (2) the verbal score on some standardized test, such as the Graduate Record Examination. Although these are not absolutes, a candidate who does not meet the minimum standards in each case will usually be admitted to a program of studies on a probationary basis contingent upon satisfactory performance in the first term of studies.

The last point to consider is the outcome of the program of studies to be pursued. Will it be a collection of graduate hours, a type of certification not previously held, an advanced degree, or some combination of these?

Many students who have taken graduate work end up with merely a collection of graduate hours, but it is not usually by design that this occurs. In most instances this is the result of poor planning at the outset. Among the unpleasant consequences are the following:

1. The failure to obtain an advanced degree may harm one's chances for advancement.
2. Most districts recognize acquisition of an advanced degree with additional remuneration, and failure to obtain one can result in significant financial loss.
3. Some states now require a planned fifth year of studies in order to achieve standard certification. By simply accumulating an unplanned sequence of courses, a student could conceivably end up with neither an advanced degree nor regular certification.

An advanced program pursued by many educators is the Fifth Year Certification program. Some of our more progressive states now require a planned fifth year program for regular certification and, in addition, ask that a teacher earn renewal units every fourth or fifth year to continue his certificate.

Three advanced degrees usually offered in post-baccalaureate studies in education include

1. *The Master's degree.* This is usually a fifth-year program consisting of approximately 45 hours of graduate work. It may culminate in a thesis.

2. *The Specialist degree.* This usually requires another year beyond the Master's degree. Ordinarily a field study is a part of this kind of program.

3. *The Doctor's degree.* This represents the terminal professional degree. It typically requires four years of training beyond the Bachelor's degree, as well as a scholarly dissertation.

In each instance the candidate can be either a specialist or a generalist. Most often the last two degrees are undertaken with a specific professional position in mind. Obviously, then, graduate study offers a wide range of choices to those who would pursue it. The most critical aspect is adequate forethought and planning prior to beginning a program of studies.

In-Service Study

A realization that is quickly brought home to the beginning teacher is that his preparation is far from complete. It has become an article of faith today that the changing nature of our society requires virtually all citizens to gain new skills and intellectual orientations throughout their lives. No group is more affected by the need for continual self-renewal than the members of the teaching profession. There are various definitions for in-service education. The one that follows serves well the intent of this discussion.

a planned program of continuous learning which would provide opportunities for growth through formal thinking and informal on-the-job experiences for all professional personnel within a school district.

Historically, the majority of in-service training has come from three sources. They are (1) the colleges and universities, (2) the school districts, and (3) the professional organizations. Generally, colleges and universities offer extension classes in the local school districts within their service areas. The local districts, either singly or in cooperation with one another, can usually have special courses designed to meet their needs. An advantage for classroom teachers, under this arrangement, is that college credits are usually accepted in all districts and can be transferred from place to place should a teacher move elsewhere. Another advantage is that this kind of in-service credit can ordinarily be applied toward both advanced degrees and to additional types of certification. For example, if a classroom teacher aspires to become a supervisor or an administrator, he can often use this type of in-service training to that end.

Most school districts are active in providing in-service training. When an activity or workshop is established by a district it is usually addressed to the specific needs of local groups or individuals, more so than are courses offered by college and universities. The fact that faculty planning groups, functioning in cooperation with the administration can perform needs assessments permits the planners to accurately determine what the staff members want and need. As a result, responsiveness to local needs is a distinct advantage for district sponsorship. Most districts also offer what is generally termed *cycle credit* for staff participation in these kinds of activities. This type of credit allows a teacher to advance on the district salary schedule, but it is ordinarily not transferable to other districts if a teacher should move elsewhere. Cycle credit may also be applied toward renewal of continuing certificates, in those states that have put such regulations into effect.

Professional organizations represent the third major group involved in in-service training. In the larger cities, these groups may be very active at the local level. Smaller communities often do not have highly organized professional organizations, but the state level usually assumes this function. The focus of these groups tends to be topical, and on a year-by-year basis. Some areas frequently dealt with include supervision, curriculum development, educational research, and so on. The larger and more well-known organizations enjoy a number of advantages in the in-service area: (1) financial resources adequate to insure quality offerings, (2) an administrative structure capable of organizing programs for large numbers of persons, and (3) a membership that often represents some homogenous interests with respect to additional training.

Promotion Opportunities

A prospective teacher may wonder what opportunities exist for promotion within a school district. The various positions available for advancement are more easily understood if they are viewed in terms of a two-by-two matrix. The categories used here include teaching, supervision and administration, school building, and central administration. A diagram of this matrix is shown as Figure 11-2.

Cell *A* of the matrix represents promotion opportunities for teachers who wish to remain in the classroom and actually teach children. Teachers who desire to go this route would find most opportunities for promotion in schools that employ differentiated staffing patterns. Figures 11-3 and 11-4 illustrate two varieties of differentiated staffing patterns. Some of the responsibilities that might be assumed by a career teacher in the differentiated staffing promotion approach include

1. *Teaching Curriculum Specialist.* Works directly with all instructional personnel for the improvement of instruction. This could be combined with the position of Teaching Research Specialist, in a small school.
2. *Senior Teacher.* The teacher's teacher serves as a subject head or team leader, and spends at least one-half time with students.
3. *Staff Teacher.* Full-time teaching responsibilities with students, this is the position most like that of teachers in nondifferentiated staff patterns.
4. *Associate Teacher.* A beginning teacher who performs regular teaching duties under the direction of a senior teacher.

		Place of Assignment	
		School Building	Central Administration
Type of Assignment	Teaching	A	B
	Administration and Supervision	C	D

Figure 11-2 *Promotion Opportunities Matrix.*

				Nontenure	REGULAR SALARY SCHEDULE
				TEACHING RESEARCH ASSOCIATE Doctorate or equivalent	Twelve Months
			Nontenure		
			TEACHER CURRIC. ASSOC. M.S., M.A. or equivalent		Eleven Months
		Nontenure			
		SENIOR TEACHER M.S., M.A. or equivalent			Ten to Eleven Months
	Tenure				
	STAFF TEACHER B.A. degree plus 1 year				Ten Months
Nontenure					
ACADEMIC ASSISTANT A.A. or B.A. degree					Ten Months
Some teaching responsibilities	100% teaching responsibilities	4/5's staff + teaching responsibilities	3/5's-4/5's staff + teaching responsibilities	3/5's staff + teaching responsibilities	
EDUCATIONAL TECHNICIANS					

Figure 11-3 *Proposed Differentiated Staffing Model.*

5. *Assistant Teacher.* Skilled paraprofessional or teacher intern who may instruct in special areas, maintain physical materials, grade papers, and supervise student study.
6. *Educational Technician.* Manages and operates learning-resource equipment, helping teachers in its use and in preparation of specialized materials.
7. *Teacher's Aide.* Keeps records, duplicates materials, types, checks attendance, monitors student activities, and otherwise assumes clerical and housekeeping tasks formerly consuming much teacher time.

As can be seen in Cell *A* of the matrix, in the more traditional schools the promotion route ordinarily leads to the departmental chairmanship at the secondary level, or the team leader's position in the elementary school. Another route to be considered is that of administration and supervision at the building level represented as Cell *C*. There are a number of positions at that level to which a teacher may aspire. Included among them are the following:

1. *Dean of Boys/Girls.* These positions are a combination of administration and counseling. They serve a student personnel function in such areas as guidance, discipline, and attendance. A Master's degree in either counseling or administration, and successful teaching experience, are usually required.
2. *Assistant principal for administrative affairs.* This position is concerned with at least two functions: (1) the business affairs of the school and (2) directing the activities of the deans and others responsible for student personnel services. A Master's or specialist degree in administration and successful teaching experience are usually needed.

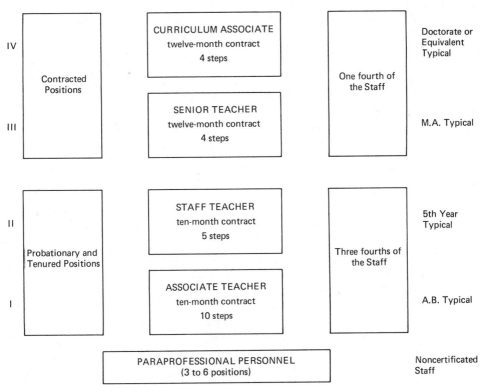

Figure 11-4 *Proposed Teacher Hierarchy Based on Differentiated Compensation and Responsibilities.* [Source: M. John Rand and Fenwick English, "Towards a Differentiated Teaching Staff," *Phi Delta Kappan,* 49:266 (January 1968)]

3. *Assistant principal for curriculum and instruction.* This position is concerned with improvement of the content of the school curriculum and upgrading the skills of the instructional staff. A Master's or specialist degree in administration and successful teaching experience, representing a broad background in curriculum planning and administration, are usually required.

4. *Principal.* The principal is regarded as the instruction leader of the school and is ultimately responsible for all the activities carried on there. He deals with such diverse matters as curriculum, student personnel activities, instruction, personnel questions, public relations, and school financial matters. For this position, one must hold at least a Master's or specialist degree, and probably would have held other leadership positions before arriving at this point.

There are some differences between positions on the secondary and elementary levels. Ordinarily, an elementary school has a principal who must personally carry out most of the functions just described. This is because many elementary schools have only three to four hundred students, and cannot support additional administrative staff members. In the junior and senior high schools, however, the picture is somewhat different; enrollments are much larger and therefore a more comprehensive administrative structure can be used.

At the central administration level there are numerous opportunities for promotion, and, depending upon the size of the district, there may be several specialized positions available. Those most frequently found in an average-sized school district are (in Cell *B*):

1. *Curriculum Supervisor.* A curriculum supervisor may deal with the entire range of the curriculum or only a single subject-field. Most often, a school district will have two or more persons in this position, with responsibilities divided according to elementary and secondary levels. Requirements for this position usually include a Master's degree and successful teaching experience.

2. *Assistant Superintendent—Curriculum.* This position is concerned with over-all responsibility for curriculum development at the district levels. He or she is concerned with developing and field-testing new programs, and revising existing programs. Improvement of instruction is also often one of the responsibilities. This person is usually trained to the Master's or specialist level, and, in many instances, may be expected to have completed the doctorate. It is also customary to have had both prior teaching and administrative experience.

3. *Assistant Superintendent—Business.* In this position, the primary concerns are the financial matters: school district budgets, bond issues, and related activities. With the increasing concern for accountability throughout the country, the influence of this position is growing. Training in a business-related area, and educational administration at the M.S. level or above, is usually required.

4. *Assistant Superintendent—Personnel.* The person holding this position deals with the certificated and noncertificated staff in matters relating to salaries, benefits, and working conditions. Hiring new staff and conducting in-service programs for the existing staff are also his concern. The requirements usually are a Master's or specialist degree, and previous teaching and administrative experience.

5. *Superintendent.* The superintendent is the chief school officer, who has the ultimate responsibility for all aspects of the school program. The superintendent must represent the school to the community, and see to it that there is accountability for each tax dollar spent. An increasing number of superintendents hold the doctorate and the specialist degree is becoming a minimum requirement. Years of teaching experience, as well as a number of increasingly responsible administrative positions are generally considered prerequisite for the position.

There are many other positions of responsibility that we have not dealt with. They include the areas of counseling, support services—such as special education —and other specialized fields. The numbers of these positions, and their requirements, vary with each district.

The Challenge of Teaching—Geographical Considerations

The educational enterprise in America is extremely vast and diverse. Nearly fifty million elementary and secondary pupils attend schools taught by more than two million teachers. The variety of professional positions in the enterprise is also vast, but the majority of those involved in public school work are regular classroom teachers. There are many ways in which faculties are organized: by departments, grade levels, teams, specialities, and so on. The regular teachers usually are supported by an auxiliary staff in a variety of ways. Counselors, media specialists, psychologists, social workers, general- or special-subject consultants, specialists working with handicapped, and nurses are examples of support personnel, some of whom are present in most schools. The number of faculty and staff members, and the way they are organized, makes each school truly unique.

In addition to the differences in staffing patterns are demographic differences. Schools have different characteristics, depending on their urban, suburban or rural location. Each type of setting offers unique problems, challenges, and opportunities. Each requires personnel that understand the community and students. Teachers must respect the cultural diversity of our country and work within any of the settings in a way that does not deprecate people from other locales.

The sizes of schools vary greatly. The range is a few schools with less than a dozen in each, to many schools with several thousands in each school. Schools differ in terms of how traditional or experimental they are. The wealth or poverty of the community has a strong bearing on the school and its offerings. So do the school's alumni, their loyalty and interest in the school and their later experiences in the world of work and post secondary education have an influence.

A good point for a potential teacher to remember is that one's personality, talents, and training should be considered when looking for a school. The characteristics of schools differ in urban, suburban, and rural America. Whether the school is in a large or small district, has a traditional or innovative curriculum, or is culturally diverse, with a homogeneous student population, are factors to consider when choosing a school to suit oneself.

Other areas in education which might be attractive to the more adventurous are the Peace Corps and Vista programs. Perhaps not as well known are the private international schools. These use English as a major language, and flourish in major cities around the world. Some are supported by large corporations and others by the U.S. Department of State. The U.S. Department of Defense also operates overseas schools for dependents living on major military installations.

The business world abounds with positions that are educational-related: sales, product development, instructional materials, and so on. In particular, technology is rapidly entering and influencing schools and teaching.

A wide range of opportunities and challenges exists within the schools and in education-related fields. Examine, research, and prepare yourself for the area that attracts you.

ADDITIONAL INFORMATION

Journals

The following journals are published for teachers in specific disciplines. Subscriptions at a considerable reduction are available to prospective teachers in these disciplines. (Some subscriptions are available only with student membership in the professional organizations concerned.)

The American Biology Teacher, % Merry Lightner, Sec.-Treas., Great Falls High School, Great Falls, Mont. 59401.

American Teacher Magazine, American Federation of Teachers, AFL-CIO, 716 North Rush Street, Chicago, Ill. 60611

The Arithmetic Teacher, National Council of Teachers of Mathematics, 1201 Sixteenth St., N.W. Washington, D.C. 20036

Business Education World, Gregg Division, McGraw-Hill Book Coompany, 330 West 42nd Street, New York, N.Y. 10036

Dramatics Magazine, National Thespian Society, College Hill Station, Cincinnati, Ohio 45224

Elementary English, National Council of Teachers of English, 508 South Sixth Street, Champaign, Ill. 61822

Exceptional Children, The Council for Exceptional Children, 1201 Sixteenth St., N.W., Washington, D.C. 20036

The French Review, American Association of Teachers of French, Sec.-Treas., J. Henry Owens, Eastern Michigan University, Ypsilanti, Mich. 48197

The German Quarterly, American Association of Teachers of German, 334 Huntington B. Crouse Hall, Syracuse University, Syracuse, N.Y. 13210

Hispania, American Association of Teachers of Spanish and Portuguese, James Van Rooy, Printer, South Memorial Drive, Appleton, Wis. 54910

Journal of Health, Physical Education Recreation, American Association for Health, Physical Education and Recreation, 1201 Sixteenth St., N.W., Washington, D.C., 20036

Mathematics Teacher, National Council of Teachers of Mathematics, 1201 Sixteenth St., N.W., Washington, D.C. 20036

The Modern Language Journal, National Federation of Modern Language Teachers, Inc., 5500 Thirty-Third St., N.W., Washington, D.C. 20015

Music Educators Journal, Music Educators National Conference, 1201 Sixteenth Street, N.W., Washington, D.C. 20036

NEA Journal, National Education Association, 1201 Sixteenth Street, N.W., Washington, D.C., 20036

The Quarterly Journal of Speech, Speech Association of America, William Work, Ex. Sec., Statler Hilton Hotel, New York, N.Y., 10001

The Science Teacher, National Science Teachers Association, 1201 Sixteenth Street, N.W., Washington, D.C. 20036

Organizations and Offices

The following organizations and offices have a primary interest in teachers and teacher preparation.

American Association of Colleges for Teacher Education, One DuPont Circle, Washington, D.C. 20036

American Federation of Teachers, AFL-CIO, 716 North Rush St., Chicago, Ill. 60611

Association of Teacher Educators, 1201 Sixteenth St., N.W. Washington, D.C., 20036

ERIC Clearinghouse on Teacher Education, Suite 616, One DuPont Circle, Washington, D.C. 20036

National Council for Accreditation of Teacher Education, 1750 Pennsylvania Ave. N.W., Suite 411, Washington, D.C. 20006

National Education Association, 1201 Sixteenth St., N.W., Washington, D.C. 20036

United Nations Educational, Scientific and Cultural Organization, Place de Fontenoy, 75 Paris, France 7e

U.S. Office of Education, Department of Health, Education, and Welfare, Washington, D.C. 20202

Activities to Pursue

1. Interview a teacher to find out about his teaching certificate. How had he initially earned it? For how long was it valid before he needed to renew it? What does it qualify him to teach? What is necessary for renewal?

2. Review your college catalogue to determine what kinds of accreditation are in effect for your teacher education program.

3. Check references in your library concerning NCATE (National Council for the Accreditation of Teacher Education). Can you find a listing of states that will issue teaching certificates to candidates who have completed an NCATE accredited program?

4. Ask your advisor or an Education Department faculty member how basic requirements for teacher preparation are established in your state.

5. Visit an area school and ask for a copy of the current salary schedule. Write to schools in the area where you would like to teach and ask for copies of their salary schedules. Write to the school board association in your state and ask about the availability of any salary studies they have conducted.

6. Interview a teacher friend or acquaintance to find out what fringe benefits are a part of his compensation.

7. Write to the organization in your state that is affiliated with the American Federation of Teachers, or to the National Education Association, to find out what the statewide goals are in terms of teacher welfare.

8. Visit your college placement office. Inquire whether a recent teacher placement report is available to you. Ask if there is information indicating the degree of teacher surplus in various areas, whether some shortages exist, what special training seems to be in demand (media training, reading training, and so on) and if certain combinations of subject areas are sought more than others. Find out the per cent of placement for candidates during the past several years in the field of your interest.

9. Write to your state department of education and ask for recent reports on teacher supply and demand.

10. Interview a principal or other school official. Determine his perceptions of surplus or shortage of teachers. Find out what specialized training is needed, and sought, when interviewing candidates.

11. Join your campus chapter of either NEA or AFT affiliation. Your dues as a student will be only a few dollars, a fraction of what it costs a teacher in the field. You will receive publications, liability insurance, and access to conferences and meetings. You may become a leader in your local group and represent your college at state, regional, or even national meetings.

12. If your campus does not have a student chapter of the organization you prefer, get some friends together and establish a chapter. Write to the appropriate state unit and ask for assistance in getting started.

13. Review the undergraduate teacher education curriculum at the institution you currently attend. Is any provision made for introducing the prospective teacher to the field of research?

14. Talk to some teachers in your local community. Ask them if they have conducted any classroom research in the last year; if they have read, in the last 30 days, any research-oriented professional journals. Ask them on what basis the current curriculum was selected over other competing curriculums.

15. Visit with the Dean of Graduate Studies at the college or university you are attending. Find out what the requirements for admittance to an advanced program are. Project your current GPA and other information to the time you will graduate. Will you qualify for admittance?

16. Visit a school district in your area and talk to the Personnel Director. Find out if an advanced degree is recognized on the salary schedule. Ask him what proportion of the teachers hold an advanced degree. Compare this with the proportion of the administrators possessing such a degree.

17. Write to your State Department of Education. Determine the degree requirements for certification in the various positions available in the typical school district.

18. Write down your short-range and long-range career objectives in education. What are the academic requirements for each?

19. Visit with the Director of Continuing Education at the college or university you are attending. Find out what arrangements he or she has with the school districts in his service areas for meeting their special needs. Are courses and workshops taught in the local communities? What is the source for instructors? Are they regular college staff members, or adjunct faculty from other professional backgrounds? Determine whether the costs to individual teachers are the same as for on-campus students.

20. Visit a school district in your area and speak with the person in charge of in-service education. Find out whether they have a planned program of in-service activities for all staff members. Ask what proportion of the school district staff annually takes advantage of the activities. How do the school district workshops relate to salary schedules and to renewal of continuing certificates?

21. Find the names of the professional organizations in the school district in your present community. Talk to the directors of these groups and find out whether they have, or are thinking of sponsoring, any in-service activities for teachers. How does the range of topics compare with that offered by the colleges and universities? the school district?

22. Talk to teachers at both the elementary and secondary levels in your community. How do they feel about in-service education? Were their responses consistent with what you had predicted they would be? If not, write down why you think this was so.

23. Visit with the Personnel Director of the school district in your local area. Ask what kinds of promotions are available to classroom teachers who wish to remain in teaching. Find out what proportion of the teaching staff this represents at the secondary level and at the elementary level. Ask him what types of administrative positions exist and the requirements for each. Is teaching experience needed in order to be considered for these positions?

24. Write to your State Department of Education and ask for a copy of the certification handbook. What requirements are mandatory for the various positions?

25. Develop a written statement in the form of a contract in which you stipulate the services you can offer to a school in return for being a short-term paraprofessional within that school. For example, you might offer to work one week full-time in the school, directly responsible to an assigned teacher. You might offer to correct papers, prepare bulletin boards, duplicate materials, tutor a student, prepare instructional materials, operate audiovisual equipment, and so on, in return for the right of observing in the classroom and learning more about the role of instructional and supervisory staff members.

26. Visit your college placement office to determine what unique vacancies are available. Ask about vacancies other than domestic, and other than in public schools.

27. Secure a copy of a school district telephone directory and look over the variety of job categories. Arrange to interview a person in the sort of position that seems to interest you.

28. Go to your library and find out how to use ERIC (Educational Resources Information Center). It will take you only a matter of minutes to find out how this system of information cataloguing and retrieval operates.

29. Once you understand how to locate ERIC documents, you will find that the *Thesaurus of ERIC Descriptors* has the following subject listings under "Teachers." Select several subjects of the greatest interest to you and then scan the titles under that subject heading in the monthly publication *Research in Education.* You may find very recent information of special interest to you.

TEACHERS
UF Instructors
NT Beginning Teachers
Chemistry Teachers
Coaching Teachers
College Teachers
Cooperating Teachers
Elementary School Teachers
Foreign Language in Elementary
    Schools Teachers
Former Teachers
Homebound Teachers
Industrial Arts Teachers
Language Teachers
Lay Teachers
Master Teachers
Mathematics Teachers
Methods Teachers
Minority Group Teachers
Negro Teachers
Nun Teachers
Part-Time Teachers
Partnership Teachers
Preschool Teachers
Professors
Remedial Teachers
Resource Teachers
Science Teachers
NT Secondary School Teachers
Special Education Teachers
Student Teachers
Teacher Interns
Teacher Nurses
Television Teachers
Vocational Education Teachers
Women Teachers

BT Instructional Staff
Professional Personnel
RT Academic Rank (Professional)
Adult Educators
Counselor Educators
Employees
Home Visits
Instructor Coordinators
Noninstructional Responsibility
One-Teacher Schools
Professional Occupations
Specialists
Student-Teacher Ratio
Student-Teacher Relationship
Teacher Aides
Teacher Attitudes
Teacher Background
Teacher Characteristics
Teacher Distribution
Teacher Education
Teacher Employment
Teacher Evaluation
Teacher Exchange Programs
Teacher Experience
Teacher Guidance
Teacher Housing
Teacher Improvement
Teacher Motivation
Teacher Orientation
Teacher Participation
Teacher Placement
Teacher Programs
Teacher Promotion
Teacher Qualifications
Teacher Recruitment

Teacher Response	Teacher Stereotypes
Teacher Responsibility	Teacher Supervision
Teacher Role	Teacher Transfer
Teacher Salaries	Teacher Workshops
Teacher Selection	Teachers Colleges
Teacher Seminars	Teaching
Teacher Shortage	

SUGGESTED READING

Hyman, Ronald T. *Ways of Teaching.* Philadelphia: J. B. Lippincott Co., 1970.

Nelson, Lois N. *The Nature of Teaching.* Boston: Ginn and Company, 1969.

Palardy, J. Michael. *Teaching Today: Tasks and Challenges.* New York: Macmillan Publishing Co., Inc., 1975.

Postman, Neil, and Charles Weingartner. *The School Book.* New York: Delacorte Press, 1973.

Rubin, Louis J., Ed. *Improving In-Service Education: Proposals and Procedures for Change.* Boston: Allyn & Bacon, Inc., 1971.

Von Haden, Herbert I., and Jean Marie King. *Innovations in Education.* Worthington, Ohio: Charles A. Jones Publishing Co., 1971.

Weigand, James E., Ed. *Developing Teacher Competencies.* Englewood Cliffs, N.J.: Prentice-Hall, Inc., 1971.

POST-TEST

In all of the following, circle one.

1. Certificates issued to persons applying for initial certification are usually valid.
   a. for a short period of time.
   b. until revoked for cause.
   c. only if accepted by a board of education.
   d. for a minimum of ten years.

2. Renewal of existing certificates is the responsibility of
   a. the school district in which a teacher is employed.
   b. a professional organization.
   c. NCATE.
   d. the individual teacher.

3. Teaching salaries are
   a. uniform in school districts across the country.
   b. dependent upon school district wealth and attitude toward education.
   c. likely to vary according to the grade level at which teachers are.
   d. individually negotiated with each teacher.

4. Salary increases are usually the result of
   a. popularity with students.
   b. the number of hours worked.

    c. additional training and experience.

    d. the recommendations of one's colleagues.

5. Tenure means that

    a. a teacher is guaranteed a job forever.

    b. a teacher is protected against arbitrary dismissal.

    c. one has freedom to do as he pleases.

    d. only your peers can criticize your performance.

6. The current demand for teachers is

    a. at an all-time high.

    b. low in all fields.

    c. about the same in all academic areas.

    d. higher for some grade levels and subjects than for others.

7. Future projections show that

    a. the demand for teachers will continue to decline.

    b. a sharp demand for beginning teachers will be felt in 1978.

    c. there will be an increased demand for teachers at all levels by 1980.

    d. identical changes in school enrollment are occurring at all levels.

8. Nationally, teachers

    a. are represented by two major organizations.

    b. are not represented.

    c. have many major groups that represent their interests.

    d. are poorly represented.

9. The federally funded regional educational laboratories and research and development centers have

    a. had a major impact upon teachers and teaching.

    b. been primarily concerned with college-level problems.

    c. been highly successful in having their findings disseminated.

    d. had only a minimal influence on the schools.

10. It is generally felt that a classroom teacher should

    a. be familiar with and proficient in all types of research.

    b. not concern himself or herself with research or its findings.

    c. have an overview and understanding of the various types of research.

    d. never conduct research.

11. Most teachers seem to

    a. rarely read research journals.

    b. continually conduct research.

    c. have had adequate training in research.

    d. be informed about new research findings.

12. It is generally felt that

    a. all institutions of higher education offer comparable quality graduate programs.

    b. there is a wide difference among institutions regarding the quality of their graduate programs.

    c. the Eastern colleges and universities are superior.

    d. state universities are more expensive to attend than other types.

13. A master's degree in professional education
    a. requires three full years of study.
    b. can be completed in a summer session.
    c. typically take about a year of study.
    d. is the only type of advanced degree available to teachers.

14. The admissions criteria established by most institutions for graduate study include
    a. a minimum of ten years of successful teaching experience.
    b. a *C* average as an undergraduate.
    c. evidence of verbal proficiency as measured by a standardized test.
    d. possession of an Associate of Arts degree.

15. The terminal professional degree in education is
    a. the Doctor's degree.
    b. the Master's degree.
    c. the Bachelor's degree.
    d. the Specialist degree.

16. The majority of in-service training for teachers has come from
    a. industry.
    b. the community.
    c. colleges, school districts, and the professional organizations.
    d. organized political groups.

17. In-service training is
    a. generally unnecessary.
    b. essential for self-renewal.
    c. for administrators only.
    d. available only in the Western states.

18. To receive a promotion in the field of education
    a. it is necessary to leave classroom teaching.
    b. one must enter administration.
    c. a teacher must work in the central office.
    d. is possible in a variety of ways.

19. Education in America is
    a. a relatively minor undertaking.
    b. vast and diverse.
    c. the business of teachers only.
    d. similar from coast-to-coast.

20. An individual considering teaching as a career
    a. has a limited set of choices before him.
    b. should plan on living in a rural community.
    c. will never have an opportunity to come in contact with a foreign country.
    d. has a great range of opportunities and challenges that are world-wide.

The Effective Teacher

Harry L. Brown

Leonard H. Clark

Jersey City State College

module 12

Pattern of Good Teaching / What the Effective Teacher Knows / Skills the Effective Teacher Has / Personal Characteristics

RATIONALE

Teaching, Gilbert Highet tells us, is an art, not a science. Every time one teaches the situation is different, and so there can be no hard and fast rules by which to indicate how to make teaching effective. Neither are there any special personal characteristics that differentiate between effective and ineffective teachers. All sorts of people have been effective teachers and all sorts of people have been ineffective teachers. Supervisors are always being surprised at how new teachers turn out. Beginners they expect to be outstanding sometimes turn out to be less than mediocre, and others of whom they expect little turn out to be outstanding.

Research on teacher effectiveness has been largely inconclusive. Probably this has been, at least in part, because of the nature of the research projects, which have in many cases concentrated on superficial characteristics rather than on essentials, and have usually lacked a sufficient theoretical base. The data gathered from such research projects do not give us information adequate for drawing dependable far-reaching generalizations. Another difficulty is that in teaching, as in many other human activities, so many factors influence the outcomes that it is difficult to say what influence any single factor may have.

Nevertheless research, observation, and educational theory do point to a number of generalizations concerning teacher effectiveness. These generalizations include conclusions about what effective teachers do, what effective teachers know, what skills effective teachers have, and what kind of people effective teachers are. Any teacher whose behavior is compatible with these generalizations will be more effective, other factors being equal, than he would be if his behavior were not.

In this module we shall try to show you what an effective teacher does, by presenting a model of the teaching-learning cycle. Then we shall point out some characteristics of effective teachers as seen from a theoretical point of view. Although many of the conclusions presented are based on solid research findings, others are based only on theoretical considerations and the opinions, gleaned from their years of experience, of extremely skilled educationists. They can be considered to be quite valid.

Objectives

Upon your completion of this module it is expected that you will be able to:

1. Explain what a teacher needs to know in order to be most effective.
2. Explain what skills a teacher needs in order to be most effective.
3. Explain what is meant by *structure of the discipline*.
4. Explain the following terms and their significance to effective teaching: *factual control, general control, fluid control*.
5. Explain why one needs to know many strategies, tactics, methods, and techniques.
6. Explain the principles and components of group structure.

7. Explain how the components of group structure and process contribute to a positive social atmosphere.
8. Describe the principal characteristics of pupils and how they learn.
9. Describe at least a half dozen ways of learning to know individual pupils.
10. Explain what is meant by structuring one's teaching.
11. Point out personal characteristics that make teachers effective.
12. Show why flexibility is considered to be such an important characteristic.
13. Show why it is important that teachers have well-defined goals.
14. Express the need for empathy with the pupil.
15. Describe the need for acquiring a strong theoretical knowledge of pedagogy.
16. Point out the advantages to the classroom teacher of experimentation with methods and strategies.

MODULE TEXT

As we have already pointed out, educational research has not been able to determine exactly what makes the difference between ineffective and effective teaching.

Does it surprise you that there is very little we can say with assurance about what makes up a "successful" act of teaching? Think about some of the teachers you have had whom you considered good. What was it that made them stand out in your mind? When one asks that question, one usually gets some or all of the following responses: "He was fair." "She really made American history come alive for me." "I don't know, it must have been his enthusiasm." "You could really tell that she loved her subject." "He didn't talk down to us." "She made the work fun." "She made us work, but she made us know that we could do it." "He helped us see why we were studying the stuff." "She had a sense of humor." "She didn't take herself too seriously."

Do these responses square with your experiences? Let us examine some of the responses. "He was fair." Is a tendency toward "fairness" in human relations a natural behavior? We think it probably is not. It seems not unreasonable to guess that the teacher whose students characterized as "fair" at one time decided, on the basis of his direct experiences or his studies, that the principle of *fairness* was a significant one to emphasize in his own life activities and in his teaching. To paraphrase a current soap commercal, "Don't you wish everyone used fairness?"

Or consider, "You could really tell that she loved her subject." Does not this statement imply deep insight into her subject? Does it not suggest that this teacher had gone beyond the words and the facts? Does it not suggest that she had grasped its grandeur, and that somehow she was transmitting that to the student? We think so, and we think it is not unreasonable to make these connections between what students commonly say about the teachers they considered good and the point of view about good teaching and its requisites, which we shall be developing.

The foregoing examples seem to point up a startling conclusion made by Jack Frymier as a result of his research on teaching. Of all the variables that may influence pupil learning in a classroom, the one that seems to make a real difference is the teacher—not class size, not materials, not method, but the personality who teaches.[1] Evidently it is how an effective teacher does what he does, and the kind of person he is, that make the difference.

In spite of all we know about teaching and teaching methods today, much of the teaching in our schools is slipshod. All too few teachers are really professionals because too many teachers are not really learned in their profession. When all teachers attain truly professional competence, then teaching will become effective. That time will come only when teachers understand the methods of teaching and the theories underlying them.

Pattern of Good Teaching

In this module we shall try to examine the characteristics that make teachers effective. We shall begin by examining the general pattern of teaching that the most effective teachers follow. (In all likelihood, these patterns were developed by gifted teachers, who did not realize there *was* a pattern to their teaching.)

Module 1, you recall, briefly describes a general pattern of good teaching. The pattern consists of five phases or steps. These phases, with their substeps are

1. Diagnosis.
   a. Gathering the data.
   b. Interpreting the data.
2. Preparation.
   a. Planning.
   b. Setting the stage.
3. Guiding learning.
4. Evaluation.
   a. Measuring.
   b. Interpreting.
5. Follow-through or follow-up.

The pattern provides an organized, systematic approach for setting aims and objectives for a course, unit, or learning episode; selecting teaching strategies and tactics consistent with the desired outcomes; providing for the availability of resources needed to carry out the instructional strategy; and arranging for the application of the evaluative activities required to assess the effectiveness of the approach, in order to provide a basis for following up where necessary. Let us now examine each of the steps in more detail.

Diagnosis. Diagnosis is the step in which the teacher determines what should be done. In this step the teacher tries to find out such things as what the pupils know, what they can do, what they need to learn, what they are ready to learn, what their strengths and weaknesses are, and where their interests lie.

It is particularly important for the teacher to be able to build on present abilities and knowledge. There is little point in teaching pupils skills they have already mastered. Neither is there much profit in trying to teach pupils concepts until they have the necessary background for them.

In other words, people learn best when they are ready to learn. Although the psychological concept of readiness has many ramifications, for our pedagogical purposes readiness can be defined, rather simply, as the combination of maturity, aptitude, ability, prior learning, motivation, and attitude necessary to facilitate

[1] Jack R. Frymier, *The Nature of Educational Method* (Columbus, Ohio: Charles E. Merrill Publishers, 1965), p. 278.

learning in a specific situation. A person is ready to learn a certain thing when he has matured sufficiently, when he has mastered the prerequisite knowledge and skills, when he has the appropriate attitudes, and when he is sufficiently motivated. A kindergarten child is not ready for calculus; a youth who despises poetry is not ready to appreciate Byron's *Don Juan;* the boy who is afraid to recite in class is not ready to take the lead in the school play; and so on. One essential role of diagnosis is to find out what pupils are or are not ready for.

Diagnosis is a two-step process. First, one must gather the data; second, one must interpret or evaluate the data. As we have seen, one needs many kinds of data to consider if one is to make reasonably intelligent diagnoses, because there are so many variables in any teaching encounter.

The first of the variables are the objectives. There are several kinds of objectives. The kind of goal for which one is striving makes a great difference in one's strategies. Different goals in the same domain may also require different approaches, both in teaching techniques and in teaching content.

The pupils themselves also make up a variable. Each is, of course, unique. Each has his own interests, abilities, attitudes, potentials, background, goals, and style of learning. Consequently, the teaching content and techniques suitable for one pupil may not be suitable for another.

But the teacher's decisions are influenced not only by his knowledge of pupils, they are also influenced by his knowledge of group dynamics, especially as they pertain to his class group. Because all groups do not necessarily behave in the same way, an understanding of interpersonal relationships in the group one is teaching can be especially helpful.

Another variable is the nature of the subject matter. This includes not only the structure of the disciplines but the organization of the subject matter for teaching, and one's philosophical basis for teaching it.

Another variable is the available technology. By *technology* we mean both the techniques and tools of teaching.

Still another variable is the environment of the school. This includes both the community in which one lives, and society at large. Indeed, the environment within the school is also important. A physically dingy school, with the majority of students hostile or indifferent to learning, usually requires somewhat different techniques from those which are suitable for well-kept schools with eager, nonhostile students. In this respect, the organization of the school must be considered. The comprehensive high school of the United States undoubtedly requires the development of many different teaching strategies and techniques that are unnecessary in the selective schools of Europe.

The other variable is the teacher. Like everyone else, every teacher has strengths and weaknesses, likes and dislikes. One's decisions invariably are influenced by one's inclinations. These in turn are influenced by one's competence, ideals, general attitudes, and personality. Individual differences in teachers cause individual differences in teaching style. It is only natural that a teacher should follow the style of teaching he or she finds compatible. Within reason, it is right that he or she do so.

Preparation. Once he has diagnosed the teaching-learning situation the teacher is ready to prepare for the teaching encounter. At this point the teacher prepares his plans, and both the physical and intellectual setting for learning.

In planning, the most important thing is to select the specific instructional objectives that the diagnosis indicates will be most effective under the circumstances. These instructional objectives are different from the objectives used as data for the diagnosis in that they are more specific—limited to the lessons or unit to be taught. In this stage, also, one selects the content and strategies for the lesson or unit that one believes most likely to be fruitful, in view of the results of the diagnosis. The teacher's criterion for choice is his best judgment but always in view of the results of the diagnosis. The effective teacher then welds these elements into a plan that outlines how the lesson, unit, or course will be conducted: sequence, time limits, use of equipment, and so on.

In addition to the planning, during this step the teacher prepares the setting for learning by assembling the materials and tools to be used. Thus, he attempts to provide a physical as well as an intellectual climate favorable to learning. In short, in the preparation step one sets the stage for the actual teaching that is to follow.

Guiding Learning. After the planning is done and the stage is set, the teacher must conduct the teaching-learning activities he has planned. It is at this point that he actually meets with the pupils and teaches them. This we call the guiding-learning phase.

Evaluation. After the teaching, one must find out how successful the teaching has been, that is, how far the pupils have progressed. This step is the evaluation phase of the teaching-learning cycle, and it is absolutely necessary as a basis for deciding what to do next. Unless one evaluates, one has no way of knowing (1) how well one is doing and (2) what one should do next.

Evaluation involves two steps: The first is measurement, wherein the teacher uses measurement devices and techniques to gather information on his success and the pupils' progress. The second is to interpret the data and make judgments on the basis of these data.

You will undoubtedly have made two observations as you read the description of the evaluation phase. First, that the evaluation and diagnostic phases are very similar. To be of any real value in teaching, evaluation must be diagnostic. Second, although we refer to *evaluation* as a phase or step, evaluating, in one form or another, is a constant element in teaching.

Following Through. The final step in the teaching-learning cycle is follow-up or follow-through. It is in this step that teachers summarize, review, devise new

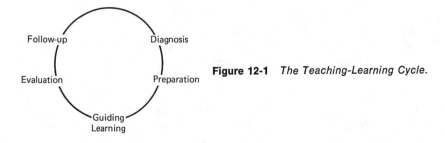

Figure 12-1   *The Teaching-Learning Cycle.*

Figure 12-2 *A Teaching-Learning Cycle Continuum.*

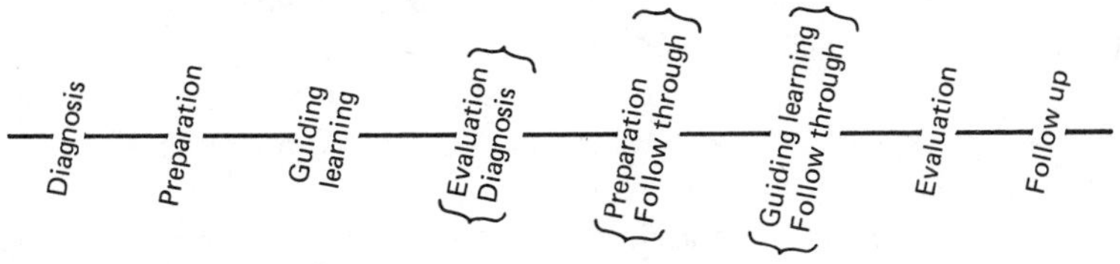

Figure 12-3 *Overlapping Teaching-Learning Cycle Continuum.*

applications, fill in gaps, reteach, or correct errors. The follow-up phase is the one in which learning is clinched.

Although each of the foregoing steps is essential for effective teaching, sometimes in the hurly-burly of active teaching the steps are combined in one operation. Frequently, the teacher will carry on two or more steps at the same time with different pupils. And often some of the steps in succeeding sequences tend to run together. Consequently, instead of forming cycles in which each step follows its predecessor in clockwise fashion (see Figure 12-1), the steps in one cycle merge into the next cycle, making it difficult to tell when one cycle ends and the next begins. (Figure 12-2) In fact, in some cases the steps become well mixed with other steps in preceding, or subsequent teaching-learning cycles (Figure 12-3). All of the steps actually take place, but they merge with one another. This does not really matter, so long as the teacher adequately diagnoses, prepares, guides learning, evaluates, and follows through.

No matter how charismatic he may be, or how interesting and exciting his classes, the teacher who neglects any of these steps will not be as effective as he could be.

What the Effective Teacher Knows. The most effective teachers are knowledgeable in at least three areas: (1) their subject matter, (2) the theory, methods, and materials of teaching, and (3) the psychology and characteristics of students, including how they learn. It is possible for a teacher to be fairly effective even though he is deficient in knowledge in one of these areas, but there is no doubt that a teacher who is knowledgeable in each of these areas is more effective than he would otherwise be. In fact, Peronto found that "of the characteristics believed to differentiate good and poor teachers, only knowledge of subject matter and pupils and professional knowledge appear to be definitely established as discriminating between good and poor teachers."[2] That Peronto should have come to this conclusion seems only natural. After all, when a teacher teaches, he must teach something (subject matter) to someone (the pupil) by some means (professional theory, materials, and methods).

[2] Archie L. Peronto, "The Abilities and Patterns of Good and Poor Teachers," in A. S. Barr, et al., *Wisconsin Studies of the Measurement and Prediction of Teacher Effectiveness: A Summary of Investigations* (Madison, Wis.: Dembar Publications, Inc., 1961), p. 98.

Knowledge of Subject. That teachers should know well the subject matter they are teaching seems axiomatic. But the fact that many teachers do not really understand their subject is probably the cause of much of the current dull, dreary, anti-intellectual teaching. The pupils subject to this quality of teaching seldom do more than recite what they were supposed to have learned from the "book" the night before. This sort of teaching is not good enough! Even if it results in pupils' mastering the information—and it usually does not—they probably do not learn the major ideas, the important intellectual skills, and the essential relationships of the subject being studied; nor do they learn to dig for information, organize data, and draw their own conclusions.

Because all knowledge is tentative and subject to change, teachers must understand what is sometimes called the *structure* of the discipline they teach. The scholarly disciplines are rather arbitrary divisions of knowledge. Over the years, scholars have shaped each discipline into a somewhat artificial pattern of ideas and scholarly methods. According to this pattern of ideas and methods, scholars place facts into categories, show how facts relate to each other, explain the meanings of facts and their relationships, and test the truth of phenomena. When new facts are discovered, the process is repeated, with variations: the meanings of old relationships are re-examined, and new meanings are drawn from both old and new facts and relationships. Therefore, to understand and use the structure of a discipline requires a considerable depth of knowledge in that discipline. Without it, teaching is usually a collection of dry facts and unrelated concepts.

As Joyce and Harootunian, the authors of *The Structure of Teaching,* point out, teachers need control of their subject matter at three levels: factual control, general control, and fluid control.

Generally speaking, we can say that, in guiding and directing his students, the teacher must display at least three types of control over knowledge. He must first have *factual control.* This means being able to handle facts and details easily and knowledgeably and to provide students an organized access to facts; this does not mean, as we earlier noted, that the teacher's mind must be an encyclopedic dispensary. Factual control, the ability to handle many details of knowledge in an organized fashion, can be critical to many kinds of lessons, such as teaching the specifics of grammar in English or in a foreign language.

Second, the teacher must display *general control*—that is, control over the generalizations or organizing concepts encountered by the learner. Does the teacher know the important ideas, the relationships defined within the subject field? Some teachers seem to have relatively good factual control but nevertheless lack familiarity with the general ideas that hold the facts together. It is little use knowing a good many things about the observable behavior of magnets, for instance, without having general control over the theories of magnetism as a branch of science.

The third and more subtle type of control over knowledge is *fluid control,* by which we mean the extent to which the teacher holds knowledge flexibly and easily, incorporating new or conflicting information, tolerating dissonance and ambiguity, and keeping the door open to alternate points of view. Fluid control enables the teacher to help children handle information in an openminded way, tolerating and exploring incongruities. Quite frequently, when a teacher presents a certain idea to his students, they respond variously with ideas slightly different from the one presented. The teacher has to compare his idea with those of his students and help bring the ideas closer together. If his control is fluid enough, the teacher can approach a topic from many angles until he finds one that his students can accurately respond to. Such should be the fluidity of his methods and attitudes.[3]

Professional Knowledge. Professional knowledge includes both the theory and practice of all the pedagogical arts. To be most effective, the teacher needs to be thoroughly grounded in the theory and method of instruction, the group process, the tools and materials of instruction, and tests and measurements. He also should be an expert on the curriculum and curriculum-building, for the really effective teacher does not limit himself to the classroom. He also is active in what Joyce and Harootunian call the "shaping of the school": that is, curriculum-building and the making of school policy and customs.

Knowledge of Strategies and Tactics. The basic problem in teaching is selection, or decision making. In every lesson, unit, and course the teacher must[4]

1. Select the instructional goals.
2. Select the strategy by which he hopes to reach these goals. In mapping out this strategy he must select both
   a. Content.
   b. General method or approach.
3. Select specific tactics by which to carry out the strategy.
4. Select the materials and tools of instruction.
5. Select procedures by which to evaluate the success of his teaching and to complete the follow-through.

Consequently, the teacher must have a thorough knowledge of the available teaching strategies, tactics, methods, and techniques, so that he may select those most appropriate for the teaching-learning situation. Intelligent decision making is of vital importance because there are so many strategies and tactics from which to choose.[5]

Selecting the proper strategy is further complicated by the fact that different kinds of subject matter require different kinds of strategies. Some subject matter is to be remembered, some is to be used, and some is to be appreciated; therefore, you should not expect a particular strategy to work well for all subject matter. What works well for one may fail completely for another. Similarly, strategies and tactics that are excellent for one group of pupils will not be suitable for another group. And, of course, individual pupils respond differently to one's strategies and tactics.

Knowledge of Group Structure and the Group Process. Because to be most effective a teacher must match his strategies and tactics to the groups he teaches, it is important that he understand (1) the structure and behavior of groups; (2) methods for teaching and influencing groups; group-process techniques; and (3)

---

[3] Bruce R. Joyce and Berj Harootunian, *The Structure of Teaching* (Chicago: Science Research Associates, Inc., 1967), pp. 40–41.

[4] Leonard H. Clark, *Teaching Social Studies in Secondary Schools: A Handbook* (New York: Macmillan Publishing Co., Inc., 1973), p. 3.

[5] See Module 1.

methods for improving group relations, group processes, and the group climate. Let us look briefly at some of these.

NEED FOR A POSITIVE CLIMATE. Learning seems to occur best in groups with a *positive social climate,* that is, an atmosphere in which the group members accept each other, cooperate with each other, understand their group roles and responsibilities, and take satisfaction in their roles. A positive social climate is neither authoritarian nor overly permissive; it is democratic and supportive. In such classes pupils are encouraged to try even though they may make mistakes; moreover, the pupils are supported in whatever activities they are pursuing. The amount of teaching structure the teacher should provide depends on the nature of the group and a number of other factors which we shall discuss momentarily.

GROUP LEADERSHIP. Part of a group's social climate are other group characteristics, such as its leadership, the attraction of its members to each other, its norms, its communication patterns, and its cohesiveness. All of these factors influence group functioning and consequently the learning of group members. Teachers who understand these factors can use them to increase their teaching effectiveness.

Leadership is the result of a process not of a position. A teacher does not necessarily become the leader of a class just because he or she is its teacher; other pupils may be as influential, or even more influential. As a rule, pupils tend to follow people they like, and those who are skilled in the leadership functions: initiating and selling ideas, encouraging, and harmonizing and compromising in order to facilitate interpersonal relationships. Therefore, the effective teacher seeks the help of the natural leaders among the pupils in addition to cultivating his own leadership skills. Teachers find it easier to lead in classes where the students have some part in the decision making.

CENTRAL VERSUS DIFFUSE GROUP STRUCTURE. Groups may be centrally structured or diffusely structured. In the centrally structured class there is a small "in" group of pupils with high status, and a large "out" group of pupils with low status. In the diffusely structured group there is not so sharp a division between the "in" and "out" groups; as a result, pupils in diffusely structured groups have better opinions about themselves. And, because self-esteem tends to foster good performance, and good performance builds self-esteem, diffusely structured classes tend to provide the happy, positive social climate that encourages learning. Centrally structured groups are more likely to be threatening and repressive.

In an attempt to structure classes diffusely, teachers use pupil-centered teaching strategies and teaching techniques that (a) force pupils to know each other and to associate with many different pupils, (b) spread leadership roles and responsibilities widely among the pupils, and (c) build up their self-esteem. For this purpose, small-group activities and committee work are excellent.

GROUP COHESIVENESS. Groups are more productive when the pupils feel that they belong. Some groups are merely aggregates of people who happen to be in the same place for a time. College classes may be like that. Day after day, the students come, listen to the lecture, and then leave, without ever getting to know or even to speak to each other. Groups in which the members not only know each other but share common interests, concerns, purposes, and work provide a much better learning environment. In such classes, group members are more likely to have high morale, good feeling toward the group, and strong goals. They know where they stand with each other, and where they are going.

Teachers can increase classroom cohesiveness by diffusely structuring their classes and having clear teaching goals. Pupil-centered techniques that involve pupils in planning and decision making, and which build pupil self-esteem, can be used by teachers to build cohesiveness.

IMPORTANCE OF GROUP NORMS. Pupils have preconceived notions of what school and classes should be like. If a class differs too much from these norms, the pupils react negatively. When the group norms are flexible, allowing for wide ranges of behavior and individual differences, the classroom atmosphere is usually positive. Narrow, rigid norms are repressive and threatening, but flexible norms encourage tolerance, good feeling, and support. Fortunately, with a little luck and perseverance, teachers can influence pupil groups to adapt norms favorable to a positive learning environment. Encouragement, support, reinforcement of desirable attitudes, value-clarification activities, and cooperative planning are among the techniques that can be used to change group norms in the desired direction.

GROUP COMMUNICATION PATTERNS. Obviously, the communications patterns within a group have a great effect on its climate and teachableness. Optimum communication does not occur in highly teacher-centered or centrally structured classes. Communication needs to be free and open, with plenty of interaction, feedback, and mutually supporting dialogue between teacher and pupils. To establish this kind of communication pattern, the teacher can use not only the various strategies and techniques already mentioned for structuring classes diffusely, but can teach communication skills per se.

Knowledge of Pupils. Teachers with a deep knowledge about the characteristics, needs, and learning processes of children and youth should be able to build curriculums, courses, units, and lessons that have genuine value and meaning for their pupils. And teachers who know their pupils as individuals should be able to adapt curriculums, courses, and strategies to their individual needs. If the teacher understands the general principles of learning listed here, and bases his choice of teaching strategies and tactics on them, his teaching will presumably be more effective than if he does not.

SOME PRINCIPLES OF LEARNING.

1. Pupils learn best when they are ready. A pupil who is not ready to learn something cannot learn it efficiently at the time. *Readiness* has been defined as a combination of maturity, motivation, experience, ability, perception, aptitude, and other factors that make one ready for a given learning. If one uses the proper procedures, it is possible to prepare pupils who are not yet ready.
2. Learning proceeds more effectively when the learner is motivated to learn.
3. Individuals learn at different rates and in different styles.
4. Pupils learn how to learn. Therefore, how one now learns usually determines how one will learn in the future.
5. One's perception of a situation determines his conception of the situation and behavior in it.
6. The whole learner is involved in the learning process. Cognitive and skill-learning have affective overtones and vice versa.

7. Learning always takes place in relation to some goal. Pupils learn better if the instructional goals are the same as their own goals and if they are consciously working toward these goals. Teachers make little headway when they are combatting powerful student goals incompatible with the instructional goals. Once pupils have reached the goals they have set for themselves, they seldom progress further until they have set higher goals for themselves.

8. Learning depends on reinforcement. Both reward and punishment may be reinforcing, but punishment is not dependable and may do more harm than good. A sense of self-satisfaction from having done something well, and a chance to participate in new, stimulating activities, are among the most powerful rewards. To be most effective, reinforcement should follow learning immediately.

9. To learn, one must do something. Anything one does may result in learning, but most school learning must be purposeful, hard work.

10. Pupils react unfavorably to overdirection.

11. Learning that does not transfer to new situations is useless. Learning inspired by incentive—that is, extrinsically motivated learning—does not transfer well.

12. Learning is not additive; it is integrative.

13. Pupils seem to learn more readily from their peers than from adults.

14. Pupils try hardest when the task they are to perform is within their range of challenge—that is, when it is neither too hard nor too easy.

15. Time spent in recalling something is more effective than rereading.

16. Pupils learn what they expect to be tested on.

17. Information that confirms one's opinions or attitudes is learned more readily than information that refutes them.

18. The opinion of one's peer group is a powerful motivation.

19. In order to form concepts, pupils should encounter specific situations in which the distinctive attribute is present, as well as others in which it is not present so that they can infer the concept from specific situations. Then they should apply the concepts.

20. Skills learned in isolation do not function.

21. One learning product does not guarantee another.

22. Meaningful material is more easily learned and transferred.

23. Everything else being equal, teaching by means of direct experience ordinarily is more effective than teaching by means of vicarious experience.

24. Psychomotor learning occurs best when there is explanation, demonstration, and meaningful practice.

25. Pleasant experiences are more useful for changing attitudes than unpleasant experiences.

26. Cognitive learning can be achieved both by rote association and by discovery techniques.[6]

LEARNING TO KNOW INDIVIDUAL PUPILS. To know pupils well enough to adjust one's teaching to their individual needs and personalities requires consid-

---

[6] Derived in part from the findings of a Wisconsin study group reported in *Wisconsin State Department of Public Instruction, Learning Principles* (Madison, Wis.: 1964).

erable effort and alertness. For this purpose the effective teacher may use the following techniques and data-gathering devices:

1. The cumulative record folder.
2. Observation of the pupils—individually and collectively—both in class and at other times.
3. Pupil conferences.
4. Parent conferences.
5. Written or oral autobiographies, themes, essays, questionnaires, and so on.
6. Tests and other diagnostic devices. (Both standardized and homemade tests are excellent sources of information. Use them as diagnostic devices.)
7. Sociometric devices. (Sociometric devices are useful for showing the structure of groups and subgroups in a class, and for showing the relationship of an individual pupil to the group and to his associates.[7])

KNOWLEDGE OF TOOLS AND MATERIALS. The effective teacher is knowledgeable about teaching tools and materials. He knows what is available and how to make the best use of it. He knows that some materials are too difficult for his pupils; that some material is boring and some challenging and exciting; that some material is well-suited for his objectives and that some is not—and he knows which is which. Teachers without a working knowledge of their teaching tools and methods are doomed to dull, boring classes; teachers who do know them can make their teaching exciting and productive.

Skills the Effective Teacher Has

Skills in Methods and Techniques. The effective teacher is skillful. The kinds of knowledge we have surveyed in the foregoing is essential, but it is useless unless the teacher is a master of the skills of teaching. What are these skills? Little hard evidence derived from experimental research is available. However, we can turn to an increasing body of research data on teaching, teaching behavior, and classroom climate for clues. Two teams of researchers, Rosenshire and Furst in 1973 and Dunkin and Biddle in 1974, have reviewed most of the studies completed up to the present time that have attempted to relate student learning to teacher behaviors. The following list of statements reflects the findings of these two teams of researchers, as well as theoretical formulations describing teaching and experiment-based judgments about teaching set down by professionals who have thought seriously about the science and art of teaching. We hope you will find them helpful to you as you develop your own thought about teaching and what contributes to effectiveness in teaching.[8]

1. Students learn better when the teacher is committed to and persists in teaching the content that he is supposed to teach.*

[7] Sociometric devices are described in *Foundations of Education.*

[8] Extensive use has been made of material from Thomas L. Good, Bruce L. Biddle and Jere E. Brophy, *Teachers Make a Difference.* (New York: Holt, Rinehart and Winston, 1975), pp. 58–61.

* The emphasis upon student learning in these statements is intended to reinforce the idea that the criterion by which teaching is to be judged is student learning.

His behavior is businesslike without being overbearing.

His commitment to his subject and his task is unmistakable.

He expects positive achievements from his students.

He pursues the instructional goals until students have learned.

He is successful in holding students accountable for attention and learning.

(He attends carefully to verbal responses as well as written work and other work products so that students know that their performance is monitored.)

2. Students learn better when the teacher is well-prepared and organized in his instructional behavior.

The clarity of his instructional goals and procedures give structure to his work and contribute positively to student learning.

In general he follows his plan for the learning episode and thereby avoids confusing students and allowing disruptions to develop.

He is able to sustain proper lesson pacing and maintain group momentum.

3. Students learn better when the teacher is enthusiastic and skilled in motivating students.

He uses praise frequently to encourage effort and reward achievement.

He avoids criticizing students for learning errors and lapses.

He is able to keep the group alert by asking questions frequently and by presenting novel or interesting materials regularly.

He consciously employs devices to generate enthusiasm directly and often.

He plans for variety in work assignments and general classroom activity.

4. Students learn better when the teacher sets instructional tasks in such a way that students are actively engaged in productive activities. There are few periods of inactivity or confusion.

In his instruction he emphasizes strategies and tactics that involve students as active participants in the learning processes: questioning procedures, as opposed to lectures, and procedures that encourage pupil-to-pupil interaction. He involves himself in the learning process as a clarifier and to provide the structure necessary for student inquiry to proceed effectively and efficiently.

He frequently works with smaller than class-size groups for short periods of time.

5. Students learn better when the teacher uses techniques that maintain the climate for learning in the classroom.

He is alert to what is going on in the classroom at all times.

He is able to sustain more than one learning activity at the same time.

In short, their findings seem to corroborate A. S. Barr's 1948 hypothesis that the skills that help to make any teacher more effective include

Skill in identifying pupil needs.

Skill in setting and defining goals.

Skill in creating favorable mind sets (motivation).

Skill in choosing learning experience.

Skill in following the learning process.

Skill in using learning aids.

Skill in teacher-pupil relations.

Skill in appraising pupil growth and achievement.
Skill in management.
Skill in instruction (general).[9]

The importance of teaching skills is illustrated by the model of the teaching process proposed by Charles W. Ford. (See Figure 12-4.) In this model the inner circle represents knowledge of the subject to be taught; the second circle represents the basic teaching skills, and the third circle represents the more sophisticated abilities within the teaching process.

Need for Skill in Structuring Teaching. The effective teacher is skillful in adjusting the teaching structure to his purpose and the classroom situation. By *teaching structure* we do not mean the structure of groups or the structure of the disciplines. Teaching structure, as Frymier defines it, is the amount the teacher determines "ideas, expectations, communication patterns, decisions, and the ways in which they are reached and the nature of the problems to be employed." The more the teacher makes the determinations, the more the teaching structure; the more the pupils are on their own, the less the teaching structure. Frymier continues his explanation of teaching structure by pointing out six different types of structuring: manipulative, directive, persuasive, discussive (both exploratory and decisive discussions), supportive, and nondirective. Each of these types of structure is useful and should be used in teaching, according to Frymier. The trick is to use the right kind of structure at the right time.[10]

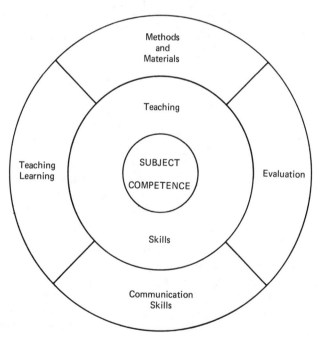

Figure 12-4 *The Teaching Process.* [Charles W. Ford, "Mirror, Mirror on the Wall. Who Is the Best Teacher of Them All?" *Educational Technology,* **15:**43 (March 1975).]

[9] A. S. Barr, "The Nature of the Problem," in A. S. Barr, et al., op. cit. pp. 14–15.
[10] Frymier, op. cit., Chap. 6.

Of course, no teacher can be proficient in all techniques and tactics, methods and strategies, but unless one is skillful in many, he is not likely to be maximally effective. A prime characteristic of the effective teacher is flexibility; unless one is skillful in many methods and techniques, one cannot be very flexible.

Need for Skill in Communicating. The effective teacher is a skilled communicator. Learning depends on successful teacher-pupil communication. It is not so much what the teacher says as it is what the pupils think the teacher says—or means—that is important. Therefore, teachers should avail themselves of all the techniques and knowledge developed by communications researchers. From a communicator's point of view, the classroom presents a difficult problem. Each class is made up of a greatly "varied group of receivers," the pupils, each of whom is different. But that is not the teacher's only communications problem.

In addition to facing the ordinary problem of communicating with a varied group of receivers, the teacher is trying to combine a dozen or more channels in the average day's work—the spoken word, the written word, the blackboard, pictures, textbooks, films, "acting it out," etc. This act of combination is not simple, and is not well understood. To make it harder, the teacher is dealing with messages which carry not only "facts" about subject matter and "demonstrations" of skills, but also "concepts" of life, roles, values. Furthermore, the teacher is dealing with a functional group or series of groups, so that all communication within the classroom must have reference not only to individual needs and interests, but also to group norms and group dynamics. . . . Finally to make the situation as difficult as possible, all receivers in the class are subject to a very large amount of uncontrolled and uncoordinated communication outside the class, some of which undoubtedly conflicts seriously with the communication they receive in class.[11]

Communication is the heart of teaching. Much of it is verbal. The teacher who fails to communicate well cannot be effective.

Personal Characteristics

Although there is little proof that one sort of person makes a better teacher than another, observation indicates that certain personality traits do seem to make teachers more effective.

The Need to Be Flexible. One trait we have already mentioned is flexibility. The effective teacher is one who can adjust to new and different situations relatively easily: a strict disciplinarian on some occasions and permissive at other times. He does not allow himself to be imprisoned by routine or mired in the ruts of comfortable familiarity. He can cope with situations of all sorts by adjusting his approach to meet new and different contingencies. Although he finds certain approaches easier and more comfortable than others, he can and does use others

[11] Wilbur Schramm, "Education and Communications Research," *Educational Leadership,* **13**:503 (May 1956).

when necessary. In fact, he has a great repertoire of strategies, tactics, methods, and techniques that he can use with confidence when the situation demands. Because of his thorough theoretical knowledge, he is not limited to the practical, old solutions to new problems. He understands the "why" of pedagogical problems and possible solutions, and consequently can be more versatile.

The Need to Be Purposeful. The effective teacher knows what he is doing. He knows exactly what his objectives are and how to attain them. He is not satisfied with soft pedagogy, that is, teaching that drifts along aimlessly getting nowhere. He does what he must to reach the objectives he has set for himself and his pupils, and he uses these objectives as the basis for the evaluation of pupils' achievement and progress.

All this does not mean he is traditional, academic or conservative. Much of the softest teaching is most conservative and traditional. The teacher who is not purposeful is unlikely to be effective no matter how traditional or progressive his philosophy of teaching or how structured or unstructured his class.

Not only does the effective teacher understand what his objectives are, he makes sure that his pupils know what they are, too. When pupils know what the teacher is trying to do, usually they not only accept the teacher's goals but set up compatible goals of their own. As a well-known educationist, Roy O. Billett used to say, most students would be glad to do what the teacher wanted them to do if they could figure out what it was.

The Need for Empathy. The effective teacher empathizes with his pupils. In his *High School Students Speak Out,* David Mallery tells the story of "Mr. Smith and the Shop Kids."[12] Mr. Smith was in some ways a disaster. His lessons were the worst sort of dull workbook exercises. The curriculum material he used actually got in the way of pupil learning. Yet in his classes the pupils worked hard to do their best. Why? Because he was skilled in human relations and interested in his students. He had a light touch, he called students by name, he encouraged them, and he expected them to do well. There was no patronizing. To him all pupils were individual human beings whom he treated with genuine respect. He was a teacher who, as one of the boys said, "made you feel like a man as soon as you entered the room." His treatment of his pupils—no matter how bad their reputation or their academic past—made all the difference. As another of the boys said, "I think the best thing here at the school is the really sincere ones—teachers— who go all the way to understand the kids and give them a break."

Effective teachers, then, treat their pupils as human beings. They do everything they can to make pupils feel adequate. Pupils do not learn well in an atmosphere in which they feel threatened. Anxiety is not conducive to learning, therefore, to be most effective the teacher must keep anxiety and fear at a minimum. Of course, pupils come to class inadequate in many ways: some are poorly prepared, others have poor attitudes, and so on. But the effective teacher accepts the pupil as he is; by adapting content, materials, and methods, and by attempting to build

[12] David Mallery, *High School Students Speak Out* (New York: Harper & Row, Publishers, 1962), pp. 57–61.

the pupil's self-confidence and morale with worthwhile successes, he helps the student to learn.

The Need to Be a Whole Person. The effective teacher is a whole person. He feels adequate. He has confidence in himself and his abilities. Consequently, he is open-minded and is not threatened by new ideas or by change. Nor is he fettered by too rigid a system of values. He is interested in what is going on in the world; he reads, studies, and uses the media to keep well-informed about developments in his profession, the community, and the nation. By being an interested, productive human being and citizen, he is more likely to be an interesting, stimulating teacher.

Because of his open-mindedness he can understand and sympathize with other points of view, even though he may not accept them. And as a well-integrated person, he is likely to be mentally vigorous, enthusiastic, emotionally stable, sympathetic, and democratic.

The Need to Experiment. The effective teacher is likely to be an experimenter. He is willing to try new and exciting techniques and materials. By continually evaluating himself and his methods of teaching, he keeps himself from repeating old mistakes and from becoming stuck in unproductive ruts and wearisome routines.

Experimentation and innovation are beneficial for specific reasons. The very newness of an experiment or innovation may bring on the "Hawthorne effect"— that is, when pupils know that what they are doing is new, different, and somewhat special, this makes them think that they are somewhat special, too; therefore, they become more interested, more eager, more willing, more receptive, and, in general, more highly motivated.

Experimentation and innovation also rid one of old impedimenta. Simply because what one is doing is new and different, one need not be bound by restraints that previously held one back. Moreover, experimenting and innovating are usually fun. They teach the teacher a lot about himself, his pupils, and his subject. These new insights, along with the sense of well-being that comes from trying something new, can make learning and teaching exhilarating.

The Need for Diligence. Obviously, effective teachers work hard at their jobs. Effective teaching does not come easily; it takes diligent preparation, careful following up, much study, and many hours of work. To do all this requires a high level of motivation. For the most effective teachers, this motivation is intrinsic— the fact is, they love their jobs.

Summary

The main concepts presented in this module are pretty well summarized in the fifteen suggestions Homer V. Loucks proposed as ways teachers "can help students achieve the maximum from their high school experience."

1. The teacher must be competent in his field. Competence can best be described as the ability to think and do in a given field, and the ability to teach others to think and do.

2. The teacher must know how to teach. Competence alone does not guarantee that

teaching will be successful. The art of teaching must be developed through continuous planned effort.

3. The teacher must be willing to read. Every discipline has its disciples who are constantly exploring, researching, and testing. Teachers are no exception.

4. The teacher must be able to communicate. Communication is more than speaking and writing. Gestures, facial expressions, and actions, as well as verbal and written communication, all convey messages.

5. The teacher must listen. Teachers must learn to listen not only to answers that are requested, but to statements, questions, and answers that reflect need, evaluation, and a choice of direction.

6. The teacher must be able to see. Such a teacher sees the student for who he is, what he needs, and for what he wants. The teacher also sees himself in terms of what he should do, what he can do, and the resources he can command.

7. The teacher must be able to ask the "no right answer" question and feel comfortable with the answer received. If students are expected to make judgments by interpreting the facts, then questions must be asked that will encourage decision making.

8. The teacher must be able to establish standards and maintain them. If any discipline is worth teaching, then the integrity of the discipline must be maintained through standards.

9. The teacher must be able to exert leadership. Students in high school can be led into renewed enthusiasm and effort. All they need is a leader.

10. The teacher must adjust to numbers. It is not uncommon for a secondary teacher to face 150 students each day. No class can meet the needs of everyone, so priorities of time, material, and attention must be established.

11. The teacher must be able to adjust to change. In our rapidly changing world, teachers are forced to change. When change occurs, teachers must be ready and able to direct the change instead of merely succumbing to it.

12. The teacher must be able to state and work toward objectives. If teachers are going to be effective, they must know what they want to do, state their objectives, plan a procedure, implement it, and evaluate it.

13. The teacher must have professional values. Without professional values based on student needs, the teacher soon finds himself without control over his thoughts or his actions.

14. The teacher must be committed to education. High school students today are a series of contradictions—respectful and barbaric, eager and bored, confident and troubled, ad infinitum. Only teachers with a strong commitment to education and to young people can reach these students.

15. The teacher must have well-developed personal values. To live and work effectively in a climate of court action that has liberated teachers socially, economically and politically, they need personal values that serve as guidelines for action.[13]

The paragon we have described as the effective teacher may not really exist in the flesh. Even the most effective teachers have their faults. Some teachers are able in some areas and not in others. However, it seems to be pretty certain that to be maximally effective, a teacher must have reached a reasonably high standard in each of the areas of competence and personality we have discussed in the module, even though he may not be a whiz in every specific minor category. Evidently, teaching is a combination of general and special abilities. Probably one's teaching effectiveness is dictated principally by the level attained in these general and special abilities.

---

[13] Homer V. Loucks. "Fifteen Suggestions for High School Teachers," *NASSP Spotlight* (Jan. 1975).

SUGGESTED READING

Barr, A. S., et al. *Wisconsin Studies of the Measurement and Prediction of Teacher Effectiveness.* Madison, Wis.: Dembar Publications, Inc., 1961.

Biddle, Bruce J., and William J. Ellena, Eds. *Contemporary Research on Teacher Effectiveness.* New York: Holt, Rinehart & Winston, Inc., 1964.

Brauner, Charles J. *American Educational Theory.* Englewood Cliffs, N.J.: Prentice-Hall, Inc., 1964.

Broudy, Harry S., and John R. Palmer. *Exemplars of Teaching Method.* Chicago: Rand McNally & Co., 1965.

Dale, Edgar. *The Humane Leader.* Bloomington, Ind.: The Phi Delta Kappa Educational Foundation, 1974.

Frymier, Jack R. *The Nature of Educational Method.* Columbus, Ohio: Charles E. Merrill Publishers, 1965.

Hyman, Ronald T. *Ways of Teaching,* 2nd Ed. Philadelphia: J. B. Lippincott Co., 1974

Joyce, Bruce R., and Berj Harootunian. *The Structure of Teaching.* Chicago: Science Research Associates, 1967.

Miel, Alice, Ed. *Creativity in Teaching.* Belmont, Calif.: Wadsworth Publishing Co., Inc., 1961.

Stinett, T. M., and Albert J. Huggett. *Professional Problems of Teachers,* 2nd Ed. New York: Macmillan Publishing Co., Inc., 1963.

Trevers, Robert M. W., and Jacqueline Patricia Dillon. *The Making of a Teacher: A Research-Based Plan and Manual for Students.* New York: Macmillan Publishing Co., Inc., 1975.

Walton, John, and James L. Kuethe. *The Discipline of Education.* Madison, Wis.: University of Wisconsin, 1963.

Wilson, Elizabeth C. *Needed: A New Kind of Teacher.* Bloomington, Ind.: The Phi Delta Kappa Educational Foundation, 1973.

POST TEST

1. List the five phases in the teaching-learning cycle, in order.

a. _____

b. _____

c. _____

d. _____

e. _____

2. Diagnosis is a two-step process. What are the two steps?

a. _____

b. _____

3. One of the ingredients of readiness is maturity. Two other ingredients are

a. _____

b. _____

4. The module mentions seven variables that might be considered in one's diagnosis of a teaching-learning situation. Four of them are

a. _____

b. _____

c. _____

d. _____

5. In preparing for a learning encounter, one must plan and _____

_____

6. The phase in which one does the bulk of the actual teaching is the _____

_____ phase.

7. The basic reason for evaluating is _____

_____

8. The two steps in the evaluating phase are

a. _____

b. _____

9. What is the purpose of the follow-through step?

_____

_____

10. Sometimes teaching-learning cycles overlap. In this case, should the teacher omit the diagnostic or follow-through processes?

_____

11. According to Archie Peronto, the only characteristics definitely established as discriminating between good and poor teachers are

a. _____

b. _____

c. _____

12. The arbitrary pattern of ideas, their relationship, and processes used in studying a discipline is called _____.

13. According to this module, one of the causes of the inconclusiveness of research on teacher effectiveness is that it has been superficial. Another is that

it has lacked sufficient _____.

14. What is the structure of a discipline?

_____

_____

15. What does fluid control of subject matter mean?

_____

_____

16. How does fluid control of subject matter differ from factual control of subject matter?

_____

_____

17. It is important that teachers have a thorough knowledge of many tactics and strategies. What is the principal reason for this?

_____

18. Which seems to be preferable, a diffusely structured class or a centrally structured class?

_____

19. One component of group structure is the group leadership. Another is _____

_____

20. Why should the direct teaching of communication skills help improve the structure of the group?

_____

21. To create the most desirable group structure, is it better to concentrate leadership roles in a few pupils or spread leadership roles widely?

_____

22. Which type of class is usually more cohesive, the diffusely structured or the centrally structured class? _____

23. When the pupils' norms differ greatly from those the teacher is trying to promulgate, pupils usually react negatively. Name two techniques that might be used to change the group norms in the desired direction.

_____

_____

24. List four things a teacher can do to learn about his pupils.

a. _____

b. _____

c. _____

d. _____

25. Teachers must be skillful in using teaching techniques (methods, strategies, and tactics) and in using the teaching tools. Name at least two other things they should be skillful in, according to this module.

a. _____

b. _____

26. Complete the diagram of the *Teaching Process* by placing the names of the "more sophisticated abilities within the teaching process" in the spaces provided.

a. _____

b. _____

c. _____

Methods and Materials

Teaching

Subject Competence

a

b

Skills

c

27. An essential for teaching success is flexibility. Why?

_____

_____

28. Another essential trait for teaching success is having clear teaching goals. Why?

_____

_____

29. Why is a teacher who experiments with teaching methods more likely to be more effective than one who does not?

_____

_____

30. How would having a strong theoretical base help one become a more effective teacher?

_____

_____

Post Test Answer Key

Module 1

1. Education includes all the learning experiences that shape one throughout life; schooling is that portion of education that one receives in school.

2. None.

3. Church, family, clubs, work, news media, entertainment media, and so on. Take your pick.

4. No. It should include all facets—the affective, the skills, the ethical and moral, and so on.

5. Broad.

6. In a changing world, one's pre-adulthood education may leave one obsolescent.

7. Readiness to profit from new learning experiences; it includes skills and attitudes conducive to learning in new situations.

8. To provide a place in which children could learn the customs, traditions, skills, and so on, necessary for their becoming good members of society. In short, to preserve the society.

9. Probably not. Schools were invented to preserve the social order, not to change it. Schools are basically conservative institutions. Whether or not they should be is a different question.

10. Only a relatively short time. It was not until after World War I and the Great Depression that the notion became really popular.

11. Health, Command of the Fundamental Processes, Worthy Home Membership, Vocation, Citizenship, Worthy Use of Leisure Time, Ethical Character.

12. None, really. The differences are only in nomenclature and editorial organization.

13. To develop the rational processes, i.e., to teach pupils to think and give them something to think with.

14. Everything a teacher does as part of his job.

15. To help pupils learn.

16. Because it is so complex and personal. Most teaching is quite subjective, although decisions are made on the basis of theoretical knowledge, and because good teachers are masters of many skills.

17. A strategy is a plan or approach; a tactic is a method, technique, or operation by which one attempts to carry out a strategy.

18. Diagnosis, preparation, guiding-learning, evaluating, follow-up.

19. The teacher.

20. Performs guidance functions, mediates the culture.

21. To carry out the routines necessary to make the system work.

22. Teachers and pupils.

23. (1) Teaching specialty, (2) Children and youth, (3) Learning, (4) Society and culture, (5) Teaching method and technique, (6) Evaluation.

24. A professional's work requires much more theoretical understanding.

25. There is no best way to teach anything. The teacher must choose the method, content, and techniques that seem best to him in view of the total situation.

26. Members of the educational community make unique contributions. Unless they work together as a team the results will be less than satisfactory.

27. Whatever stand seems right to him, after careful study and consideration of the question.

Module 2

1. c. (The provision of increased opportunities for schooling.)

2. a. T   **b.** P   **c.** T   **d.** T   **e.** P

3. j. (a,b,d,e,g, of above)

4. a. S   **b.** S   **c.** L

5. f. (all of above)

6. f. (a,c,d,e, of above)

7. True

8. True

9. False

10. e. (a,b,d, of above)

11. a. False   **b.** True   **c.** True   **d.** False   **e.** False

12. f. (all of above)

13. g. (all of above)

14. i. (c and f of above)

Module 3

I. 1.d   2.a   3.c   4.b   5.c   6.d   7.e   8.b   9.c   10.b
   11.d   12.d   13.e   14.d   15.e   16.e   17.a   18.c
   19.d   20.d   21.e   22.b   23.a   24.d   25.e

II. (Items are not listed in order of importance.)
   1. Technology.
   2. Moral values.
   3. Urban education.
   4. International harmony.
   5. Overpopulation.

Module 4

1. a	**2.** a	**3.** d	**4.** b	**5.** a
6. c	**7.** b	**8.** c	**9.** b	**10.** b
11. c	**12.** a	**13.** d	**14.** a	**15.** b
16. a	**17.** c	**18.** d	**19.** d	**20.** d
21. c	**22.** c	**23.** b	**24.** b	**25.** c
26. d	**27.** a	**28.** c	**29.** d	**30.** c
31. c	**32.** a			

Module 5

1. The Tenth Amendment.

2. "promote the general welfare."

3. a. Federal Court decisions;
   b. U.S. Office of Education;
   c. Direct aid federal programs;
   d. General federal aid.

4. U.S. Office of Education.

5. Supportive.

6. Jurisdiction of education.

7. State boards of education.

8. State commissioner or state superintendent.

9. Financial.

10. 24,000.

11. Policy making.

12. a. Appointed; **b.** Elected.

13. Superintendent.

14. Local property tax.

15. Principal.

Module 6

MULTIPLE CHOICE

1. b	**2.** b	**3.** a	**4.** b	**5.** b
6. a	**7.** c	**8.** c	**9.** a	**10.** b

COMPLETION

11. The superintendent of schools.

12. a. The education plan.
 b. The expenditure plan.
 c. The revenue plan.

13. a. Science.
 b. Mathematics.
 c. Foreign languages.

14. Locally designed projects.

15. a. *Serrano* v. *Priest* decision (California).
 b. *Cahill v. Robinson* decision (New Jersey).

16. a. It is easy to collect.
 b. It is a relatively "painless" tax.
 c. The revenue from sales tax tends to increase at the same rate as income increases.

17. a. It has "regressive" tendencies.
 b. A sales tax may discourage influx of industry.
 c. A sales tax, once enacted, tends to pyramid—because it is easiest to increase legislatively.

18. Income Tax.

19. a. It is most directly related to the taxpayer's ability to pay.
    b. Adjusts readily to earning power of taxpayer.
    c. Can be adjusted to individual circumstances through the exemption system.

20. a. The income from this tax usually goes down at a faster rate when the economy recedes than do other sources.
    b. Often it is more vulnerable to administrative "loopholes."
    c. It is politically unpopular.

21. Local.

Module 7

DEFINITIONS

A. All the learning experiences that have been planned by, and are under the direction of, the school.

B. 1. *Scope* is the "what" that is to be taught in the curriculum.
    2. *Sequence* is "when" the concepts included in the scope are to be taught.
    3. *Articulation* refers to the smooth progression from grade to grade and from class to class.
    4. *Balance* refers to the designation of equitable time for all educational areas in the curriculum.

MULTIPLE CHOICE	MATCHING
A. 2	**A.** 4
B. 2, 3, 5	**B.** 6
C. 3	**C.** 1
D. 5	**D.** 3
	E. 2
	F. 5

RECOGNITION

1, 2, 3, 4, 5, 6, should all be checked.

Module 8

Answer Key for Elementary School Curriculum.

MULTIPLE CHOICE

A. 2   **B.** 1   **C.** 3   **D.** 5

LISTING

A. (Any five of these seven.)
1. State laws and regulations.
2. NEA
3. Local citizens groups.
4. Regional accrediting agencies.
5. Textbook authors.
6. Standard testing programs.
7. American foreign policy and international commitments.

B.
1. Language arts.
2. Social studies.
3. Mathematics.
4. Art.
5. Science.
6. Music.
7. Physical Education.

C.
1. Reading.
2. Spelling.
3. Writing
4. Speaking.
5. Listening.

D. (Any six of these seven.)
1. history.
2. anthropology.
3. economics.
4. sociology.
5. psychology.
6. philosophy.
7. political science.

E.
1. National Science Foundation.
2. National Defense Education Act.

F.
1. music.
2. art.
3. physical education.
4. foreign language.

G.
1. A standard learning cycle with pretesting, behavioral objectives, multiage grouping, and diversified learning activities.
2. A special decision-making structure with multiunit organization, team teaching, and differentiated staffing.
3. Stronger home-school communication.
4. League linkages for schools geographically close to each other.

H.
1. Independent study.
2. One-to-one.
3. Small-group instruction.
4. Large-group instruction.

I. (Any six of the ten listed.)
1. Classroom practices should be guided by rather clearly discernible educational objectives which, in turn, should reflect the larger school-wide and system-wide agreement on school functions.

2. Classroom instruction, particularly in the early years, should be guided by emphasis on "learning how to learn."
3. The subject matter employed to teach children how to learn should evidence considerable intrinsic appeal for pupils.
4. The golden age of instructional materials is almost everywhere evident in the schools.
5. Today's schools pay considerable attention to and make substantial provision for individual differences among students.
6. Today's teachers make rather substantial use of basic principles of learning and instruction.
7. Today's classrooms should be laboratories in group dynamics and productive human interaction.
8. One should find flexible standards of evaluation, with increasing attention to the actual performance of children, rather than comparison with grade, age, or group norms in today's classrooms.
9. One should expect to find comparable flexibility in determining both the appropriate settings for learning and the most appropriate persons to participate in instructional activities.
10. One should reasonably expect to find the traditional reading and listening activities of the primary years considerably expanded and enriched, not only by more vibrant attention to mathematics, but also by considerable attention to the natural and social sciences and, perhaps, to a lesser degree, the arts.

Answer Key for Secondary School Curriculum.

MULTIPLE CHOICE

A. 4	**B.** 3	**C.** 2	**D.** 1	**E.** 5
F. 5	**G.** 3	**H.** 2	**I.** 1	**J.** 2

LISTING

A.

1. Health.
2. Command of fundamental processes.
3. Worthy home membership.
4. Vocation.
5. Worthy use of leisure.
6. Citizenship.
7. Ethical character.

B.

1. Fundamental skills of communication, arithmetic, and mathematics.
2. Appreciation of our democratic heritage.
3. Civic rights and responsibilities.
4. Respect and appreciation for human values.
5. Ability to think and evaluate constructively.
6. Effective work habits and self-discipline.
7. Social competency.
8. Ethical behavior.
9. Intellectual curiosity.
10. Aesthetic appreciation.

11. Physical and mental health.
12. Wise use of time.
13. Understanding of the physical world.
14. Awareness of our relationship with the world community.

C.
1. Business English.
2. Composition.
3. Journalism.
4. Creative Writing.
5. World Literature.
6. Mythology.
7. Speech.
8. Dramatics.

D.
1. Sociology.
2. Psychology.
3. State History.
4. International Relations.
5. Regional History.
6. Anthropology.
7. Current Events.

E.
1. General Math.
2. Algebra I, II, III, IV.
3. Geometry—Plane and Solid.
4. Trigonometry.
5. College Mathematics.

F.
1. General Science.
2. Biology.
3. Chemistry.
4. Physics.

G.
1. Biological Sciences Curriculum Study (BSCS).
2. Chemical Educational Materials Study (CHEM).
3. Chemical Bond Approach (CBA).
4. Physical Sciences Study Group (PSSG).

H.
1. General Music.
2. Music Appreciation.
3. Band.
4. Orchestra.
5. Instrumental Classes.
6. Choir.
7. Glee Club.

I.
1. Business Mathematics.
2. General Business.
3. Typing I, II.
4. Shorthand I, II.
5. Accounting I.
6. Business English I, II.
7. Business Principles.
8. Office Practice.
9. Office Management.
10. Consumer Education.
11. Retail Selling.

J.
1. Woodworking.
2. Plastics.
3. Electronics.
4. Metalworking.
5. Drafting and Graphic Arts.
6. Automobile Mechanics.

K.
1. Home Management.
2. Family Management.
3. Interior Decorating.
4. Social and Community Relations.
5. Child Development.
6. Consumer Education.
7. Sex Education.

L.
1. Painting.
2. Drawing.
3. Modeling.
4. Weaving.
5. Construction.
6. Crafts.

M.
1. Animal Husbandry.
2. Farm Forestry.
3. Gardening.
4. Horticulture.
5. Landscape Gardening.

N.
1. Office Occupations.
2. Distributive Education.
3. Trade and Industrial Education.
4. Technical Education.
5. Agricultural Education.
6. Health Occupations Education.

O.
1. Marketing.
2. Sales Promotion.
3. Salesmanship.
4. Advertising.

P.
1. Full time counselor for each 250–300 pupils.
2. Eliminate tracks.
3. Require 4 years of English, 3–4 years of social studies, one year of mathematics and one year of science for all students.
4. Eliminate homogeneous grouping.
5. Provide to graduates a record of courses taken.
6. Increase emphasis on English Composition.
7. Increase emphasis on marketable skills.
8. Give special consideration to slow readers.
9. Require at least 15 hours of homework.
10. Provide Advanced Placement courses.
11. Make an annual academic inventory.
12. Have not less than 6 periods in school day.
13. Require prerequisites for advanced courses.
14. Eliminate ranking.
15. Publish honors list.
16. Establish Developmental Reading Program.
17. Establish summer schools.
18. Extend foreign language courses.
19. Require at least one year of science for all.
20. Keep same home room for four years.
21. Require 12th grade social studies course in economics or Problems of American Democracy.

Q.
1. Team Teaching.
2. Independent Study.
3. Ability Grouping.
4. Differentiated Staffing.
5. Flexibility.

Module 9

1. b	**2.** a	**3.** a, b	**4.** a	**5.** a
6. a, b	**7.** d	**8.** d	**9.** a	**10.** a, b
11. a	**12.** c	**13.** a	**14.** a	**15.** a
16. c	**17.** a	**18.** a, c	**19.** a, c	**20.** b
21. b	**22.** a, d	**23.** a	**24.** a	**25.** a
26. a, c	**27.** a	**28.** a, b	**29.** a, b	**30.** a, c
31. a	**32.** a	**33.** a, b		

Module 10

MULTIPLE CHOICE

1. e	**2.** d	**3.** b	**4.** c	**5.** b
6. a	**7.** b			

MATCHING

8. c, a, b

MULTIPLE CHOICE

9. c	**10.** a	**11.** a	**12.** b	**13.** b
14. c	**15.** b	**16.** d	**17.** e	**18.** c
19. e				

MATCHING

20. Traditional: a, b, e, i, c
Emergent: d, f, g, h, j

MULTIPLE CHOICE

21. d	**22.** f	**23.** d	**24.** f

Module 11

1. a	**2.** d	**3.** b	**4.** c	**5.** b
6. d	**7.** c	**8.** a	**9.** d	**10.** c
11. a	**12.** b	**13.** c	**14.** c	**15.** a
16. c	**17.** b	**18.** d	**19.** b	**20.** d

Module 12

1. **a.** Diagnosis.
   b. Preparation.
   c. Guiding learning.
   d. Evaluation.
   e. Follow-through.

2. **a.** Gathering the data.
   b. Interpreting the data.

3. Any two of the following:
   Motivation ability.   Attitude.
   Prior learning.   Aptitude.

4. Any four of the following:
   The objectives.   The technology available.
   The pupils themselves.   The school environment.
   The nature of the group.   The teacher himself.
   The nature of the subject matter.

5. Set the stage for learning.

6. Guiding learning phase.

7. To find out (1) how well one has taught and (2) what the pupils have and have not learned. In other words, diagnosis.

8. **a.** Measurement.
   b. Interpretation.

9. To correct, drive home, tie up loose ends, and so on. (If your answer indicates that the teacher makes sure that the learning was effective, your answer is correct.)

10. No. The good teacher does not omit a step, but he may merge two steps.

11. **a.** Knowledge of subject.
    b. Knowledge of pupils.
    c. Professional knowledge.

12. Structure of the discipline.

13. Theoretical base.

14. The pattern of concepts and their relationships, plus the processes by which one tries to find out the truth in that discipline.

15. Fluid control comes when one has so mastered the content that he can easily use it and adjust new ideas to fit it.

16. A person having factual control knows the facts but he has not so mastered the concepts that he can move freely in the area, using the facts and ideas easily and adjusting to new ideas. The person who has fluid control can.

17. In order to be able to select those most appropriate for each occasion.

18. Diffusely.

19. Any of the following: cohesiveness, communication pattern, group norms.

20. It should improve the communication pattern and lead to a more positive climate.

21. Spread leadership roles (for a more positive climate).

22. Diffusely.

23. Any two of the following: (1) value-clarification activities; discussion of values; (2) encouragement; (3) support; (4) reinforcement of desirable attitudes; (5) cooperative planning.

24. Any four of the following:
    Consult the cumulative record.   Thought sheets.
    Observe.   Questionnaires.
    Pupil conferences.   Tests.
    Autobiography.   Diagnostic devices.
    Reaction sheets.   Sociometric devices.
    Value sheets.

25. Any two of the following:
    Communication skill.
    Skill in structuring.
    Skill in reading signs.
    Skill in adjusting strategies to situation.

26. The blanks should be filled in by the following. The order does not matter.
    a. Teaching learning.
    b. Communications skill.
    c. Evaluation.

27. Flexibility allows one to adjust to different situations and to do well under a variety of circumstances.

28. If you have good teaching goals, you can aim your teaching, select the most suitable materials and methods, and evaluate your progress.

29. The teaching is more likely to be exciting, interesting; one may find new and better ways to teach; and it may produce the Hawthorne effect.

30. A theoretical base helps one to be more fluid and to adjust teaching to the situation.

NOTES

NOTES

NOTES

NOTES

NOTES

NOTES

NOTES